CRADLE-LAND

OF

ARTS AND CREEDS

CRADLE-LAND

OF

ARTS AND CREEDS

OR

NOTHING NEW UNDER THE SUN

CHARLES J. STONE

GYAN

Published by

GYAN

Gyan Publishing House
5, Ansari Road
Daryaganj, New Delhi-110002
Phone: 011-47034999, 9811692060
E-mail: books@gyanbooks.com

Distribution Network
gyanbooks.com
India, USA, Canada, UK, Australia, France

ISBN: 978-81-212-9328-0 (PB)
First Published, 1880

2nd Impression 2023

Printed at: Gyan Press, Delhi.

CRADLE- LAND OF ARTS AND CREEDS OR NOTHING NEW UNDER THE SUN

Author: CHARLES J. STONE

CRADLE-LAND OF ARTS AND CREEDS

CRADLE-LAND

OF

ARTS AND CREEDS

OR

NOTHING NEW UNDER THE SUN

BY

CHARLES J. STONE,

BARRISTER-AT-LAW, INNER TEMPLE; AND LATE ADVOCATE,
HIGH COURTS, BOMBAY

"Who keeps the keys of all the creeds.
. . . . .
Dost thou look back on what hath been
. . to clutch the golden keys.
. . . . .
Eternal process moving on,
From state to state the spirit walks."

ALFRED TENNYSON, "In Memoriam."

LONDON
SAMPSON LOW, MARSTON, SEARLE, & RIVINGTON
CROWN BUILDINGS, 188 FLEET STREET
1880

CONTENTS.

CHAPTER V.

CHAPTER VI.

CHAPTER VII.

CHAPTER VIII.

CHAPTER IX.

CHAPTER X.

CHAPTER XI.

CHAPTER XII.

CHAPTER XIII.

CHAPTER XIV.

CHAPTER XV.

CHAPTER XVI.

CHAPTER XVII.

CHAPTER XVIII.

CHAPTER XIX.

CHAPTER XX.

CHAPTER XXI.

CHAPTER XXII.

CHAPTER XXIII.

CHAPTER XXIV.

CHAPTER XXV.

CHAPTER XXVI.

CHAPTER XXVII.

CHAPTER XXVIII.

CHAPTER XXIX.

CHAPTER XXX.

CHAPTER XXXI.

CHAPTER XXXII.

CHAPTER XXXIII.

CHAPTER XXXIV.

CHAPTER XXXV.

CHAPTER XL.

CHAPTER XLI.

CHAPTER XLII.

CHAPTER XLIII.

CHAPTER XLIV.

CHAPTER XLV.

CHAPTER XLVI.

CHAPTER XLVII.

CHAPTER XLVIII.

CHAPTER XLIX.

CHAPTER L.

CHAPTER LI.

CHAPTER LII.

CHAPTER LIII.

CHAPTER LIV.

CHAPTER LV.

CHAPTER LVI.

CHAPTER LVII.

CHAPTER LVIII.

CHAPTER LIX.

CHAPTER LX.

NOTE.

The "Indian Museum," to which allusion is made on page 55, has ceased to exist. But the photographs of the excavated Temples, etc., are to be retained in the same edifice; which has become an annex to the South Kensington Museum. The ancient Buddhistic sculptures, described upon page 315, have been relegated to the British Museum; so that ancient Indian art remains may be contemplated in juxtaposition with those of Greece, etc. The specimens of natural products in the Indian Museum have been sent to Kew.

INTRODUCTION.

In a treatise on the romantic poetry of the Italians, adduced by Lord Byron in the notes on his translation of Pulci's *Morgante Maggiore*, a passage is quoted from the Italian poet of the fifteenth century, which demonstrates that glimpses of our modern revelations in astronomical and geographical science were caught in the general darkness of the Middle Ages. Before the discovery of the New World by Columbus, and previously to the promulgation of the Copernican system and the persecution of Galileo by the Church of Rome, some rays of scientific truth had fallen upon the art-loving and commercial civilisations on the Mediterranean. In the words of Mr. Merivale's translation, the author of the *Morgante Maggiore* wrote, "The water is level throughout its whole extent, although, like the earth, it has the form of a globe. Mankind, in those ages, were much more ignorant than now. Hercules would blush, at this day, for having fixed his columns. Vessels will soon pass beyond them. They may soon reach another hemisphere, because everything tends to its centre; in like manner as, by a divine mystery, the earth is suspended in the midst of the stars; here below are cities and empires which were ancient. The inhabitants of those regions were called Antipodes. They have plants and animals as well as you, and wage wars as well as you."—*Morgante*, c. xxv. st. 229, etc. Ugo Foscolo observes, "The more we consider the traces of ancient science, which break in transient flashes through the darkness of the Middle Ages, and which gradually re-illuminated the horizon, the more shall we be disposed to adopt the hypothesis suggested by Bailly, and supported by him with seductive eloquence. He maintained that all the acquirements of the Greeks and Romans had been transmitted to them as the wrecks and fragments of the knowledge once possessed by primeval nations, by empires of sages and philosophers, who were afterwards swept from the face of the globe by some overwhelming catastrophe. His theory may be considered as extravagant; but if the literary productions of the Romans were not yet extant, it would seem incredible that, after the lapse of a few centuries, the civilisation of the Augustan age could have been succeeded in Italy by such barbarity. The Italians were so ignorant that they forgot their family names; and before the eleventh century individuals were known by their Christian names. They had an indistinct idea, in the Middle Ages, of the existence of the Antipodes; but it was a reminiscence of ancient knowledge. Dante has indicated the number and position of the stars composing the Polar constellation of the Austral hemisphere. At the same time he tells us that, when Lucifer was hurled from the celestial regions, the arch-devil transfixed the globe."

It has been conjectured that civilisations existed in the present Polar regions, under different geographical and climatic conditions. Their remnants may have descended as seeds to fructify in the ancient civilisations with which we are acquainted. But this appears to refer us to times too remote; before the present climacteric of the earth.

It has been assumed that a continent occupied the existing Indian Ocean; and Oriental traditions seem somewhat to countenance this thesis. Buddhist historians have imputed to earthquakes the submersion of vast regions. A disturbance of the coast of Ceylon is alleged to have taken place B.C. 2387, and a subsidence of the shore adjacent to Colombo 200 years later. On account of the wickedness of Ravanna, the monarch of Ceylon, 25 palaces and 400,000 streets were related to have been overwhelmed. A gradual submergence might seem to have occurred some 10,000 years ago, or thereabouts. A tradition is extant that a submersion took place, at a remote period, on the east coast of Ceylon, wherein the island of Giridipo, mentioned in the first chapter of the Mahawanso, was engulfed; and that the dangerous rocks, known as the Great and Little Basses, are remnants of it.[1]

No account is given in our sacred volume of the dawn of the sciences, nor of the revelation of the art of obtaining fire. With this, perhaps, the Adam may be presumed, in primal perfection, to have been acquainted. In classic legend Prometheus is narrated to have climbed the heavens by the assistance of Minerva, and stolen fire from the chariot of the Sun, which he brought down upon the earth at the end of a ferula.

Undoubtedly the discovery of the capability of obtaining fire at will upon the earth was a golden key which unlocked the entrance to the progress in civilisation of the human race. Whether divinely revealed or apprehended under man's own ingenuity, it was the first step which ennobled Humanity in science, and exalted man far above the lower animal life. Beyond this story of Prometheus we have no record of the genius who first evolved fire from the rubbing together of two sticks, or secured its transient flash when flints were struck. It was his discovery which afforded to man the capacity for expansion throughout the world; for the garden of his innocence would seem to be necessarily situated where fire was not required. Though in Christianity we no longer worship the Sun, we can find no higher simile for the object of our adoration than the Light of the World. Still do the lamps and tapers of the altars of Christendom attest that the presence of the divine is felt to be typified with sublime truth in the burning lights.

[1] See Appendix VII.

And the history of our civilisation, and the growth of religion upon the earth, may be shown to have commenced in the awe and admiration felt in the presence of the mysterious power, which enabled man to summon the divine-seeming spark to his presence to serve him at his pleasure.

In the most ancient Scriptures of our Aryan race, in hymn 11 of the first book of the Rig Veda, we find the fire of the altar, the fire possessed by humanity, adored as the divine messenger, as calling the gods to earth, as the loved lord of men. The fire stolen by Prometheus from the chariot of the Sun was reverentially retained and invoked as a god bearing up man's vow to heaven. This topic will be introduced again in the course of this work.

CHAPTER I.

The Eden of the Human Race—Whether Civilisation originated in Egypt and Babylon?—India, the Madhyama[1] or Centre Land—Originals to be found in India—Quotation from E. Burnouf as to the tracing back of a story to the Sanskrit through fifteen languages—Grandeur of the Indian Empire of Victoria.

WHERE or what was the actual primeval garden of blissful innocence? In what part of the world was original sin actually or metaphorically committed through our first mother being tempted by the serpent to pluck the fruit of the tree of knowledge of good and evil? Or where, if we adopt the materialistic theory, did mankind emerge into dawning civilisation from the ape-kind? Where was the central land, in which the Omniscient communicated to man that information which has resulted in our ancient and modern civilisations, or wherein the human intellect grasped the first ideas of science? Where did we begin to cultivate the soil, employ weapons of warfare, and adore the divine under the dispensation of labour?

We have accepted the region of the Euphrates and the Valley of the Nile as the earliest homes of the arts and sciences. On the plains of Shinar, and in Egypt, humanity has been considered to have commenced the invention of those artificial contrivances for its progress or comfort which have culminated so far in telegraphs, telephones, and torpedoes. The origin of Babylon upon its drained, and of Egypt upon its irrigated, district, have been allowed to remain, like certain articles of our religious creed, as incomprehensibles. We have been contented with contemplating the mists concealing the tracts through which our predecessors in culture have passed; and regarded the region in which science was

[1] The Sanskrit words introduced in the book, in their English rendering, have only been accentuated when requiring to be thus differenced.

first self-mastered, or else revealed by the divinity, as a wonder-land. According to the Bible narrative, and the orthodox chronology adopted from Archbishop Usher, about one hundred years after the destruction of humanity in the universal deluge, Noah's descendants were still "of one language, and of one speech" (Genesis xi. 1). "And it came to pass, as they journeyed from the east, that they found a plain in the land of Shinar; and they dwelt there. And they said to one another, Go to, let us make brick, and burn them thoroughly. And they had brick for stone, and slime had they for mortar. And they said, Go to, let us build us a city and a tower, whose top may reach unto heaven; and let us make us a name, lest we be scattered abroad upon the face of the whole earth" (Genesis xi. 2, 3). After commencing this attempt, they are related to have been confounded and dispersed.

About 260 years subsequently to this event, according to our accepted chronology, viz. about the year 1985 B.C., Abraham is described as being rich in cattle, silver, and gold, and is narrated to have come from Ur of the Chaldees. He was ordered by the Lord to go into the land of Canaan, but a famine occurring in that land, he went down into Egypt, and we know that, at least by this period, Egypt was flourishing in its fanciful civilisation. Architecture of a stupendous and art of a highly elaborate character were already in existence, as has been demonstrated by the evidence of their remains. The Assyrian Empire has been allowed to have been also founded by this period, and acquaintance likewise to have been made there with the arts and sciences. Mankind in these regions, according to the orthodox view, would appear to have arisen to civilisation in all the majesty of original genius. The districts upon which they had settled demanded artificial aids to the convenient existence of man; and man immediately invented them. He is neither recorded to have gone through any preliminary process in lands habitable by humanity without the artifices of civilisation, nor to have enjoyed any especial revelation from the Almighty. The simpler, nomadic and pastoral, life of Abraham and his dependants obtained the divine favour, or was more consonant with the divine will, according to the Bible. The devices of art in Babylon and Egypt would seem to have been of merely human origin, according to the account in our Sacred Scriptures. They appertained to the diabolical, or at least the idolatrous, rather than to the truly divine. Originating in the vicinages of the Euphrates and the Nile, rendered suitable for man's abode by highly artificial means, in aiding or restraining the rivers' inundations, it has been supposed that their influences spread eastwards. The comparatively vast and habitable districts of India and China have been held to have acquired all their varied arts from these instinctively mechanical, and art-inventing, Babylonians and Egyptians. As the Euphrates is mentioned amongst the four rivers which watered the Garden of Eden, a site has been assigned to the abode of happiness, in innocence, somewhere about the sources of that river. The regions of the Euphrates and Nile have been regarded as the central portion of the earth, in which sprang the original fountains of civilisation. The question has, indeed, been debated, as to whether Egypt borrowed from India, or India from Egypt, in those points in which their ancient civilisations seem to be akin. But the science of the nineteenth century appears generally to have admitted a more remote date for the authentic monumental records of Egyptian than of Indian civilisation. Of late years the ancient Indian language has been allowed to be a collateral ancestress of our Latin, Teutonic, and Slavonic dialects in Europe, thereby establishing a relationship between ourselves and the Aryan race in India. We vaunt our modern European civilisation as the most advanced and progressive in the arts and sciences which our world has known. But we have, still, generally ascribed the origin of the arts and sciences to the races anciently inhabiting the shores of these rivers; with which races we recognise no kinship. We have considered that our precursors in India, Greece, etc., originally learnt the arts and sciences from these Semitic or African people. These collateral ancestors of ours are admitted to have formed admirable languages in India, etc., and to have left a voluminous literature. Still the original instances of Greek architecture have been recognised in Nubia, and the southern temples of India have been alleged to have been suggested by the architecture of Assyria. The arts and sciences are considered to have been perfected only, not invented, by our race. And true religion is believed to have been solely revealed to, or apprehended originally by, the Hebrews of Palestine. Histories of the civilisations of the world have been written without any introduction of India or China as links in the progressive chain of civilisation, east and west. Yet these two countries possess physical capacities for containing populations threefold those of Europe and the western and northern parts of Asia combined. England, as a small country, has indeed carried the commerce and culture of modern times to extensive and remote regions; but England is virtually part of Europe. We are, however, beginning to trace back the originals of many matters of our civilisations to sources which, like those of the Nile, have long been hidden in mystery. The revelations of the Sanskrit language are beginning to display the continuation backwards of our literary history, and we are astonished at the antiquity of many ideas which we had conceived to be new and original.

To offer the familiar, literary instance of our dramatic art—we have often read upon a theatrical playbill some such announcement as the following:—At the Theatre Royal Olympian will be presented a new and original comedy entitled All the World's a Stage, by the author of So and So, etc. etc.—We have presently found the piece to have been adapted from the French, and have been contented to imagine it original in France. But if we had continued our researches into its origin, we might have ascertained that it had been appropriated by the French from the Spaniards. Still continuing our investigations, it is not unlikely that we should have discovered the story in the Arabic. Finally, or at all events, so far as living literature goes, the original idea might probably be even discerned in the Sanskrit. M. E. Burnouf has cited a curious example of continuous adaptation in a different sphere of literature—viz. in the account of the canonisation of an Indian personage by the Roman Catholic Church. He adduces a book in existence under the title of *Barlaam et Josaphat*; which has been successively translated into Arabic, Armenian, Hebrew, Latin, French, the Languedoc language, Italian, German, Irish, Swedish, English, Spanish, Bohemian, Polish, and finally into an Indian dialect. It contains the history of an Indian king converted to Christianity by a monk. We now possess the original Sanskrit from which all these have emanated; it is the Lalita Vistâra, which existed in the third century B.C. The Sanskrit names in this have all been replaced by the Syriac; and the hero of the story is no other than the Buddha, Sakya muni. Besides those of literature, and the pictures of life presented on the stage, we shall find the originals, in a much more complete form than we have supposed, of scenes, incidents, and situations of the actual dramas of the world's theatre. That history repeats itself has been acknowledged as an aphorism, but we have not duly realised the extent to which the repetition may be traced in some of the most important matters affecting our lives. It was a shock to our sympathies to be informed that Shakspeare had merely improved upon stories in existence in his time, sometimes even in the form of dramas, although he had magnificently and completely improved upon them. We now discover the leading incident of the Merchant of Venice so far back as the Sanskrit; which had assumed a position in India, like that of the Latin in mediæval Europe, at the time of Christ, or even 300 years before the commencement of our era. In fact the sacred language of Hindustan appears to be the original stream in which all the rivers of Aryan fancy have flowed. The revelations which we are receiving further seem to relegate the arts, sciences, and traditions of all those nations, formerly comprehended under the appellation of Caucasian, to fountain-heads farther eastwards. There may have been springs in some region which has become altogether obliterated in the mists of antiquity. But of the known world, arts, learning and poetry and religion, as we possess these, seem to have commenced amongst the pre-Christian Aryans of the East; and to afford in their archaic aspect very distinct types of their successors in mediæval and modern Europe.

Victoria, in 1879 Empress of India, rules over a country nearly equivalent, in dimensions and population, to Europe without Russia and Sweden. We are nationally proud of our Indian Empire; still it has wearied us as a topic. It has often emptied the House of Commons, and obtained but a scant and cursory recognition in the English press, except upon extraordinary and sensational occasions. But let us dismiss from our thoughts the Anglo-India of the nineteenth century, with its "competition wallahs," and its curry and punkahs, its quaint superstitions, and people enervated by long periods of conquest and by the parsimony of their diet. Let us contemplate the ancient India—of an epoch centuries before the annexation of England by the old Romans. We shall here find the oldest originals of, or else the strangest coincidences with, the coeval and subsequent developments of the European nations in religion, romance, state polity, and even social habits. We shall find similitudes of old England.

Instead of India we ought to style it Great Bharata, or Jambu-dwipa, the Island of the Rose Apple. The peninsula of India is almost an island; for the sources of the Ganges and Indus and Brahmaputra seem in juxtaposition amongst the eternal snows of the Himalayas; whence, curling round, the rivers take their very diverse routes on either side of the great northern plains. It was also styled Madhyama, or the middle land; and not only figuratively but actually, this last epithet can be applied to it with more truth than to any other district on the earth. It was not uttered in mere boastful vanity; for India is the most central in its situation of the countries of the eastern hemisphere, taking into consideration continents and islands.

CHAPTER II.

Revelation of past Civilisation in the Indian Epic, the Ramáyana—Sketch of that Poem, quotations from it, and comparisons with Homer's Iliad and Milton's Paradise Lost.

Great revelations of the buried past arise at intervals. The exhumation of Pompeii from its volcanic ashes of 1800 years is one of the most interesting. The discovery, in 1877, at Mycenæ of the golden paraphernalia of the great Agamemnon, or of some magnificent chieftain, whose tomb is, at all events, a revelation of bygone splendour, is another. In the exhumations of Troy, again, we have revelations of stirring import. The discoveries of classical literature during the mediæval ages, and the consequent renaissance of classical art and learning, led to our present advancement in science and culture; while the printing of the Bible was virtually a revelation of the deepest significance to the masses of the people. Now, a revelation of mighty consequence seems to be continuing in the opening of the literary stores of the Sanskrit to European knowledge. The Rig Veda is considered the oldest existing work in this dead language, and is held to have been collected in its present form in about the fifteenth century B.C. Positive evidence forbids its being relegated to a materially later date than this period, *i.e.* the period assigned by theologians to the exodus of the children of Israel from Egypt. Now, this book would appear to contain, not the mere outpourings of the simple awe, devotion, or superstition of a rude and uncivilised race, but the systematised collection of religious utterances of a people profound in philosophical meditation, and versed in arts, civil government, and the refinements of warfare. It exhibits a civilisation which would seem to have required a vast duration for its growth, if originating amongst the countrymen of the authors of the hymns, or else it must have been a descendant of the civilisation of one of the empires of sages and philosophers who, according to Bailly's supposition, may have been swept from the face of the earth by overwhelming catastrophe.[1]

It must be remembered that the Vedas—*i.e.* the books of knowledge—in their entirety, are not merely collections of hymns, but rather compilations, corresponding to our Prayer-Book, with carefully ordained ritual, religious festivals, or periods of ceremonies, regulated by a calendar of the seasons, duly ordered according to astronomical observations. And what our commentators have styled the sacrificial ordinances seem, in part, rather to correspond to those concerning the sacrament of our Christian altars than to sacrifices in the sense of offering to the deity the blood of slaughtered animals.

We have in these Vedas distinct evidences of settled civilisation, commerce, roads, money, chariots, and carts, ploughs, etc., in combination with its various vices, and notably gambling.

These books altogether suggest that, if compiled in their present form, at about the fifteenth century B.C., they are likely to have been the product of many centuries of civilisation, of systematisation of the arts of life, with their mingling influences of good and evil.

Later than the Vedas by, at least, some centuries, upon the authority of comparative philology, etc., we have the two great epic poems in the classical Sanskrit. One of these has been placed within the reach of the mass of English readers by a translation of Mr. Griffith's, head of the college of Benares.

If the estimate which he appears, in his Introduction, to have adopted of the antiquity of this poem be correct; if it was really written, as he argues, and as European criticism has, in part, admitted, about the twelfth century B.C., with the exception of certain easily-perceived interpolations, or alterations shown in a later recension, this poem must be accepted as a most important revelation of the history of our civilisation and religion.

Whether buried States existed at the Poles or in the Southern Ocean or not, here, at all events, in India, seems to

[1] See Appendix V.

have been founded a civilisation distinctly leading up to our classic and Gothic European polities.

This epic unveils original forms in the old realm of Bharata, or Madhyama, of many ideas and manners of men, hitherto traced no farther back than mediæval Germany or ancient Greece. Indications of customs appear in it which seem to belong to our actual ancestry.

The Trojan war is supposed to have taken place about the commencement of the twelfth century B.C., and Homer to have celebrated it in the tenth century. If the Ramáyana was really written by Valmiki in the twelfth century, he would appear to have been a more wonderful and original man than either Homer or our great Milton. There are suggestions in his poem of both the Iliad and Paradise Lost; and whatever may be its chronological position in regard to the former, it certainly cannot be held to have been indited after the latter. It is considerably longer than the Iliad and Odyssey combined, or the Paradise Lost and the Paradise Regained; for it contains 24,000 epic verses of twenty-four syllables. It is, at the lowest estimate, a grand and extraordinary literary monument of a remote period, and, as we have proclaimed empire over the whole peninsula of Hindustan, it may be esteemed as British national property.

In the twelfth century B.C. Troy is related, or fabled, to have fallen under the combined Grecian chieftains, and Æneas to have found his way, through many marvellous and supernatural adventures, to the shores of Italy, where he founded the Roman Empire. Israel was still under the government of the Prophets; Samson being chronologically considered to have exhibited his extraordinary and divinely-endowed strength about the commencement of the century; while the power of David arose at about its termination. The Argonautic expedition and the labours of Hercules are related to have occurred in this same period. The Assyrian and Egyptian monarchies were powerful, and highly advanced in civilisation; but their literary remains, so far as at present discovered, have struck few chords of sympathy in our own intellectual life, except in the interest attaching to the finding of biblical legends.

We gaze upon the sculptured or painted records of Assyria and Egypt, and feel ourselves in the presence of civilisations, enterprising in their conceptions, noble in their works, and picturesque in their arts, but we have no fellow-feelings with them. From five to ten centuries later we find ourselves more at home in the presence of Greece and Rome. We have adopted the architecture of these last. We constitute their literary remains the text-books of our schools, and embody our conceptions of ideals, or transcendental abstractions, under the appellations of their divinities. Jove, Minerva, and Diana, Venus and Cupid, live, although they no longer enjoy divine honours; but Osiris, Isis, and Astarte are virtually defunct. Germany, France, and England, in the twelfth century B.C., have not yet arrived at any historical consideration whatever; while India and China have been treated as having had little or no influence upon our western civilisation. If, however, this Indian epic, the Ramáyana, was written in this age of the world's history—*i.e.* the twelfth century B.C.—in a language exhibiting remarkable affinities to the Greek and to our modern European languages, it proves that we must look for the originals of many of our ideas in the earlier period, in ancient India, besides that of the story of Barlaam and Josaphat.

The Ramáyana narrates the history of a son of the king of Ayodhya, the modern Oude. This son is named Rāma, and he is said to be an incarnation of Vishnu, which word signifies the all-pervading. Vishnu is, of course, familiar to us as one of the persons of the Hindu threefold manifestation of Brahm, the eternal, universal, and absolute spirit, as Brahma, Vishnu, and Siva, the Creator, Preserver, and Destroyer, or, more correctly speaking, changer of forms. The poem is rendered a revelation by the fact that, although produced at what we have been taught to consider so early an age of the world's history, it contains continual allusions to the matters of ordinary everyday life of the period. These exhibit a civilisation not contemptible in comparison with our European civilisation, putting aside steam and electricity, which have only been developed in the last half-century. On the other hand, the description of the solemn horse sacrifice with which the work opens, and the general aspect of religion throughout, appear to indicate a remote age. It certainly appears to be an epoch farther removed than the invasion of India by Alexander the Great in the latter half of the fourth century B.C., because we have Grecian evidence as to the aspect of the country in his time. A city is depicted in this poem as constructed "with chess-board line and even square." Allusion is made to the watering of the roads and to public gardens, to curtained screens, folding doors, golden statues and inlaid floors. The expression, "houses of gods at cross roads" seems familiar to us; while "warlike engines which slay 100" quite emulate our weapons of Christian civilisation in the nineteenth century. Allusion is made to music with "sevenfold notes and triple measure." Palaces, terraces, ramparts, triumphal arches, gold and silver plates, ladles, vases, couches, chambers inlaid with lazulite and pearl, and numbers of similar institutions of pomp, luxury, and taste, are mentioned, certainly with more suggestiveness of their modern form than we find in articles of furniture, etc., in Homer's Odyssey. The expressions, "fair sculptured stone in twin images," and "temples bright and fair as white clouds, towering in the air," "walls that split and beams that blaze," "shrinking wood and heated stone," seem to refute an allegation set forth in Mr. Fergusson's History of Architecture that stone structures were unknown in India before the third century B.C. In many respects the descriptions seem as if they might have been taken from some mediæval European romance. The squares of Ayodhya, on a festive occasion, overflow with mimes, dancers, and minstrels. Of the Queen of Beauty and Fortune it is said that "the glory of her hair flowed down," which seems suggestive of similes in Tennyson's idylls of King Arthur's days. Golden armour and helmets, a long enumeration of weapons, heralds, the rich dresses of women, a feast on venison after a sacrifice, accompanied with wine-drinking, "mettled steeds," the similes of "a vessel with her rudder lost," and "the state wrecked and tempest-tost" as indicating sea-voyaging; also an allusion to "a tall ship upon the main,"—the mention of a bride's dower, of servants trained to heat baths, of needles and razors, and richly brocaded dresses, with wreaths of flowers on ladies' brows,—of envoys sacred by the law of nations, of wine and mead distillers, and of boiled, stewed, and roasted meats, and of a sort of rockets or firearms, etc. etc., seem altogether to represent an archaic civilisation leading to that of Greece,

Rome, and mediæval Europe. In sequence Greece, Rome, and mediæval Europe have combined to form ourselves.

The peers of state meet for debate, and King Bharat announces to them that the eldest son should succeed to the throne. Brahmins are described as chanting text and prayer. "Scripture-learned" is applied as an epithet of praise, and allusions to heaven and hell, and to "the wicked washed clean," appear to be prototypical of Christianity; while the following verses, uttered by the "self-existent Sire" at the revelation of Rama's divinity, might almost be introduced into a modern hymn:—

> "High bliss awaits the devotee
> Who clings in loving faith to thee;
> Who celebrates with solemn praise
> The Lord of ne'er-beginning days:
> On earth below, in heaven above,
> Great joy shall crown his faith and love."

Modern poetry is anticipated by the constant celebration, throughout the epic, of the grandeur and beauties of nature, especial praise being bestowed upon the charms of forests and flowers. The scented yellow blossoms of the champac, the red flowers of the asoka and others of the gorgeous floral world of India, are continually introduced into the poem with admiration and delight, and employed in similes, as for instance—

> "That wreath of women lay asleep
> Like blossoms in a careless heap."

In fact, in the epic of the Ramáyana, as in the disinterred Pompeii, not only the gods and the heroes, the temples and the forums, but the house furniture and articles of personal adornment, the stewpans and the gewgaws are revealed to us. In the tombs of Egypt, and in the exhumations of Assyria, departed civilisations are displayed to us, but, as has been observed, they present aspects utterly foreign to our habits and tastes. Those shown in Pompeii and the Ramáyana epic scarcely appear more distant and different from our own than those of our actual European ancestors of five centuries ago. What a transformation England exhibits from the days of ordeals, trial by *battel* and tournaments, of castles and monasteries, of hermitages in the forests, Canterbury pilgrims, and benefit of clergy extended to all who could read! An old English aspect is especially imparted to the warriors of this old Indian poem by their skill in the use of the ancient English weapon, the long bow.

There is no allusion to *sati* in the epic, that is to say, to the custom of widows immolating themselves on the funeral pyres of their husbands, although the descriptions of manners and customs throughout are so constant and minute, and although the enormous amount of slaughter during the war affords ample opportunities for its introduction. We have the testimony of Megasthenes to the recognised existence of *sati* at the time of Alexander's invasion B.C. 327, so that a powerful argument is thereby added to the reasoning in favour of the Ramáyana's antiquity. The regular series of Vishnu's incarnations does not seem to have been known to the author.

Stupendous natural machinery is introduced, but our European mediæval romances also dealt extravagantly with the transcendental. The tales of chivalry in which Don Quixote delighted, the narratives of the valiant deeds of King Arthur and the Knights of his Round Table, and the Legends of the Seven Champions of Christendom, similarly abound in marvels; so that, in this respect, there is no absolute excess of eccentricity in the Indian work. Don Quixote's favourite knight of the burning sword, who, with one back blow, cut asunder two fierce and mighty giants, was not essentially less prodigious than Rama, who, with his arrows, checked in their flight trees and other ponderous missiles hurled at him by his Titan-like foes.

And it must be remembered that the great epic poet of the Augustan age of Latin literature indulged largely in the supernatural. The episodes of the Ramáyana are not more fanciful than the quaint enchantments of Circe, and the other picturesque embellishments of Ulysses' narrative also.

Ravanna, the demon monarch of Ceylon, or Lankā as it is styled in the poem, a word signifying the equinoctial point, has obtained, by tremendous austerities, the promise from Brahma that his prayer shall be granted.

It may be parenthetically remarked that India undoubtedly possesses the precursors or originals of all Christian asceticisms. The Protestant, contemning bodily austerities, contents himself with some amount of negation of the flesh on the Sabbath. The Roman Catholic and Ritualist practise abstinence more arduously, and have occasionally indulged in vigorous mortifications, flagellations, etc., with a view to the purification of the soul in the punishment of the body. But the Hindu tortures his body to the extreme limits of endurance. It is not from mere superstition that he swings, suspended by hooks in his flesh, or rigidly retains his limbs in fixed positions till they become immovable. It is in demonstration of his soul's hatred and contempt for his body that he thus mortifies his members, and in the belief in the power of austerity even over the divine will.

Brahma cannot revoke his word, and is self-compelled to grant Ravanna his request—the possession of such power, that not even the gods shall prevail against him. This power he uses to the anger of the divine beings and the destruction of mankind. To counteract his evil influence Brahma is obliged to resort to the subterfuge of sending Vishnu to be born of woman, for Ravanna, despising mankind, has neglected to secure himself against human interference. Vishnu assents to his incarnation, and while seeming only a promising young prince, and himself unconscious of his divine birth, he is ordered into banishment by his father, the King of Ayodhya, owing to machinations of his stepmother. His bride Sita refuses to become what Anglo-Indians have styled a grass-widow, and, with one of his brothers, accompanies him to exile in the distant forests. For some time they live contentedly in recluse life, Rama enjoying the consolation of Sita's society. But their tranquil joys are presently terminated by Ravanna carrying Sita off to Lanka. The distracted Rama seeks her in vain, till, in the south of India, he obtains the aid of Hanuman, monarch of the monkeys or satyrs, who discovers her situation, and, with his powerful, though grotesque army, aids Rama in her recovery. A main incident, therefore, of this story resembles that of the Trojan war, but, besides this incident, there is little in common between the Ramáyana and the Iliad, except indeed the vigour and personal prowess exhibited by the heroes in both epics. The leading idea of the Indian poem appears to be the destruction of the enemy of the gods by the incarnate Vishnu, whereas the wrath and majesty of Achilles is the main feature of the Greek. The abduction of the heroine and consequent siege may have been suggested from the one to the other. But, as Mr. Káshináth T. Telang of the Bombay Bar has observed in a printed lecture upon this topic, read before the Bombay Students' Literary and Scientific Society, there can be little comparison between the ravisher of Helen and the dreaded enemy of the gods, the ravisher of Sita, or between the coquetry of Helen and the purity of King Janaka's child. If it be contended that the elopement of Helen with Paris to Troy is an actual fact, and that the Indian romance must therefore have been adapted from the Grecian, the answer is, that the existence of Rama is no less implicitly credited in India. Indeed it survives as a matter of faith to this day. Sacred places, from Oude to Ceylon, continue to attest the scenes of the poem. Explanations by European critics contend that the work illustrates the southward progress of Aryan civilisation, and the reduction of the rude aborigines, or the conquest of the south by Rama, etc. etc.; but to the Hindus the epic is a divine gospel.

As no critic has yet had the temerity to assert that the Ramáyana is the production of some clever Brahmin of modern times, "craftily" plagiarised from Homer, Milton, Buddhist stories, etc. etc., Milton's great poem must be therefore of course regarded as posterior. Just as the abduction of Helen in the Trojan story accords with that of Sita in the Ramáyana, so does the assent of Vishnu to the descent into the flesh, to deliver gods and men from the power of Ravanna, strangely correspond to that of Christ to redeem mankind, as expressed in the Paradise Lost. The Creator is represented by Milton as speaking thus:—

> "Say, heav'nly Powers, where shall we find such love;
> Which of ye will be mortal to redeem
> Man's mortal crime, and just th' unjust to save?"

And silence prevailed in heaven till the "Son of God" offered Himself. Vishnu responds to the appeal of Brahma in strikingly similar terms. Again, Ravanna, for vengeance and hatred, carries away Sita; Satan, from the same motives, tempts Eve, and succeeds thereby in destroying the happiness of the pair in their garden of bliss. Moreover, the description of the purity and placid enjoyment of the lives of Rama and Sita, amid the lovely scenery of their forest dwelling, closely resembles that of the lives of Adam and Eve in Eden. The delineation of "Ayodhya the blest" is also in essential resemblance to that of Milton's immortal abodes. In perusing the Ramáyana the European reader can scarcely fail to acknowledge the grandeur and beauty of much of it, while it must be confessed that many parts will appear preposterous and unnatural without being sublime. Can it be asserted that Milton's noble work will not also present contrary aspects to an Asiatic, if not to a European reader? For instance, the materialistic transformation of the spirits of evil into serpents in the full assembly of Pandemonium—who all suddenly lose their old dark angel forms, and hiss the expected response to Satan's address — is undoubtedly related in magnificent language in Book x. of the Paradise Lost; but we might have considered it rather ridiculous if the majesty of Brahma had transfigured Ravanna and his giants in similar fashion. The making the future of the human race dependent upon a fruit temptingly suspended within the reach of the original pair, as the test of obedience unto righteousness, may seem out of character with a due conception of the Supreme Being, to the Hindu, unendowed with faith. It may also be averred that the European poet has displayed less reverence for woman's character than the Indian. Satan, in his machinations, attempts and succeeds in overcoming Eve as the weaker vessel, but Sita remains unswerving in constancy, courage, and devotion, throughout her life. The highest precepts of Christianity and the noblest purposes of chivalry are continually illustrated in this Indian, or, more correctly speaking, ancient Aryan poem. In both Valmiki's and Milton's epics magniloquent and materialistic descriptions of the powers and numbers of the contending hosts are given. The vast multitudes of the sylvan troops of Hanuman adapt forest trees as clubs, and fling whole summits of hills as missiles, and the demon giants encounter them with equal vigour. Milton, in similar fashion, says,

> "Millions of fierce encount'ring angels fought
> On either side."

And Milton also bestows upon them tremendous power in the use of materialistic weapons.

Altogether, the Ramáyana contains suggestions for the Paradise Lost. Milton cannot reasonably be supposed to have seen or heard of the former, but its leading ideas may be held to have filtered through the various strata of Aryan imagination from about the twelfth century B.C. to the seventeenth century A.D. Some of Milton's conceptions have also been traced in the Dutch Vondel, author of a Mystery play; and in the Lucifer of Marlowe's "Faustus."

CHAPTER III.

Rama as an Incarnation of Vishnu—Idea of the Incarnation in the Institutes of Manu; and Civilisation of the Twelfth Century B.C., as illustrated in the Epic and Institutes as to Commerce, etc.—Quotations from the Institutes as to the Unity of Deity and the Christian Spirit.

IT has been surmised by modern critics that the portion of the Ramáyana relating to the descent upon earth of Vishnu as Rama, and to the revelation of the latter as the incarnate second person of the Hindu Trinity, may be interpolations of a later age, after the story of Christ had been brought to India. Rama, unlike Krishna, the later incarnation of Vishnu, is not aware of his own divinity till it is declared to him by Brahma descending from heaven for that purpose. Although thus rendered cognisant of his divine nature, he does not immediately ascend to heaven. He inaugurates a happy reign of 10,000 years over his humanly paternal city of Ayodhya. The idea, however, of a divinity incarnate in humanity is expressed in the Institutes of Manu, the first Indian code of laws, which is still held to be an authority by the Hindus, and recognised by our High Courts in India when dealing with their affairs. Sir William Jones, the earliest translator of these Institutes, assigned them, upon astronomical, philological, and other evidence, as a compilation in their present form, to about the ninth century B.C.; and modern investigations at all events allow this to be the most ancient of existing Indian law-books, and that its antiquity is unascertained. It is generally admitted to belong to some centuries B.C. in virtually its existing form. It is observed therein that the "very birth of Brahmins is a constant incarnation of Dherma the God of Justice;" and that a "king, even though a child, must not be treated lightly, from an idea that he is a mere mortal; no, he is a powerful divinity who appears in human shape." A conception, therefore, of the divine in the human was in existence in India, seemingly the natural growth of ideas which are found in the Vedas, and undoubtedly pre-Christian. The sequence of ideas, again, from the Incarnation of Justice in a typical monarch to that of Vishnu, actually incarnate in the prince Rama, seems natural. Also, in the Institutes of Manu, it is said that a king is formed by the rule of the universe, of particles drawn from the substance of Indra, Yama, Surya, Varuna, and other deities. The original notion, in fact, seems here apparent of our old idea of the divine right of kings.

These Institutes may possibly have been known in the Roman Empire, and at all events they are antecedent[1] to those of the Roman Justinian. The codes of Manu and Justinian have been two great central and remarkable promulgations of defined law amongst the Aryan race east and west.

Doubtless in India, as in Rome, the laws had long been in existence before they were collected into an authoritative volume. This was accomplished under the imperial authority in the Roman Empire, and under Brahminical influence in India.

In England we have not yet codified our laws authoritatively, though this has been effected by the Anglo-Saxon race in America. We still regulate our rights and liberties by multitudinous arrays of statutes of Parliament and recorded judicial decisions, together with irregular numbers of doubtfully-ascertained ancient customs. King Alfred is, however, narrated to have instituted a code in the dawn of our national history, which seems to have consisted of transcripts of the existing ordinances of the race upon the continent of Europe.

We find in these Institutes of Manu ample confirmation of the existence of an advanced stage of civilisation at about the epoch to which the Ramáyana epic has been attributed. Allusions to the insurance of sea-going vessels testify to the actuality of the sea voyages indicated in the poem. Provisions for the support of widows corroborate the opinion that the Institutes, like the epic, were formed before the system of *sati* was introduced, this having been in existence, as has been observed, in the time of Alexander the Great. The law of bailments and other niceties of jurisprudence in the Code, and the general

[1] See Appendix I.

rules for the disposal of property, are evidences of the existence of an orderly and commercial community in India about the ages of Solomon, Sardanapalus, and Codrus of Athens. Our common chronological tables state that the mariner's compass was known in China at about this time. The evidence altogether points to an advanced condition of human culture in Asia to the eastwards of the Indus. The following verses, translated by Mr. Griffiths from the Rig Veda, 1-48, suggest careful and correctly-ordered conduct of life :—

> "She (the dawn) hath dwelt in heaven of old,
> May we now her light behold,
> Which, dawning brightly from afar,
> Stirreth up the harnessed car ;
> Like as merchant folk for gain
> Send their ships across the main.
> Morning comes, the nurse of all,
> Like a matron at whose call
> All that dwell the house within
> Their appointed task begin."

The language of the Madhyama, or, as it was also styled, with the other epithets which have been adduced, the Arya varta, the noble, excellent, or cultivated land, from the same root as the Latin *arare*, to plough, had not attained its full classic excellence and elegance in the period of the Institutes of Manu. Of this Sanskrit language the historian Heeren observed that it appears to have received its grammatical structure at a very remote period of antiquity, as the Hindus take their oldest grammarians far back into the fabulous ages. Schlegel said that "in its grammatical structure the language of India is absolutely similar to the Greek and Latin, even to the minutest particulars. But the grammatical forms of the Sanskrit are far richer and more varied than those of the Latin tongue, and more regular and systematic than those of the Greek. In its roots and words the Sanskrit has a very strong and remarkable affinity to the Persian and Germanic races of language."

He remarked that the Institutes of Manu are composed in a measure of most primitive simplicity. By the Hindus themselves this Code is referred to absolutely prehistorical antiquity. Professor Weber observes that traditions display reminiscences of its various remodellings, and that its precepts agree with allusions to judicial cases in Vedic literature. He comments on the degree of perfection of its judicial procedure. Altogether it demonstrates that many centuries before the time of Christ the people of India had established laws and a judicial procedure, etc., then seeming ancient.[1] They had engaged in foreign commerce, produced poetry, and constructed a language in harmony with the subsequent efforts of our Aryan race in the same directions. Yet we have scarcely estimated their civilisation in considering the ways of God to man, and the history of humanity upon our globe. Not only law but liberty and justice in the fullest sense seem to have been perfectly apprehended by them. Although the distinctions of caste are most carefully promulgated in this evidently Brahminical code, there is no slavery recognised in it. The kingly authority is to be tempered by the advice of the Brahmins, for whom the strictest discipline is enjoined. And what may be termed constitutional checks seem intended to prevent either the Brahminical or warrior and kingly class from obtaining undue preponderance.

Although Brahm, or Brahma, and Vishnu appear in both poem and Institutes, the Indian Trinity is not promulgated in them. Vishnu is introduced in both as a subordinate Deity, but not as identified with the Supreme Spirit. The unity of the Almighty, as adored in the regents of the elements or guardians of the universe, in fact the religion of the Vedas, is still in vogue. "Of all duties," it is ordered in Manu, "the principal is to acquire a true knowledge of one supreme God; that is the most exalted of all sciences because it ensures immortality." "In this life as well as the next the study of the Scriptures to acquire a knowledge of God is held the most efficacious of duties in procuring felicity to man; for in the knowledge and adoration of one God, which the Scripture teaches, all the rules of good conduct are fully comprised." "The Divine Spirit alone is the whole assemblage of gods; all worlds are seated in the Divine Spirit; and the Divine Spirit no doubt produces, by a chain of causes and effects consistent with free will, the connected series of acts performed by embodied souls." "He must consider the supreme omnipresent intelligence as the Sovereign Lord, a spirit by no

[1] See Appendix VIII.

means the object of any sense, which can only be conceived by a mind wholly abstracted from matter." "Him some adore as transcendently present in elemental fire; others in Manu, lord of creatures, or more distinctly present in Indra, regent of the clouds and the atmosphere; others as the most high eternal Spirit." "Thus the man who perceives in his own soul the supreme soul present in all creatures, acquires equanimity towards them all, and shall at last be absorbed into the highest essence, even that of the Almighty Himself." Moses did not propound the truth of the unity of Deity in words more distinct than these, and he less unequivocally expressed the hope of a future life. Christianity has alleged the laws of Moses not to be due to an accretion of human wisdom, but to direct divine inspiration. It would rebuff the Hindu assertion of similar aid. If the code of Manu, as we have it, can only be referred back with certainty to four or five centuries B.C., the analogies of legal history, etc., would then suggest the origin of its statutes and measures in ages antecedent to the time of Moses, *i.e.* to the fifteenth century B.C.

That the practical teaching of Christianity was not unrecognised at this Ramáyana and codification period may be inferred from the following texts quoted, like the above, from Sir W. Jones' translation of the Institutes:—"Let not a man be querulous though in pain, let him not injure another in deed or thought, let him not utter a word by which his fellow-creatures may suffer uneasiness, since that will obstruct his own progress to future beatitude;" and much English Protestant teaching is anticipated in the observation that "since so far as a man studies completely the system of sacred literature, so far only can he be eminently learned."

In these Institutes, moreover, a great deal of modern sanitary legislation is forestalled in the command, "Let nothing impure be thrown into water."

Briefly, let us return from the ethics of this age, probably at least some 3000 years ago, of Bharata, now British India, to its social and various aspects as illustrated in the Ramáyana. Allusions to grammar, prosody, and astronomy, should commend it to our educationists, while religious ritual should hallow it in the eyes of our High Church party. The well-ordered streets and noble roads of Lanka should gratify the Board of Works.

One-eyed giants emulate the classical Titans. An aged votaress says that she shall repose in bliss through the grace of Rama, after having seen him, the godlike one, which, with the expression used by the gods to Vishnu, "incarnate as his seed be born," seems suggestive of our sacred histories. Bharat, the brother of Rama, goes to meet him with 9000 elephants, 60,000 cars, and 100,000 archers—an army not unworthy of modern times; war-chariots at this epoch in India, as in Homeric Greece, being the precursors of our modern cavalry. Boiled, stewed, and roasted meats, with deer, peachick, jungle-fowl, sauces, and soups, and ardent liquors, would prevent the period from becoming too contemptible in the contemplation of a modern gourmand. Tooth-brushes, mirrors, combs, umbrellas, sandal-powder for the skin, evince due regard for the culture of the body. Hermits with coats of bark and matted hair, on the other hand, exhibit already a religious contempt for it. In a prayer to the goddess of a stream, the classical Naiads seem anticipated. Lovers of one faithful spouse are commended. We find rivalry in shooting with the long bow. Guards with truncheons transfer us from old England to our modern police-tranquillised State. Merchants' shops, holy fig-trees in the open squares, trees bearing lamps, awnings, crowds with garlands, a chapel in Rama's mother's mansion, coloured banners, a chieftain's cap with coronet, a fight with fists, wreaths and grain thrown on conquerors as they enter the city, the auspices taken after the sacrifice of a goat, a public assemblage of suitors for a maiden's choice, a wishing tree, Rama's name engraven on a ring, a shipwrecked sailor, grottoes, picture-rooms, waggons for draught, dames commended for being clad in "modest raiment simply neat," brickmakers and physicians, combine to present a jumble of matters which seem to introduce us to an age which has anticipated many features of both our classical and Gothic civilisations. These cannot be all considered as merely instinctive in the whole human race.

The importance of these considerations seems to be that in the Ramáyana and the Institutes of Manu we perceive the great idea of the Divine Incarnate for man's preservation published in a form incomplete in comparison with the Christian idea, yet distinctly suggestive of it. In the subsequent incarnation of Vishnu as Krishna, the recognition while on earth of his own divinity, and the inculcation of the doctrine of salvation through faith in himself, present a closer resemblance to our gospel message. Humanly speaking, the idea might seem to have been gradually developed. Protestant Christianity will now generally admit that science has incontestably demonstrated that it has been the Almighty pleasure to create our world and its vegetable and animal life in successive stages, extending over periods numbered at least by thousands of years. It seems scarcely as yet prepared to allow that mankind has been slowly educated to the mature apprehension of the complete Christian doctrine. But either this was partially comprehended by the old Indian Aryans, or else the Brahmins, by an ingenious grafting of the idea of the Incarnation into this ancient poem and other works, curiously made a large portion of the Hindus unconscious Christians.

Not only has Rama been adored as sacred to modern times, but miracle-plays have been performed in honour of him, which might seem to be the originals of those represented by the monks of mediæval Europe.

CHAPTER IV.

The idea of the Incarnation in Krishna—His Name (the Black One) as brought into juxtaposition with that of Christ—Also affinities to Apollo—Apprehension in India of portions of Christian doctrine in times previous to the Revelation of Christ—Krishna as a prototype of Christ; and similarities in his history.

IF the Hindus believe that the Almighty has taken flesh and dwelt amongst them, for their spiritual as well as bodily welfare, we must surely admit that they have knowledge of one of the essentials of Christianity. They undoubtedly obtained this knowledge, or conceived this idea, before the advent of Christianity in Palestine; but they may have realised it under that aspect, which seems to embody the most sacred truths of Christianity, at a later period. Rama is adored as divine, but, in the incarnation of Vishnu, the All-pervading one, as Krishna, the whole Universal and Absolute Spirit of God is affirmed to have been upon earth in human form. Even the appellation of Krishna might be either a prototype or resemblance of the name of Christ in its similarity of sound and aspect. The latter is very variously pronounced in different languages, and can scarcely be approximately spoken by some peoples. The nearest sound to it which the Chinese are said to be capable of uttering has been represented as Ki-li-se-tu. Krishna is worshipped as the Preserver, the cowherd lord of the world, etc., and he is related to have demonstrated his divinity by many miracles. Some of these appear to us exceedingly fantastic, but it must be remembered that fanciful narrations of the life of Christ were current amongst the early Christians; to be found in the Apocryphal Gospels, which soon appear to have been discarded by the Church. Kṛishṇa in Sanskrit literally means black, and he is represented as black in his effigies. But Godfrey Higgins, that grand and voluminous but eccentric and occasionally fanciful author, makes a suggestion concerning his name and that of Christ which may seem startling, but which is perfectly in accordance with the letter of our New Testament. He urges, in his Anacalypsis, that it is open to question as to whether the appellations of both Krishna and Christ may not be really derived from some old Aryan word, bearing the same significance as the Greek χρηστὸς (chreestos), which means good, benignant. He remarks that Suetonius alludes to the followers of Jesus as Chrestians, not Christians. A text of St. Paul's (Philippians i. 21),—"For me to live is Christ, and to die is gain,"—accords more reasonably with this meaning than the orthodox signification of "anointed." The word in the verse may have simply been χρήσον or χρήστον, but, if its rendering by Christ be faithful to the writer's meaning, it would certainly infer the interpretation of good rather than anointed for that word; for the employment of the word gain distinctly points to an antithesis, suggested by the appellation—For me to live is good, and to die is gain, sounds reasonably; but, for me to live is anointed, and to die is gain, does not seem sensible.

St. Paul altogether preaches our Lord as the benignant rather than the anointed One. In St. John iv. 25, where the woman of Samaria says "that Messias cometh, which is called Christ," it does not seem to be a necessary inference that Christ is an actual translation of Messias, but that the Messias has had that appellation applied to him.

But, whatever may have been the original signification of Krishna, in those mists of antiquity in which his real or apocryphal being arose, the later signification, at all events, is black. But again, in regard to this we are confronted by the coincidence that amongst the ancient images of European churches black virgins and bambinos are to be seen, so painted as to leave no doubt that the colour was intended.

The Sanskrit verb *kṛish* means to plough, to allure, to subdue, etc. *Kṛishta* signifies cultivated. The origin of the meaning for *Kṛishṇa*, of black or dark blue, appears to be dubious, but to be susceptible of derivation from *kṛish*. It would seem as if the divine name, represented by old tradition from an archaic dark race, may have given the original signification to the noun, rather than the noun to the divinity. The name may have arisen in accordance with this surmise of Godfrey Higgins, or from the derivation of *kṛish*, to cultivate, etc.

As from the verb signifying to pervade came the sacred name of Vishṇu, so from that meaning to plough may have been derived the name of the Aryan all-preserving deity's great incarnation in the ancient Eastern civilisation. In fact, under his eighth of the ten principal incarnations he is held, in Indian story, to have taught the cultivation of the earth. This is attributed to the third Rama, who seems, however, to be equivalent to Krishna, as a co-existing incarnation. So the classic Bacchus was narrated to have first instructed in the culture of the soil and of the vine.

With this great schooling in the commencement of civilisation may have been associated the idea of benignance. The word Christian, now used as an adjective, is undoubtedly held to signify good in the highest sense, not anointed, either actually or figuratively. So from the name of the Indian incarnation of the divine, originally representing the teacher of the cultivation of the earth, may have firstly proceeded the notion of benevolence as attached to the word, and secondly, from the blackness of the material representations of the idea—*i.e.* of the images of Krishna—a word with that signification, to which the poet of the epic applied his fanciful or legendary reason. Krishna also presents affinities to Apollo, the sun god of Greece, the deity of the silver bow, slaying the serpent as Apollo the Python, etc., as if the latter had been an adaptation of the earlier and more earthly conceptions of the former. In old Irish *Creeshna* or *Krishna* has been applied to the sun, and the name has been held to have been derived from the sun in *Aries*. At the time when the Mahabharata epic was written, which appears, probably, to have been later than 1400 B.C., the name of Krishna was supposed or conceived by the poet to have been bestowed on account of the blackness of the infant's complexion. The two brothers, who were at the same time incarnations of Vishnu or Narāyana, etc., were respectively born—white in the case of Bala Rama, and black in that of Krishna. Vishnu plucked two hairs, according to the poet's fanciful account, which entered into Devakī and Rohini. The one was black, and became Krishna; from the other, white, issued Bala Rama, his brother, the twin incarnation, though the divine honours seem only to have been, in their fullest extent, bestowed upon or reverenced in Krishna.

The Princess Krishnâ is also related, in the Mahabbharata, to have obtained the appellation of black, in its feminine form, on account of having been born of that colour. Blackness is here undoubtedly associated with, or not held incompatible with, the attribute of beauty, for she is styled the beautiful.

The regularity of contour in features, and brilliance of eyes and smile, in the dark races of the lands of the sun, are not deprived of their fascinations by the darkness of hue. They may be even enhanced by the purity of that blackness. The notion of disease may be associated with whiteness amongst dark people.

In India the darker people are black, the lighter of the complexions of the south of Europe. The Indians may perceive beauty in both, just as we may equally admire the charms of a dark Italian signora and fair German fräulein.

Still there certainly seems to be a suggestiveness in the story of Krishna of some ancient application of the name, with other than a mere signification of colour, such as teacher of cultivation, or the benignant one, as parallel to Buddha, the enlightened. And such a signification seems not less worthy of Christ than that of the anointed one; which was also applied to Cyrus, who is called the Lord's anointed in the book of Isaiah, xlv. 1.

The general history and doctrine of Krishna distinctly suggests the apprehension or acceptance of main features of Christianity by the inhabitants of ancient India. The more fanciful and elaborate framework in which they have invested the Idea may have been divinely ordered as adapted to the eastern, before it was revealed to the western world. It may have been our vanity which has caused us to pay insufficient attention to the divine command—"Judge not"—and condemned the Indians as votaries of degrading, feeble, or ungodly superstitions, before fitly examining their creeds. We may conceive a sort of imitation of our revealed and Christian doctrine to have arisen in their imaginations without the Truth being in it. But if a notion of religious doctrine, similar to our own though in fanciful form, arose in their minds without divine revelation, it would seem that it might have arisen in our own, in the purer form suggested by the circumstances of our lives in the west.

We may assert that it is a merely specious resemblance—that no real resemblance exists, as did the missionary Ward at the commencement of this century, or ascribe it all to the wiles of the devil. At all events, the Indian idea of the divine incarnate for man's sake may be argued not to differ more from our own proportionately than their general fashions of life, and aspects of nature, from ours. It distinctly seems to present the appearance of a prototype to our own Revelation.

We may, indeed, maintain that the Indian conceptions of the incarnation, under their more divine expression at least, have been borrowed from Christianity, yet if they could conceive the cruder forms of the idea, it seems consistent with the progress of the human imagination to suppose that they could intensify the divine attributes, and, from depicting a Rama, create or credit a Krishna. He may have had an historical basis of truth, and been raised to his divine majesty, when time and the accretion of poetical narratives concerning him had exaggerated his heroic or benevolent deeds. At all events, there is the belief in his divinity as a fact. It may be asserted to be different from, or unworthy to be compared with, the Christian doctrine. But it distinctly exhibits as similar a form, when passages in the Mahábhárata and our Gospels are compared, as that European doctrine could be likely to display in India, supposing that the two had originated from the same source, taking into consideration the diversities in the outward aspects of Indian and European life, under the influences of climate.

The Roman Catholic missionaries are said to have attributed to the instigation of the devil the remarkable affinities, which they could not avoid noticing, that the ritual of Buddhism presented to their own. We may make the same assertion in regard to the affinities afforded by Krishna to Christ, or we may allow that the Hindus really do possess a highly embellished form of Christian doctrine, introduced into India 1800 years ago, by St. Thomas or some other apostolic missionary. We are then confronted by the remarkable fact that they at that time rapidly adopted the Christian idea, expressed it under a nomenclature, and in numerous additional narratives of their own, or adaptations to it of the old legends of their black idol Krishna, yet that they now almost utterly refuse to modify their faith in accordance with the true form of it, which our modern Apostles are zealous in endeavouring to impart to them. It is wonderful that they should then have been so ready to accept what they are now so reluctant to modify. If they could then be persuaded so rapidly to change their religions, why are they so conservative now? Why did the divine grace irradiate their hearts so much more freely then than now?

It is more consonant with the testimony to believe that the divine spirit of Christianity, before our religion was promulgated on the shores of the Mediterranean, was apprehended in more archaic form on the banks of the Ganges. The arguments for the Indian autochthonity of the story of Krishna are exceedingly powerful. The doctrine of the incarnation of the divine in the human is also apparent in ancient Egypt, and under a materialistic form in Greece and elsewhere. But nowhere is it displayed in a progressive series of ideas so indicative of original growth as in Hindustan.

And, not only in the principal idea of God incarnate in man, but in the narrative of the man in whom the Almighty is born upon earth—in the actual story—the religion of Krishna has resemblances to that of Christ.

Krishna is represented as the incarnation of deity, considered as preserving, vivifying, and all-pervading, while Christ is termed in Christianity the Son of God. But Christ, like Krishna, is said to be the Almighty Himself, the Supreme Spirit of the universe. Although Christ is the Son, none the less is He God, One in Three.

In the Nicene Creed He is styled God of God, Light of Light, etc. etc. In fact the sonship remains only as a mystery, sublime and incomprehensible in human thought. In both Christianity and Hinduism the deity is distinctly adored, as having been born in man, in the persons of those who have been named Christ and Krishna.

A massacre of innocents attends the birth of the Indian Preserver, by order of Kansa, tyrant of Madura, who has been informed that one of the children of Devaki, Krishna's mother, will be born for his destruction. His birth is attended with supernatural manifestations. Amongst other miracles he pronounces remarkable words over the corpse of a child and restores it to life. His death is suggestive of that of the classical Achilles, whose mother Thetis, one of the Nereids, was an immortal. Like Achilles, Krishna dies from an arrow-wound in the foot, in fulfilment of a prophecy. He is suspended after death upon a tree, to become the prey of vultures, but ascends to Heaven and re-assumes his divinity. The name of his mother, Devaki, seems to bear the signification of divine; which is also apparent in that of his father, Vasu-deva.

CHAPTER V.

Introduction of Buddhism into China—Reformers in India preaching salvation by faith only in Krishna—The Mahábhárata Epic, and description of an ancient Picnic—Quotations from the Bhagavad Gita, which present the aspect of Christian doctrine—Quotations from other parts of the Epic, setting forth the divine nature of Krishna.

At about the period in which Christianity was preached in Palestine, Asia Minor, Greece, and Rome, a religion, confessedly of Indian origin, was introduced into China. No modern critics have denied that Buddhism—the Chinese religion of Fo—arose in Hindustan, at least some centuries B.C. In this religion we find, not only a correspondence with the Roman Catholic ritual as has been observed, but also a grand Lama, a spiritual potentate curiously similar to the Pope. We also see monasteries and nunneries of celibate votaries, etc. etc. Moreover, there is again a resemblance in the events related of Gautauma Buddha to those recorded of the Founder of our faith—for instance, in the temptation of the Evil One. But Gautauma Buddha, or Sakya muni, is not generally adored as an incarnation of the Divine, but only as a man, who through successive transmigrations has purified his soul of all desires of the flesh and attained the blissful repose of Nirvana. There have been many discussions amongst European critics upon the precise nature of this Nirvāna. It may perhaps be best apprehended as a blissful, holy state, in which desire is lost in tranquillity. Buddhism has conceived or adopted heavens of reward and hells of punishment, though neither seem to be eternal; and it by no means remains content, as has been supposed, with only a nihilistic future. It inculcates the doctrine of future happiness to be obtained, and present contentment, in a thorough change of the heart and desires. Krishna, the incarnate Preserver, who is worshipped by so many amongst the 200,000,000 of our great dependency, is a Divinity of light and liberty. In that temple of Juggernaut even, name so associated in our minds with the horrible observances of gross superstition, Dr. Hunter has shown us, in his work on Orissa, that all caste distinctions are levelled, and even the shedding of a drop of blood is absolute defilement to the sanctity of the place. In the vast concourse of pilgrims at the great festivals many lives are sacrificed to fatigue and disease, especially of women who throng to this sanctuary. But Juggernaut, "the Lord of the world," does not demand such sacrifices.

Juggernaut, as we have coarsely rendered Jagañātha, is merely one of the numerous names of Vishṇu, or the Almighty considered as all-pervading or preserving. Not only do we find an apparently more original Christianity in India, but also a more original Protestantism. Wickliffe appeared in England in the fourteenth century A.D., and Luther in Germany more than a century later. Several reformers arose in India between the twelfth and fifteenth centuries of our era, who preached faith in Krishna as the manifestation of the Supreme Spirit and the way to salvation. The inward man was to be the essential care, temples and images were to be considered useless, or actually prohibited. The followers of Kabir observed none of the Hindu rites and ceremonies; their homage consisting chiefly in chanting hymns. No visible objects of worship were admitted. Ramanuja, in the twelfth century A.D., removed all restrictions from his followers as to bathing and eating. The chief religious tenet of the Ramanujas, says H. H. Wilson in vol. xvi. of "Asiatic Researches," is the assertion that Vishnu is Brahma, "that he was before all worlds, and was the cause and creator of all." Chaitanya was born about the fifteenth century A.D., in Bengal, and admitted all castes, even Mohammedans, amongst his disciples. The whole religious and moral code of his sect is comprised in the word Bhakti, signifying a union of implicit faith with incessant devotion. Amongst the adorers of Krishna solitary mortification is practised; and there are monasteries with superiors, resident disciples, and endowments of land.

As the Ramáyana records the history of Vishnu incarnate in humanity as Rama, so does the other great Indian epic, the Mahábhárata, narrate that of the Preserver in Krishna.

It is considered to have been written subsequently to the Ramáyana, for it contains the story of Rama. But Professor Weber ascribes it to an earlier date in respect to its original purport. Its bulk reaches the gigantic size of 120,000 epic verses, or, according to Professor Monier Williams, of about 220,000 long lines; and no Englishman has yet had the enterprise to attack it bodily in translation. This poem and the compilation of the Vedas, and other works, are attributed to the divine sage Vyāsa, who has a mythical aspect—his name meaning arranger or compiler. European critics have pronounced the work to be by several hands, but it does not appear to have undergone any strictly critical examination. So have Homer, Shakspeare, and other poets been held to be names of mere collections. Its colossal proportions, and the extent of episodical matter in it, appear to be the chief arguments for that view. But if the author wrote with a religious purpose he would naturally have become episodical; like the writer of a modern novel with a purpose. The Brahmins have displayed such literary fertility that there would appear little reason for their interpolating an old poem rather than inditing a fresh story. It may be argued that the sanctity of the poem urged them to this. But the sanctity of the work appears to be owing to the portions considered interpolations. Fifteen years' labour, about the time bestowed by Gibbon on his History of the Decline and Fall of the Roman Empire, would complete the work at the rate of some fifty lines per diem, allowing for holy days. Then let us consider Sir Walter Scott's series of novels. As the poem, with its luxuriance of imagery and wealth of description, becomes occasionally prolix, and seems to exhibit little effort at condensation, the more arduous labour of writing is little apparent, and fifty lines per diem constitute no exaggerated quota. When we contemplate the examples of ancient Indian constancy in work, in the elaborate productions of the chisel in the granite rocks of Ellora, etc., the proportions of the poem seem less stupendous. However, some additions must be admitted to exist in it. It professes that "no narrative on earth is not founded on this epos." It is "the great manual of all that is moral, useful, and agreeable." The author may have industriously striven to epitomise all legends and didactic morality existing in his time. He may have been styled Vyāsa, in regard to this, and his other literary work in connection with the Vedas, and so his proper nomenclature have been lost in the mists of antiquity. The name of Vaisámpáyana is also associated with the poem. Professor Weber adduces the express intimation in it that it consisted formerly of 8800 slokas only. This he appears to consider an argument against the production of the epic by the author, or authors, to whom it is attributed. Of course the transcripts of an antique work must be supposed to contain alterations, emendations, and additions. We acknowledge one at least in our New Testament (1 St. John v. 7), but in the natural process of writing an author amplifies his own work. It is even quite consistent with acknowledged facts of authorship to conceive him composing it originally as a narrative, and subsequently interlarding it with the didactic morality, or heightening the divine or supernatural element. Pope printed the Rape of the Lock without the machinery of the Sylphs, and extended it to five cantos in the subsequent year. Byron retouched and largely amplified his poems. Shakspeare's Hamlet was a creation of growth. A poet attempting to embody the legends of Krishna would naturally find an accretion of them as he continued, and the diviner and purer aspects of his doctrine, such as those displayed in the Bhagaveda Gita, could, humanly speaking, have only proceeded from the matured contemplation of the attributes of the character. The contrasts presented by the Catholic Lent and Carnival are as marked as those in the religious aspects of the Mahábhárata.

Mr. R. Mitra, who is esteemed about the most learned Hindu antiquarian of our time, has recently given a picture from it in a magazine article. He observes of this, that it is so different from what we now behold in Hindustan, that we might imagine the people portrayed in it to be sea kings of Norway, or Teuton knights; yet they are Hindus of the Hindus—incarnations of the divinity and a holy sage who had abjured the world for constant communion with his maker, also the author of a law treatise. Baladeva, Krishna, and his favourite disciple and friend Arjouna, accompanied by a party of eminent persons, visit a watering-place on the west coast of Gujerat. They come with their families and courtesans, and betake themselves to feasting, drinking, singing, dancing, and bathing, with most western-like ardour, and in a very promiscuous manner. Baladeva was the only constant person, and he was drunk. Ladies of pleasure joined the orgies, and they danced or romped till they tottered and fell. Strong spirits were introduced, including rum, which seems to have been drunk neat, with fried birds and sugared cake by way of refection. A roast buffalo, which, remarks Mr. Mitra, was a favourite viand with Hindus in former days, formed the *pièce de resistance* in the banquet, and venison appeared, boiled and garnished with mangoes and condiments, besides other meats and curries. Sweetmeats and cheese were introduced, and the ladies were present, at all events at the dessert, contrary to modern Hindu custom, and indulged in spirits and roasted birds, besides the sweets. Maidens, however, do not appear to have been there; and the heroes danced with their wives. They bathed in the sea together, adorned with flowers, and jubilant with draughts of wine, not, however, without their garments. Krishna and his 16,000 wives played in the water, and they sported on floats, etc., apparently thus constituting prototypes to the bathers in gay modern French *bains de la mer.* Then they entertained themselves in boats, in "large vessels with commodious cabins, painted inside with gardens, trees, festal halls, etc.," and gay in flags outside. Baladeva is described as being dressed in two pieces of sky-blue cloth. The Brahmin sage Narada made them all laugh, and the ladies showered on him pearls, garlands, etc. Altogether, unless the poet had a marvellous imagination, the people amongst whom such a description could have been written may be accepted as predecessors of, or kindred to, the gay, voluptuous, and valiant Greeks, and hardy, hard-living, romantic Northmen, without violence to the understanding. They certainly existed before the latter, and it is difficult to conceive them as being Hindus subsequent to the time of Alexander's invasion. Yet in the Bhagavad Gîtâ, or divine song, an episode of this Mahábhárata which has been published in an English translation by Mr. J. Cockburn Thompson, the most benignant and philosophically divine words are uttered by Krishna to Arjouna. As has been remarked, they seem as complete in contrast to this revel of the Harivansa as the Catholic austerities of Lent to the wild indulgence of the preceding Carnival.

"I," says Krishna, "whenever there is a relaxation of duty, O son of Bharata, and an increase of impiety, reproduce myself for the protection of the good and destruction of the evil-doers. He who truly comprehends my divine birth and action does not undergo regeneration (*i.e.* transmigration into another human or animal life) when he quits the body, but comes to me. He who professes faith acquires spiritual knowledge. He who ignores the truth, and is devoid of faith and of doubtful mind, perishes. I am the sacrificial butter"—the clarified butter offered with the sacrificial cake corresponds to the wine of the mass service—"and the whole sacrificial rite. He who, remembering me at the moment of death, quits the body and comes forth, enters my nature."

Arjouna said to Krishna, "Thou art the supreme universal spirit, Creator and Lord of all that exists, God of gods, Lord of the universe."

The Holy One spoke, "They say that the eternal sacred fig-tree grows with its roots above and its branches downwards; he who knows this tree, the leaves of which are Vedic hymns, knows the Vedas; when one has hewn down this sacred fig-tree, together with its wide-spreading roots, with the steady axe of indifference to the world, then may that place be sought to which those that go return no more. I declare the truth to thee; abandoning all religious duties, seek me as thy refuge. I will deliver thee from all sin. Be not anxious. Thou art very much beloved of me, and, therefore, I will tell thee what is good—'They who devoutly worship me are in me, and I in them.'"

Although the story of Krishna and the narratives of the previous incarnations be demonstrated to have originated in India, it may still be held that the divine expression of the idea thus propounded in the Bhagavad Gita, this episode of the Mahábhárata, may have been brought to India after its promulgation in Palestine in the Gospel of St. John. Professor Monier Williams, of Oxford, and the Rev. Mr. Hardwicke, in *Christ and other Masters*, appear to entertain the view that this "divine song" of the Hindus was suggested by, or taken from, the Gospel. The legend of the success of St. Thomas's mission to India may have a firm foundation of truth. But, undoubtedly, numerous ancient Aryan writings in India, including these two great epics apart from this episode, seem to lead up to its doctrines by a natural procession of ideas. Abstractedly there would appear to be no greater improbability in the Almighty revealing His truths amongst the population of India than amongst that of the Roman Empire, of which Palestine was a province at the time of the Gospel dispensation.

It is by no means in the Bhagavad Gita only that the conception of the divinity of Krishna, and the Christ-like nature of many of his words and attributes appear; and a curiously elaborate system of interpolation must be conceived. And why again, if they took so much trouble to incorporate Christian ideas with their own then, do they not more eagerly adopt our religious expressions now?

In the *Sabha* division of the Mahábhárata, Krishna, as the incarnate Vishnu, as *Narāyana*, moving on the waters, is hailed as Invisible nature, as the Eternal, as the Superior to all beings, as the Intelligence, the Heaven, the Earth, etc. It is said that "in effect, the generation and fortune of worlds is in Krishna; this universe and all that exists, movable and immovable, is in Krishna."

Again, under another name, Vishnu, incarnate in Krishna, is styled Vāsudeva, the truth, immortality, purification, and sanctity itself; also the eternal Brahman, the supreme certainty, the light without end, from whom the sages have related the divine works.

The poetical and fanciful element, however, which is so distinctly present in Milton's descriptions of the heavenly host, and in the engagement of the Son of God to take humanity upon Himself for the redemption of mankind, accompanies these spiritual conceptions. In concert with the *Devas*, Indra, the divine regent of the firmament, made with Narāyana arrangements for his particular descent upon earth; corresponding to the manner in which the angels are introduced in Milton's work. Narāyana is also called the ancient one; who has had no birth, nor will he have end; whom spirit cannot measure, who is everything under infinite forms. The sun and moon, the constellations, the cardinal points, all are said to subsist in Krishna.

In this poem a passage mentions the condonement of all sin, except the sin against Mahadeva, the great god, equivalent to Siva, the third person of the Hindu Trinity, which seems exactly correspondent to the text in the New Testament concerning the forgiveness of all sins but those against the Holy Ghost. Allusion is made to Krishna as he from whom the universe derives its origin, who is the commencement and the development, who is the birth, death, and resurrection of beings. The description of the youth of Krishna, in the Harivansa, a sort of addenda to the Mahábhárata, is so charming that it is not wonderful that the Hindu women have been said especially to adore him. In this he is called the "universal pastor of the world," the sovereign of heaven and earth, uniting his divine nature to the human.

As the missionary Ward wrote, "According to the Shree Bhaguvutu, Muhabharutu, and other works, the god Krishnu, a form of Vishnoo, was incarnate to destroy Kings Shishoopalu and Kung-Su, and a number of giants;" but he was also incarnate to found virtue on the earth, and conduct souls to the bliss of heaven. He, who was without beginning or end, the creator of the world, and its universal soul, has been adored as giving to those that sacrifice the fruit of their piety —as being at the same time the sacred offering and the supreme spirit, and as being honoured in prayer, while himself the prayer. The mystic doctrine of the Roman Catholic mass service seems here suggested.

In the description of Krishna's city of Mathura we find ministers of state, priests, and heads of corporations. The staircases of the houses are decorated with paintings. A triumphal arch is erected, and the streets are adorned with flags, garlands, and vases filled with water perfumed with the sandal. The women are represented as saying that although he did not possess the crown he was worthy of the title of King of kings, for he had protected Mathura against its enemies.

The Mahábhárata, altogether like the Ramáyana, seems to introduce us to an age which may be truthfully defined as cultured.

CHAPTER VI.

Continued quotations from the Mahábhárata as to the divinity of Krishna—Divine birth of the heroes of the poem—The doctrines of Christ not diminished in significance by the pre-existence of the Incarnation theory amongst our Aryan race in India—Considerations as to the Brahmins having copied Christian expressions.

PROFESSOR MONIER WILLIAMS says in his treatise on the Indian epics that these poems contain evidences of high civilisation; and that "nothing can be more beautiful and touching than the pictures of domestic and social happiness in the Rámáyana and Mahábhárata. Children are in them represented as dutiful to their parents, younger brothers are respectful to their elders, and husbands and wives are mutually tender. He remarks that the diction of the Indian epics is more polished than Homer. Heaven and hell are prominently assigned as the reward or punishment of the deeds of this life. Escape from hell and from earthly transmigrations to eternal life, in the latter through faith in Krishna, is not only promulgated in the Bhagavad Gita, which has been asserted to be an interpolation during the Christian era, but elsewhere distinctly appears in the Mahábhárata. According to a French translation of the epic by M. Fauche, which seems to be the most complete which has been published, Krishna is addressed under one of his names as follows:—"Tu es habile, Keçava, tu es le commencement et la fin de tous les êtres." "Tu es, meutrier de Madhu (the demon), la route suprème et la tête des Dieux." "Il n'existe en toi, meutrier de Madhu, ni colère, ni envie, ni mensonge ni cruauté." "L'homme qui a mortifié son corps est exalté sur la voûte des cieux. La est la pure Dwaravati, on reside le meutrier de Madhu." "Il est le Dieu antique, descendu sur la terre, il est le devoir eternel. Les Brahmes qui savent les Vedas, les hommes qui ont la science de l'âme universelle assurent que la magnanime Krishna est l'eternel devoir. Govinda (Krishna's name as the herdsman) est appelé le plus grand des purificateurs." Krishna says to the Princess Krishnâ, "Himalaya se fendu, la terre n'être plus que des fragments et le grand tapin des eaux se dessécher que ma parole être vaine Krishnâ."

Professor Weber of Berlin asserts that this translation of M. Fauche can only pass for such in a qualified sense. But he, at all events, seems to allow the Christian aspect of matter in the poem, though he ascribes it to interpolations after Christianity may have been promulgated in India.

Krishna is concerned with the great wars described in the Mahábhárata; but he endeavours to act as mediator between the contending parties.

According to the ancient Aryan system, which admits of the personification, in the thought, of lesser deities as emanations from the supreme, not only is Krishna an incarnation of deity itself, but the virtuous princes, whose side he espouses, are incarnations of inferior divinities. They are called the sons of Pandu, but they are in reality the sons of Pritha, Pandu's wife, by the divine influence of Dharma, Vayu, and Indra, regents respectively of justice, the wind, and the firmament, and of the two Aswins, twin sons of Surya, the Sun. A curious ancient tradition is evidently set forth in the account of the marriage of these five princes with the Princess Krishnâ, a polyandrous proceeding totally repugnant to the ordinary ancient Aryan, or modern Hindu notions. But it is reconciled by explaining that these deities, the parents, are in reality only one, and that their incarnations upon earth are in reality only one.

The doctrine of punishment in life for the sins of a former existence is very materialistically expressed in regard to this princess. It is said that the damsel was born under an unhappy destiny, in chastisement of her actions in a former state, so that, notwithstanding her beauty, she could not find a husband. Her earnest prayers for a spouse, in five emphatic repetitions, resulted in her obtaining these five husbands.

At the birth of the eldest of the Pandu princes, a voice from heaven exclaimed, "This is the best of virtuous men." At the birth of Arjouna showers of flowers fell from heaven, and celestial minstrels filled the air with harmony. We see the faith of Yudishthira in Krishna combined with his support of the Brahmins when he says that "the whole earth has indeed been conquered through reliance on the power of Krishna, by the favour of the Brahmins." Rules for obtaining final emancipation are enunciated in a didactic discourse, in which Krishna joins.

It is observed in this poem, "occupied by duty, which has for its object the final emancipation"—*i.e.* from future transmigrations. The prevalence of infidel opinions before the end of the world is prophesied. The ancient legend of the deluge and ark appears in the Mahábhárata as assigned to Vaivasvata, the seventh Manu.

The magnificent vigour and prowess ascribed to the heroes in the use of the bow, club, and other weapons, argue traditions of a physically powerful race, and wine is even recommended by Krishna, again a seeming parallel to the incident in our Lord's life of producing the wine. After the death of Krishna, and the restoration of the princes whom he had favoured to their sovereignty, the divine purpose of their lives is illustrated by their finally abandoning the earth and seeking the sacred mountain by which they shall reach heaven; and a kind of Pilgrim's Progress, suggestive of Bunyan's journey of Christian, concludes their histories.

Altogether, under the exhibition of prolific imagination presented to us in the Mahábhárata, and in its evidently prehistoric legends, the story of Deity incarnate upon earth for man's benefit is beautifully set forth; in a casket elaborate but nevertheless containing essential doctrines and narratives corresponding with those of Christ. In fact, if the essential doctrines of Christianity were revealed by Providence to the ancient Aryan civilisations of the East, in a shape appropriate to the wants of the time, the old difficult problem of the destiny of the virtuous heathen would be in the way of solution. We may find assurance that light is shed upon our old ignorance upon this point, and that the esoteric teaching of the divine in the human has been diffused more widely in the world than we have supposed. Four hundred years ago we were in utter ignorance of the existence of America, and its advanced central civilisations. Devout Christians were practically unacquainted with the Bible; and a large number, not of the lowest ranks in life, would have been unable to peruse it for themselves, if presented to them. Its publication encountered great opposition, and Christianity was declared to be endangered by any attack upon the Roman Church. Now that these scriptures of our own race, long trusted by them as divinely inspired, are being promulgated, it may be surely hoped that Christianity, educated in the science of the age, and warned by the example of old Catholic bigotry, will not refuse at least to investigate them impartially. If the divine word is to be discerned in them, it need not destroy our faith in the true doctrine of Christ, but only induce us to recognise a scope in the influences of the Spirit of Righteousness larger than we had attributed to it. There is no abstract reason why the influence of holiness should not have rested upon the inhabitants of east as well as west. Here are, at all events, the phenomena that a Trinity in unity, and Incarnate Preserver, are found in the religion and sacred books of the people of India; and that these people profess and appear to have entertained faith in them from an age more remote than that of the revelation of our Saviour in Judæa. And it was amongst our own Aryan race, in the region of Palestine, that the Christian doctrine is shown to have been most widely embraced. Our four Gospels have descended to us in the Greek, not in a Semitic language. The Aramaic dialect seems to have been the ordinary language of Palestine at our Lord's epoch. He is thought to have quoted from the Aramaic version of the Jewish Scriptures. We have indeed a bare statement by Papias, a father of the Church, that St. Matthew wrote a gospel in Hebrew, and we have the Peschito version, attributed to the second century, in Syriac. But it is in a language akin to the ancient Sanskrit of India that the gospel narratives appear to have become generally diffused in the rising Christendom of the Roman Empire. Nor does the ordinary life of the Hindus, moreover, especially as exemplified in the village communistic system, exhibit antagonism to the Christian dispensation, as proclaimed by Christ. No people on earth so strictly fulfil our Lord's command to render unto Cæsar the things that be Cæsar's, and, according to their faiths, unto God the things that be God's. Even the images reprobated by Protestants, in common with Jews and Mohammedans, are not universally employed amongst them, as has been shown. However Protestantism has styled Roman Catholic Christianity idolatrous for the use of images, so that the Indians are the less able to complain that irrational superstition is attributed to them, upon that score.

It may be urged, in fact, that the passages in the Mahábhárata and other works which appear to afford comparisons with the moral teachings of the New Testament, or which seem to present Krishna in a light similar to that in which Jesus is set forth, are imitations. It may be alleged that they were adopted by the Brahmins, and interpolated amongst the portions of this poem and other literary productions, which are acknowledged to be more ancient than the time of Christ. The Brahmins may be supposed to have been thus desirous of adding sanctity and weight to their object of idolatrous devotion, Krishna. But if they so clearly recognised the value, or divine characteristics, of the New Testament teaching, it is curious that they did not adopt the story of Jesus in its entireness. As according to their religious theories incarnations of the Divine are frequently occurring, and, as Krishna is not an object of adoration in the Vedas or Institutes of Manu, Christ might have been altogether instead of partially accepted by them. The notion of their interspersing their old literature with a number of didactic observations and episodes seems altogether founded upon prejudice rather than evidence. There was no necessity for it; for the Hindus might have accepted the moral truths as revelations of a recent incarnation, according to their theories.

There does, indeed, appear to have been an incarnation of the Deity credited in the south of India, which exhibits, in some respects, still closer affinities to the incarnation of our Lord. This will be given in a subsequent chapter. It has been thought to have been actually a legendary history of Christ, naturalised in India. If therefore the Brahmins adopted the maxims of the New Testament, and the more spiritual view of the Incarnation, as appearing in St. John's Gospel, it seems remarkable that they did not attribute them to this incarnation. But it may of course be held that the Hindus of the northern district of India still desired to believe in the Krishna, whom they had idolatrously deified, that they were wise enough to perceive the merits of Christ's perfect doctrine, and that therefore they clothed him in the benignant and moral garb of our Saviour. Once acquainted with the divine idea, delivered amongst the Jews, our Aryan forefathers, or collateral ancestors, according to this view, eagerly amplified it, and interspersed it largely amongst their voluminous sacred literature. Like the Jews, however, they have claimed the direct inspiration of the Almighty in their own scriptures. We have allowed this assertion of the Jews alone to be divine truth. But then we have only recently become acquainted with the scriptures of the race whose language is in affinity with our own. Part of Christendom still proclaims that God only speaks through the Pontiff of the Church of Rome, as the only true interpreter of the Old and New Testaments. The Standard of Faith may again alter without destroying Christianity.

CHAPTER VII.

Character of the Hindus—Comparison of aspects of Hinduism with Mediæval Christianity—Krishna and marriage—His Incarnations in the Bhagavat Purana—Battle between the Angels and Evil Spirits in that book—Quotations from the Sanskrit, displaying similitudes to texts in the New Testament—Remarks by Dr. Muir upon that point.

In regard to the general habits and demeanour of the Hindus, they do not, at the worst, compare disadvantageously with those of Protestant England. If we conscientiously perambulate our great towns, or even our rural districts, observing all classes, especially that caste for which the gin-palace displays its usually gorgeous interior, even on what we style the Lord's day, we shall not find much occasion for the vaunting of moral superiority. The Indian coolies present but a mean and barbarous appearance, with only a poor waist-cloth for raiment, but they are usually sober and hard-working. They may be heard in Bombay lightening their labours on the English works with quaint songs and choruses, in excellent "time." Their wives sing gaily, also, as a party of them, for instance, flatten down the chunam floor of a house; and they trot along with their heavy burdens on their heads, or their little bright-eyed naked children seated astride of their hips, with pleasant contented faces, though probably, like the men, they have but one, or, at the most two, meals of coarse grain or other frugal aliment in the day, even in periods of no famine pressure, with a few sweetmeats on rare occasions. They are certainly cleanly in their habits. Lord Northbrook, late Governor-General, said publicly, on July 18, 1876, that "the millions of people of India commend themselves entirely to the affections of those who govern them. He did not think that there existed a more contented people—a people more ready to obey to the letter, and feel a confidence and trust in those placed over them. All do their duty to their friends and relatives in times of difficulty, and all live peaceably with one another. No man who has had charge of a district goes away without a feeling of affection for them."

They remain constant to their faiths as a people; and their numbers are about equivalent to those of the nations of Europe, without Russia. In comparing the polity under which they appear to have existed from time immemorial with that of the inhabitants of Europe, there appears to be an obvious concordance with that of the 70,000,000 of the Greek Church in Russia. These have a village communistic system and a hereditary married clergy of Brahminical aspect. The kingly and warrior caste had, however, depressed the Russians to utter subservience; and a monkish celibate clergy has occupied the higher position in the church. The wilder religious ceremonies of the Hindus, whether ancient or modern—the revelry depicted in Mr. R. Mitra's quotation from the Mahábhárata, in contrast with the religious fervour expressed in the Bhagavad Gita—do not seem so disconsonant with Christianity when compared with mediæval practices. Miracle plays, boy bishops, dances of death, etc. etc., present us with performances of religious origin which are quite as eccentric as those of the Hindus. They have partially reformed; but, subdued as they have been by the terrors of conquest, they cannot be expected to have ameliorated their conceptions of propriety in the expression of religious emotion so rapidly or completely as ourselves. The Indian Krishna, amongst his performance of miracles, and his utterance of noble discourses, is concerned in wars and worldly questions, and he largely departs from the moderation enjoined to some castes and recommended to others, in the Institutes of Manu, of having only one wife. Gautauma Buddha, however, the corresponding and virtually collateral object of adoration in India at the time of Christ, as presenting, like Krishna, perfection in humanity, is related to have abandoned wife as well as throne, and to have preached the religious value of ascetic celibacy; as, indeed, did many followers of the voluptuous-seeming Krishna. Brahminism, in its code, enjoined marriage; and it has frequently recounted the praises of the society of women, and the truth and beauty of their instincts.

"It is not the house itself which is called a house; the housewife is declared to be the house. Without a wife a householder's house will be empty, though crowded in every part," is said in the Mahábhárata. Also, "A wife is the half of a man; a wife is a most excellent friend; a wife is the foundation of the three objects of life—*i.e.* virtue, pleasure, and wealth; a wife is the foundation for him who seeks to be redeemed (from this world)." "These sweetly speaking women are friends in solitude; they are fathers in matters of duty; they are mothers to those who are in distress; they are a repose to the traveller in the wilderness. The wife who is devoted to her husband always follows him when he dies and departs hence, when he is alone and in misfortune. The wife who dies first, after death expects the coming of her husband; and when he dies first, the good wife follows him (as a sati)." "Until he finds a wife a man is only half (of a whole). The house which is not occupied by children is like a cemetery." "For these women are by nature instructed; whilst the learning of men is taught them by books."

The above are quoted from Dr. Muir's translations of texts from the Mahábhárata and other Sanskrit works.

When Krishna (the incarnate Vishnu) enters the city of Dwarka in triumph, as described in the Bhagavat Purana, he is attired in yellow, with a garland of flowers. He first pays his respects to his parents, and then retires to domestic felicity amongst his wives. But although this book, in recounting the story of Krishna, here portrays him in materialistic manner, it affords a highly spiritual or metaphysical, though fanciful, conception of the incarnation altogether. Bhagavat, says M. Emile Burnouf, translator into French of the Bhagavat Purana, is the most elevated and holy of the names of Krishna, signifying the possessor of all perfections. When Bhagavat took the form of Intelligence, Brahma proceeded from him. Krishna alone of incarnations is Bhagavat entirely, who by the divine Mâyà, desire of the sovereign Intelligence, manifests everything in the universe. Bhagavat is always mentioned as united with Mâyà, the union of Spirit and Illusion seeming the creation of mind. Mâyà is also defined to be Invisible Nature. In his sixteenth incarnation Bhagavat purged the earth of the tyrannical kings of the warrior caste; in his nineteenth incarnation he was Krishna, and in his twentieth, Buddha; and as Kalki, the horse, or as mounted on the horse, he is yet to come. Under the incarnation of Krishna, he is invoked as having returned to bear the burden of the earth, and to offer a perpetual subject of meditations to those that know him, and have no other object of thought. Adoration is offered to Krishna, son of Vasudeva, cherished child of Devaki, to the young shepherd of the pastor, Nanda.

In this book we find the devas, or angels, victorious over the Asuras or evil spirits, which again appears like an anticipation of Milton's conception; while the variety of ingeniously tormenting hells mentioned in it seems to forestall Dante. The originality of these ideas in India must be admitted at all events. It cannot surely be contended that the allusions to them in this Purana, even if it be ascribed to a recent epoch, have been suggested by the great Italian and English epic poets.

Like the Jews and Christians, as has been observed, the Hindus have absolutely claimed divine revelation as the inspiration of their sacred scriptures. It is difficult to discern any intrinsic spiritual difference between the following and texts of similar purport, which have been held to testify to the divine teaching of the New Testament.

"Thou, even thou, art my mother, father, kinsman, friend. Thou art knowledge and riches. Thou art my all, O God of gods."

"He by whom swans are made white, and parrots green and peacocks variegated, will provide thy subsistence."

"Amass that wealth which has nothing to fear from king or from thief, and which does not abandon thee when thou art dead."

"Hear the sum of duty which is declared in a million of books; helping others is to be esteemed as virtue, oppression of others as sin."

"Hear the sum of righteousness, and, when thou hast heard, ponder it; do not to others what would be repugnant to thyself."

"The good, when they promote the welfare of others, expect no reciprocity."

"Let no man do to another that which would be repugnant to himself."

"What virtue is there in the goodness of the man who is

good to his benefactors; he who is good to those who do him wrong is called good by the virtuous."

"A good man who regards the welfare of others, does not show enmity even when he is being destroyed; when it is being cut down the sandal tree imparts fragrance to the edge of the axe."

"Innumerable are the men who know the faults of others; a few, too, know their merits. But it is doubtful if any one knows his own faults."

"O king, thou seest the faults of others though only as large as mustard-seeds; but seeing, thou seest not thine own, though of the bulk of Bilva fruits."

"Skill in advising others is easily attained by all men. But to practise righteousness themselves is what only a few great men succeed in doing."

"The carrying of the triple staff, silence, a load of matted locks, shaving, a garb of bark or skins, religious observances, oblations, the *agni-hotra* offering, abode in a forest, the drying up of the body—all these things are false if the disposition be not pure."

"By his own kindred a man is regarded as one like themselves; by strangers he is looked upon as a person of merit. Hari (*i.e.* Vishnu, under another of his numerous appellations, regarded as incarnate in Krishna) was regarded by cowherds as a cowherd, but by gods as the lord of the universe."

"How can the man who loves ease obtain knowledge? The seeker of knowledge can have no ease. Either let the lover of ease give up knowledge, or the lover of knowledge relinquish ease."

These texts have also been quoted from Dr. Muir's translations. He says, "They have been taken in some instances from the Mahábhárata epic; the other works which I have quoted are of much more modern date, but the germs of many of the maxims which occur in them are to be found in older works; and the fact that so many sentiments in the latter should have been repeated in the more modern books, affords some proof that they are congenial and natural to the Indian mind."

He afterwards remarks that the Sanskrit literature of India presents, like the literature of other countries, a mixture of good and bad, pure and impure.

CHAPTER VIII.

The excavated Temples of India — Temple at Karli, and description of it by Bishop Heber — His imputation of idolatry in an answer of a Hindu boy, which does not seem to be fairly imputed—The English Cathedral of Bombay, and the figures on its stained glass windows — The Chinese traveller, H. Thsang, in India — Temple of Kennery, in Salsette, and arguments as to antiquity of excavations.

THE excavated temples of India, most venerable in their aspect, have been held to be revelations of the art of bygone forgotten civilisations. But Mr. Fergusson, the well-known writer on historical architecture, and of a treatise on these temples, has ascribed them to a comparatively modern epoch; though he has said that the stone of the rock-cut temples affords more durable material than any other in the world. They may be contemplated or studied in the excellent series of photographs in our Indian Museum with very complete realisation.

Heeren observed of these excavations, in his "Historical Researches," that "even Nature has impressed the marks of venerable age upon them, and many of the sculptured representations on the walls are so dissolved by the action of the atmosphere that they can with difficulty be recognised." He also remarked that "the rock out of which they are hewn is a clay porphyry, one of the very hardest kinds of stone."

As Buckle said, the great divergencies of opinion entertained by modern critics upon antiquarian Indian topics is alone sufficient to indicate their extreme age.

Sir Richard Phillips observed in his "Facts" that "Strabo joins Herodotus in saying that the Egyptians and Phœnicians were the first who erected temples, but the Indian caverns are presumed to be more ancient, and of unknown origin." And again, that the rock-cut temples of Elephanta and Salsette, near Bombay, and of Ellora, near Aurungabad, are gigantic works, dedicated to Siva, and presumed to be more ancient than the Egyptian ruins, which they resemble."

The freedom, natural grace, and regularity of Greek art, and the pointed picturesqueness of Gothic architecture, have been considered to have been perfected by the genius of the Greek and Gothic people respectively. The former, at least, is held to have been suggested by Egyptian art, while the latter arose out of the earlier style adopted from the basilicas of the Roman Empire; seeming, however, to claim originality in the slender pointed arch. In the mountains on the western side of India are not only numerous temples but also monastic abodes, excavated out of the solid rock. These distinctly present, under two great generalisations, the appearance of affording prototypes of these diverse styles, or else curious coincidences of shape. As no reliable accounts, or legends, of the dates at which these were formed, have been discovered, the first Europeans who, with wonder, contemplated them, were disposed to allow to them an approximation to the antiquity of many thousand years, claimed for them by the Hindus. But later investigators have been sceptical upon this point, and Mr. Fergusson has assigned them to ages between the first and tenth centuries of our era; with the exception of some of the smaller and ruder descriptions, for which he admits a few more centuries.

In the island of Salsette, between Bombay and the mainland, is one of these religious excavations, which he has ascribed to a period which might be as recent as the tenth century of our era. General Cunningham, however, chief of the Archæological Survey in north-western India, has lately attributed inscriptions upon it to about the first century.

Even Mr. Fergusson admits that the so-called Buddhistic cave temple at Karli, which is of corresponding but superior execution to that in Salsette, was probably excavated in about the first or second century of our era. Situated in the precipitous hill-side of a wide valley amongst the uplands of the Western Ghauts, between Bombay and Poona, the visitor enters it, and is astonished to find himself in the seeming choir of a Gothic cathedral. The outer world constitutes the nave, but the face of the rock has been opened in most suggestive resemblance to the mediæval rood screen. Above the rood loft, which, like the whole work, is excavated in the rock, an arch, in horseshoe shape, with toothed ornaments, rising to the height of some 50 feet, admits the light to the interior, which is 126 feet in length by 45 in width. There is a dark aisle on either side, formed by a row of 41 octagonal columns, which, in semicircular sweep, constitute an apse at the upper end. These columns are surmounted by capitals, carved into the figures of elephants with their riders, with good workmanship. From these the arched roof springs, which, although hewn out of the integral rock, has been curiously decorated, as if for support, by slender ribs of timber in the same curve. In the position which would be assigned to the altar in a Gothic church a piece of the rock has been left standing, carved into a dome, and surmounted by a wooden umbrella, now warped by age.

In fact, if the umbrella-topped rock at the upper end were cut down to an altar and reredos, stalls inserted on both sides, and an organ placed over the entrance, the place would altogether present the appearance of the choir of a Gothic cathedral of the Church of England, that is to say, of an ancient cathedral without the objects which the reformed church has considered superstitious. Bishop Heber observed that it would make a noble temple for any religion. The Gothic languages having been pronounced by philologists related to the Indian, and an eastern origin admitted for the Germanic races, it seems not unreasonable to surmise that we here behold an original specimen of the form ordinarily adopted for the Gothic choir. The first edifices of the kind having been probably constructed of timber, an imitation of them was excavated in the rock before the stone was quarried and erected in similar fashion. It seems easier to believe that the descendants of the excavators built the churches of Europe, than to hold the similarity of shape to be a mere coincidence, taking the corroborative evidences of language, etc., into consideration. In the umbrella we perceive the archetype of that which still figures conspicuously in Buddhistic ecclesiastical ornamentation. An umbrella may also be seen in St. Peter's at Rome, borne above the Pope's head, in the elaborate ceremonial of the Catholic Church.

A remarkable instance of the unfairness with which the religious beliefs of those whom we style the heathen may be treated, even by so elegant a mind as Bishop Heber's, may be found in his Indian Journal, in the account of his visit to this excavated temple of Karli.

"The approach to the temple," says the Bishop, "like that at Kennery (Salsette) is under a noble arch. . . . Within the portico, to the right and left, are three colossal figures, in alto-relievo, of elephants, their faces looking towards the person who arrives at the portico, and their heads, tusks, and trunks very boldly projecting from the wall. On each of them is a *mohout*, very well carved, and a howdah with two persons seated in it. The internal screen, on each side of the door, is covered, as at Kennery, with alto-relievos very bold, and somewhat larger than life, of naked male and female figures. I asked our young guides what these deities represented, and was surprised to hear from them in answer: These are not gods, one god is sufficient; these are viragees (religious enthusiasts or attendants on the deity). On asking, however, if their god was the same whom they worshipped in the little temple before the steps, and if he were Mahadeo, they answered in the affirmative; so that their deism merely extended to paying worship to a single idol only. There is certainly, however, no image either of Buddh, or any other mythological personage, about this cavern, nor any visible object of devotion except the mystic *chattah* or umbrella, already mentioned at Kennery."

The Bishop classes this boy's religion as idol-worship, and there was doubtless some sort of image in the little temple to which he alluded; just as the crucifixion and Madonna are to be seen in Roman Catholic chapels. But the boy could not possibly have answered with greater propriety. He said that one God was sufficient, and that he worshipped Mahā Deo, which simply and literally means the Great God. If, after this answer, idolatry was still imputed to him, he could not possibly have made any response, without a lengthened explanation, which could have averted the imputation.

At the east end of the cathedral of the Church of England in Bombay is a fine painted window. Its centre light depicts the Crucifixion. Above this is a full-sized representation of a bearded and majestic figure of regal aspect, seated, and bearing a sceptre in his hand. It appears intended to represent either the First Person of our Christian Trinity, or the Second Person glorified and reigning in heaven. During the evening service the interior lights of the edifice cause these designs to be distinctly visible from the exterior. The Hindus, Parsis, or Mohammedans of Bombay may be seen to pause in passing as they hear what must seem to them the stupendous music of the organ. It is not improbable, when they see these pictured representations, and catch a glimpse of our white-robed priests through the open side windows, that they suppose us to be adoring these painted figures in an idolatrous manner; especially as they may perceive priests and congregation kneeling, and occasionally bowing towards them. Adjoining both to the temple of Karli, and the similar excavation in Salsette, are a number of square and flat-roofed chambers excavated in the hill-side, sometimes on terraces. A portico with plain pillars usually opens to an inner room, containing a recess, in which may be seen a life-sized statue supposed to be Gautauma Buddha. Many of these cells still retain their cisterns well supplied with water. Some of the apartments are larger, contain more carving, and appear to have been council or lecture rooms, or refectories. In fact, the archaic monastery seems to be here displayed to us.

The Chinese traveller, H. Thsang, of the seventh century A.D., who has left us an exhaustive account of the Buddhistic monasteries of that period, seems by no means to show that excavations were then the ordinary abodes of the Buddhist monks. He describes the monastery of Tillarah as having four courtyards, and as being ornamented with verandahs, three-storied pavilions, lofty towers, and a series of gates. "It was built by the last scion of the house of Bimbisara, who was a man of more than ordinary attainments, and who assembled around him men of talent and worth from every quarter. Men of letters from distant countries flocked there in crowds." "There are 1000 recluses here," he relates, "who study the doctrines of the Greater Vessel. In the road which leads to the eastern gate there are three viharas, each of them surmounted by a cupola hung with bells. These buildings are several stories high, and are surmounted with balustrades. The doors, windows, rafters, and columns are covered with bas-reliefs, etc., in gilded copper, and decorated with still choicer ornaments. Stone beams support a roof consisting of huge slabs of granite and basalt. The pillars are of great variety of design; some are square at capital, base, and shaft; some have square bases and capitals, with octagon shafts; others are oval, and covered with the richest ornamentation."

At the epoch of this Chinese traveller—viz. the seventh century A.D.—the Roman Empire was flourishing in luxury and literary civilisation; and the monastic system was becoming stereotyped in the Catholic Church of Christendom. As the latter certainly did not arise out of the educational system of the empire, but from exoteric sources, it is not unreasonable to suppose that the extensively developed monasticism of India travelled westward. In the Buddhistic monastic edifices, which have been recently unearthed by General Cunningham in the north-west of British India, we behold the predecessors of those of western Asia and Europe.

As, at this time, the Indians had begun to erect such ornate structural edifices as that described by the Chinese pilgrim, it seems improbable that they were still continuing to excavate so elaborately, according to the view which would assign the works at Karli, Ajanta, etc., to centuries within the first nine of our era. Cities, known to have been then in existence in the vicinity of the Western Ghauts, and thriving in commercial civilisation, forbid the supposition that this part of India was behind the age. The Hindus are conservative in respect to retaining their own manners and customs, but they have evidently changed considerably in the march of centuries. They have ceased to excavate temples now, and it would appear from the evidence that they are scarcely likely to have been continuing to excavate them so lately as 1000 years ago. It would altogether seem that far greater antiquity must be attributed to the mythological excavations of India than recent authorities have allowed to them.

And Egyptian, Assyrian, Persian, Grecian, and Gothic, may be as reasonably supposed to have emerged from them, under their two great divisions, as the English architecture of the nineteenth century from the classic and Gothic styles which have preceded it in Europe. If, on the other hand, these excavations were copies, it is strange that structural edifices of stone were imitated in this manner. It seems much more probable that the excavations were suggested by wooden buildings, and that they, in their turn, suggested structural stone architecture. In reference to the excavation of Kennery, in Salsette, an inaccuracy is observable in Bishop Heber's Journal; which appears to have been edited by his wife after his death. This is calculated to be misleading, in respect to the question of the rapidity of decay in the work. He describes the dhagob and the timber rafters of the supposititious roof of the temple as still remaining, as in the temple of Karli. The brothers Daniel, however, whose sketches of Indian scenes were published in the year 1800, some twenty-four years previously to the Bishop's visit, have represented the interior, in an elaborate painting, as precisely similar to its present appearance. A few jagged pieces of wood, projecting from the sides of the roof, indicate the former presence of the timber merely. Only a slight excrescence at the summit of the dhagob suggests an umbrella similar to that of Karli. Moreover, Forbes in his "Oriental Memoirs," published in 1774, describes the roof as fluted concave, without mentioning timber. He considered the dhagob (dome-shaped altar-piece) as a lingam, which appears to demonstrate that there was no umbrella then upon it.

He supposed these caves to have been the abodes of Brahmins and their pupils; an opinion for which grounds exist in an inscription upon a similar excavated temple; which will be quoted in a subsequent chapter.

CHAPTER IX.

Cave Temple of Elephanta—Description of its mutilations, and argument as to its antiquity—The Trinity in unity shown in its principal sculpture—Arguments as to the amount of injury done to the Temple by the Portuguese—Bishop Heber's visit—Portuguese statement concerning it—Remains of adjacent edifices—Antiquity of brickmaking in India—Banasura, traditional founder of Elephanta, 3000 B.C. or 1500 B.C.

BUT even if the centuries between the first and tenth of our era be admitted for these excavations of Gothic aspect at Salsette, Karli, and elsewhere, they still assume priority to the edifices constructed in similar style in Europe. The builders of our magnificent and picturesque churches may still be traced to India, upon this point of evidence as well as upon that of affinity in language. Another question of race and art history is to be answered by the other, and very different, class of excavations in western India; of which the temple of Elephanta may be taken as an example. These exhibit similarities to the styles both of Egypt and of Greece.

The cave temple of Elephanta has become quite a common resort for Bombay excursionists. Picnic parties are frequently held there. On the occasion of the Prince of Wales' visit it was illuminated, and a grand banquet held in the interior, at which he was present. The Hindus still perform rites in it, which seem rather to merit the epithet of superstitious than religious. Still its venerable interior appears as ill adapted to a banquet as the unrestored nave of an old English cathedral. Bishop Heber, Mr. Fergusson, and others have, however, rather contemptuously pronounced it to be probably not more than 1000 years old or thereabouts. Its worn and ruinous appearance has been ascribed to the rapid action of water and the iconoclastic zeal of the Portuguese.

This temple has been excavated in the sloping hill-side of

the little tropical verdure-clad island of Elephanta, as we call it, in Bombay harbour. The excavation measures about 220 feet by 150, and is 18 feet in height. Four rows of columns divide it into aisles. These have square bases to about half their height, above which symmetrically rounded, fluted and swelling shafts, terminate in rounded capitals. At the upper end, in the position assigned to the high altar in a Catholic chapel, is a recess containing a colossal three-headed bust, rising from the floor to the roof. Right and left of it, and in compartments on all sides of the temple, are life-sized carvings in high relief representing allegorical topics. The whole has been carved out of a stone resembling porphyry, which Mr. Burgess, conductor of the Archæological Survey of this part of India, has styled a hard compact trap.

Of the twenty-six columns, cut in the integral rock, about a third are gone, the capitals of some and parts of the shafts of others still adhering to the upper rock or not quite levelled with the lower. Many of the sculptures in the compartments are in a very mutilated and defaced condition. These marks of ruin have been ascribed to the Portuguese, except the loss of the tip of the nose of one of the three heads of the great central bust, which is said to have been knocked off by an Englishman within Anglo-Indian historical memory. A custodian has long been appointed by Government to take charge of the place, and sixpence is demanded for admission, visitors being now narrowly watched to see that they do not inscribe their names, or damage it in any way. Now, with regard to the mutilations observable in the cave, and attributed to the Portuguese, two or three points arise in what may be termed cross-examination. These seem to discredit the hearsay sort of evidence upon which the Portuguese are credited with them. It can only be supposed, taking the climate and circumstances into consideration, that they assaulted the work from desire to destroy the vestiges of idolatry, not from mere wantonness or exuberance of spirits. But why in any case did they wreak their vengeance on pillars, and comparatively obscure sculptures, and leave the central image standing, which must have appeared to them as an idolatrous imitation of their own sacred Trinity, or, at least, as a tempting object to assault. This and its flanking sculptures are in comparatively excellent preservation. If they had left it untouched on account of its being a Trinity in unity, though an idolatrous and impious one, surely they would not have fatigued themselves, especially in that tropical atmosphere, with attacking the massive columns of the excavation. Surely they could not have been so utterly devoid of penetration as not to have perceived that even if they did destroy columns which were part of the integral rock, the roof would not fall in; supposing their design to have been to have compassed the total ruin of the whole. Besides, the task of filling up the entrance, which is some 100 feet in width by 15 in height, would have been obviously easier. Supposing, however, that they did attack the columns, under the impression that they really supported the roof, what was their method of warfare? It has been alleged that they dragged a cannon up the hill and fired into the cave. But that, in this case, they should have entirely avoided firing straight up it, at the three-headed figure, which presents a most tempting target, and that they should have only aimed right and left of it at the pillars, is too preposterous. Mr. Burgess, in his recently published account of Elephanta, annexed to an admirable series of photographs of the excavation, has assigned to the Portuguese the following method of destruction. He informs us that they filled the cavern with combustibles, and, when the pillars were thoroughly heated, threw cold water upon them, thus causing the stone to split and fly into fragments.

The immense stones of the old British temple at Abury are stated to have been broken up by this sort of process, to render them available for modern use. Godfrey Higgins, in his Celtic Druids, relates that fires were lighted under them, lines of water drawn along them, and the stones then split by strokes of a sledge hammer, but the amount of fire and force required is said to have been excessive. In contemplating Elephanta it is difficult to believe its partial ruin assignable to such a cause.

That in the climate of Bombay, moreover, the Portuguese should have selected such an elaborate method of destroying an idolatrous temple seems almost incredible. What a fierce and continued bonfire must have been requisite to heat sufficiently these columns, each about a yard in diameter, in this wide though low cavern. The stifling smoke cannot have been endurable for unfortunates entering to throw the water upon them, for we can hardly suppose them to have applied our modern fire-engine processes. And after all their pains the essentials of the Temple are unimpaired. The great triune figure, and Siva's dome-shaped emblem, the *lingam*, in an inner chapel, remain virtually uninjured.

Bishop Heber, half a century ago, had not apparently heard of this incendiary attack of the Portuguese when he visited the cave and recorded his impressions in his Journal. He remarked that "the rock out of which the temple is carved is by no means calculated to resist, for any great length of time, the ravages of the weather. It evidently suffers much from the annual rains;" and he adds, that "these ravages are said to have greatly increased within the memory of persons now resident in Bombay, though for many years back the cave has been protected from wanton depredation, and though the sculptures rather than the pillars would probably have suffered from that vulgar love of knicknacks and specimens which prevails amongst the English."

But an anonymous writer of about Bishop Heber's time has recorded the remark, that the custodian of the cave had informed him that he had seen only one small piece of stone detached during six years. In drawings which have descended to us of the cave at the commencement of this century, it appears the same as at present. Although the water percolates through the upper rock to considerable extent of dropping during the rainy season, yet the rainy season only lasts for four months, and the action of the high winds which then prevail can scarcely have momentous effect upon the interior. The excavation can hardly have fallen into its present state of decay, aided by an occasional battering upon the noses and other members of its carved figures, within a thousand years or so. Time must have accomplished the partial ruin which we observe in it, in far longer space. If we may be permitted to deny that all civilisation started from the plains of Shinar, after the confusion of tongues at the tower of Babel, B.C. 2247; if it can be admitted that this peninsula or continent of India, with its voluminous ancient literature, can have had a remote past in art and science, the cave temple of Elephanta may most reasonably be admitted to be a witness to it. What different aspect, it may be asked, could an ancient and elaborately carved excavation present, supposing it to have fallen into dilapidation by the slow decay of thousands of years? While many of its massive columns are gone, crumbled apparently in great part into the dust, one of those standing now is to be seen split, and in seeming process of disintegration, occasioned perhaps by the action of water.

The sculptures are not only broken, but they and the bases on which they stand, and the steps on the four sides of the little chapel sacred to the Sivaic emblem, are worn down till, in places, they have almost returned to their natural rock, yet with the impress of art still distinctly remaining on the stone—the worn-down traces of a perfect sculpture in relief, not the first outlines of one to be created. Traces of European damage may be discerned; but they are mere additions to the great work of time's gradual destruction. The grand Trimūrti, the conjunction of Brahma the Creator, Vishṇu the Preserver, and Ṣiva the Destroyer, or, as it perhaps ought to be styled, the image of Siva, or Mahādeva, to whom the temple is dedicated, represented as the threefold deity, is in superior preservation, because the sculptors were probably careful to stop at an especially good stratum of stone for their most sacred and prominent figure. At all events, it is in superior preservation, which seems more compatible with such an argument than with the iconoclastic proceedings asserted of the Portuguese, which left the central idol intact.

When the Puritans broke the painted windows of our cathedrals, they did not leave the images of the high altars uninjured. They do not appear to have vented their zeal upon the pillars, except in the case of the cathedral of St. Andrews, which they almost entirely levelled with the ground. If the Portuguese had intended the utter ruin of the Elephanta temple by breaking its columns, when they found that the roof did not fall in, they may reasonably be supposed likely to have attacked these principal images. On one side of the entrance is a life-sized figure, similar to those supposed to represent Gautauma Buddha, in ancient Indian art. It is also in good preservation. In fact, as in most ruins, decay has been partial throughout.

No interior could possibly be more venerable in aspect,

more solemn, more grim and gray with the apparent wear and tear of ages, than the Cave Temple of Elephanta; and the figures seem to appertain to a prehistoric race. The men have massive figures. The women are small by comparison, but voluptuous in form, and both possess handsome, powerful faces, with full, rich under lips. Their bearing seems stately and dignified. The full under lips merely suggest the vigour of the race; and their general carriage seems worthy of the great Aryan sources which may have been anciently allied to them before it rolled its streams to the north-westwards, in compassing the conquest of our globe. The profusion of jewels, in bracelets, anklets, gemmed girdles, etc., which adorn their otherwise naked bodies, and the elegant tiaras of the chief personages, do not display a race corresponding to our modern Zulus, but a grand people, with highly cultured artificers amongst them. The most remarkable feature in their personal equipment is, that, with the exception of the regally divine persons, who are distinguished by the tiara, and guards who wear a sort of coroneted cap, the men wear a head-dress resembling the British bar-wig—that is to say, the wig which was in general European fashion amongst the upper classes during part of the eighteenth century, but which has latterly been the especial head-dress of our lawyers. One, of exalted and judicial aspect, who is seated, has a full-bottomed wig, after the style of those worn by the Speaker of the House of Commons, and by our Judges and Queen's Counsel on State occasions. This curious phenomenon in the sculptures is continued so as to complete the resemblance of their heads to those of the European modes in the eighteenth century, by the aspect of the women. These have their hair combed upwards from the top of the head, and stiffly curled at the sides, after the manner of the head-dresses which we see in the portraits of Reynolds and Gainsborough. The difference between the wigs and the natural hair elaborately dressed, seems as distinctly marked in the sculptures of Elephanta as in the pictures of those artists. Besides the stately figures in the foreground of these sculptures, which are in such high relief as to exhibit their full proportions, there are smaller, and often allegorical representations, in low relief in the background—such as four-faced Brahmas seated on lotus thrones; Kāma, the Indian Cupid, upon an elephant; Vishnu, with four arms, etc. And there are a number of grotesque dwarfs, who appear to be intended as jesters in attendance upon the superior persons. These are presented with humour, suggestive of that which our mediæval monkish sculptors lavished upon their gargoyles, etc. Now, it cannot be assumed that these evident wigs and lofty ladies' head-dresses have been sculptured since they were worn in Europe. And the whole aspect of the sculptured figures, including the wigs, seems to take the modern beholder back to days coeval, at least, with the old wig-wearing and beard-trimming Assyrian and Egyptian hierarchies. But the style of art displayed in them is spirited, and approximating to the higher Greek art in freedom of handling. The mouldings of doorways, etc., have an appearance of being ancestral to the Greek style.

Da Couta, a Portuguese author of the commencement of the seventeenth century, has recorded that these temples were executed under Banasura, son of Bali, King of Kanada, who also constructed adjoining palaces. Vestiges of these palaces remained in Da Couta's time, and are still to be discovered. A red tile of venerable aspect, glazed with blue enamel on one side, is to be seen in the library of the Sassoon Institute in Bombay; which tile was found in the island of Elephanta, and is evidently a vestige of ancient structural work.

The antiquity of brickmaking in India is, at all events, unquestionable. The largest bricks in the world are said to be those found at Hastinapur, measuring twenty inches in length by ten in breadth, and two and a half in thickness. This excess in dimensions over the bricks of Babylon may be considered an argument, in conjunction with other reasons, for assigning the priority in brickmaking to India. Brickmaking must surely have been suggested as a substitute for quarried stones. The Holy Bible indicates that the builders of Babel were acquainted with brickmaking on their arrival in the plains of Shinar; for they at once proposed the employment of bricks, as has been observed.

By connecting these works at Elephanta with Banasura, they appear to be referred to the age of Krishna, placed by the Indians themselves at 3000 B.C., and by English criticism at 1500 B.C. His connection with them has therefore been rejected, on account of the reluctance of English critics to admit for them so remote a date.

The Portuguese are said to have taken a stone from the entrance to the excavation, with an inscription in characters which no Hindu could decipher, and sent it to Portugal, where it seems to have been lost.

It does not appear improbable that the Portuguese may have vented their religious animosity in attacks upon the sculptures, and that broken heads and limbs may be results of their rage. That the missing columns, and general time-worn aspect of the place, with decay marked upon steps, pedestals, and the carved work throughout, can be their handiwork, seems hardly possible from the evidences.

Mr. A. B. Frend, the architect, has considered that the excavators must have bored into the rock to the depth of the cavern, and then worked backwards in widening it. This would explain the excellent material of the central figure at the end. They would have taken perfect rock for their extreme point; but they would have been unable, in sculpturing their work with regularity, to select all their future strata. He supposes that they must have been acquainted with geometry.

CHAPTER X.

Arguments for assigning the Birthplace and original seat of the Aryan Race to India itself—India shown to be the most central land—Elephanta possibly a remnant of the race which conveyed civilisation to Babylon and Egypt, out of which the Sanskrit-speaking and Greek peoples subsequently proceeded —5000 or 10,000 years B.C. no excessive period to have elapsed in India, in civilisation leading up to the period of the compilation of the Vedas—Egyptian civilisation likely, from the evidences, to have come from India—Classic altars, etc., amongst the natives of the Bombay district—Westward course of the greater part of ancient as of modern Aryan emigration.

APART from any preconceived notion that Egypt, Assyria, and Greece were the original fountains of the arts, this Cave Temple of Elephanta might reasonably have been recognised as preceding these structural edifices of Egypt, which resemble it in style. It would not appear improbable that the people which could form the Sanskrit language, and write so many works of philosophy, science, and imagination in it, should have left art remains of an age antecedent to that in which the elaboration of their speech and literature took place, as has been the case amongst the Aryans of Europe. The Sanskrit is acknowledged to be an older branch of the Indo-European, or Aryan family of languages, than the Greek. The art of the cave temples, when resembling Greek art, seems similarly to claim seniority to the ancient Greek ruins. The sculptured figures of Elephanta, however, do not appear to appertain precisely to the Aryan or any other historical race. They rather suggest some powerful prehistorical people; perhaps those who spoke the parent speech, from which Professor Max Müller has surmised the Greek, Sanskrit, Zend, Lithuanian, Old Sclavonic, Gothic, and Armenian languages to have been derived. They might even seem relics of a race preceding that people; of a race from which both Aryan and Dravidian predecessors were derived. Professor Max Müller and others have placed the seat of the archaic Aryans in what has been termed Central Asia, *i.e.* the region of the ancient Bactria, or modern Balkh. But the real centre of the populations of 2000 B.C., if we include China, the Indo-Chinese countries, the Asiatic islands, and Africa, in our estimate of the Eastern Hemisphere, is to be found in the peninsula of Hindustan, not in the comparatively arid regions to its north-west. There seems to be no reason for supposing any change so essential as to have affected civilisation, to have occurred in the relative aspects, during the last 5000 years, of Hindustan and the district of Balkh. It has been observed of the latter, that the soil has the general characteristics of a desert land, with parts rendered fertile by irrigation. In the whole of the Gangetic plain the prevalent soil has been described as a rich black mould of alluvial origin.

Practically, the most central portion of the habitable earth, the true centre of populations and of pre-Christian civilisations, is India, rightly, though self-consciously, termed the Madhyama by its inhabitants. It even retains that position now that Victoria of England reigns there. Looking at a map of the Eastern Hemisphere, and making allowances for the deserts of Caubul and Arabia, we find that the Chinese Empire balances in territory and population western Asia and Europe, while the Asiatic islands and Africa oppose the land of northern Asia and Europe. Delhi has more fertile soil and more extensive populations to its south than to its north. The expanse of territory in northern Asia is vast, but the greater portion is composed of regions almost profitless to man. The ocean to the south of India has rendered its position veritably central, by affording highways for commerce between the most fruitful regions of the world. The Chinese, with a civilisation as orderly and historically ancient as our own, are estimated to equal nearly the combined populations of India, western Asia, and Europe. We have considerably despised them, and forced ourselves and our opium upon their acquaintance with bullet and bayonet, though we seem to have imitated them in respect to competitive examinations. We usually consider the aspect of their civilisation contemptible by the side of our own, though we are compelled to admit that it is a civilisation. But its influence seems scarcely to have been taken into sufficient account in considerations respecting the origin and progress of our Aryan civilisation; in regard, for instance, to forcing the increasing Aryans to a necessarily westward course in emigration. In this central land in Hindustan, all those advantages of fertility of soil and convenience of sea-coast exist, which have caused modern civilisations to arise and flourish. We find here remains of past ages. These have every appearance of antiquity, and there are no records in the country respecting their origin. We reject their evidence as bearing upon the history of our civilisation and religion, on account of a theory that their sculptures represent phases of the Hindu faiths, which did not come into vogue till about the time of our Christian era. But the Hindus themselves have constantly asserted the antiquity both of the works and the religion which they illustrate. It is reasonable to conceive that the ancient language changed to the comparatively modern Sanskrit in India itself, just as the English language has become altered in England. The Brahminical Aryans seem to have descended from the north-west by literary and traditional evidence, but it does not appear to be the region to the north-west, beyond Hindustan, and its mountain barriers. Vedic hymns indicate an authorship in the district watered by the Indus and its tributaries. By arms or arts they subdued, or they gradually interpenetrated, the peninsula; but there is no evidence against their having originally sprung out of its general population, though the Brahminical system may have arisen into a powerful organisation in the north-west. The Aryan Greeks returned from their fertile sea-girt land on the Mediterranean, and failed in an attempt to conquer the old Aryavarta. The English Aryans have sailed from our home in the extreme north-west and succeeded. The intellect of the Brahmins, and the valour of the warrior caste, invigorated in the more northern climate, obtained sway over the peninsula. They, like ourselves, may have returned rather than advanced to overcome the south. Elephanta would seem to be the remnant of the civilisation out of which the Sanskritic and Greek people emerged, and from which the Egyptian civilisation simultaneously or previously came. The faces of the Elephanta figures do not differ more from the general Indo-European type than the pronounced Celtic from the Teutonic or Latin races.

The two great divisions of our Aryan race in Europe have adopted widely-varying forms of Christianity. India being virtually equal in dimensions to our continent without Russia and Sweden, also appears to have contained two great religions —branches of the earliest recognition of the all-sustaining Spirit of Nature. While Brahm and the Vedic deities of the elements were invoked on the plains of the Indus and Ganges, Mahadeva, the "great God," seems to have been worshipped, perhaps, under the triune form of Creator, Preserver, and Destroyer, in the peninsula south of the Nerbudda. The grandeur of the first was especially recognised in the Sun, and adored in Agni, the fire upon earth, in Indra of the air, etc.; the second (Mahadeva) was reverenced in the above-mentioned dome-shaped emblem of creative power. From the coalition of these, as Brahminical influence spread through the country, may have come the representation of Brahm under the three-fold aspect of Brahma, Vishnu and Mahadeva, or Siva. This last appellation, which has been associated with the idea of destruction, signifies, in Sanskrit, happy or auspicious. At a later period the Preserver was worshipped as incarnate in Rama, Krishna, and other forms, for man's protection on earth and eventual redemption from the woes of the material world. In Buddha humanity was recognised as overcoming the lusts of life, and becoming tranquillised in the divine. The general appearance of the excavated temple of Elephanta might admit of an antiquity of 5000 years, or perhaps of a far vaster period; and the character of the figures harmonises with such prehistorical antiquity. A third of the columns, cut in the integral rock, might reasonably be supposed to have been disintegrated and destroyed by the dripping of water, or its soaking into the rock during the rainy seasons in some such lapse of time. At the rate of three generations per century, 5000 years would only require 150 generations of men, no inconceivable or preposterous number to have inhabited this region in some sort of civilisation, to minds unimbued with the biblical interpretations of two or three centuries ago, and not more than seem required to account for the old-world aspect of humanity in the sculptures. The symbolism of modern Hinduism which appears amongst them, considering how immaterially the Hindus have altered since the historical epoch of Alexander the Great, might have been several thousand years older than his time. The Trinity in unity, distinctly and grandly carved, in the most prominent situation of this temple, certainly looks as if it might probably be the earliest of existing representations in the world of this idea or truth.

Supposing the compilation of the Vedas in their present form to be referred correctly to about the twelfth or fifteenth century B.C., there is no reason for rejecting evidence in favour of the Sivaic form of adoration having existed in the south of India for many previous generations. Surely men are likely to have sculptured rocks into allegorical representations for many centuries before they collected their sacred writings into volumes, and noted their sacrificial ordinances with regular rites performed in accordance with astronomical periods, as in the Vedic ritual. The ancient symbolism of India seems not unlikely to have survived through several phases of the adoration of the divine; just as our Christian symbolism has passed through Roman Catholicism to the Anglo-Catholic Church. If the Egyptian civilisation came from India, the invention of hieroglyphics in Egypt would show that writing was not yet in vogue in India, when the conquerors or colonists arrived in Egypt. Laws are likely to have been reverenced under the sacred name of Manu, passing into the Egyptian Menes, before these were written or systematically codified. The Vedic religion must have preceded the actual volumes, or systematised recitations of the Vedas, by long ages. It cannot be reasonably supposed that it occurred to the archaic religious to define canons of Scripture, within merely a few generations after feeling impelled to lift up their voices to the mysterious power of life and death. The sanction of ages must have been given to these utterances before they became canonised. The glories of nature must surely be allowed to have inspired the poet long before his words were accepted as the actual inspiration of the Supreme Spirit. Again to quote a translation of Mr. Griffith's, the following hymn to the Sun may have been naturally suggested in the contemplation of its grandeur. Its adoption into a canon of Scripture would seem to have been of artificial contrivance, appertaining to an advanced age of law, order, and class privileges.

"Risen in majestic blaze,
Lo! the Universe's eye,
Vast and wondrous host of rays,
Shineth brightly in the sky.

Soul of all that moveth not,
Soul of all that moves below;
Lighteth he earth's gloomiest spot,
And the heavens are all aglow.

"See he followeth the Dawn,
Brilliant in her path above;
As a youth by beauty drawn,
Seeks the maiden of his love!
Holy men and pious sages,
Worship now the glorious Sun;
For by rites ordained by ages,
Shall a good reward be won.

"Look! his horses mounted high,
Good of limb and swift and strong;
In the forehead of the sky,
Run their course the heaven along.
Praises to his steeds be given,
Racing o'er the road of heaven!

"Such the majesty and power,
Such the glory of the Sun,
When he sets at evening hour,
The worker leaves his task undone;
His steeds are loosed, and over all
Spreadeth Night her gloomy pall.

"When he rides in noontide glow,
Blazing in the nation's sight,
The skies his boundless glory show,
And his majesty of light;
And when he sets, his absent might
Is felt in thickening shades of night.

"Hear us, O ye Gods! this day.
Hear us, graciously, we pray.
As the Sun his state begins,
Free us from all heinous sins.
Mitra, Varuna, Aditi!
Hear, oh hear us, graciously.
Powers of ocean, earth, and air,
Listen, listen, to our prayer!"

This hymn suggests the combined inspiration of the aspect of the sun and of the rites which were considered by the poet to be of ancient ordinance. It then would seem to require the sanctity of its own antiquity to elevate it into the rank of the divine. If it was composed and adopted by the church of the period, like a modern hymn sung in our services, it, at all events, sets forth the antiquity of the ritual. It seems absolutely suggestive of the Grecian ideas respecting the chariot of the sun, and of the pantheon of their Olympus.

An argument against the derivation of Indian civilisation from Egyptian may be discerned in the probability that if the hierarchy of Egypt was imitated in Brahminism, the laws of Menes in the Institutes of Manu, the adoration of Osiris in the worship of Siva, and the architecture of the Nile in the columns of Elephanta and the other ancient excavations of western India, hieroglyphics would also have been adopted there.

If Egyptian art-remains can be referred back to 7000 B.C., or to some remoter period, the Indian arts at Elephanta can be carried back before them; as their date is a mere matter of conjecture, and their dilapidations might make allowances for 20,000 years, or more. Indeed, the process of destruction by the natural decay of the rock, in a cavern, aided by the rains extending over a third of the year, might seem to require what we have considered geological rather than historical periods.

At about a quarter of a mile from the great temple of Elephanta, near the summit of a wooded hill, is a much smaller excavation. A portico, some 16 yards in width by 8 in depth, supported by four columns of a plain classical order, opens to three doorways, with straight Grecian mouldings. These give access to three chambers, each of about five square yards in dimensions, two of which are without sculpture and empty. The centre chamber contains an altar, without figures or ornaments beyond simple square entablatures. This place appears to have been long used as a cowhouse for the cattle of the villagers on the opposite side of the hill. It is only approached through thickets of brushwood, and it has been scarcely visited or criticised by Europeans. Not only in this excavation, but in the villages of the district near Bombay, may be seen, in the gardens of the mud-walled, palm-leaf-roofed houses, small classical altars. Plain, with straight, simple mouldings, they have horns at the four corners and a tulsi plant growing at the top. This is sacred here to Krishna as the laurel was to Apollo; Krishna's coy nymph having been turned into the former as Apollo's into the latter plant. They certainly have not been copied from Christian altars. It is difficult, if not impossible, to conceive that they should have been due to the temporary presence of the Greeks, at some hundreds of miles' distance, in the north-west provinces, even though they extended down to Gujerat, or to a small short-lived commercial settlement related to have been formed by them on the west coast, near Bombay, but speedily expelled by the inhabitants. The European settlements in Bombay for more than two centuries, Portuguese and English, appear to have induced so little imitation that it is hard to imagine that Greeks or Assyrians can have been copied in former times. The Hindus can imitate our work if they are set to do it, but their general intense conservatism seems scarcely compatible with former imitativeness in the manner of their lives, or general art efforts. The Indian pottery, too, assumes classical forms. The Greek republican idea seems to be existent in the village communistic system, with its species of jury of five persons to settle disputes. When art, altars, language, etc., present Greek affinities, the doctrine of coincidence appears scarcely tenable. The people to whom these things appertain are not of the caste of the Brahmin invaders, as they have been called. They are more likely to be the conservative descendants of the above-mentioned race, which, after the foundation of Egyptian civilisation, arose into the Sanskrit-speaking Indians, and, by emigration, became the Greeks; while in the south, with less change of language, they remained as, or became what have been styled the Dravidian, Telingan, or Tamulian races of India. They are conservative because they are autochthonous—because their usages were developed amongst them in the long course of ages. Amongst these agriculturists—a class most disposed to be conservative of the inhabitants of all countries—are still to be seen the archaic customs which have developed so widely with the more stirring life of the north-west. The warrior and commercial classes, pressing to the inviting climates of the Mediterranean, arose into the civilisations which have culminated in Great Britain.

To the eastward and north-eastward were the great Mongolian and Chinese civilisations. In the western parts of Asia the Semitic races occupied, chiefly as nomads, the comparatively scanty fertile spots. These seem likely, in the ages preceding the Indian literary, legal, priestly, mercantile, and art-attempting generations, to have scattered themselves over those regions.

To the people from whom are descended the various Indo-European nations, Europe, with its early Finnic populations, the races of which we have evidence in the Swiss lacustrine dwellings, offered the same openings for expansions which America, Australia, etc., have afforded to Europe in our own days. Like the ancient Indian emigrations, our modern European colonisations have been mainly westwards. In South America the Latin Aryans have established republics and the Brazilian Empire. In the north the Anglo-Saxon and Germanic races have founded a mighty republic. Similarly does it appear that the republics of Greece, the Roman Empire, and the warrior kingdoms of northern Europe, previously proceeded, in course of time, from the original cradle of the race in India. At all events, India affords infinitely more natural qualifications for being the original school of our civilisations than any other part of the world, except perhaps China, from which we evidently did not emerge. India, like Europe and America, is a region of rugged mountains and fertile plains, noble rivers and sea-coasts available for commerce, forests and wealth of herbage, and climates varied by sunshine and rain. The districts of Balkh and the Caucasus, which have been assigned for the first growth of our civilisations, seem neither to afford the physical conditions under which that growth has continually advanced, nor to contain relics or records of its commencement or existence therein. There are, indeed, ancient caverns at Bamian, near Balkh, but they appear to be Buddhistic in style, and therefore appertaining to a religion allowed to have originated in Hindustan.[1]

[1] See Appendix II.

CHAPTER XI.

Mr. Fergusson's theories respecting the Aryans and architecture—Excavated temples at Baug, with art of Greek character—Considerations as to whether the so-called Buddhistic excavations may not be Brahminical, as evidenced by an inscription—Apparent absence of antagonism between Brahmins and Buddhists in this inscription.

MR. FERGUSSON has advanced the theory that the early Aryans did not care to cultivate architecture, and that their ceremonial worship was conducted in the open air, without images or temples. This appears to have been so, but certainly, in the Institutes of Manu, as well as in the epics, there are allusions to temples. Architecture, in the later history of the Aryan race, appears to have been the precursor of literature. Our cathedrals were systematically erected before the regular commencement of our literary history. Why should we suppose the sequence of human intellectual work different in the earlier times of our race? Mr. Fergusson has attributed to a Dravidian element in Greece the architectural excellence of that country. Here in India is undoubtedly an intermingling of Aryan and Dravidian elements about this Bombay neighbourhood which may have produced the two divergent styles which we perceive in these excavations; or from the people which in the remote past diverged into these races, and contained the elements of both, may have proceeded the earliest efforts at architectural excellence. But taking into consideration the works carried on by what we term our Aryan race, and looking at those which have been lately disinterred in the north-west of India, it would scarcely seem that this view respecting the want of inclination or capacity in the race for architecture can be sustained.

The Elephanta caves do not stand alone in ancient aspect and dilapidated condition in the western side of India. There are many other excavations presenting these semi-Egyptian, semi-classical styles. It is difficult to imagine that the Portuguese can have managed to wage an ecclesiastic war with such zeal upon all of them. There must have been numbers of the ordinary Hindu pagodas at hand, such as we now behold throughout the country, upon which to wreak their religious hatred. They can scarcely have bestowed such immense pains upon wrecking these mysterious caverns. Their aspect of venerable antiquity cannot be invariably fallacious. The excavation of Baug, about eighty miles from Oojein, on the road to Gujerat, is 84 feet square by 14½ feet in height—the light being only admitted through doorways. Its roof is thought to have been evidently painted in square compartments. It contains four rows of columns, with a recess at the upper end, in which are carved figures. An interior apartment, measuring 20 feet by 17, has the dome-topped dhagob, which is supposed to demonstrate Buddhistic origin.

Parenthetically it should be observed that even if it can be proved that Buddhism was really founded by Sakya muni, about the fifth century B.C. according to the Ceylonese chronicles, it does not necessarily follow that the symbols of the religion have been invented since that period. Buddhism arose out of Brahminism—perhaps more definitely out of Sivaism—and it may have retained things of ancient usage. The Anglo-Catholic Church has preserved the altars of the Roman Catholic communion in their eastern position,. which had been adopted for them in the Western Church, merely abrogating their ornamentation.

A third cave at Baug, measuring 80 feet by 60, has had the walls, roof, and columns covered with a fine stucco, and ornamented with paintings in distemper, of considerable elegance, chiefly in *chiaro oscuro.* The figures and the Etruscan border, as it has been styled, have been coloured with Indian red. Indications of groups of peaches and peach-leaves are observable on the roof, and, beneath brilliant traces of the Etruscan border, surrounding the tops of the columns, are represented dragons fighting. The design is finished with festoons of small flowers. On the lower part of the wall and columns male and female figures have been painted, of a red or copper colour. The whole cave is stated to be in a very ruinous condition, with many columns, described as massive and beautiful, borne down by the falling in of the roof. It has been remarked that the dilapidated state of the caves might be received as evidence of their high antiquity, did not the soft argillaceous nature of the stratum of rock above them, owing to which the roof has given way, render this evidence very equivocal. But in other places are elaborately sculptured caverns, greatly decayed, and without assertion of either Portuguese or Mohammedan destruction, or any special frailty in the material in which they have been excavated.

If these sculptures, and the paintings of Baug, are ascribed to Greek influence, after the establishment of the Greek kingdom of Bactria, when the literature of the country informs us of structural stone edifices and sculpture in towns, it seems almost incomprehensible that they should have applied these borrowed Greek ideas to the adornment of excavations which are in themselves so original, so peculiar in conception.

There is nothing in that essentially Brahminical production, the Institutes of Manu, to forbid the supposition of Forbes, to which allusion has been made, that the so-called Buddhistic excavations were in reality ancient colleges of Brahmins. Retirement for meditation is recommended at the close of life; and all young Brahmins are directed to enter upon a studentship under some learned Brahmin. We find universities established, in later times, at Benares and elsewhere, in which this appears as the prototype of the Oxford tutorial system. Meditating on the Supreme Being, the reading of the Scriptures and abstinence from indulgences of the body, are represented in the Institutes as of more consequence than merely ceremonial acts. The adoration of images is nowhere enjoined in them. The figures sculptured in the recesses of the seeming refectories, lecture halls, and monastic cells of the Salsette and other caves might as reasonably be held to represent Manu, to whom the Institutes are declared to have been delivered by the Deity, in his turn imparting them to disciples, as Buddha. The figure formerly representing Manu may have been afterwards assigned to Buddha, just as the sacred effigy of St. Peter, in his church at Rome, is said to have formerly done duty for Jupiter, or some classic divinity. The resemblance of figures in these places to those now reverenced as Gautauma Buddha, seems to be unreliable evidence for ascribing the date of their excavation to a later period than that which we have adopted for this era. The domed Dhagob may have been a religious symbol long before the modern expression of Buddhism; possibly as an adaptation of the lingam, which it appears to resemble when considered without the umbrella or the ornament at the summit.

A motive for these reflections is afforded by an inscription on a cave, of the character supposed to be Buddhistic, near Nassick, which seems to be distinctly Brahminical. Fragments of it, which contain the points indicating this conclusion, are as follows:—"To the Perfect Being, may this prove auspicious —By the son of king Kshaparata, of the Kshatrya tribe, etc., a gift of cows . . . constructor of this holy place, for the gods and for the Brahmins, to mortify their passions . . . there is not so a desirable place, etc.—where hundreds of Brahmins go on pilgrimage, etc.—nor at the city of Pratisraya, where there is a Buddhistical monastery. . . . These venerated by man—viz. the Sun, Sutha, and Radhu,[1]—were in their exultation when the gift was bestowed." No antagonism is apparent in the mention of the Buddhistical monastery. It seems rather to be introduced as displaying the desirability of the city of Pratisraya. In fact, it does not appear to be a correct inference that, because the Brahmins preserved the purity of their own class, and assumed their own spiritual superiority, they protested against monastic constitutions amongst those of other castes. Their creed has been liberal; admitting of the divine appealing to the human in many ways. Or again, is it not possible that Buddhistical may simply express the cultivation of wisdom rather than asceticism; and that a monastery dedicated to the Buddha, as we understand him in later times, was not intended? As *budh* simply means to know, a narrowing of the entire application of the word to the faith formulated in historical times seems not unlikely to be erroneous. The Buddhist sacred books suggest that Gautauma founded orders resembling, or rather precursors of, the mendicant friars of the thirteenth century in Europe; not that he first conceived the idea of religious societies.

[1] See Appendix VI.

The date of the above inscription is, of course, an important consideration. The dates of old inscriptions, and styles of caligraphy, and the identifications of ancient monarchs seem often susceptible of various renderings. The concluding sentence of the inscription does not seem to appertain to the Buddhism of Gautauma, *i.e.* Sakya Muni.

CHAPTER XII.

Difficulties in conceiving the origin of the Aryans in the Balkh district, or the artificially created Babylonia and Egypt being primitive abodes of civilisation —Our Scriptures not contradicted by placing the Eden of the human race in the garden-like tropical islands to the south of India, and tracing the rise of civilisation in India from natural causes—Fire first obtained by the rubbing together of two sticks—Early Chinese civilisation—Natural advantages of India.

THE old astronomers encountered constant difficulties so long as they supposed the earth to be stationary, and the sun and stars revolving round it. So soon as they perceived that the earth itself revolved, the system of the heavens became comprehensible. In placing the origin of civilisation in Babylon and Egypt, and in supposing the Aryan race to have developed as such in some district to the north-west of India, from which they invaded India and penetrated into Europe, we are confronted with the difficulty of conceiving the first steps of these civilisations. In their artificially sustained oases amidst barren wildernesses the Babylonians and Egyptians, by the pure force of their imaginations, in a manner which we credit rather than comprehend, have been supposed to have leaped into the execution of high art. The Aryans are said to have acquired a religious, orderly, and pastoral civilisation amongst the comparatively sterile regions beyond the Hindu Koosh, and then to have entirely abandoned a home which they had occupied with so much advantage. As these high Asian regions have since only produced nomadic tribes, and a few commercial towns or occasional agricultural settlements, the creation in prehistoric times of our own race must also be placed amongst the mysteries which mankind has not considered itself called upon to understand. But if, like the astronomers, we reverse the order, and if, instead of pouring all the old civilisations into India to conquer or educate people now so intensely conservative of their own customs under conquest, we regard the so-called Madhyama as indeed the central land, we shall be able to perceive reasons for the commencement.

It has been lately admitted in the orthodox world that, without derogating from the sublimity of our Holy Scriptures, we may infer that the facts of natural science are not explained in them. The orthodox, as well as scientific, world may not make the same inference in respect to the history of humanity. Like the biblical narrative of the sun and moon standing still, and others, the story of the resuscitation of mankind by Shem, Ham, and Japheth, with the commencement of post-diluvian architecture in brickwork in the plains of Shinar 2348 B.C., seems absolutely to require transmutation. Even if Indian legends could be demonstrated to be mere inventions of the Brahmins, it would be difficult to dispute the authenticity of Chinese history, which goes back to within a century of the epoch ascribed to the universal deluge. Without being branded as heretics, we may now admit the creation of our world in the successive stages of geological records, during periods not inconsistent with those relatively enormous numbers which the Hindus have assigned to their first ages of the world's history. These numbers have been often quoted as ridiculous. But to allow, at all events, a duration of man's growth in civilisation during 7000, 10,000, or 20,000 years B.C. is not abstractedly preposterous, either in relation to these geological ages of its physical progress, or in comparison with the eternity which has been taught in Christianity as the future of our conscious and individual existences.

With an esoteric meaning we may adopt the story of Eden, while considering the world under its present geographical aspect, without offering any violence to the facts of science. We must include in our volumes of its history such records as have been written in the remains of the old dwellers in the villages constructed on piles in the Swiss lakes, and in flint instruments, etc. The quadrumana, which approach nearest to man in aspect of all the animals, are found in the tropical islands of Asia and in the interior of Africa. If, by the Almighty Power, man was first placed in a garden, such a region may be discerned in the lovely and luxuriant tropics as would afford him a careless existence—though perturbed by his natural enemy, the serpent—on the simple bounty of nature in her fruits, without the necessity of toil. Surely, whether man was physically made in the image of the Almighty, and placed by Him in a garden to eat of all its trees, except the tree of knowledge of good and evil, or whether he developed from an anthropoid ape, a tropical rather than temperate climate would be the scene of his commencement. In Genesis iii. 8 the Lord God is described as walking in the garden in the cool of the day, which certainly suggests this inference. If man had originated in a temperature similar to that which now compels him to wear clothes, would he not have been endowed by nature, all-wise under the divine, with a protecting skin? If the Eden story be admitted, one of its essentials is that the primitive pair were without garments, and as they were in a blissful condition of course they were not shivering with cold. It is, indeed, said that savages endure a great degree of cold in the extreme south of America, with naked bodies; but humanity in general has, in a chilly temperature, warmly clothed itself, adapting the hides of beasts for covering when in the coldest climates. In the tropics the aprons of Adam and Eve remain, frequently as the only articles of attire.

There is, however, a verse in our Holy Writ (Genesis iii. 21) which suggests a provision against cold, and at the same time shows that our primeval hides were not weather-proof. After God has said to Adam "Cursed is the ground for thy sake," and "In the sweat of thy face shalt thou eat bread," it is recorded that "unto Adam also and his wife did the Lord God make coats of skins, and clothed them." Then they were banished from Eden, and we are told, three verses subsequently, that Abel had become a keeper of sheep and Cain a tiller of the ground.

This keeping of sheep seems to indicate a climate wherein coats of skins might be desirable; and the progress of civilisation in the colder parts of the earth would seem to be thus briefly allegorised. That the writer of Genesis iv. did not intend it to be literally accepted that only Cain and Abel had been born, as might be conceived from Genesis iv. 2, would seem evident from verses 14, 15, wherein a population is distinctly inferred.

According to the article on Java in Hamilton's East India Gazetteer, with the species of the monkey genus called the Wow-wow the Javanese pretend to have a fellow feeling, there being a tradition amongst them that their ancestors originally sprang from this species of ape. In this work it is remarked of the ourang-outang of Borneo that "some authors assert that he is also a cooking animal."

Primeval man, whether physically an advance upon the cleverest ape's form, or created from dust by the divine *fiat*, with woman formed from one of his ribs during his sleep, may be conceived to have learnt to walk erect, to have obtained some definite command of language, and some respect for the rights of property, while living in happy indolence, comparatively speaking, on the bread fruit and plantains, cocoa-nuts, and sufficiently nourishing tropical fruits in general. Fishing, and attempts at increasing the growth of fruits, may have added to his means of sustenance. He would, in accordance with his unrestrained natural desires, become acquainted with crime, in the shape of murder and robbery, induced by the passion of anger, and the natural craving for food or property in others' possession. With a recognition by the community of rights in property, and in the settled union of husband and wife, civilisation would commence. The Asiatic islands are the richest portion of the globe in the life-sustaining fruits, and parts of the Indo-Chinese peninsula seem to offer equal advantages. There is no novelty in the idea of assigning primeval man to the tropics, but it does not appear to have been duly connected with the next links in the chain of human education, India and China. Canoes, such as we see in the South Sea Islands, would easily transport man over seas calm for the greater portion of the year. As mankind multiplied, the limits of the bread-like fruits must have been passed, the boundaries of the gardens of the earth must have been overstepped, and we find that two great civilisations have grown up, or become established, just to the north of these tropical regions, viz. those of the Indians and Chinese. Each of these affords every indication of autochthonity. It is impossible to contemplate the ordinary Hindu, seated on his ankles monkey-fashion, and observe his gradations, in peaceful and primitive-seeming civilisation, from the simple cultivator of the soil to the Brahminical philosopher and poet, and hold him otherwise than aboriginal. And in his art, from the rude hut, and idol of a mere block of wood but slightly shaped, and the small pyramidal pagoda, up to the elaborate architecture, fanciful ornamentation, and imagery, to be found side by side with the primitive style throughout the land, the successive steps may be discerned. And the Chinese have a similar aspect of authochthonity. In these two sub-tropical regions the natural fruits are not sufficient to support man without regular labour, but the fertility of the soil must have afforded him subsistence, in the dawn of civilisation, without any advanced effort of thought or artifice of manual toil. Both are watered by magnificent rivers. They have contained within well-defined limits 200 and 400 millions of inhabitants respectively. Two great peoples would seem in them to have formed the second great strata in man's history. India would seem first to have offered the most obvious suggestions for man's transition from the mere savage state to one ordered by labour, and improved by archaic commerce. The plains of the Ganges must either have afforded cereals in a wild form, or coarse grasses to be developed into them, when mankind discovered that their seeds had nourishing properties. Small ingenuity and the rudest cultivation would seem to have been sufficient. Again man spread forth. From India, and the Indo-Chinese peninsula, he reached the barren steppes and regions where existence could only be maintained by the chase. Weapons of a superior description to those by which the wild animals of the tropics had been kept back, warm clothing and fire, began to be absolutely requisite to his existence. Then the horse was subdued. The rubbing together of two sticks to produce fire must be accepted as an earlier method than the striking of flints, or, at least, as coeval. As has been observed, it survived as a ceremony of the Aryan altars, as shown in extracts which will be quoted in a subsequent chapter from the Sanskrit, given by M. Emile Burnouf, Principal of the College of Athens, in his publication entitled Les Sciences des Religions. It seems, at all events, to have been the method in which fire was obtained by man in the tropics, being still employed there in our time.

Meanwhile, in Africa races were growing, which did not find the peculiarly civilising influences of India similar to those which have continued the Aryan education in Europe, and their intellectual capacity seems but slightly to have expanded in comparison. Gradually, from the range of tropical Asiatic islands or regions had proceeded those who have become Mongols and Fins, and all the various developments of some five or ten races, considered more or less distinct by ethnographists, which have appeared upon the earth. The inferior tribes either had remained in their original tropical homes, or were pressed onwards, as civilisation advanced, towards the more barren north. In both the extreme tropical and in the high latitudes, we find a low degree of human culture comparatively to our own.

So long ago as 2200 B.C. the Chinese appear to have made and recorded astronomical observations. Abel Rémusat says that the Chinese history goes back with certainty to the twenty-second century before our era. Ages previously, one of their early patriarchs is related to have discovered the use of fire by rubbing two sticks together. In later days they claim to be the most original of nations in the matter of printing, as the text of the Chinese Annals assigns the year answering to A.D. 952 as the date of the printing of the first edition of the Nine Kings or Scriptures by means of wooden types. "The historical import of the early legends of the Chinese," says Pritchard, "represents that people as a tribe of barbarous nomades, destitute of the most simple arts of life, and roving about in the forests of Shensi, at the feet of the high mountains of the Tibetan border, without settled dwellings, clothed in skins, ignorant even of fire, and feeding on insects and roots, in a state hardly less abject than that of Bushmen and Australian savages. Philosophers, wise rulers, and law-givers gradually converted the rude condition of existence into the Chinese thoroughly utilitarian manner of life. They claim to have had a code of laws as long ago as 2205 B.C. Here, as amongst the Aryans, the north-western portion of the country, adjacent to sub-tropical regions, with stimulants to toil in its temperate climate, and soil capable of affording due return for labour, produced the leading instructors in the arts of life. If we have somewhat ridiculed the Chinese civilisation, a compliment which they have returned by styling us foreign devils, they have, at all events, managed to multiply to the extent of about 400,000,000 by steadily making the most of their advantages.

They have cultivated their territory to the utmost extent of its capacity, producing works of art and literature; the former of which have certainly been valued in Europe for their beauty as well as their quaintness.

The Mohammedan emperor, Mahommed III., who reigned at Delhi in the fourteenth century A.D., is related to have adopted the Chinese custom of using paper for currency, with the royal seal appended.

While China, even at about the year 2000 B.C., had arrived at positive scientific knowledge, reasons combined to render the progress of Aryan civilisation in India stronger, more comprehensive, and more knowledge-embracing. In the comparative barrenness of much of its southern tropical territory toil would be rendered requisite for the growth of humanity, of a more arduous and thoughtful character than in the richer tropical regions. Of the half of the world containing most land it is, as has been remarked, for all purposes of commercial intercourse the most central region. Including the islands it is geographically the most central. To its east lay the great China, populous and rising in education. To the south-west were large islands to which the Indian influence extended; as testified by the ancient temples in the midst of the thick jungles of Java, and on the mainland in Cambodia. To the south-west lay Africa, in which Colonel Moor discovered Sanskrit names, probably bearing witness again to Indian enterprise or extension. To the north-west were districts, widely sterile, capable of affording sustenance to a comparatively small settled population, except where commerce passed. To the farther west, still more arid districts only admitted the existence of the nomadic Arabs; perhaps the earliest wanderers beyond the Indus. Amidst these, great settlements were founded as mankind increased in science.

How could Babylon, existing by a system of drainage, be a primitive city; an abode of man just emerging from the uncultured life of savages? When those whom we now term the Aryans had formed their civilisations, and had multiplied beyond the limits of India; which is only calculated, by reason of its mountainous and barren regions, to support about half as many inhabitants as China, they found it requisite to extend by way of the Red Sea, Persian Gulf, or north-western overland route, into the fertile temperate Europe, pressing northward the Finnic people, or the "stone and bronze races," of whom we have found vestiges. From Indians of the age in which the cave temple of Elephanta was excavated may have come emigrants into Egypt. From those of between about 3000 and 1800 B.C., and after classic forms had been introduced, perhaps exiles on account of an exodus occasioned by the Mahábhárata war, which may apparently be safely accepted as a fact, followed others into Asia Minor and Greece. The civil and religious wars of India, like those of France and England, may be reasonably supposed to have resulted in the expatriation of many of the conquered, as Mr. Pococke has urged in his "Greece in India." Simultaneously, or at a later period, the more northern Aryans were spreading by the shores of the Caspian into northern Europe; but the Aryan race has in its two regions of India and Europe not more than equalled, or surpassed by about a fifth, the population of the Chinese in their more compact territory.

The Tartars, associated with the Chinese, appertain to the Asiatic regions to their north, so the Semitic races, formerly classed with our own as Indo-Caucasian, inhabit the sandy, ever sun-bright realms to the west of India. The Persian Aryans, however, occupied the more fruitful territories towards the Caspian. Here sylvan scenes abound; but they have not the advantages which those of India possess for aiding the advance of human education, in the propinquity to the tropical life-sustaining vegetation.

Our European civilisation has been due to the general fertility of our soil, our varying rainfall, our temperate climate, and our seas and rivers. Indian civilisation was induced by the same combinations, but with this difference, that it contained within itself not merely the incentives to improve but the suggestions of nature actually to commence culture. Progress must have been incited in the avenues of civilisation by its magnificent and navigable rivers, its seas enjoying mild and equable winds for eight months in the year, and its prolific cereal-producing river plains. In its varieties of hot and genial climates all grades in vegetable and animal life teem beneath the glowing sunshine; tempered as it generally is by the moisture equally requisite in their nurture. There the cotton-pod invitingly opened and displayed its stores of thread, almost as if asking to be extracted and utilised for raiment. The cocoa-nut palm, comprehensive in its utility, fringed its southern shores. Where can we find, in the so-called Central Asia, in the districts of Balkh or the Caucasus, though they contain beautiful and fertile places, any regions with all these incentives to civilisation—for conducting man from the life on nature's gifts alone to that supported by artifice? The Almighty in these might seem to have communicated with man, not after the fashion we have vainly imagined, in thunder from the mountains, but by the prompting voice of nature, working then, as we recognise it now, by its laws and constant forces.

In evidence for these theories, as opposed to the notion of the development of civilisations on the inland uplands, the long-conserved archaic culture of India, and its art and literary remains, are offered.

CHAPTER XIII.

Universality of the aspect of Indian architecture—Arguments as to relegating to India the origin of science, etc., with illustrations of the argument from Bombay—Tropical and sub-tropical attributes of India; and arguments as to the priority of its temples to those of Nubia, etc.

WE find in India architecture which contains suggestions of every form which it has assumed in Europe, Egypt, or Assyria. We have the Greek, Roman, Italian, Romanesque, Gothic, and more fantastic Oriental styles. We have the simple and ponderous, the light and fanciful. We have art occasionally comparable to classic, and occasionally similar to the varied or grotesque forms of Gothic. We find languages related to all the Aryan languages of Europe. We have discovered within the last century a literature in ancient forms of those languages, the Sanskrit and Pali, which contains essays on astronomy, music, medicine, etc. etc., epic poems, romances, dramas, and moral and didactic scriptures. We find in religion a Trinity in unity, and the conception of Deity incarnate upon earth. We see kingdoms, warlike republics amongst the ancient Rajpoots, an hereditary priesthood as in Russia till the present day, and a celibate one in Buddhism as in the Church of Rome. We read a code of laws, indubitably of many centuries B.C., in the present—a later form of it, with regulations for commerce and rules for the honourable conduct of warfare, etc. etc. Yet it has been considered that the germs of all these existed in archaic, pastoral Aryans, issuing from some region near the Caspian to conquer India on the south-east and Europe on the north-west, and produce, on the two sides, these similar civilisations. Surely it is much more reasonable to surmise that the one actually proceeded from the other. Surely the diversities of climate would otherwise have produced more intrinsically as well as extrinsically different civilisations. As it is not contended that the Aryans arose in Europe, and the literature of India distinctly exhibits its priority to our own, we ought altogether to acknowledge India as the parent, not the mere elder cousin, of Europe in respect to our Indo-European race and its culture. Steam and electricity are amongst the modern realisations to which we do not seem to be indebted to our parent; but geometry, algebra, the decimal system, etc., are now relegated by science from the Arabs to the Indians.

If we contemplate the native streets of Bombay, we perceive carved woodwork upon Hindu houses which might be old English. Other houses are painted in broad borders and panels, which recall to the mind the houses of Pompeii. The Hindu women of the wealthier classes are to be seen in richly-tinted and delicately-embroidered garments, which rival the Grecian peplum. If these are imitations, it is incomprehensible that, although this island, about eleven miles in length by two in width, lying outside a wild and thinly-populated part of the mainland, has been settled by Portuguese and English for three centuries, there is scarcely a trace of copying our habits and customs amongst the Hindus. If we pass through the English suburb of Malabar Hill, we arrive at a holy village of Brahmins. Temples and houses are clustered round a tank, situated on a narrow promontory, terminated by a residence of the English Governor's. Although thus isolated amidst European influence for many years, it seems utterly unaffected by it. The Japanese have rapidly adopted many European aspects. The Hindus, as a people, do not exhibit the slightest inclination to imitate our appearance or borrow our customs. Some of them learn our language to perfection, and many adopt some European habits; and they act as clerks in our banks, our law courts, and our business houses; but, as a people, the Hindus remain constant to their own fashions in life. Can then this race have been copyists in those ancient monuments in which we find a resemblance to Assyrian, Egyptian, Classic, or Gothic art? Is it not more likely that these all emanated from them? They are of our own inventive race. They still exist amongst their ancient works. Why should the Babylonians, Egyptians, and Greeks of the past be esteemed their teachers? Although their outward aspect is now so different from our own, there will be found intrinsic similarity in essential respects.

In all Asia to the westward of China—indeed we may say in the whole world—there is no space of earth so likely, from its natural attributes, to have afforded the sources for our streams of Aryan civilisation, whether sparkling in fancy or placid in progressive utility. As the scene of the first development of agriculture, no more probable situation can be conceived than that of the *Arya varta,* the cultivated land. It has been observed that Hindustan presents beautiful plains and fields, adorned with luxuriant harvests, which are gathered twice in the year. The inundations of the Ganges and Brahmaputra impart great fertility to the ground; in many places requiring no such aid, as consisting of vegetable soil to the depth of six feet. The "Modern Traveller" observes:—"To its rare vegetable treasures, no less than to its mineral riches, this country has owed the distinction of being in all ages the fountain of mercantile wealth and the focus of commercial enterprise." The luxuriance of herbage is scarcely equalled in any other region of the globe. Wheat, barley, maize, millet, and twenty-seven varieties of rice, here reward the husbandman's labour. Vegetables, fruits, and spices abound, amidst as picturesque foliage as the world can show. Flowers of every hue not only bloom upon shrubs and creepers, but, magnificent and more brilliant in blossom than our rhododendrons, on forest trees. Vast regions will look arid and sun-baked before the rains; but a few days of tropical downpour will carpet them with delicious verdure. Not only geographically is India a centre land, but as possessing attributes intermediate between those in which nature supplies food without what can be termed toil, and those in which she demands unremitting attention. Here there must be labour, but no carefully artificial aids to it are demanded in the great part of the country. Here hermit life can be sustained on the roots and hot peppers; and the contemplative faculties allowed to exult in an almost total suspension of bodily cares. A scanty garment round the loins is sufficient raiment for the greater part of the year in most parts of the land.

If man was actually ejected from a garden by the Almighty, and a cherubim placed at the gate, with a flaming sword which turned every way, as our Bible informs us, and if it was commanded to him "In the sweat of thy face thou shalt eat bread, till thou return unto the ground," India is exactly adapted to his first labours. If, according to the development theory, he emerged from savage life under the promptings of his own intelligence, urged by the necessity of procuring food for himself and children, whom he had begun to love with affection more enduring than that of the beasts towards their offspring, India again affords the most obvious suggestions for the application of his toil. And, for the pastoral life, for the maintenance of those flocks and herds which, as Professor Max Müller has demonstrated, are testified by the Vedas to have been the chief feature of archaic Aryan wealth, it is equally adapted. Still, as in the dawn of civilisation, cattle constitute a main resource of Indian peasant life. Early legislators enforced, as a religious duty, the necessity of their preservation, and ordained that they should only become food for man after being solemnly sacrificed to the deity. Pickering, in his "Races of Men," observed that "it is a mistake to suppose, with many, that the pastoral or nomadic life is a stage in the progressive improvement of society. The condition is inscribed upon the face of nature; and widely extended regions minister to the wants of man, where, nevertheless, cultivation is impossible. But in India the pastoral life was not nomadic, but settled and conjoined with the tillage of the ground. Fertile as India generally is, however, it still extensively requires irrigation, and is liable to famine, consequent upon drought. Canals and tanks, constructed by its ancient inhabitants, sometimes measured by miles, though artificially embanked, attest the recognition of this fact, works which the English do not appear to have continued so zealously as our constant assertion of our beneficial influence in the country would have suggested. But these water-works were undertaken by men who had observed the luxuriant herbage resulting from the extensive scheme of natural irrigation in their vicinity, and from the copious rainfall of ordinary years. Surely it is more probable that agriculture and its concomitant civilisation originated here than in Egypt or on the plains of Shinar, where the fertile river territories are bounded by vast deserts, where the artifices of irrigation and drainage have to be very ingeniously applied, and where no wealth of forest timber animated the first efforts of architecture.

There are productive and beautiful regions in the vicinities of the Euphrates and Nile, and the date-palm is there a beneficent friend; but they cannot supply that abundance of life-sustaining fruits which enriches the tropics within the region of the monsoons. Their gardens have been created by man rather than endowed by nature; the gift of the Supreme Spirit.

It cannot be reasonably supposed that the stonework and bricks of Egypt and Babylon were employed till mankind had previously comprehended how to raise columns of wood by shaping trees to their uses. A tree is nature's column, supporting a leafy roof; and to cut it down, to raise it again in support of a more impervious covering, seems no great effort for archaic man's imagination. Mr. Fergusson has most ably illustrated in his history, and asserted the growth of stone architecture from wooden forms; yet, when he traces resemblance between the Southern India and the Assyrian styles, he surmises the latter to have been the earlier. Surely the tropical Asia, with its varied and vast extent of forest timber, is more naturally likely to have been the original than the comparatively small wooded and fertile districts amongst deserts, where the inhabitants dwell in tents or temporary huts, as is the case in great part of the western and northern Asia, where commercial settlements have not been formed, and upon the sands about Egypt.

The ancient Nubian and Egyptian temples present aspects distinctly homogeneous with Indian architectural works. The systems of caste and of religion and philosophy prevailing in the two countries, would appear to be too analogous to be due to mere coincidence. Egypt has been styled the mother of the arts and sciences; but the manner in which she arrived at her offspring has not been apprehended. If we allow them to have come from India, on the other hand, we can trace the successive stages in their rise, through man's gradual education by the influences of Nature around him. The supposition seems to be justified that the populations of the two countries may have had the same proportions in the past ages; that is to say, about 200,000,000 in India to 7,000,000 in Egypt. *Primâ facie*, it seems most rational to conceive that the greater produced the civilisation, and then conveyed it to the lesser—the mere fertile valley of a river running between barren mountains and sandy wastes. It is difficult to conceive primeval man in Egypt maturing within his mind all the artificial aids to existence which we find recorded in its lasting granite monuments. The Egyptians may have originated as a race in Africa itself, India, or elsewhere; but if in the former, they may still have adopted civilisation from the latter, although keeping to their own language. Old Egyptian art is dead; old Indian art still lives.

Just as the Aryan empires of Macedonia and Rome stretched grand works of civilisation into the arid Asian regions, so at an earlier age the Aryan empires in India sent forth arts and culture. That the inhabitants of the Madhyama should have formed or influenced the artificially sustained settlements on the Euphrates by proceeding up the Persian Gulf, seems geographically natural, and consonant with the literary evidence as to sea voyaging; while, as has been shown, it is in accordance with the brief biblical account.

The Aryan race has acquired roots which seem likely to endure with the habitable globe, for itself and its works, in the most fertile portions of the earth, with the exception of eastern Asia, where the great Chinese Empire supports almost as extensive a people.

CHAPTER XIV.

The Indian Manu, the Egyptian Menes, the Cretan Minos—Comparison of the laws, etc., of Moses with those of Manu—The Dravidian or Tamulian race of India—The Ramáyana and our mediæval romances—Advantages presented by the Monsoons for archaic commerce—Our minds cramped by the reception of Archbishop Usher's scheme of biblical chronology.

WE find that the first recorded promulgation of law in India has been made under the name of the Institutes of Manu. In Egypt the foundation of civilisation and law was ascribed to Menes. By the Greeks Minos, King of Crete, son of Jupiter and Europa, was believed to have established laws so equitable that he was elevated, after death, to the office of supreme judge in the infernal regions.

Egypt appears to afford us no definite account of this Menes. He has been affirmed, on the scientific authority of M. Mariette Bey, to have been actually the first king who sat upon the throne of Egypt, who claimed to be only a mortal. A reign of sixty-two years is assigned to him, after which he was killed by a hippopotamus. But no monuments can be attributed with certainty to him and his family. The "Saturday Review" of October 20, 1877, inquires, "Was Menes of the people of the land, or did he and the first dynasty which he founded come from the scene of some still older civilisation, to introduce law and order in the Nile valley? This question seems to be answered by referring the name attributed to the monarch to the appellation of the laws which he promulgated." The divine birth of Minos, and his position after death, would seem to relegate him to the domain of the mythological with certainty. In India the code of Manu still lives, in such a form that it would seem impossible to consider it otherwise than as indigenous. The inference that Menes and Minos both really refer to Manu, appears to be obviously reasonable. The laws of Manu were adopted in Egypt and Crete, and, in process of time, the name applied to mythical monarchs, as indicated by the uncertainty respecting Menes, and the fact that Minos was related to the son of the highest of the Grecian deities.

Manu or Menu is the prophet and spirit, creative thought and lawgiver of Brahma. The name is derived from the Sanskrit *man*, signifying to think. This derivation, combined with the present existence in India of these laws, acknowledged to be referable in their present form to the literary cycle succeeding the Vedic, must surely be sufficient evidence of the priority of the promulgation under the name of Manu.

When we compare the cosmogony of Moses with that of Manu—the laws concerning purifications and the Levites, etc., with those respecting the Brahmins, etc.—it is not unreasonable to surmise that the framer of the one should have been acquainted with the other.

It may be conceded that the Almighty imparted wisdom to Moses, by the same process as that by which it is communicated to our leading minds in these later days, without derogating from the sublimity of his feeling the inspiration of the Most High on Sinai. The statement in the Acts of the Apostles, that he was learned in all the wisdom of the Egyptians, will account for his mind having become imbued with these ancient Aryan laws. They contain no trace of deity regarded under the aspect of Trinity in Unity. It is conceivable that Moses may have retained the Unity of the Absolute Spirit as expressed in them, while dissenting from belief in the existence of the subordinate deities, which they set forth as occupied in the government of the universe, apparently as actual existences, though only emanations from the Supreme. He also seems to have abrogated the theory of the transmigration of souls set forth in them. He seems to have presented merely temporal rewards and punishments, and consequences of acts descending for good or ill upon the children. In both the codes of Manu and of Moses the brother is ordered to raise up seed to the deceased by his widow; under the Mosaic law, in respect for his inheritance, in the Hindu, in order that he may offer up the sacrificial cake for the repose of the putative father's soul. In this last regulation we may perhaps recognise the original of Catholic masses for the dead.

It does not seem to be certain that the Aryan, Tamulian, Semitic, and even ancient Egyptian languages, will not admit of a common origin in the remote past. But if it be held that the two latter are shown by their formation to be incapable of having proceeded from the same source as the first, since that age, at all events, when language had arrived at such a point of completeness as to be worthy of the dignity of the appellation, it is possible that Indian civilisation and arts may have been adopted by the Semitic or Egyptian people, and modified by their circumstances, just as European and American civilisation is being nowadays received by Japan. Affinities again have been recognised between the Asiatic and ancient Central American civilisations. It is possible, or even probable, that these were due to Asia, if not actually to India. The westerly winds which commonly prevail across the Pacific Ocean to the north of the tropical trade wind region appear to render likely the approach from Asia to North America and Mexico, especially as they are aided by the current. But the return for the comparatively rude sailing vessels, or rowing galleys, probably in use, would be difficult, if not impossible, in the same latitude. It is more difficult to conceive that the Mexicans or Peruvians brought civilisation to India by the line of the South Sea Islands.

The Dravidian or Tamulian race seems to have developed a literature of its own in India, south of the Vindhya mountains, apart from Brahminical influence. Before the Vedas were compiled, before alphabetic writing was in vogue, before the laws were codified by the Brahmins under the name of the Institutes of Manu, before the Sanskrit language assumed even the ancient form in which it appears in the Vedas, as they have come down to us, there may still have been great civilisations in India, which may have transmitted arts and sciences to Egypt. Judging from the epoch of Roman history at which Justinian's code was compiled, many ages of law and order may be assigned to India before the appearance of such a succinct promulgation of laws as that which has descended to us. Observations of the heavens, architecture, sculpture in wood and stone, working in metals, regulations for the order of society, conceptions of the deity, and settled forms of approaching him in adoration, must have long preceded literary treatises upon these matters. Philosophy must have been orally discussed and inculcated ages before men, in the earliest civilisation of the world, thought of recording in writing their opinions, for their wider diffusion in their own days, and the benefit of posterity. Literature is only a convenient method of conveying instruction in or noting opinions upon these topics. It merely obviates the fatigue of retaining an essay, poem, or narrative in the memory. Even the Ramáyana epic professes to have been delivered by word of mouth, and learnt in its entirety by the first receiver of it. Our own ancestors of five centuries ago became statesmen, able chieftains, and accomplished gentlemen, in music, dancing, and warlike exercises, without knowledge of letters. Yet their relics seem to show that they were not destitute of sense of beauty or elegance. For their romances they listened to the bards.

In our mediæval romaunts wild sylvan regions are assumed to exist within a knight errant's reach on horseback from Caerleon on Usk, or any other chivalrous capital. Giants, dragons, and enchanters, in a world of mystic spells, await the adventurous knight. In considering the peninsula of India in the eleventh century B.C., the date of the Ramáyana, according to the translator Mr. Griffiths, it is not necessary to hold it to have been then inhabited by savages merely in the south, because that narration poetically describes it as such, or rather as peopled by supernatural beings who may be thought poetical pictures of uncivilised men. Indeed the apes or satyrs, which compose the army of Hanuman, the monkey-faced divinity of India, appear in the poem to be by no means necessarily intended to allegorise barbaric inhabitants of the country. They would rather seem to be presented in poetical treatment of the monkey race, which is held sacred.

It may be that they are so esteemed on account of the poet's imaginative treatment of them; or perhaps he may have depicted them as Rama's warriors, because they were regarded with superstitious veneration previously to his conception. The monkeys of India are weirdly manlike. Fanciful ideas concerning them would appear to be naturally engendered. Surely the idealisation or embodying of existing faiths has usually been the poet's province rather than the actual inventing of them. The poetical fervour would appear likely to have been excited in a similar manner in all ages. Shakspeare did not invent his fairies, neither did he probably introduce them as types of other beings.

Perhaps the Darwinian theory is to be dimly discerned amongst the numerous philosophical systems of the country. This reverence may be half unconscious respect for monkeys, as descended with the human race from collateral ancestry, but who remained amongst the trees, and have not improved in culture. The distinct allusions to commerce beyond seas, as well as inland, in the Institutes of Manu, must render the existence of extensive trade previously to the compilation of the code a certainty. Indeed it would seem consonant with the historical progress of the human race that this people, which produced the Indian civilisation, should have perceived the advantages offered by the steady winds of the monsoons, blowing with constancy upon their coasts, and taken advantage of them, and of seas only periodically ruffled by tempests. To coast around the Arabian Sea and ascend the Red Sea or Persian Gulf, is no very adventurous undertaking for the rowing galleys which, like the Greeks, they appear to have employed.

Our minds have been so cramped by Archbishop Usher's biblical chronology that they hesitate to accept even 10,000 years backwards from the present time, 300 generations, for the growth of civilisation from its childhood. Such a period, with 10,000 or 20,000 previous years for the development of civilisation from its birth to the termination of what may be considered its infancy, is less incredible, however, than what we have been taught, in orthodox Christendom, in respect to other matters in which time is a feature.

From the date of the deluge, 2348 B.C., to the confounding of tongues at the dispersion of humanity from the Tower of Babel, only about 120 years have been allowed in the accepted biblical chronology. The impression that a considerable number of persons were at the building of the tower is certainly made by the biblical narrative. No miraculous interposition is recorded to account for the three sons of Noah, and the three wives, multiplying so rapidly. And the short date, therefore, seems to demand a higher effort of faith than these extended periods, especially as the 20,000 or 30,000 years of civilisation are as easy to credit as the lives of the antediluvian patriarchs of the Bible, which are extended to about 900 years. The duration of time presents nothing contrary to our scientific knowledge. The lives of the patriarchs are contrary to our experience.

CHAPTER XV.

Wooden forms of architecture traced by Mr. Fergusson in the sculptured cave-temples—Excavations of Ellora, and their semi-Egyptian, Classic, Gothic, later Italian, aspects in archaic work—Excavations and wall-paintings of Ajanta—Hindus as described by Megasthenes—General appearance of antiquity of Indian civilisation.

IT would altogether appear that, in these mythological excavations, as they have been styled, scattered through the Western Ghauts, and more sparsely existing in other parts of India, there is evidence to indicate that we possess a key to the locked pages of the early civilisation of the world. Mr. Fergusson has traced in them, as has been observed, an imitation of wooden forms of architecture, as if the only structural edifices with which the sculptors were acquainted were of that material. What surely can be a more probable sequence of ideas, to man emerging from barbarism, than the use of the timber of a luxuriantly wooded country to construct habitations, and then the enlargement and adornment, or imitation, in excavation, of the natural caverns in which he had previously and simultaneously found shelter? That he should proceed to carve the stone in imitation of the easier and more obvious process of wood-carving, which is found to prevail amongst the more intelligent savage nations, may surely be conceived likely to have happened ages before letters can have been invented. Surely man must, humanly speaking, have carved in wood or stone the resemblances of persons and things which occupied his fancy for ages before he learnt to paint in colours, or thought of perpetuating in writing his words or ideas, or even constructing regular poems for recitation. Instead of a later date being assumed for the cave-temples on account of passages in the history of Krishna or in the Sivaic legends being found in them, it would rather appear that an earlier date should be assigned to the development of those religious narratives from the illustrations of them found in the excavations. Our modern archæologists have suggested that when these caverns contain representations of topics taken from the Ramáyana and Mahábhárata epics, they must be posterior not merely to the original stories, which may have given birth to the poems, as the old tales of Hamlet, Romeo and Juliet, and others inspired Shakspeare's plays, but to the actual epics.

Certainly if these are to be considered solely as romances, culled absolutely from the luxuriance of the individual poet's fruitful imaginations, this must be so. But if it be held that these, like our own great European epics of Milton and Dante, were metrical renderings of and additions to stories or ideas existing at their epochs, and which may have already been illustrated in stone or paint by numerous archaic artists, there is no reason why the carvings of the caverns may not have preceded them.

Macaulay's New Zealander of the future, lounging meditatively over the broken arches of London Bridge, might erroneously ascribe all our acquaintance with the battle between the angels and devils, for instance, and the victory of St. Michael over Satan, to a period subsequent to the publication of the Paradise Lost.

It may be equally wrong to argue that the incidents related of Rama in the Ramáyana, or of Krishna in the Mahábhárata, were necessarily unknown to the world of Bharata before the inditing of these works.

The most extensive and remarkable series of these excavated temples are to be found at Ellora and Ajanta, some 200 miles to the east of Bombay; which may be conveniently studied, as has been observed, on the walls of our Indian Museum; which contains numerous and admirable photographs of these and other cave-temples, besides copies of the wall-paintings which are so remarkable in the Ajanta caverns. The Brahmins assert that the cave-temples of Ellora were formed by Eelloo, rajah of Ellichpore, 7900 years ago; but a Mohammedan tradition of the neighbourhood assigns them to a period shortly preceding the Mohammedan conquests, which commenced in the eleventh century of our era.

As the Brahminical statement disagrees with our orthodox age of the creation of the world B.C. 4004, we have, naturally, preferred the Mohammedan date.

"The first view of the desolate religious city" (Ellora), wrote Mr. Erskine, "is grand and striking, but melancholy. The number and magnificence of the subterranean temples, the extent and loftiness of some, the endless diversity of sculpture in others, the variety of curious foliage, of minute tracery, highly-wrought pillars, rich mythological designs, sacred shrines and colossal statues, astonish but distract the mind. From their number and diversity it is impossible to form any idea of the whole; and the first impressions only give way to a wonder, not less natural, that such prodigious efforts of labour and skill should remain, from times certainly not barbarous, without a trace to tell us the hand by which they were designed, or the populous and powerful nation by which they were completed. The empire, whose pride they must have been, has passed away and left not a memorial behind it. The religion to which we owe one part of them, indeed, continues to exist, but that which called into existence the other, like the beings by whose toil it was wrought, has been swept from the land."

Some of these caverns, like Elephanta, present the semi-Egyptian, semi-Classic, or perhaps later Italian aspect in their columns, caryatides, and spirited sculptures. Others, like Karli, suggest the Gothic type, and contain only an image of Gautauma the Sage, in attitude of meditation or benediction. Most wonderful of all, worthy certainly to be ranked as an eighth wonder of the ancient world, the mountain has been hewn away to leave an area some 300 feet in length by 150 in width, with a solid piece of rock remaining in the centre. Out of this a pagoda of most elaborate and delicate workmanship has been sculptured, 100 feet in height, and over 500 feet in circumference. Colonnades, obelisks, bridges connecting one part of the temple with another, niches occupied by statues, porticoes, pillars, pilasters, flights of steps, and infinite varieties of architectural ornaments, are all carved in one immense monolith. The whole is supported on the backs of elephants, alternately with tigers and griffins; forming altogether one stupendous bit of most profuse carving. The rock on which this and the cavernous excavations have been effected, is variously described as granite or basaltic, not being entirely of the same nature.

From the more elaborate style of the workmanship at Ellora these excavations have been ascribed to a later period than Elephanta. This is corroborated by the fact that while the sculptures in the latter are greatly decayed, and one third of the columns totally wanting, in the former an occasional absent pillar or partially shattered sculpture may be observed. It would be difficult to attribute dilapidations here to the cannon or bonfires of the Portuguese, but, of course, the Mohammedans may be asserted to have vented their rage upon a column or two, or to have battered the base of a statue while sparing its countenance. Otherwise the venerable and old world aspect of the sculptures here again might seem to stamp them as veritably antique; appertaining to an age which might have been ancient at the time of Alexander, 2000 years ago.

With regard to the Buddhistic caves, however, those resembling, in their general style, that which has been described at Karli, the modern archæologist may again observe that they at least cannot be earlier than a few centuries B.C., because Gautauma Buddha only enunciated his doctrines about 550 B.C. But even if the figures can be proved to be Gautauma's, the precise accuracy of this Ceylonese date for the founder of Buddhism has yet to be verified. It does not emanate from ancient India, in which the religion is held to have originated; and the tribe of the Sakya to which he, Sakya Muni, is related to have belonged, has not been discoverable at that epoch. Moreover, he is styled the seventh Buddha, and it is by no means impossible that the essential doctrines of Buddhism, in its distinction from Brahminism—viz. the antagonism to the Vedas in respect to blood sacrifices, and to the Brahmins in regard to the privileges of caste—are more ancient by many centuries than 550 B.C. The personages represented in the wall-paintings of the Ajanta caves would seem suggestive of ancient Saxons or Teutons rather than of modern Hindus. They certainly may be easily conceived to be the people from which the Teutonic races have been derived. Making allowances for the darker complexions, the result of the tropical climate, and a concomitant occasional scantiness of attire, the general effect of the figures recalls to the mind those of our ancient illuminations. Many of the patterns in foliage and general ornamentation look precisely likely to have been the product of the people who have produced subsequently the graceful, delicate, and fanciful varieties of Gothic architecture and decoration. Many grotesque figures here again seem evident precursors to our quaint mediæval gargoyles, etc. A comical dwarf, seated amongst flowers, aptly illustrates the fairy Puck. The conical cap, straight sword, cross-gartering on the legs, and the wide drinking goblets, the moustaches of military aspect, in fact the whole style of the figures, seems well enough adapted to the revellers described in the scene which has been quoted from the Mahábhárata, and capable of producing the warriors of mediæval Europe. As Brahminical influence is alleged to have occasioned the expatriation of the old pure warrior and merchant castes, it seems certainly to be a reasonable conclusion, in conjunction with the evidence of language, etc., that in Greece, Germany, England, etc., we must look for them. In India it would seem that the prevalence of the priestly and agricultural castes, which remained in the country with natural conservatism, has ended, in the turn of Fortune's wheel, by their falling under the invading, really returning, descendants of the ancient warriors and merchants.

The gaily-adorned pavilions depicted in some of the Ajanta pictures appear to be constructed of wood. This may corroborate the supposition that the caverns were excavated in resemblance of timber edifices.

We may reasonably allow that the inexhaustible variety of form in the foliage and floral world of India, produced its imitation in wood-carving and afterwards in stonework, in the sombre recesses of these mountains. We may surely then admit that the Egyptians and Assyrians on their sunburnt plains, vivified by no perennial outburst of dense tropical rain, producing this infinite assemblage of vegetable life, received from India the art in stone-working, which had been first acquired in the easier process of wood-carving. The course of art history thus seems to have become conceivable. Now that the process of shaping detached blocks of stone for structures or statues has become thoroughly comprehended, men no longer delve in the rocks to image forth their conceptions of the Sublime and Beautiful.

The Hindus described by Megasthenes at the period of the invasion of Alexander the Great seem to present a decided similarity to those of the present day. Elaborate structural temples in India can be traced back to about the eighth century of our era, which appear to exhibit a complete mastery of stone architecture, as Mr. Fergusson has observed. The allusions to architecture in stone, in the pre-Christian literature of the country, appear altogether to be sufficient to demonstrate a long antiquity for it.

If these grim mythological excavations of unknown origin, solemnly and mysteriously beautiful in their decay, shattered not only in their quaint and profuse sculptured decoration, but in their massive columns left standing in the integral granite, also exhibit only an antiquity of 1000 or 1800 years, it is strange that the conservative Hindus should have abandoned this species of religious work. It is remarkable that they should have exhibited such zeal and perseverance in forming them, some 1200 years ago, yet now have ceased even to use them regularly as temples. Elaborate pagodas have been lately constructed in all the fulness of the structural style which Mr. Fergusson admits to have been in existence about 1000 years ago. Why have they deserted the system of excavation? In constructing some late examples of their more extensive and elaborate edifices, and in the little pagodas scattered numerously through the land, the models afforded them by the religious edifices of their conquerors appear to have had no appreciable influence.

This side of India, in about the sixth century of our era, is far from exhibiting to us an uncivilised region, such as would have been unlikely to have left positive records of such vast and elaborate works as those at Ellora. A commercial and literary civilisation is clearly displayed to us.

CHAPTER XVI.

The ancient city of Kalyan—Trade between Egypt and India under the Ptolemies—Lists of exports from India, as given in the Periplus, and by the Prophet Ezekiel—Buried city of Bhulabai.

In a poem of A.D. 696, entitled "The Garland of Jewels," Kalyan, on the west coast, within 200 miles of Ellora, is celebrated in the ornamental and mechanical arts, and the walls of its houses are said to have been covered with coloured pictures; and public schools were there provided. It is related to have been a great city long before the Christian era.

Bishop Butler observes that many places were known to the ancients on the coast of the peninsula of Hindustan. The promontory of Comaria, he says, is unquestionably Cape Comorin, and Taprobane is the island of Ceylon; and Maliarpha is Maliapur, near Madras.

Under the Ptolemies the maritime trade with India had been extensively opened by Egypt. The merchants of Alexandria established lines of navigation down the Red Sea, by Berenice to the port of Moosa, and through the Straits of Babel Mandeb to the excellent harbour of the modern Aden, which possesses great tanks, constructed of solid masonry, in the old magnificent spirit. Thence the voyage was continued to Muskat and Rasel Had, on the Arabian Sea; but, after passing the Persian Gulf, they appear to have trusted to the steady breezes of the monsoons. After entering ports called Minagara and Barbarike, at the mouth of the Indus, they passed by the gulf of the modern Cutch, dreaded for its swell, shallows, and bad bottom, and sailed northwards up the modern gulf of Cambay. Here was Barygaza, a grand Indian emporium thirty miles up the river, in a territory, the capital of which was Ozene (Oojein). Both here and at Minagara it was necessary to propitiate the king by liberal presents of the best wine, cloth, perfumes, plate, musical instruments, and female slaves, which system of presents still survives in India like so many other features of about 2000 years ago; a custom which has been brought home to us in 1876 in the noble collection of the Prince of Wales. The exports which they embarked at the Indus were composed of silk and cotton, emeralds, sapphires, spikenard, etc., and from Barygaza they took muslin, porcelain, and pepper in addition. In fact, the list of exports given in the Periplus, of about A.D. 64, affords a curious comparison with those which are conveyed up the Red Sea, in the modern iron steamers constructed to go through the Suez Canal. Amongst these are striped cloths, adamant and sandal wood, silver plate, arsenic and aromatics, ivory, spices and ginger, incense, fine muslins, cassia, cinnamon, tin and nard, coral, crystal and alabaster, porcelain, pearl, betel, quills and bark, knives or daggers, brass or copper articles, sugar, honey, myrrh, purple cotton and black silk, both Indian and Chinese.

To go back to an earlier age, we find in the 27th chapter of Ezekiel another apparent inventory of the principal Indian exports, as conveyed both overland and by sea, by Persian and Syrian merchants, or Sabean and Phœnician traders, B.C. 588. These consist of ivory, ebony, and precious clothes, spices, gold and precious stones, cinnamon or sugar cane, etc. etc. Nine hundred years previously the productions of India may be discerned in the Egyptian markets; and 240 years earlier (B.C. 1729) we find an Arabian caravan, as recorded in the 37th chapter of Genesis, transporting to Egypt balsam, myrrh, and spices, probably from India. Sailing southwards, the navigators touched at Kalliana, near Bombay, then proceeded down a long extent of coast infested by pirates; and they terminated their voyage, after entering Mangalore, at the modern Nelisuram, which seems to have been the chief emporium of the south-western part of India.

In the year 1018 A.D., when Mahmoud invaded India for the third time, with 100,000 horse and 30,000 foot, raised in Turkestan, Khorassan, etc., when he had with difficulty conducted his army through the mountains and entered the plains of Hindustan, driving all opposition before him, he saw in Kanouje, says the Mohammedan historian Ferishta, "a city which raised its head to the skies, and which, in strength and structure, might justly boast to have no equal." This city, in the beginning of the sixth century A.D., is said to have become so populous that it contained 30,000 shops in which betel was sold, and 60,000 musicians and singers paid a tax to the government. Bhulabai city, now buried to the depth of eighteen feet, is described as having cyclopean walls thirty leagues in circumference. Then there was Gaur. And, in fact, from one end of India to the other, continued success appears to reward the exploring archæologist, and demonstrate the completeness of its ancient civilisation and the populousness and architectural excellence of its cities.

CHAPTER XVII.

Kalidasa's dramas—Dialogue from "Sacontala, or the Fatal Ring," illustrating the old Indian habit of drinking—Argument that if Art be modelled on Nature, India contains the suggestions for it, especially.

THE era in use in northern India commences B.C. 56, from the reign of the potent Vicramaditya, who, remarked Sir W. Jones, gave encouragement to poets, philologers, and mathematicians; nine men of genius, commonly called the nine gems, attended his court, amongst whom the dramatic poet Kalidasa is allowed to have been one of the brightest. Some of his contemporaries and other Hindu poets, even to our own times, have composed so many tragedies, comedies, farces, and musical pieces, that the Indian Theatre would fill as many volumes as that of any nation in ancient or modern Europe, says Sir William Jones. He was personally acquainted with thirty plays, amongst which were "The Malignant Child," "The Taming of Durvasas," "The Seizure of the Lock," and five or six dramas on the adventures of their incarnate divinities. The more exalted personages in these spoke Sanskrit, the women Prakrit—a soft and familiar form of it, while the common people talked in the vulgar dialects. Modern critics have discovered arguments for relegating Kalidasa, and the Vicramaditya under whom he flourished, to some centuries after the commencement of our era, but whether he wrote in or about the last century B.C., or within the first seven centuries afterwards, he would belong to a period subsequent to the Grecian and Roman dramatists whom we venerate or admire in Europe, but previous to the development of the drama in mediæval and modern Europe. It may therefore be said that he owed his inspiration to the presence of this Greek kingdom on the north-west of India. But certainly his plays appear to present the aspect of being the forerunners of those of modern Europe, rather than the successors of those of the classic countries. The drama of "Sacontala, or the Fatal Ring," which has been translated by Sir W. Jones, in its dramatic situations, constant changes of scenes, opportunities for stage effect, in its mingling of the sentimental and humorous, in its language abounding with allusions to the charms of nature, and in its introduction of graceful supernatural beings, seems to suggest Shakspeare's Tempest or Midsummer Night's Dream. Religion is in it more distinctly introduced than in the plays of our great dramatist; but the king's favourite buffoon is a reverend Brahmin, which indicates that the professors of religion were held to be open to satire then as in modern times. The art of perspective is apparently shown to be comprehended in India in this period by the description of a landscape painted with foreground, etc. And a damsel is introduced, who is skilled in painting. A box of pencils and colours are also mentioned. Allusion is made to the case of a merchant of extensive commerce, who has been ruined by shipwreck, in order that the king's wisdom and justice may be recognised in a decision which he passes thereupon. The general religious allusions and the description of an ascetic apply to the Hindus of the present day. Kalidasa has distinctly expressed the Trinity in Unity. As quoted by Professor Max Müller, he wrote:—

> "In those three Persons the one God was shown,
> Each first in place, each last, not one alone.
> Of Siva, Vishnu, Brahma, each may be
> First, second, third, among the blessed Three."

It would appear that either Brahminical precept, Mohammedan example, or the poverty occasioned by many centuries of foreign conquest and spoliation, have abrogated a free English or American like manner of drinking together—of what is called "liquoring up," in slang phraseology—which seems then to have prevailed amongst the class in India which, in England and America, might now be expected to have recourse to it upon an occasion of celebration. The Fisherman who has been the means of restoring to the King the Fatal Ring, receives money in recompense, and he says to the officials who had conducted him to the monarch, "Here's half the money for you, my masters; it will serve to purchase the flowers you spoke of, if not to buy me your good will."

Januka. "Well, now, that's just as it should be."

Superintendent of Police. "My good fisherman, you are an excellent fellow, and I begin to feel quite a regard for you. Let us seal our first friendship over a glass of good liquor. Come along to the next wine-shop, and we'll drink your health."

Altogether, Kalidasa's dramas seem to have possessed much more of the modern European freedom in respect to stage arrangements than the Greek dramas, and to be aptly reducible into the category of being prototypes or originals of our European dramas. Lassen has supported the view of the origin of the Indian drama, as it has continued, in religious spectacles resembling our mediæval mysteries. The Sanskrit word for "player" literally signifies "dancer." If Kalidasa was the first Indian dramatist of more comprehensive range, marvellous genius must be imputed to him for so far perfecting the dramatic art. But it would seem that, like Shakspeare, he eclipsed his predecessors rather than that he had none.

CHAPTER XVIII.

India to be considered a continent rather than a country—That it probably continued in agricultural, commercial, and literary civilisation for some 2500 years before the Mohammedan conquest—Wealth found in it by Mahmoud—Subsequent wars and peace from England.

CONSIDERING the amount of literature in India of antochthonous aspect extant in the ancient Sanskrit, and attributed by our modern critics to the interval between the fifteenth century B.C. and the commencement of our era, it would indubitably appear that we must allow a period measured by thousands of years to have elapsed, during which civilisation progressed to such a point as the commencement of this epoch. Otherwise the miraculous interposition of Providence or of some superhuman genius seems requisite, or the previous growth of civilisation in some sort of submerged southern continent. But the existence of such has been based upon little beyond conjecture.

In the Bible we have been taught to recognise God's revelation to man of his early history on the globe; but the Bible ignores India and China, though their combined populations appear to have been numbered by hundreds of millions at about the time of Solomon. We have affirmed the wisdom of the Bible to have been personally delivered by God to man, which explains the sudden leap of human intelligence to its high altitude. Our European nineteenth century has come from 3000 years of art, literature, and science since the time of Homer. What period of growing civilisation is required to have produced the Vedas?

Our knowledge of Greek and Assyrian history extends backwards to about the commencement of this Indian literary period, when hymns were chanted to set religious ceremonial. It does not seem to promise, in the story of the Tower of Babel, or of the Greek Deucalion, a satisfactory solution of the question. Egyptian monuments are referred to about 5000 B.C., or earlier. In the earliest of these it may, of course, have been that the imagination of man aroused itself to art. But if art is modelled upon nature, which it seeks to idealise, applying the varied forms of the natural world to the sympathies, wants, and fancies conceived in the human mind, then undoubtedly India contains a multitude of natural suggestions to progress in science and art in which Egypt is deficient. The same remark will apply to the districts of Balkh and the Caucasus, and to the notion of our Indo-European race there acquiring the rudiments of the civilisation which it now exhibits.

The slowly-changing India, still retaining forms of the ancient Aryan civilisation, in spite of 800 years of foreign dominion, would seem to afford incomparably more evidence of antochthonity than any other territory in our globe. We have been too much inclined to consider it as a country divided among tribes rather than as a continent partitioned amongst nations. We have talked of the languages prevailing in India as if they were the strongly-marked *patois* of provinces, instead of languages distinguishing geographical limits as distinct as those of Europe. The greater part of our continent has been compelled, in a Charlemagne and Napoleon, to acknowledge one emperor; so India has been claimed by a sole monarch; but its independence has never been entirely lost, or even proclamation made of empire throughout the peninsula, till that of the British in 1876. The Rajpoots and Mohammedans of the Deccan were still retaining the names at least of independence; and portions of the land appertain to the Portuguese and French. The Sikhs had maintained their national liberties till they were lost, about the year 1848, in the sanguinary battles of Chilianwallah and Goojerat. This continent, then, containing a large portion of the great Aryan race, presenting both in its historical and continuing religion and civilisation, language and literature, a parallel to that of Europe, has been supposed to have been the settlement of one of the two great branches of the Aryan family. These have both been thought to have emerged from what has been called Central Asia; deserting entirely their original abode, and each, by some sort of instinct, developing into aspects exoterically different, but esoterically similar in their intrinsic forms.

In the Mohammedans, who, between the tenth and fifteenth centuries of our era, issued from regions akin to that of Balkh, and conquered, after hard fighting in both, the fair southern settlements of the Roman Empire in Constantinople, and of the Hindus in Delhi, we do not find that the mere change of climate, and superior luxury of situation, has occasioned any absolute alteration in ideas and manners, though it may have produced deterioration in hardihood. But the Indo-European race must be supposed to have contained in itself peculiar instincts, or else to have had two special revelations made to it by the Almighty, causing it to adopt, under somewhat different forms, the adoration of a Trinity in Unity of Deity, and an Incarnate Preserver or Saviour, in each branch of the race. It certainly appears more consonant with reason to allow that in the tropical paradise of food, without delving or hunting for it, the morning of Order arose upon humanity; and that in agricultural labour and pastoral care civilisation was chiefly developed in the sub-tropical district of India, the most conveniently situated and comprehensive sub-tropical tract of land in the world. As the present Indo-European grew beyond its limits, he travelled in search of new habitations in the direction most available to him, as China was occupied, namely the north-west, taking with him, in successive emigrations, his old ideas; or adapting and continuing the archaic conceptions of the original land.

From that age of the world's history which we have assigned, upon the authority of our biblical interpreters, to Moses and the exodus of God's chosen people from Egypt, and to the establishment of the state of Athens by Cecrops, 600 years before the end of the Assyrian monarchy under Sardanapalus, India, at the very least, was settled in orderly and cultured life. From that period, 1555 B.C., to the invasion of Hindustan by Mahmoud, 1001 A.D., that is to say, for some 2500 years, the Hindus maintained an agricultural, commercial, and literary civilisation, as evidenced by the Vedas, etc. These afford testimony to it at the former epoch.

The warlike element seems to have been less prevalent throughout the country than in Europe, though the rules of civilisation in war were established, which shows that it was regarded as an institution liable to be recurring. The Persian and Greek invasions seem merely to have affected the north-west. It must be remembered that Europe, from the days of Charlemagne to the present time, has only lasted some 1100 years, not half of the above period. As a specimen of the riches of India at the latter part of it, in a fort chiefly inhabited by priests, and used as a depository for the wealth belonging to the neighbouring temples, Mahmoud found 700,000 golden dinars, 700 maunds of gold and silver plate, 40 maunds of pure gold in ingots, 2000 maunds of silver bullion, and 20 maunds of various jewels set, according to the account of Ferishta—the least maund in India being equivalent to about 40 pounds avoirdupois.

In the great battle which occurred near Peshawur, the elephant on which the Hindu generalissimo rode is related by Ferishta to have taken fright at the report of a gun, and, by his flight, occasioned a panic in the Hindu army. The Eastern civilisations thus seem to have had the priority in the use of firearms, though we have continued their improvements to such extent of destructive power.

Some description of weapons of fire, as has been observed, is mentioned in the Ramáyana.

At the end of this period of 2500 years we find India exhibiting every appearance of having been able to sustain ample populations in the general culture of civilised existence, during its continuance, presenting, meanwhile, in religion these seeming prototypes or archaisms of our own doctrines. Then the successive inroads of Mohammedans, and the attacks of Rajpoots upon the Mogul power, the rise of the Mahrattas and the establishment of the kingdom of Tippoo Saib, etc. etc., imparted an aspect of perpetual warring to the old Madhyama, from which we boast to have delivered it.

CHAPTER XIX.

The pretensions of the Brahmins to periods of vast antiquity—Their present Age (Yug), and its commencement 3000 B.C.—Their preceding Ages and astronomical cycles—Quotations from Mr. R. Mitra and Sir W. Jones as to the antiquity of the adoration of Vishnu as incarnate in Krishna—Not repugnant to the spirit of Christ's teaching to suppose that man may have arisen gradually to the conception of the Incarnation—The doctrine of Regeneration Indian as well as Christian—The expression of the Divine as *I am*, in India.

THEOLOGIANS have talked glibly of eternity. Geologists and astronomers refer us to periods measured by hundreds of thousands of years, to account for the physical conformation of our globe. The history of the world which we have been taught, in the Christian Church, to esteem as sacred, displays to us only the civilisations existing on the Nile and on the Euphrates, at about the twentieth century B.C. It describes God's chosen people as settling, after their wanderings, in a province on the shore of the Mediterranean, bounded by deserts on the other side, and about 180 miles in length by 60 in width. Their entry upon the Promised Land is ascribed, by our interpreters of biblical chronology, to the fifteenth century B.C., *i.e.* the period to which modern science has assigned the compilation of the Vedas in India. The general deluge is said to have taken place some eight centuries previously. But the discoveries of geology, and the revelations of that science in regard to the structure of the earth, seem to demonstrate in a matter-of-fact manner, that we must regard the interpretations of the Bible in respect to the flood, and the duration of the early history of mankind, etc., from a new point of view; such as we have already admitted in astronomical considerations. Human remains and relics have been discovered in situations in Europe, which necessitate the antedating of man's existence on our world to periods beyond the old theological data. We have been accustomed to deride the pretensions of the Brahmins to acquaintance with ages of antiquity, which we have considered absurdly imagined. Yet if we place the commencement of our actual Aryan civilisation in arts, laws, etc., at the date which they have ascribed to the beginning of the Kali Yug, the Black or Iron Age, we shall apparently be approximating decidedly nearer to the truth than the interpreters of the old Biblical school. This, 3001 B.C., is about the date at which the apotheosis of Enoch has been placed, 700 years before the universal deluge. At about this time, the adoration of the great spirit in fire, and in the dome-shaped emblem of creative power, the devotional hymns of the Vedas, the ordinances and moral axioms afterwards collected as the Institutes of Manu, the separation of classes, the amenities of commerce and the consequent braving of the ocean, the observation of the heavens, necessary not only at sea, but in the sandy pathless deserts of western Asia, the veneration of rivers as the means by which man was enabled to flourish in the hot but yet not actually tropical climates in which he was maturing in education, in fixed settlements, and perhaps the actual invention of letters, from systematised symbolisation, were progressing, or perhaps had been long in progress. Unless the testimony of the Vedas can be shown to be fallacious, or a direct revelation from the Most High asserted, to account for the rapid origin of Aryan civilisation, there must have been the gradual advancement. The Madhyama has been surmised, from the later Sanskrit works, the Puranas, to have comprised four rich and powerful kingdoms, at about 2000 B.C., virtually independent of each other, though generally confederate under one common head, or emperor. If the Vedas, in their present form, are to be assigned to the fifteenth century, and the Institutes of Manu and the Ramáyana epic to a few centuries later, as seems to be reliably evidenced, 3000 B.C. certainly seems by no means too remote a date for the commencement of the present Age of the world; that is to say, for the commencement of that civilisation which has resulted in our own, 5000 years or 150 generations afterwards. But the Vedic mythology, and many of our arts, may be reasonably conjectured to be many centuries older.

If we take the preceding Age, which the Indians termed

the Dwaipar Yug, corresponding to the classical Bronze Age, we find a period indicating that lapse of time which we may allow for the development of man, from a mere savage, living on the spontaneous products of the earth, to an agricultural, pastoral, and social being, inhabiting abodes constructed by his own ingenuity. Their previous periods, corresponding with the Gold and Silver Ages of Greece, will sufficiently accord with geological and astronomical Ages for the formation of the earth. In fact, the Brahminical theories, allowing for the poetical colouring under which they have been expressed, are nearer to scientific truth than the short interval which we have been educated, in our church, to accredit between the creation of the world in six days, and the present time, *i.e.* from 4004 B.C. to the nineteenth century A.D.

The Brahmins have been ridiculed for their astronomical cycles; but our brief history of humanity, extending only to the 6000 years, with an intervening total destruction by water, somewhat over 4000 years ago, is really more grotesque. It would seem impossible for humanity, with its seventy years of life, to exaggerate the duration of the earth, which rolls so steadily upon its orbit. Hundreds of thousands of years would seem little in considering the mere universe, as revealed by the stars, putting aside eternity. But we have dwarfed our conceptions to 6000 years, not ninety Psalmist lifetimes. The evidence of Brahminical literature in the Sanskrit is powerfully supported by Buddhist literature in the Pali. Allowing Buddhism to have been founded actually in the sixth century B.C., a long anterior civilisation must be admitted from its history. But the dates which have been assigned to the manifestation of Gautauma Buddha, have varied, according to Professor Wilson, from about 2420 B.C. to 453 B.C.

"Vaishnavism has been associated with Hinduism from remote antiquity," says Mr. R. Mitra, the author of "Orissan Antiquities," "as shown in the Zoroastrian writings, in the earliest Veda, and in the later scriptures as an appellation of the Almighty. Panini, the grammarian, at a low estimate, places knowledge of Krishna at the sixth century B.C." The doctrine of Vishnu, incarnate in Krishna, contemplated as God upon earth, undoubtedly seems to have been revealed by the Almighty, or apprehended by man, under some form or other, in times vaguely remote.

Sir William Jones, writing at the close of the last century, has recorded his observation that, in the Sanskrit dictionary, compiled more than 2000 years ago, we have the Incarnate Deity, born of a virgin, escaping in infancy from the reigning tyrant, etc.

To argue that humanity has gradually arisen to the conception of the divine truth of the Supreme Being apprehended by man, in His Spirit taking flesh and dwelling amongst us, not once only but as often as may be requisite to guide civilisation into religion, is surely not repugnant to the spirit of our New Testament. Christ therein reveals His divinity; but He does not mention the world beyond the Roman Empire, in the brief accounts of His discourses which have been preserved to us. We find Him constantly using the Indian expression of regeneration, which appears so anciently as to be in the Institutes of Manu. He adopts the Indian custom of washing the body as preparatory to seeking for spiritual cleanliness; as shown in the institution of baptism.

Though the doctrine of the Deity incarnate for man's sake is only developed in later Hindu sacred writings, into belief in union with the Supreme Spirit through faith in His manifestation upon earth in the flesh, the Christian idea of the Word, the Son of the Almighty, as expounded in the Gospel of St. John, seems dawning in the earlier scriptures. In the *Yasur Veda* it is said—"Knowing the elements, and recognising all regions and quarters to be Brahma, and worshipping speech (or revelation), the first born, the votary pervades the animating spirit of solemn sacrifice by his own soul. Let the wise man know that Brahma, in whom the gods attain immortality . . . is our venerable parent, and the providence which governs all worlds." In the writings of the Old Testament, ascribed to about the same epoch, no equivalent can be discerned, so illustrative of the doctrine delivered in the Gospel. M. E. Burnouf observes that "l'Arya seul a conçu l'être, la pensée et la vie dans leur unité absolue. C'est donc lui qui est le veritable auteur de la religion, et son plus ancien livre de metaphysique est la Vêda." As to the extreme east, he remarks that it has long been converted by Buddhism, and that Buddhism has issued from India.

We may surely, without irreverence, grant that the Christian doctrine, under archaic developments, may have been revealed some thousand years earlier than we have supposed. We have accepted Christ, the anointed one, as the Messiah of the Jews, who have rejected Him—by that very rejection constituted our own Saviour. Is it irreverent to say that we have not yet entirely apprehended the fulness of the divine message, and that we may also receive Him, in the omnipotency and omnipresence of the Supreme Spirit, as the Divine Incarnate also for our own ancestors and kindred, as the Spirit of holiness communicating with all flesh in all time, not only Christ the anointed, but Chrest the benignant, the good?

If the name Krishna was originally derived from that same Aryan word, we may realise the reception by the leading race in the world's civilisation, as we may venture to assert our own to be, of the divine grace in this revelation, within a sphere only bounded by barbarism little educated above the quadrumana. All the old civilisations, even in Central America, will have known it under some form. And this should surely not be held to derogate from its dignity. It ought only to render us more capable of opening our sympathies to all mankind, and studying without prejudice the perceptions of the divine appearing in all nations and all time. We should follow St. Augustine, as Professor Max Müller has said to us, and "feel cheered by the words of that pious philosopher, when he boldly declares that there is no religion which, among its many errors, does not contain some real and divine truth."

In India appeared also the great expression of the divine as *I am*. It is thus expressed in the Bhagavat Purana:—"Even I was even at first, not any other thing: that which exists unperceived: supreme, afterwards I am that which is; and he who must remain am I."

CHAPTER XX.

Extract from Sir R. Phillips as to Indian literature—The adoration of Krishna; with quotations from Sir W. Jones, More, Mrs. Graham, and Wilford—The Indian origin of baptism, etc.—Miracles credited in modern times in India.

SIR RICHARD PHILLIPS, in "Facts," published in 1836, gives the following summary of the Hindu scriptures, etc., which conveys an excellent general idea of the whole:—"In the Hindu mythology the coequal and eternal powers are Brahma, the creative power; Vishnu, the preservative; and Siva, the converting power. In other words, Brahma is matter, Vishnu spirit, and Siva time; and in other senses, earth, water, and fire. The religion of the Hindus is developed in the four Vedas. On these there are six commentaries, called *Angas;* in all, eighteen sacred books. There are then four *Upa*-Vedas and four *Up*-Angas, which include the eighteen Puranas. The Vedas are their Bible, and the Puranas contain their mythology and the historical poems; the Derma-Shastra contains the Ethics, and two other poems; the Nyaya and the Mimansa the philosophy. The whole are called the Shastra; their language is Sanskrit in the Devanagari. There is a copy of the Vedas, in eleven volumes, in the British Museum.

The poetical and romantic mythology of India is to be traced to the epics of the Ramáyana and Mahábhárata, of middle age between the Vedas, and Sacontala written in the century before Christ. Manu is a mythological personage of Hindu creation. The first was the son of Brahma; and the last, or seventh, was Satyavrata, the holy King. The religion and philosophy of the Hindus are contained in a book called the *Anbertkend,* or The Cistern of the Waters of Life; but they have nine schools of philosophy, ancient and modern.

The Hindus have no less than nine sects of philosophers,

whose principles embrace all the metaphysics and speculations of the Greeks, and the objects of controversy among modern Europeans. Three of them are atheistical, and six are partly materialists and partly spiritualists, in certain shades of difference. No justice is done to their profundity in the crude or partisan reports of Europeans.

The Vedas, or ancient books of ceremonials and morals, are palpably the foundations of Egyptian and Western knowledge.

The Hindus are now worshippers of Vishnu and Siva; the vulgar by idols, and the learned by the Spirit of God in Vishnu or Siva, for God is deemed too awful for address.

Brahma has four faces, for the four elements and the four castes—the priest, soldier, trader, and labourer. The Sun is his symbol.

The Vedas teach that Universal Being is a conscious, intelligent personality, which forms and sustains all visible and sensible things within itself and by its own energies.

The Institutes of Manu assert that the Supreme Spirit alternately wakes and reposes for thousands of ages. The Hindus believe in the unity of God, and in subordinate deities, represented by the elements, stars, and planets. They teach a fifth element, which effects attractions, repulsions, etc., and call the sun Adetyœ, the attractor.—*Sir W. Jones.*

The Hindus assert that the deity Vishnu has visited the earth in nine several incarnations, and that a tenth is to come. This opinion has the sanction of indefinite antiquity.

If the Revelation of St. John was really written by that apostle under the inspiration of the Divine, it affords evidence in favour of the Hindu assertions of divine knowledge; for, as has been remarked, this tenth incarnation of Vishnu as Kalki, accords with the description in Revelation xix. 11 of the coming of the "King of kings and Lord of lords" (v. 16) upon a white horse. The authenticity of the book was doubted in the Church of the third century. At all events, the account corresponds with the Aryan conception, in respect to this coming of the Lord to judge finally the world.

"Sir W. Jones, More, and Mrs. Graham tell us," says Sir R. Phillips, "that the Indian *incarnate* God, Chrishna, lived about 900 B.C., had a virgin mother of the royal race, and was sought to be destroyed in his infancy. It appears that he passed his life in working miracles and in preaching, and was so humble as to wash his friends' feet. At length dying, but rising from the dead, he ascended into heaven in the presence of a multitude. His father carried him over the Yamuna to escape from the tyrant Kansa, who ordered all new-born infants to be slain. Sir W. Jones fixes the incarnation of Chrishna in 1300 B.C.

"Major Wilford, and other searchers into Brahmin mysteries, prove, very plausibly, that the gods of the Egyptians and Greeks were of Hindu origin. The famous mysteries of Eleusis were concluded with the words *conx, om, pax;* and the Brahmins at this day finish their service with the words *cansha, om, paxsha.*" He also observes that the Hindu division of four ranks or castes appears to have existed in Greece and Egypt, while the Saxons also were classed as clergy, soldiery, husbandmen, and artificers. "The Hindus call their castes—1, Scripture; 2, Protection; 3, Wealth; and 4, Labour; proceeding from the mouth, the arm, the thigh, and the foot of the creator." He remarks that the forbearance of the Indian Brahmins in killing and eating animals leads to much practical benevolence—to abhorrence of all bloodshed, and to universal charity.

The Banians, or mercantile caste, are enjoined by Brahma to observe veracity, and to use no circumvention. They make their contracts by their hands under their covered thighs, after the manner of the contract described in Genesis.

Sir R. Phillips further observes that "baptism by immersion in water is of Hindu origin, and was spread by them through Asia," and that "the inhabitants of the Nicobar Islands in the Bay of Bengal, and of some others in those seas, keep a festival at every change of the moon, by which they establish, by lunar motion, a *seventh* day holyday, and an eighth day every fourth time.

He says that "when the English embassy under Elphinstone in 1806 went to Caubul, the peoples of the town and country through which he passed believed he could work miracles, and even animate sculpture. The roads were covered with the sick, lame, and blind, to be touched by him or he by them; and hundreds were reported to be cured. On his return he was obliged to change his route to avoid the accumulation of diseased persons, while no explanations could remove the popular delusion."

He observes that "Aguillaneuf was the name of a feast of the Druids, and adopted as the Catholic Christmas. At the entrance of the sun into Capricorn they went in solemn procession of priests and chief men to the forests to gather mistletoe, the preservation of which kept off evil during the year;" and that "the Druids, in authority and pursuits, resembled the sophists of Greece, the Magi of Persia, and the Brahmins of India; and there is no doubt that they cherished science and learning to an extent little understood by the Romans. Diodorus quotes Hecatæus as asserting that the Druids had instruments by which they could draw distant objects nearer, show them plainer, and discern mountains and valleys in the moon. Such an anticipation of the exact powers of the telescope could not be fanciful."

CHAPTER XXI.

Dr. Schliemann and the discoveries at Troy, as bearing upon the history of religion in India—Symbolism of the Holy Fire (*Agni*)—As to the Greeks generating fire by friction from a species of cross—Observations of Mrs. Manning and Dr. Muir, and hymns from Vedas.

An important link in the chain of evidence which connects the civilisations of the Ganges with those of the Mediterranean has been recently afforded by the discoveries of Dr. Schliemann. M. E. Burnouf and others have descanted on the ancient cross connected with the idea of the *agni*, the fire of God upon earth. This was the *arani* or *swastika*, the instrument of wood by which the lighting was accomplished by friction. As the † is the symbol of the *Agnus Dei*, so is the swastika 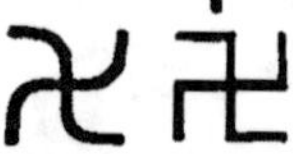 of the *agni*. On numbers of *prehistoric whorls*, exhumed from fifty feet below the surface of the soil at Troy, beneath layers of remains, in which later generations of men are traced, are various forms of crosses. These, in 1878, were placed on view in the South Kensington Museum. The cross assumes the following shape , and again , and the symbol is supposed to be equivalent to εὐ ἔστι, a sign of good wishes; also   . Flaming altars, the sôma tree, the pyramid of Siva, are also engraved on these relics. The *swastika*, again, frequently occurs in the catacombs of Rome, and is even to be seen on the pulpit of St. Ambrose at Milan; while the cognisance of the Isle of Man suggests a derivation from it. From the *Pramantha*, the instrument of friction by which the divine fire was produced, came the idea of Prometheus, who stole the fire of the gods from heaven. The Rev.

K. Brown Keer has observed that he has seen the 卐 innumerable times in the most ancient Hindu temples.

The ships of Rama had the 卍 on their prows. The symbol occurs sixty times on an ancient Celtic funereal urn discovered in Norfolk; and it is found on Corinthian columns and upon Attic vases assigned to 1000 B.C.

Dr. Schliemann observes that, after twenty-three feet in depth, the aspect of civilisation apparent in the relics increases. This would seem to suggest the same sort of movement which placed the ruder civilisation of the Goths on the ruins of the cultured Romans.

It would appear to be this higher civilisation which came from the old Aryan land of India, bringing the religion and symbolisation of the Holy Fire. This seems to have been suggestive, or prototypical in its imagery, of the human birth of the Divine in Christ, and of the great mystery and central point of our Western Aryan religion. Dr. Schliemann observes that "the discovery of the most ancient sacred emblems of the Aryan race, at all depths below the ruins of Greek Ilium, attests the common Aryan descent of all the nations that had dwelt successively on the hill before the historic Greek colony. There is an absence of any trace of Assyrian and Egyptian influence. In this central rite of the Aryan civilisation, two pieces of wood were laid crosswise upon one another before the sacrificial altars, their ends being bent round and fastened by nails, so that the wooden scaffold might not be moved 卍. At the point where the two pieces joined was a small hole, in which a third piece of wood, in the form of a lance (Pramantha), was rotated by means of a cord of cow's hair and hemp, till the fire generated."

It was said that the father of the Holy Fire was Twastri, the divine carpenter, and the mother the divine Maia. In the Rig Veda are hymns in praise of the new-born creature—the little child laid upon straw, beside it the milk and butter destined as the offering; before it the holy priest of the divine Vâyu (wind), who waves the small Oriental fan, in the shape of a flag, to kindle life in the child. Then it is placed upon the altar, the holy sôma, juice of the tree of life, poured over it and the purified butter. The child's glory shines on all around it; angels (devas) and men shout for joy, sing hymns in its praise, and throw themselves on the ground before it. On the left is the rising sun, on the right the full moon, and both appear to grow pale in the glory of the new-born God (Agni), and to worship him. As the priest laid the young god upon the altar, another poured the holy draught, the spiritual sôma, upon its head, and then anointed it by spreading over it the butter of the holy sacrifice. Thus Agni becomes the anointed, *akta,* rich in glory; he sends forth blazing flames; he shines in a cloud of smoke, which rises to heaven like a pillar, and his light unites with the light of the heavenly orbs. The god Agni, in his splendour and glory, reveals to man the secret things; he teaches the doctors, he is the master of the masters, and receives the name of Jâtâvedas—that is, he in whom wisdom is inborn.

The Greeks for a long time generated fire by friction, and the two lower pieces of wood upon which this was effected, forming a cross, were styled the *σταῦρος.*  These accounts are transcribed in Dr. Schliemann's book upon his discoveries at Troy.

It appears that in the expressions concerning and praises addressed to the holy, beneficent fire, when adored upon the ancient Aryan altars, we have absolute prototypes of the manifestation of the Light of the World in Christ.

Mrs. Manning observes, in her "Ancient and Mediæval India," that "the first duty of a pious Hindu was to kindle flames at dawn upon his domestic altar. Thus Ushas, the dawn, introduces us to Agni, fire, one of the best-beloved of Hindu gods. When 'the devout' desist from slumber, they propitiate the mighty Agni. The Vedic expressions of awe and wonder at the production of fire by rubbing pieces of wood against each other are very poetical."

Hymn II. of the first book of the Rig Veda is thus metrically rendered by Mr. Griffiths:—

"Mighty Agni! we invite
Him that perfecteth the rite.
O thou messenger divine,
Agni! boundless wealth is thine.

"Agni, Agni, with this gift,
Lo! to thee the voice we lift.
Loved, O Lord of men, art thou,
God that bearest up the vow.

"Thou to whom the wood gives birth,
Thou that callest gods to earth.
Call them that we may adore them,
Sacred grass is ready for them.

"Messenger of gods art thou.
Call them, Agni, call them now.
Fain our offerings would they taste,
Agni, bid them come in haste.

"Brilliant Agni! lo, to thee
Pour we offerings of ghee;
Oh, for this, consume our foes,
Who on demons' aid repose."

Mrs. Manning remarks, "Sun, Fire, and the Firmament (or Heavens) represent distinct powers or gods, and are invoked under various aspects, while the beautiful appearances of day-break and the terrible sounds of thunderstorms are but attendant deities. Mitra, Aryaman, Vishnu, are often only synonyms for the sun and heaven and earth. Agni appears with less of regal pomp than Indra or the Sun; but, at the same time, one feels that Agni symbolises grander conceptions of infinitude. Agni is fire. Agni carries prayer to heaven, invisible deity. Agni is the progenitor of heaven and earth. Agni forgives sin." To Agni and the other gods, who, as we have seen in the Institutes of Manu, are all in and of the one Supreme Spirit, the potent sôma beverage is offered, just as the wine upon our Christian altars. The sôma is said to be divine, purifying, joy-inspiring, a water of life. Doubtless this discovery of the exhilarating properties of the sôma juice led the way to the various distillations of spirit. This vivifying, enlivening drink, in its mysterious influence, naturally seemed to transcend the mere earthly. Dr. Muir has thus translated a hymn to it:—

"We've quaffed the sôma bright,
And are immortal grown;
We've entered into light,
And all the gods have known.
What mortal now can harm,
Or foeman vex us more?

Through thee, beyond alarm,
Immortal god, we soar."

"Viswakarman," says Dr. Muir, in the 81st and 82d hymns of the tenth book of the Rig Veda, "has become the name of a deity, if not of the deity" (vísva, whole, universal).

Viswakarman is called "wise," "pervading," the "creator," the "disposer"—the one who dwells beyond the abode of the seven Rishis. The seven Rishis, or religious sages, are the seven stars of the constellation of the Great Bear. He is invoked, according to Dr. Muir's translation, as "Our father who, a rishi and a priest, celebrated a sacrifice, offering up all these worlds—he earnestly desiring substance, veiling his earliest (form) entered into later (men)."

"What was the position, what and of what kind was the beginning, from which the all-seeing Viswakarman produced the earth, and disclosed the sky by his might?"

"The one god, who has on every side eyes, on every side a face, on every side arms, on every side feet, when producing the earth, blows it forth with his arms and with his wings."

Then Purusha, universal soul, is said to be the whole universe, which has been, and whatever shall be, and the lord of immortality. The gods performed a sacrifice with Purusha as the oblation. "This victim, Purusha, born in the beginning, they immolated on the sacrificial grass. He is recognised as having a kind of personality, himself the universe, he is offered up in sacrifice." The Supreme God produced the world by offering himself in sacrifice. We say in Christianity that He saved it by Himself as His Son.

"When the gods, performing sacrifice, bound Purusha as a victim, there were seven sticks stuck up for it around the fire."

Fire and soul are alike of God, and sin is confessed in invocations to Agni.

"May our sin, Agni, be repented of."

"Thou whose countenance is turned to all sides art our defender; may our sin be repented of. Do thou convey us in a ship across the sea for our welfare; may our sin be repented of."

Not only the sôma juice, but rice cakes are offered in the ancient ritual to Agni and Vishnu, *i.e.* to Fire upon earth, and the all-pervading spirit of deity.

CHAPTER XXII.

Professor M. Williams as to the Hindu religions—Arguments as to their Christian aspect—The doctrine of Transmigration in relation to Christianity—Controversies as to Sectarial marks amongst the Hindus, resembling our own as to Ritualism—That superstitious practices have arisen in Christianity as in Hinduism—Superstitions as to devils in India compared with the devils of the Gospels—Brahminical assertion that the Divine has given various revelations to man—As to Christ's command to preach the Gospel to every creature not necessarily referring to the ancient civilisations, not mentioned in the New Testament—The "strait way" to Heaven in the Mahábhárata—Mohammedan legend that Christ had travelled to India—Quotation from Josephus, appealing to the example of the Indians—Jews in China and Babylon at the time of Christ.

PROFESSOR MONIER WILLIAMS, in reference to his personal observations on Southern India, has defined Brahminism as the "purely pantheistic and not necessarily idolatrous creed evolved by the Brahmins out of the religion of the Vedas." It would seem, from the quotation which has been given from the Bhagavat Purana, in which the Divine speaks as "I am," etc. etc., that the pantheism is spiritual—the Supreme Spirit conceived as pervading and influencing every living organisation—the universal soul of which the material universe is the visible body. This appears to be really identical with the Almighty of Christianity—who is omnipotent and omnipresent, without parts or passions. And the spiritual expressions in the adoration of the material fire would certainly seem to suggest a further development of ideas into faiths akin to Christianity.

Professor M. Williams has again remarked that "Hinduism is that complicated system of polytheistic doctrines, idolatrous, superstitious, and caste usages, which has been developed out of Brahminism after its contact with Buddhism, and its admixture with the non-Aryan creeds of the Dravidians and aborigines of South India—one is the germ or root, the other the diseased outgrowth."

Now it appears from the Vedas and the Institutes of Manu, the latter of which are essentially Brahminical in all their ordinances, that polytheism existed under pure Brahminism in respect to the adoration of numerous divinities. These, although merely regents of the elements, emanations from the Supreme and Universal Spirit, constitute the Brahminical religion a polytheism as decided as the later Hindu faiths, in which the Supreme Spirit is certainly said to be adored under the emanations, incarnations, etc.

It would appear that there may have been a conjunction of Siva-ism and Vaishna-vism with Brahminism, and the conception of the Trinity in unity of Brahma, Vishnu and Siva. This may have proceeded from the conjunction of northern and southern religions. But whether we consider the Indian religions, as expressed in the Brahminical Institutes of Manu, or in the Bhagavad-gita, which the professor seems to suppose to have been written after the commencement of the Christian era, or in passages concerning the Trinity in Unity, the conception of the divine seems always to appear as the Soul of the Universe, in which we all live, move, and have our being. And in respect to what he terms the diseased outgrowth of Brahminism, the Roman Catholicism of the Christian Church, with its images, relics, mariolatry, and adoration of the saints, may be held to afford a precise parallel.

In fact, either in Christianity or Hinduism, we may assume those who bow down before images to be crediting the images with power, or to be worshipping a degrading conception of deity through or in the image, or we may more charitably suppose that, while fixing their attention on a mean image, they are adoring, through the concentration which it affords to their minds, the Universal Divine Spirit.

The spirit of Hinduism certainly inculcates this last view. A mere dash of red paint upon a stock or stone is said to be a point on which to concentrate the thoughts upon the divine soul of that, and all other portions of the material universe.

"The South," wrote the professor, "produced the three great religious revivalists, Sankara, Madhva, and Ramanuja. Some of Sankara's followers call themselves Saivas, as identifying the god Siva (the Dissolver and Reproducer of creation) with the one omnipresent Spirit of the universe."

But Siva is also termed Maha-deva, which means the great God. The Trinity in Unity, which is figured in the cave temple of Elephanta, either represents Brahma, Vishnu, and Siva, as three in one, or else, as has been supposed from the other sculptured representations in the temple, it represents Siva as creating, preserving, and destroying. Now, whether the carvers of the image regarded the figure as representing Siva or great God under the three attributes, or whether they sculptured two of the heads, as under the appellations of Brahma and Vishnu, the bust distinctly represents one deity under that threefold aspect which we find in Sanskrit literature. One god is here represented under a threefold aspect, not seemingly to be adored as in the religions of Christ and Krishna, in the incarnation in the flesh, but to be reverenced in the dome-shaped emblem of creative power. Siva is not only the dissolver and reproducer of creation, but He who confers happiness. He is the eternal and absolute Spirit of the universe. He is Brahma, Vishnu, and Siva. He is everything, or rather Spirit in everything—pantheism, but not materialistic pantheism.

"The adherents of Madhva," said Professor M. Williams, "call themselves Vaishnavas, as worshippers of the god Vishnu, whom they identify with the Supreme Spirit when he assumes incarnation for the preservation of his creatures, and they maintain an eternal distinction between the human and supreme soul."

The "God Vishnu" again, like Siva, is held to be the Supreme Universal Spirit, one in three, one in all divinities and all worlds, and the meaning of the word Vishnu is the all-pervading Spirit. In fact Siva and Vishnu are merely names, or aspects, of the same divine spirit; but the latter is especially revered as appearing on earth in man. In his incarnation as Krishna, he is believed, as expressed in the Mahábhárata epic, to have been all-god upon earth for man's preservation. In Christianity we call this preservation salvation; for, through Krishna, bliss hereafter, as well as in this world, or, perhaps, hereafter rather than in this world, is to be attained. Unlike those philosophising Brahmins and Buddhists, who say that when the soul obtains emancipation from transmigrations, it becomes absorbed and loses its individuality in the universal soul, these devotees of Krishna allege that it continues in personal existence. What is this faith in a triune deity, manifested in flesh upon the earth for man's salvation, but a form of Christianity; not exhibiting more differences from any one of the orthodox Christian creeds than those display amongst themselves? Indeed the Professor has observed that "this is a form of Hindooism which has more common ground with Christianity than any other," and that he had "met with many excellent and intelligent Brahmins who professed it."

Making allowances for the difference of climate, and general manner and aspect of life, it seems unreasonable to conceive the Christian religion as presenting, in India, greater similarity of appearance to that which it presents in Europe, taking both Roman Catholicism and Protestantism into consideration, than this religion of Krishna. If St. Thomas had miraculously traversed and converted the Indian land, differences of language, habits, etc., must, humanly speaking, have occasioned a great outward diversity from our own expressions of the religion in these 1800 years. Even then our missionaries could scarcely have expected to find surplices and lawn sleeves, or black coats with white ties, prayer books or hymn books, etc. But indeed the Apostles themselves must have looked much more like Hindus than English. It may not be impossible that he did so traverse it, though the evidence appears against it. The theory of the purification of the soul through many transmigrations differs, of course, from our belief in an eternity of torture in hell, awarded for the sins of this lifetime, or for incapacity to receive Christ in "saving faith." But Origen, and other early followers of the doctrines of Christ, admitted transmigration; and Christianity is now at variance with itself as to this question of future punishments. The Romish Church teaches the purification of the soul in purgatory as a prelude to eternal bliss. Protestant divines have lately expressed doubts as to whether divine justice can demand *hopeless* punishment, and divine mercy permit it; while human justice, supposed to follow divine law, punishes in hopes of amelioration, allowing to the felon condemned to death the clerical aid to eternal pardon.

Professor M. Williams remarked that "the followers of Ramanuja have divided into two parties, corresponding to those which rally the advocates of faith, or of good works, as means of salvation in Christendom." But he observed that their quarrels related more to the external marks of their sect on the forehead than to difference in fundamental doctrine.

A Brahmin visiting England, of late years, might easily conceive that the High and Low parties in the Church of England only quarrelled over the questions of white, black, or embroidered ecclesiastical vestments, and altar decorations. What research, legal acumen, and important time have been devoted by our chief judicial functionaries to these topics! What animosities have divided English congregations, and even families, upon questions which might seem to the Brahmin to relate only to garments and genuflexions! And, possibly, if he questioned some of the contentionists upon the motives of their religious enmities, he would become no wiser. By the Hindus these sectarial marks may have been accepted as the standards of belief, like the surplice, chasuble, and Geneva gown amongst ourselves.

In fact we can discover great divergencies between the Hindu adoration of an incarnate deity, one in three, and our own; but a Brahmin coming to Europe, and studying Catholicism and Calvinism, might surely conceive these to be as absolutely dissimilar. The Third Person of our Trinity seems to have an equivalent either under the name of Vishnu or Siva; for, in their expressions of the attributes of Deity, allusions to the holy all-influencing Spirit are constantly made.

The worshippers of Krishna believe that the Almighty took flesh for their sake, in their own part of the world, which contains two hundred millions of inhabitants; while we hold that He only came to us, in our part of the world, containing at present some two hundred and fifty millions; or rather in a part of Asia near to the chief Christian continent. At the time when we believe that this occurred, Europe does not appear to have been so civilised throughout its extent as India. The Hindus have the philosophical, or, at all events, philanthropical advantage over us, in the declaration in their sacred books that those who adore the Divine, under the revelation which has been vouchsafed to them, in reality worship Him in the incarnate all-pervading Spirit—Vishnu incarnate to them as Krishna—but also, in the universe incarnate under all or any forms to reveal religion.

And why need we be disquieted at discovering that the Divine has irradiated east as well as west, that the millions who have died in this ancient realm of Bharata, philologically acknowledged to be our cousins, have, like ourselves, known some form of Christian doctrine? It may indeed suggest an abrogation of the expense of missionary efforts as tending to confuse rather than enlighten; but as an educating force these are most valuable, while their labours must aid in spreading the knowledge of true—of essential—Christian doctrine and charity. Conquered and governed by invaders as the Aryans of Bharata, like those of the Roman Empire, have been for many centuries, we cannot wonder at the ancient religion having degenerated in many of its ritual observances or articles of faith. But have not Christian practices been tolerated amongst the highly cultivated art-loving Neapolitans and others in Europe, which English Protestantism has contemned as grossly idolatrous and intellectually feeble; while in England the revived ritualism has occasioned the legal warfare? As there are dissenters, like the Quakers, who widely differ from the ordinary Christian churches in their tenets and practices, so, as has been observed, there are Hindus who abjure caste usages and forms and ceremonies.

Professor M. Williams has summed up his observations in the following remarks :—"In short, Vaishnavism and Saivism constitute the very heart and soul of Southern Hinduism, Brahma being only worshipped in his alleged offspring the Brahmans."

The last part of this assertion is scarcely verified in the Institutes of Manu, which allow to the Brahmans descent from the most honourable part of Brahm, but to the other castes also a divine origin, as indeed to everything in the visible or invisible universe.

In the Christian churches also we only address God through or in Christ. We only worship the Godhead as Three in One, and in the Son, co-eternal and one with the Father, incarnate for our benefit; and we pray for the personal influence of the Holy Spirit to strengthen and comfort us. Demons are much dreaded by the Hindus, who attribute to them all evils such as drought, blight, and disease; and this, again, seems to recall the teaching of our New Testament. Ganesa, usually described as the elephant-headed deity, or, more correctly speaking, divine Regent of Sagacity, is much propitiated, according to the Professor, because he is believed to contravene the obstacles and diseases caused by devils. The demons are supposed to be propitiated by offerings of food, etc.; and it appears that the souls of the departed are thought capable of haunting the places which their bodies have inhabited. "For example, when a certain Englishman died, who was a terror to the district in which he lived, the natives were in the constant habit of placing brandy and cigars on his tomb to propitiate his spirit, supposed to roam about the neighbourhood in a restless manner, and with evil proclivities." And offerings have also been made to secure the good services of a philanthropic Englishman, after his decease. There are professional exorcisers who become gifted with clairvoyance like our spiritual mediums; and who perform wild devil dances, with painted faces, etc.

Now it must be remembered that in the eighth chapter of St. Matthew not only are two, possessed with devils and "exceeding fierce," delivered from their tormentors, but the devils are actually allowed to enter into a herd of swine, who run down a steep place into the sea. Bodily infirmities are also constantly attributed to devils. Christ, in the tenth chapter, gives His disciples power to cast out unclean spirits, and in the twenty-seventh verse of the twelfth chapter He distinctly indicates that there were those amongst the Pharisees who actually cast them out when he says, "If I by Beelzebub cast out devils, by whom do your children cast them out?"

The superstition of spirits haunting tombs, and places in which they have existed in the flesh, as ghosts, has never been absolutely discredited in England; and a number of persons in America and England profess themselves to be believers in spirits communicating by table-rapping, etc. A Brahmin in England might scarcely believe our population to be so materially in advance of, or different from, the Hindus in these matters as Mr. M. Williams would seem to have assumed, when, in the latter part of his letter, he alluded to "the depraved appetite of the Indian for mental stimulants." The Professor has remarked upon the "difficulty of convincing a Hindu of the superiority of the plain story of the Gospel to the wild exaggerations of the Ramáyana." But the story of the Ramáyana extends to a length and fulness surpassing our New Testament, combined with the discarded Apocryphal Gospels and a considerable number of ancient traditions as well. If this were purged of its exaggerations, as our Gospels have been of these excrescences, the lives and conversations of Rama and Siva, the fraternal devotion of Rama's brother, and the noble friendship of Hanuman, would be very worthy of our veneration. A Brahmin who studied Christianity in the light of monkish legends, and by the illustrations, for instance, of the ceremonies of the Holy Week in Rome, might as easily fail in Europe to be convinced of the spiritual superiority of Christianity to his own faith as in India. Their sacred words, Brahma, Vishnu, Siva, etc., have an idolatrous irreligious sound to us. But our names of Jehovah, Jesus, and Holy Spirit, must have the same unfamiliar or profane sound to them. Great God is to them as Mahadeva to us, which bears the same meaning. If we could admit, as the less narrowly thinking Brahmin has long asserted, that the Divine Spirit has given various revelations to men, adapted to their special or local wants, all of which, if pursued conscientiously, are paths leading to Him, we might not really detract from the devotion due to the all-sustaining Lord of the eternal and infinite universe. We hold Himself to be Almighty yet Himself as His son, as the divine in the human, inculcating the principle of self-sacrifice, to have suffered death in human form for our sakes. There is India, with its ancient literary and commercial civilisation, with a population virtually equivalent to that of Europe. There may be other worlds in the glittering universe which we behold at night, inhabited by beings like ourselves. May we not think, without derogating from the dignity of Christ, that the divine has suffered for or communicated with the human in all? May we not say that the human intelligence has obtained knowledge of the divine before the civilisation of the Roman Empire and our own?

But it may be replied that Christ commanded His apostles

to go into the world and preach the gospel to every creature, and that this applies to their successors the modern missionaries, by whose aid it is divinely designed to spread the gospel message throughout the world. But if this command is to be so accepted in its most literal signification, the remainder of Christ's words must be also taken literally. He says that "these signs shall follow them that believe: in my name shall they cast out devils; they shall speak with new tongues; they shall take up serpents; and if they drink any deadly thing, it shall not hurt them; they shall lay hands on the sick, and they shall recover" (St. Mark xvi. 15-18). If these tokens can be proved literally to accompany the work of modern Christian missionaries, we must admit that theirs is the only true message of salvation. As the world of our Bible is the world cognised by the Roman Empire, it is surely more consonant with the apparent cessation of these manifestations promised by the Lord to presume that the true religious state of the whole world, like its true geological and astronomical conditions, was to be gauged by human intellect in future ages; still inspired, though not just in the way that evangelical Protestantism has regarded inspiration.

But again may be adduced Christ's observation that strait is the way to heaven, and few there be that find it, and the assertion made that this indicates the circumscribed scope of revelation. But if we take this text with the whole context of Christ's teaching, so adverse to exclusiveness, so perfect in universal charity, which is love to all men, can we suppose that this applies to other than the consideration of the difficulty which all mankind must have in separating the heart from the desires of the flesh to pure aspirations after holiness? And this has been definitely recognised by the Indian teachers.

It is said in the Mahábhárata, as expressed in Dr. Muir's translation, xiv. 2784, "The gate of heaven, which is very small, is not seen by men owing to their delusion." In the Taittirīya Brāhmana, iii. 12, 4, 7, "These are the five doors of heaven. . . . Austerity guards the first, faith the second, truth the third, mind the fourth, and good conduct the fifth."

The evangelical Protestant may then urge his distinct views as to original sin, the atonement, and the crucifixion; but his views seem to differ as widely from those of Roman

Catholics, as those of the latter from the Hindus. As Christ said, the spirit, not the letter, signifies, and the mere fact of the event taking place by crucifixion, or hanging upon a tree after life had been extinguished, cannot surely alter the signification of a death in self-sacrifice.

But it is not, perhaps, to be expected that Christians, who have so vindictively slaughtered one another for instituting various minor points of belief or ritual in the avowedly same faith, are to be brought to confess that the dark-skinned Hindus, who call their preserver Krishna, and say that he appeared in the country of the Ganges instead of that of the Jordan, can be truly worshipping the Almighty through His Spirit. Our missionaries, to whom we suppose to have been entrusted the communication of the will of the Almighty to these millions of our sun-burnt cousins, who were civilised before our island was discovered by the Romans, may still find noble work to accomplish, even although this forecast of Christianity be admitted. Christ made no allusion to the facts acknowledged in modern astronomy, yet it can scarcely be maintained that the incarnate Omniscient one was ignorant of them. Similarly he made no allusions to India, or to the existence of doctrines there, possessing, at the least, such specious similitude to those which He was preaching in Judea. But, again, it cannot be averred that He knew nothing of them. Surely, if doctrines so like his own had been an imitation of man's intellect, or of the devil's prompting, He would have warned His disciples, not only of those who would afterwards come and assert themselves to be Christs (St. Luke xxi. 8), but against those who, in a country then in commercial relation with Palestine, had been already believed to have been incarnations of the all-pervading and preserving Spirit of God. But the idea of the Divine taking human flesh was not only known in India, but throughout the Aryan world, before the time of Christ; in forms sometimes spiritual, sometimes materialistic, sometimes very vague, sometimes with the positiveness of the classical stories of the union of Jupiter with mortal maidens.

A legend exists among the Mohammedans, in the northwest of India, which affirms that Jesus Christ visited that country between His manifestations in Palestine in his twelfth and thirtieth years. We have been left in ignorance of His life during this period. If in His suffering He was human, in His education we may surely, with all reverence, say that He also may have been human. If the Divine Spirit had illumined India with the first rays of Christian doctrine, the Great Master may have been humanly irradiated with them there, before reproducing them in their full glory to the West. The picture which Milton has given us in the Paradise Regained, of Christ arriving at the self-consciousness of His divinity, cannot be satisfactory to those who venture to penetrate into what most Christians distantly revere as a sublime mystery, too sacred to investigate.

That intercourse existed between India and Syria, which would have enabled Him to go to the former without miraculous interposition, seems evident.

Dean Milman, in his History of the Jews, in transcribing Josephus' account of the siege of the hill fortress of Masada by the Roman army, depicts Eleazar as thus endeavouring to raise the spirits of his soldiers: "He spoke of the immortality, the divinity of the soul; its joyful escape from its imprisonment in its mortal tenement. He appealed to the example of the Indians, who bear life as a burthen, and cheerfully throw it off."

It appears that, at this period, a colony of Jews had even found their way to China, where they settled peaceably, and became much respected in the country. While a large number had refused to take advantage of the opportunity to return from Babylon, after the Captivity, other bodies seem to have extensively occupied Asia Minor and Rome itself. Notwithstanding their veneration for their holy city, the temptations of commercial gains, or perhaps the necessity of abandoning so narrow a territory as that of Judæa, certainly drew large numbers to foreign lands, previously to the destruction of Jerusalem.

The British of the present day are carrying their national institutions, their church and their faith in England, throughout the world, and forming settlements; they seem, however, to have accompanied the ledger of commerce with the sword of conquest more constantly than the Jews. Like them, we preserve our distinctness; but with the pride of conquerors rather than the mere force of the customs and exclusiveness of our race.

Dr. Rowland Williams, in "Christianity and Hindooism," seems to acknowledge the *boná-fide* belief of the Hindus in an incarnate preserver at an earlier date than the revelation of our religion in Palestine; but to assert that their faith merely proceeds from their own imaginations, while ours, by its superiority, is shown to be actually a divine revelation. The Brahmins, with greater liberality, will allow that both are divine, both intended for the benefit of the human race, in its diverse situations. Dr. Williams, speaking in the person of a supposed controversialist with an intelligent Hindu, says—"Whatever your poets have fabled of the Divine Preserver's becoming incarnate in Rama and Chrishna, seem to me shadows of the truth that the thought of the Eternal Spirit must come to fulfilment in act, and His wisdom manifest itself to our experience embodied in a living person, before we can know the counsel of Him whose thoughts are not as our thoughts, nor His ways as our ways."

He allows, in reference to another point of Hindu doctrine, that Christianity is vague as to the soul's destination. He remarks that "some Christians fancy that the spirits of the departed enter at once into joy; others, more agreeably to the letter of Scripture, that our bodies are raised and glorified, or else that a new organisation, perhaps in some distant world, is given to the soul." He observes that "the Christian doctrine might even be reconciled with the Indian by thinking a succession of lives a succession of steps of glory.[1] Men might be born in some higher world, as in a resurrection, with organs fitted for a higher life, yet such a life, though having the seeds of immortality, might yet be finite, so as to admit of a higher one beyond it." This seems, in effect, to be the doctrine of transmigration; for stronger and healthier organs and a happier worldly situation would afford opportunities for a higher life. He says that Buddha may stand as the representation of pure intelligence, which is really worshipped; *Adi Buddha*, the perfect Intelligence, being associated with *Dharma*, the law which comes from him, and *Sauga*, the union or bond of fellowship, in which all the saints are bound to Buddha and to each other.

[1] See Appendix XIII.

He allows that the three earlier Vedas were arranged about 1400 B.C.; "for they contain a calendar, with the old Indian cycle of five years. In this the ratio of solar and lunar time is given. The zodiac is divided into twenty-seven asterisms, beginning with the Pleiades. The solstitial points are reckoned to be at the beginning of the constellation Dhanisht'ha and in the middle of Aslesha, and this, according to astronomers, was the case in the fourteenth century B.C. He admits that the epic poems, in which the idea of the incarnations is promulgated, were complete at 200 B.C. He places Rama at 2000 B.C., the great war of the Mahábhárata at 1400-1200 B.C., and Vaivasvata Manu at 4376 B.C. He ascribes the compilation of the laws of Manu to 700-500 B.C. He states that Eusebius mentions a Hindu visitor in Athens.

To continue the evidence of the universality of Indian originality, it may be added that he quotes the Indian version of the story of the judgment of Paris. Púrúravas, the son of Ilá, having to choose between Wisdom, Wealth, and Desire, selects the latter, and is persecuted by the two rejected. Dr. Williams also has recognised the evidence of ancient intercourse between India and Palestine in the biblical description of King Solomon's trade with Ophir—that *algumin*, *kophim*, and *tuchim* are, in effect, the Sanskrit words for sandal-wood, apes, and peacocks, which are Indian products.

Our modern commentators on the prophecies of Daniel, etc., have ignored the 600,000,000 existing under the ancient civilisations of India and China, and conceived that the Almighty only made revelations concerning the warlike 250,000,000 who have inhabited the regions of the Euphrates, Nile, and Mediterranean, and of Northern Europe.

CHAPTER XXIII.

Pritchard as to Vishnu in the Fish Avatar and the Assyrian story of the flood, and the Fish-god Oannes—Verses on the ten chief incarnations of Vishnu, and their relation to the physical history of life upon the earth—Sir R. Phillips as to these incarnations.

PRITCHARD observed that in the ancient historical fragments of the Assyrian or Babylonian history, belonging to the Semitic race, the Hindu fable of the incarnation of Vishnu in the Fish Avatar has a close parallel in the story of Xithurus and the flood, and the fish god Oannes, which approaches more nearly than the Indian version to the Scriptural account of the Noachian deluge. Geologists do not appear to be able to account scientifically for the fossil marine remains buried in the interior of mountains, etc., by the account of the flood in Genesis. It is evident that the whole earth, or many portions of it now land, were once covered with water; but it does not seem possible to attribute the vast changes apparent in sea and earth to this cause. The monsters called saurians, whose bones have been exhumed, were formerly styled antediluvian, under the conception that they were overwhelmed and rocks hurled upon them by the flood. But science cannot admit this, while, according to the account in the Bible, their species could not have been destroyed by the deluge, because Noah was commanded to take some of *all* living beings then on the earth into the ark with him for their *preservation.*

The Hindu fable presents strong signs of originality in its consistency. It may be a tradition of a great or universal deluge, which also survived in other Asian countries, or it may be a curious apprehension of the history of life upon the earth. In fact, the four first descents of Vishnu in the character of Preserver, as recounted in the ten principal avatars attributed to him, seem to afford some just comparison with the successive epochs of animal life, as represented in our geological history :—

1. The Fish denotes the fatal day
   When earth beneath the waters lay.
2. The amphibious Turtle marks the time,
   When it again the shores could climb.
3. The Boar's an emblem of the God
   Who raised again the mighty clod.
4. The Lion king and savage trains
   Now roam the woods, or graze the plains.

Geologists have testified to the general truths that the igneous rocks have exhibited no indications of animal life. In the next strata, commencing with the mollusc orders, the fish appears. Then amongst the armour-clad monsters, styled the saurians, we see the tortoise or turtle. The boar comes in the following series, the remains of which have been revealed to us; while the lion and feline race complete the reign of the lower animal life and lead up to the discovery of human remains. The succeeding five incarnations seem to symbolise man's progress in civilisation :—

5. Neat little man begins his reign,
   O'er earth and sky and watery plain.
6. Ram with the axe then takes his stand ;
   Fells the thick forest, clears the land.
7. Ram with the bow 'gainst tyrants fights,
   And thus defends the people's rights.
8. Ram with the plough turns up the soil,
   And teaches man for food to toil.
9. Buddha for reformation came,
   And formed a sect well known to fame.
10. When Kalki mounts his milk-white steed,
    Heaven, earth, and all will then recede.

The relics of primeval man, as seen in the lacustrine Swiss dwellings, appear to display a small race; contending, nevertheless, against the wild animals with success, as their bones are found in juxtaposition with the flint weapons, etc., according to Sir Charles Lyell's description in the "Antiquity of Man." The clearing of forests, opposition to tyrants maintaining a reign of disorder by brutal strength alone, and the growth of agriculture, succeed in due course. Krishna is represented as the brother of the later Rama, the spirit of Vishnu being in both, but in Krishna alone has the whole divinity of Vishnu, and the Almighty Spirit of the Universe, been held to be incarnate. Buddha is here admitted to be an incarnation of Vishnu. Kalki, still to come, seems to correspond with the Vision in the Revelation of St. John (vi. 2 and xix. 11).

Sir Richard Phillips observes in " Facts " that " it may be suggested that the incarnations of Vishnu are historical, and that they mean simply the successive states of Nature on our globe. Each state is considered as the preserving God, in a visible or personified form, relatively to the condition of nature at the period of each incarnation.

" The first incarnation, or embodying in nature of the Deity, was the aqueous or fish state; that is, the state in which the old continent was when the perihelion had northern declination.

" The second was the tortoise period; that is, the reign of amphibia, when the plains were generally occupied by lizards, crocodiles, alligators, sharks, turtles, tortoises, etc.

" The third was the hard-skin ascendency, when the marshes, the mud of rivers, etc., sustained myriads of pachydermata, in the forms of mammoths, hippopotami, elephants, hogs, etc.

" The fourth was the age of the ascendency of wild and carnivorous beasts, when a long war existed for predominance between them and man.

" The fifth was the first stage of the ascendency of man.

" The sixth was the age of war and conquests among men, for the occupation of certain countries, and to gratify ambition.

" The seventh was the age when man began to unite with practices of war the arts of horticulture, and the raising of fruits and flowers.

" The eighth was the age which was distinguished by the invention of the plough, and of sowing, reaping, etc.

" The ninth was the age of moral reformation, by Buddha, Confucius, Zerdusht, Taautus, etc.

" The tenth is to be the reign of the White Horse, and it commits the system on the credit of some mystical allegory."

With Buddhism the reign of benignity, inculcated as religious duty, towards all living beings, seems to have been fully entered by humanity in the East.

The future adoration of Vishnu as all-god certainly seems to be commenced in the Rig Veda. When he is contemplated as the sun, he is represented as creating and upholding the worlds.

"I declare the valorous deeds of Vishnu, who measured the mundane regions, who established the upper world, striding thrice, the wide-stepping, who alone sustained the triple universe, the earth and the sky, (yea) all the worlds."

Again, in the Rig Veda hymns it is said, "Vouchsafe to us, swiftly-moving Vishnu, thy benevolence, which embraces all mankind."

"Thrice this god by his greatness has traversed the earth with its hundred lights. May Vishnu be the strongest of the strong; for awful is the name (power?) of that immovable (being).

"This Vishnu traversed the earth to bestow it for a habitation on Manu (or man). The men who praise him are secure."

A Krishna appears in the Rig Veda, but not, it seems, to be identified with the later incarnation of Vishnu.

Professor Weber observed, "By what circumstances the elevation of Krishna to the rank of deity was brought about is as yet obscure, though unquestionably mythical relations to Indra, etc., are at the root of it. In Vedic literature he finds a Krishna, eager, as a scholar, in the pursuit of knowledge." Indra assumes a personality suggestive of actual incarnation.

There are two benevolent, youthful spirits in the Vedas, called the Aswins, who travel in a triangular, luminous car, and appear to be emblematical of the invigorating power of the sunshine. They assume many forms; they enable the lame to walk and the blind to see, and restore an aged man to youth. They rescue from drowning Bhujyu, who had gone to sea in a hundred-oared ship.

Indra, in personifying the atmospheric phenomena, as Mrs. Manning says, as the Sender of Rain, as traversing the sky with his water-laden chariot, as liberating the obstructed streams, as the showerer of benefits, as invoked also as "chief amongst men, the protection of the good," etc., seems to possess attributes that naturally fall into the subsequently all-embracing Vishnu, in his incarnation in Krishna, and revelation of himself as the supreme and universal spirit in the Bhagavad-gita.

The winds are sons of Indra, and they also are attendant upon Vishnu.

The opening for the merging of the personification of Indra in Vishnu seems to be afforded in a hymn in which doubts are raised concerning the former's existence.

In Varuna (Οὐρανὸς) the name for the personification of night and water, a high moral character appears, says Dr. Muir; and the same functions and attributes are attributed to him and Mitra, but Mitra is also king of the day. He seems afterwards to have become the Persian manifestation of deity for the benefit of mankind.

These Vedic idealisations of the spirit of the universe seem to lead naturally to conceptions of the assumption, by the preserving Spirit of Deity, of the flesh, in successive forms, for the salvation of the world.

CHAPTER XXIV.

The Chinese and Buddhism—Progression of the idea of the incarnation to be observed in India—G. Higgins as to the Book of Isaiah, and the literal application of its prophecies to Cyrus—Aryan conceptions apparent in the Immanuel, God with us, of Isaiah—Hindus and their doctrines in Rome at about time of Christ—Gospel of St. John and Bhagavad Gita seeming different promulgations of the same idea—The name Messiah—Name of Christ—His miraculous birth not apparently set forth in the teaching of St. Paul, etc.—Christianity taking the place of Pythagoreanism on the Mediterranean, just as Krishnaism superseded Buddhism in India.

WE find that the Chinese adopted Buddhism, under the appellation of the religion of Fo, at about the commencement of the Christian era. While the Aryan race was thus imparting a religion to the Turanian on one side, it was, according to the orthodox view, which has left out of sight this old doctrine, itself receiving on the other side a Semitic revelation of the divine. We have held the Christian revelation to have been the fulfilment of the prophecies delivered to the Jews alone. We have credited tho Hebraic self-assertion of being God's chosen people; yet, by what seems inconsistency, they have been believed to have testified to the especial possession of knowledge of the divine by not recognising the Messiah promised to them.

Our cousins in India have also asserted with constancy that their conceptions of religion are direct revelations from the Almighty, but they have not maintained that His favours were bestowed within a sphere limited as the Jewish. In India we trace the idea of the incarnation progressing through various stages till it assumes a form in its essence similar to that which it takes under the appellation of Christianity in the Roman Empire. In the latter, unless, indeed, indications be admitted of Christian doctrine in the adoration of the more divine aspect of Bacchus, and in the Eleusinian mysteries, we have to believe that it appeared suddenly, developed only out of the Jewish idea of a temporal Messiah, who should restore to the Jews their ancient glory. We have asserted, moreover, that the rejection of the Messiah by the chosen people was actually necessary for the Almighty scheme of salvation for ourselves; that is to say, the Jews were ordained to be especially favoured, and then especially disgraced, by the divine predestination.

It was prophesied, according to our orthodox faith, that the chosen people should fall into error, and become outcasts from the divine favour, by Isaiah and other of their prophets. Godfrey Higgins remarks, however, that the book of Isaiah literally expresses that it alludes to Cyrus, and that it was a sign for the prophet's contemporaries. If the prophet Isaiah wrote the entire book ascribed to him in the Jewish reigns mentioned in his first verse, *i.e.* between 810 B.C. and 698 B.C., he must be held to have described the conquests of Cyrus and his conduct towards the Jews in restoring them to their city, and even to have mentioned the name of Cyrus, nearly 200 years before that monarch's birth. Cyrus is distinctly styled the shepherd and anointed of the Lord (Isaiah xliv. 28, and xlv. 1). Isaiah is considered to have annexed to these prophecies relating to the more immediate temporal concerns of the Jews, those referring to our Saviour's birth under the synonym of Immanuel, His sufferings, rejection by the Jews, and reception by the Gentiles.

The meaning of Immanuel, God with us, appears suggestive of the idea of the incarnation as expressed in the Indian Scriptures. According to the descriptions of Solomon's commerce in gold and silver, ivory, apes, and peacocks; and that in Ezekiel to which allusion has been made, etc. etc.; it seems evident that actual trade was then carried on between Palestine and some part of India. We may perceive at this period a definite opening for the introduction of Aryan ideas, even if they did not previously exist amongst the Jews. M. E. Burnouf has advanced the theory, in a somewhat different form from Godfrey Higgins, that there were two elements in the Jewish race, the Idumæan and the Aryan; that the adorers of Elohim (Allah) were Semitic, and of Jehovah, Aryan, who principally existed in Galilee. From them came the prophets and the sacerdotal system. The religion of Jesus was Aryan—"L'ancienne loi contenait une portion de doctrines Aryennes que Jésus venait non point detruire mais complèter."

The prophet Isaiah may have become imbued with this grand Aryan realisation of the divine abiding in the human when he uttered those striking predictions which have so encouraged the faith of Christendom.

It seems, at all events, that communication existed between Palestine and India; and the Aryan element, subsequently observable in the Hellenistic Jews, may have been present in Judæa throughout its history. At about the time of Christ, not only was there commercial communication between India, Western Asia, and Europe, but Hindus seem to have been settled on the Mediterranean as emigrants; the Brahminical edicts against emigration, then as now, having been only held applicable to, or at least accepted by, sections of the race. Godfrey Higgins produced evidence to show that Hindu astrologers were in repute in Rome in the first century of our era, that Hindus had been brought thither as servants, and had also come in the capacity of attendants upon elephants; and some tribes of Hindus were settled in Colchis. Roman gold coins of the second century of our era have been found in India. A doctrine of transmigration of souls, similar to the Indian, appears to have been held amongst the Pharisees, while the Essenes of Palestine had a clear resemblance to sects of Hindu devotees. As the doctrine of the incarnation of the divine in man already existed in Greece under a materialistic conception, and in Persia and Egypt under mystic forms, it would really have been matter for wonder if the more spiritual Indian apprehension of the doctrine had not appeared in the Roman Empire. It was there revealed, and it, not unnaturally, gratifies our spiritual pride to believe that it was then for the first time delivered, and that it is our mission, who have been thus favoured above the rest of humanity, to carry the divine word throughout the world.

The Christian doctrine, as taught in our orthodox churches, does not seem to have been promulgated, at first at all events; according to the written evidence. The doctrine of the Word, as with the Father in the beginning, was not expressed in the earlier, the Synoptical Gospels. It was not published by St. John, according to orthodox estimates of the date of his Gospel, till he had arrived at about the age of ninety, sixty years after the death of Christ. At about this time the Bhagavad Gita, or

Divine Song, seems to have been in existence in India. The Gospel and the Bhagavad Gita have no resemblance in their general contents; but, to Christ in the one, and to Krishna in the other, are assigned the attributes of the whole divine nature, as incarnate in them, for man's sake, upon earth. According to the two authors, Christ in the one, and Krishna in the other, declare their oneness with the Supreme Spirit. These works would rather seem to have been promulgations of the same idea under different forms, than imitations or copyings of the one from the other. Our Church teaches that Christ used the exact words attributed to Him by St. John, written under the inspiration of the Almighty. Orthodoxy must affirm that words which seem to have a corresponding spiritual import in the Hindu writing were either conceived under human imagining alone, or were borrowed in some way from our Scripture. As India and China are not mentioned in the New Testament, and our scriptural world appears to be that of the Roman Empire and its neighbours, it does not seem to be disconsonant with the Supreme Goodness to conceive that the Almighty, for the benefit of the ancient civilisations on the other side of our hemisphere, had put words of similarly sacred meaning into the mouth of Krishna. At all events, they are in spirit identical. And the conception, or ideas leading up to the conception, seem so prevalent throughout the literature in the Sanskrit, held sacred by the Hindus, that, humanly speaking, it is unreasonable to insist that the doctrines must be foreign importations into India.

It is again remarkable that, if Christ's religion be not Aryan, the Greek epithet Christos should have been applied to Him. The Semitic inhabitants of Judæa might have been thought likely to have reverenced Him under the explicit name of Messiah, instead of turning the word into Greek. It appears from St. John iv. 25, etc., that He was called Christ.

It would seem not to be really of vital consequence whether we as Christians adore the Divine in the name of Christos, signifying the anointed one, or whether the true appellation was Chrestos, the benignant one, as G. Higgins surmised, or whether the Hindus adore the same universal Divine Spirit as having spoken in Krishna, the dark one, an appellation with or without some recondite meaning, or as

Bhagavat the blessed, etc. etc.; for Christ taught that it was the spirit, not the letter, which signified. If the Spirit of Goodness, the Saviour, or Preserver, under the form of humanity, is adored in spirit, throughout His universe, many names may surely be applied to Him, and many pronunciations of names. To reverence the mere name would seem idolatrous. If it be impious to doubt the absolute facts and literal application of every word in the Gospel narrative, there is still no word which denies the former belief in the incarnation of the Divine in other lands, or worlds, and the influence of the Holy Spirit upon man in previous times in other regions. The Spirit is of all time and all space. And as the Omniscient cannot have been ignorant of these imputed incarnations amongst the Aryan race, it must surely be presumed, from the silence of our Scripture, that they were admitted, as partaking of the divine ordinance. This does not militate against the order to the disciples to preach to all the world and baptize. The true religion of Christ, though apparently not intended to supersede these prototypical faiths immediately, may be held to be the completion of divine dispensations.

It may be remarked that, according to the New Testament, the history of the Virgin Mary, and the facts of the birth of Christ, as related in St. Matthew's and St. Luke's Gospels, appear not to have been prominently put forward in the earlier teaching of the Church. St. Paul is considered, according to orthodox estimates again, to have written some of his Epistles at about the same time as, or previously to, the three earlier Gospels. The history therefore of the divine and supernatural birth of the Saviour had not been widely disseminated, at all events in writing; unless the Apocryphal Gospels be considered to have been earlier publications—an opinion not seeming justified by their contents, etc. But St. Paul's Epistles make no comments upon these supernatural manifestations. Perhaps the history of the Nativity would not then have been received with the veneration which it has since attained. There were stories of divine offspring resulting from the loves of the old classical deities for mortal maidens; which might have occasioned the assertion that this story was only a development of the old idea into a more spiritual form. No mention was made of it in the Gospels themselves, except in the first two chapters of St. Matthew and the first three of St. Luke. This must at least indicate that stress was not laid upon the material aspect of the Incarnation. The stories of the infancy of Jesus, and concerning His mother, which appeared during the first few centuries of the Church, have been rejected, and apparently with discretion, except those related by St. Matthew and St. Luke. While the doctrines of Christ appear to have likenesses in those attributed to Krishna, Pythagoras, about 500 years previously, is related to have brought into Greece, from India or the East, doctrines very similar to those expounded at that period by Gautauma Buddha, in respect to the transmigration of souls, the pursuit of wisdom and virtue, etc.; or by the sect which is supposed at that epoch to have been formed by him. These doctrines appear to have prevailed to considerable extent on the territories of the Mediterranean. At the time of Christ, valid evidence, as has been said, seems to demonstrate that the doctrine of beatitude to be enjoyed by faith in the Divine Spirit incarnate in Krishna, was in existence in India, destined eventually to supersede Buddhism there. This doctrine, preached by Christ in Palestine, and promulgated by the apostles in various parts of the Roman Empire, including the great capital, seems to have taken the place, by gradual process, of Neoplatonism, the child of Pythagoreanism, and also of the more materialistic classic faiths. The old religions of Greece and Rome appear to have been the offspring of the Vedic religion, combined with the Sivaic. We find in the Vedic literature Dyaushpitar (Zeus Diespiter) and mother earth (Demeter). The Celestial Sea encompasses the world as the Ocean Stream of the classics, etc. etc. As the Buddhistic and Vaishnavic faiths appear amongst the Aryans of the East, they are followed or accompanied by corresponding religious movements amongst those of the West. Sir W. Jones' comparison in the "Asiatic Researches" of the religions of Greece and India, and a further comparison of the tenets of Buddha and Pythagoras, and then of the doctrines and histories of the births and portions of the lives of Krishna and Christ, with an investigation of the periods at which they can be historically shown to have been disseminated, eastwards and westwards, exhibit coincidences too remarkable to be due to chance.

CHAPTER XXV.

Allusion not made to the supernatural events of the Crucifixion in Roman writers on the natural history of the period—Life of Herod, without mention of slaughter of Innocents—Accounts of the eruption of Vesuvius also written soon after the destruction of Pompeii, without allusions to it—Gross exaggerations of the details of the destruction in another account—Prototype of the Christian story in Cyrus.

THE divine inculcation, in the suffering of Jesus, of those leading ideas of the world's amelioration in civilisation—self-sacrifice, courage, and devotion—does not lose its signification even by some of the accessories of the crucifixion being impeached. Humanly speaking it is difficult to comprehend the true meaning of the details as related in St. Matthew xxvii.—viz. that it was accompanied by abnormal darkness over "all the land;" that the "veil of the temple was rent in twain from the top to the bottom; and the earth did quake, and the rocks rent; and the graves were opened; and many bodies of the saints which slept arose, and came out of the graves after His resurrection, and went into the holy city, and appeared unto many. Now when the centurion, and they that were with him, watching Jesus, saw the earthquake, and those things that were done, they feared greatly, saying, Truly this was the Son of God." Two Roman naturalists have left accounts of the phenomena of earthquakes, eclipses, and the like, which happened at that period in the Roman Empire, and it is difficult to conceive why no notice should have been taken of these occurrences in the important province of Judæa; especially as an officer of the Roman army was so impressed with their supernatural aspect. Could such prodigies have happened in Calcutta in the days of Warren Hastings, and an exhaustive account of natural occurrences have been written shortly afterwards by an English philosopher without allusion to them?

Lives of Herod, again, have descended to us without mention of the slaughter of the innocents, which we find in Hindu story as attributed to Krishna. Still these are negative evidences. Sir Charles Lyell, in his "Principles of Geology," comments upon the singularity of Pliny's giving a circumstantial detail of the eruption of Vesuvius, the earthquake, and shower of ashes which fell at Stabiæ, yet making no allusion to the sudden overwhelming of two large and populous cities, Herculaneum and Pompeii—"All naturalists," he observes, "who have searched into the memorials of the past for records of physical events, must have been surprised at the indifference with which the most memorable occurrences are often passed by, in the works of writers of enlightened periods; as also of the extraordinary exaggeration which usually displays itself in the traditions of similar events, in ignorant and superstitious ages." It may have been, however, that Pliny, writing for his contemporaries, gave an exact account of the phenomena of the eruption in the benefit of science, but did not allude to so notorious a fact as the overwhelming of the cities; which had probably been widely discussed in the society of the Empire. About a century and a half after Pliny, Dion Cassius is the first actual historian who alludes to them. "Suetonius, although he alludes to the eruption incidentally, is silent as to the cities. They are mentioned by Martial in an epigram, as immersed in cinders; but the first historian who alludes to them is Dion Cassius, who flourished about a century and a half after Pliny. He appears to have derived his information from the traditions of the inhabitants, and to have recorded, without discrimination, all the facts and fables which he could collect. He tells us that, 'during the eruption a multitude of men of superhuman structure resembling giants appeared, sometimes on the mountain and sometimes in the environs; that stones and smoke were thrown out, the sun was hidden, and then the giants seemed to rise again, while the sounds of trumpets were heard, etc. etc.;' and finally, he relates that 'two entire cities, Herculaneum and Pompeii, were buried under showers of ashes, while all the people were sitting in the theatre.'"

The negative evidence therefore offered by the silence of Roman historians, and the incredulity of the Jews themselves, who must have seen or heard of these portents as related in the Gospel, which made such an impression on the Roman centurion, may not be valid. But, on the other hand, the quotation from Dion Cassius is an illustration of the rapid growth of fictions around a striking occurrence in times of excitement. These Indian narratives of Krishna and his doctrine, together with the Indian Trinity in unity, or Trinity out of unity, which is perhaps the proper expression for it, may be mere specious similitudes of the divine incidents belonging to Christ, but they undoubtedly exist as similitudes. They may have arisen from the promptings of a devil. But it seems more rational, and more in accordance with Christian charity and meekness, to refer them to the work of the Almighty, and hold that He has given to all His creatures the revelations profitable for them.

A prototype of the Christian story again, curiously, seems to have existed in Cyrus. A prophecy warns a reigning tyrant that the child is born for his destruction; and Cyrus is nurtured amongst shepherds, etc. Cyrus would altogether seem to have been another prototype of the Saviour, unless the spiritual rather than materialistic view of Christ's advent be adopted; and the actual incidents in the Christian story held to be inconsequential. Old stories certainly have passed current for new events without much questioning concerning them in all historical ages. In fact the world prefers to be interested by romance rather than enlightened by truth.

CHAPTER XXVI.

Gibbon's evidence as to the disputes, amongst the Christians of the early centuries, concerning the essential doctrines of our Church and the Roman Catholic —That we ought to be consistent in our assertions of Hindu copying—The first discovery of the means of obtaining fire a marvel in its time—Shown by quotations from E. Burnouf to have been commemorated in the Sacrament of the Veda; in which the adoration of the *Agni*, consecration of the sacred cake, and the anointing with the spirituous liquor of the Somâ, offer analogies to the Sacrament of the Mass—The *Agni* (sacred fire) suggested in the Apocalypse—The Founder of Christianity not lessened in dignity by receiving the application of a theory which existed before all history—Doctrine of the Atonement in the first ages of Christianity—Quotation from L. Jacolliot as to the symbolical sacrifice of the Sama Veda—E. Burnouf's assertion of the identity of the Christian with the Vedic ritual—Did the custom of anointing priests and kings come from the *Agni* sacrament?

THE historian Gibbon produced much evidence to show that the doctrines upon which Roman Catholics and Protestants are now agreed, as to the Trinity in Unity, and the nature, divine and human, of our Lord, were subjects of dispute amongst the Christians of the first centuries. The first five of our Thirty-nine Articles of the Church of England, which five articles are in accord with the Roman Catholic articles upon the same chief doctrines of Christianity, appear only to have become settled during the continuance of three or four centuries after the time of the Founder of the Faith. Agreed as to these main points of belief, we are now contending over questions of Church government, ritual, and the precise meaning of Christ, when He laid His hands upon the bread, and said, "This is my body." By faith we may continue to hold that the Almighty took flesh in Judæa, not quite 1900 years ago, and there, once and for all time, revealed the divine idea of the Incarnation. But we cannot refuse to admit that ancient Egyptians, Greeks, etc., apart from the Indians, had some inkling of it; though we may maintain that only our view of the Incarnation has truth in it. So again, by our old belief in the uniqueness of Greek art, we may allege that all superior art discoverable on the continent of India is due to their influence. We must then consistently continue to attribute the more fantastic art, and the caste system, to imitation of the Assyrians and Egyptians; and remain content with contemplating, with wonder, the marvellous imaginations and inventive faculties of those people. We must, in fact, consider the present autochthonous aspect of the Hindus as an indication merely of the capacity of an imitative race to become conservative in course of time.

It would seem that we ought also, in consistency, to assert that the Zendavesta was the predecessor of the Vedas, that Buddhism was derived from the doctrines of Pythagoras, and that the elegant perfection of the classical Sanskrit language was due to taking careful example by the formations which the Aryan languages had assumed in Europe. We must hold that the Indian proa is a recollection of the teaching of Phœnician mariners, and that the Institutes of Manu really display to us the laws first promulgated by Menes of Egypt or Minos of Crete. It might even appear logically deducible, that the sacred tanks appertaining to the Hindu temples were suggested by the baptismal fonts of Christian churches. If the continent of India adopted one of these things from the continent of Europe, why not the others? It seems easier to believe that India produced all in an archaic form from the suggestions of nature, for wants caused in ascending from the tropical regions; that the race which has continued to improve, first invented the arts and sciences, enlightening the Semitic and other races in ancient days as at present. If Greece could be shown to have instructed Egypt, we might place the originals in that glorious region, but this does not seem demonstrable.

In contemplating Indian scenes, whether in the reality or in pictures, how absolutely the art exhibited seems to harmonise with the aspect of the people! Let us take their art remains in the mythological excavations in conjunction with their literary remains in the Ramáyaṇa and Mahábhárata poems, and consider the civilisation suggested in both. Then let us observe the native life under Mohammedan and English rule, and compare it with the ancient aspect of life, and we must admit that the whole are in harmony, and in accord with the aspects of nature around them. It seems possible to trace man's progress in inventions from tropical India to variable England, as rendered necessary by changes of climate or progressing commercial activity, in the literary links which commence with the Vedas. From the obtaining of fire by rubbing together two sticks to the analysing of the substance of the stars by their rays of light, seems a constant chain of scientific progression in steps. This ancient method of obtaining fire must have seemed as wonderful to its first discoverers as the application of electricity to ourselves. As has been remarked in connection with the cross found graven on the Troy relics, it seems to have been commemorated in the bloodless sacrificial observances at the old Aryan altars, as M. Emile Burnouf has shown in the work of his which has been mentioned; the fire, in this ancient rite, being obtained by friction on the instrument of wood called the *araṇt*. The ceremony altogether has the appearance of being the original or prototype of the great commemorative Catholic sacrifice of the Mass, or sacramental ordinance of ritualistic Christianity.

M. Burnouf thus comments on "the unity of this central rite of the Catholic religion, with the ancient Aryan practice as set forth in the Veda."

"Blood sacrifices," he observes, "had been suppressed by the Therapeutes and Essenes, conservators of the Aryan traditions among the Jews. This had been almost accomplished in the Veda, for the *agni* fire is itself almost always offered in the fire of the altar, under the double aspect of the sacred cake and of the spirituous liquor of the *sôma*, "ou, comme on dit chez nous, du pain et du vin." He gives the following quotation from the Veda:—

A. Agni.

"La jeune mère porte l'enfant royal mysterieusement caché dans son sein . . . la reine l'a enfanté; car d'une antique fécondation c'est la germe qui s'est développé; je l'ai vu à sa naissance, quand sa mère l'a mis au monde. Oui j'ai vu ce dieu aux couleurs brillantes . . . et j'ai répondu sur lui l'onction immortelle . . . je l'ai vue s'avancer de sa place tout resplendissant . . . des enemis avaient rejétés au rang des mortels celui qui est le roi des êtres et le désiré des nations . . . que ses colomniateurs soient confondus."

This young queen, also called "la dame du peuple," is the *araṇt*, that is to say, the instrument of wood on which the fire is obtained by friction—the *swastika*, to which allusion has been made in Chapter XXI., as represented on the "prehistoric whorls" discovered by Dr. Schliemann, and exhibited in the South Kensington Museum. It may be considered a coincidence that the *Agni*, the divine fire lighted in sacrifice on the old Aryan altars, should happen to present such verbal resemblance to the Latin form of the Lamb of God, Agnus *Dei*. In the sacred unction (ânjana) fire or heat is supposed to be drawn from the milk of the cow; which heat, which is life, comes, as in plants, from the celestial Father; the priest being the human instrument. Vishnu, remarks M. E. Burnouf, is the force which manifests itself in the penetrating rays of the sun. *Agni* is the power, free, intelligent, and universal, of which all fires are the visible signs, which exists in all bodies, and even in thought. There appears, he continues, to be a strange mingling of the ideas appertaining to both the Sanskrit *agni* and the Latin *agnus* in the Apocalypse. According to the orthodox view, it must be remembered that this book is considered to have been written by St. John at Patmos about A.D. 96, *i.e.* more than sixty years after the death of Christ, so that there was ample time for the reflex action of ideas from Rome. It is said, in the "Apocalypse" of St. John, that the "holy city, the new Jerusalem" . . . "had no need of the sun, neither of the moon to shine in it; for the glory of God did lighten it, and the Lamb is the light thereof." Of course, the expression "light of the world" is very commonly applied to Christ in Protestant Christendom, and may appear naturally to be uttered of Him in His capacity as teacher; while the appellation of the Lamb is as naturally bestowed upon Him as performing the all-sufficient sacrifice for the sins of the world. But if we accept this view of M. E. Burnouf's, as he observes, the Founder of Christianity is not lessened in dignity by receiving under the name of Christ the application of a theory which existed before all history.

A true historical perception of the doctrine of the manifestation of the divine in the human, in the person of Christ, certainly seems attainable in these exhumations of ancient Sanskrit religious writings. They seem to exhibit facts of ancient practice, not fancies. Three hundred years ago the general promulgation of the Bible produced Protestantism. Further literary publications of antiquity seem to demand modifications in Protestantism as then settled.

The evangelical doctrine of the Atonement teaches the necessity of full reliance on the actual and necessary blood sacrifice upon the cross. This seems to involve the Almighty's requiring a sacrifice of Himself, in the incarnate Second Person of the Trinity in Unity, unto Himself in the First Person thereof, as an expiation for the sins imputed to mankind in consequence of the curse passed upon the disobedience of their first parents. It was not completely adopted by the converts of the first ages of Christianity. Divergencies of faith were numerous; and some conceived that Christ was offered as a compensation to the devil for his loss of the world's sinners.

Faith in the resurrection of the dead to eternal life, as assured to mankind by God in the raising of Jesus after His suffering, seems to have been made more directly prominent at all events by St. Paul. The Jews having been taught to rely upon the atonement of blood sacrifices, the transition or progress of ideas from the conception of the divine man—instructing to righteousness and rising from the grave to point the way to eternal bliss, to faith in an actual atoning sacrifice—seems natural.

It must be remembered that, according to the orthodox Church of England view of Biblical chronology, the Gospels are generally regarded as having been written, at all events in their present form, subsequently to the earlier of St. Paul's Epistles. The actual details of the manifestation, and the incidents related of the infancy of Christ, rest upon the narratives in the Gospels. If found to have been previously related of or suggested by Indian incarnations of the deity, they may surely be held to be apocryphal in portions without destruction of the divine attributes of Christ, though these had been recognised by other nations in other men.

To limit the action of the Holy Spirit is incompatible with the expression omnipresent. M. L. Jacolliot, in "Le Bible dans l'Inde," thus sets forth an Indian view of the sacrificial office of the Incarnate Divinity: "Brahma is at once both sacrificer and victim, so that the priest who officiates each morning at the ceremonies of the Sāma Veda, the universal sacrifice symbolic of creation, in presenting his offering to God identifies himself with the divine sacrificer, who is Brahma; or rather it is Brahma, victim in his son Krishna, who came to die on earth for our salvation, who himself accomplishes the solemn sacrifice."

M. E. Burnouf suggests that Vishnu, in the Veda, a symbol of the sun, contemplated by the Brahmins, became the penetrating energy in the life of thought, as well as the physical. (They say that fire is even in thought.) Siva came from Rudra, chief of the winds, etc., or was associated with that idea. Brahma represents thought, science, and religion; Vishnu life in the Divine Unity and Incarnate Spirit; Siva the law of dissolution and reproduction in continuing form. According to the Brahmins, the Divine Being himself composed the Vedas and delivered them to man. Our religion and its rites, he remarks, are only to be explained by going to India. The Sun, Fire, and Wind are the images of the Spiritual Trinity.

He writes that we find in the Nirukta of Yaska, that the more ancient Vedic authors only admit three deities—Savitri, Agni, and Vâyu, *i.e.* the father or producer, the fire of altar and hearth, and the physical and thinking life. The Fire has a terrestrial father, who bears the name of Twâstri, the carpenter, as has been observed in commenting on the Troy relics. In the maternal bosom it is conceived as Spirit, Vâyu, materially the wind and the spirit of life. The *Agni* has for mother Mâyâ, the personification of the productive power. The Twâstri prepares the pile of wood, etc., and the Soma is the mysterious influence, the spirituous liquor, which causes the fire to burn up. Before the sun rises a star is in the east. He observes: "Le centre duquel ont rayoné toutes les grandes religions de la terre est donc la théorie d'agni, dont le Christ Jesus a été la plus parfaite incarnation;" also that the rites, symbols, and legends of Catholicism are to be found in the Veda, expressed in almost the same terms as those employed in the present day; in fact, that one is astonished not at their similarity but at their identity. "On ne peut donc raisonnablement douter que le Christianisme ne soit la religion Aryenne ellemême venue d'Asie au temps d'Auguste et de Tibère, quelle que soit d'ailleurs la manière dont elle à été introduite, promulguée et vulgarisée."

Supposing it be decided that the name Christ is derived from the Greek word signifying anointed, which corresponds with the Hebrew word which we render Messiah, and which was applied by the Jews to Him to whom they looked for restoration of their temporal grandeur, and to whom, therefore, they applied the epithet of anointed—anointing being the symbol of conferring the kingly and priestly authority;—whence, in that case, came this symbol? from what was it derived? It seems reasonable to surmise that this ancient pouring of oil upon the flame in the solemn sacrifice, upon this *agni*, which was adored as the symbol of the Divine upon earth, had occasioned the custom of anointing priests and kings as the highest amongst earthly potentates. That which was at first done to give brilliance to the fire of the altar, was bestowed upon those consecrated to be the guides of men, the lights of the world, as symbolical of their sanctity. Christ became the *Agni*, the anointed Light of the world. Again, therefore, through Egypt, with the rest of the knowledge of the Egyptians which Moses had acquired, or through the traditions generally prevailing throughout the civilisations of the epoch, we may derive the reason of the epithet from the Madhyama.

If it should be argued that the anointing of kings merely signified the giving of suppleness to their limbs, as the leading warriors, it may be answered that this, at all events, does not apply to the priests.

No ceremony, surely, can have been absolutely meaningless. It is in the numerous rites of Roman Catholic Christendom, rather than in the plainer ritual of Protestantism, that M. E. Burnouf has perceived the outward resemblances of the Eastern and Western religions.

CHAPTER XXVII.

E. Burnouf as to Oriental doctrines in early Christendom—Exampled in the Catacombs of Rome—Quotation from the Rig Veda as to the *Agni*, by Dr. Muir—Arguments as to our having limited Christ's doctrine—Schlegel as to Indian and Greek religious affinities—Also Christian.

IN the fourth century, writes M. E. Burnouf, according to a letter from St. Jerome to Marcella, Palestine was a centre which was frequented by men from all parts of the world, amongst which he enumerates Armenia, Persia, and India. Shortly before, Eusebius remarks, in his Ecclesiastical History, that the Christians were styled barbarians, as belonging to a foreign religion, *barbaræ ac peregrinæ*, qualifications which would scarcely be applicable to Judæa or Egypt, which constituted part of the Roman Empire. In the third century Tertullian mentions the Brahmins and Indian ascetics as being well known in his time. Towards the end of the second century St. Hippolytus asserts that many heresies are founded on certain systems of the Brahmins of India, which proves that he was not ignorant of these systems. A short time previously Melita, Bishop of Sardis, writing in 170 to Antoninus the Pious, says to him: "The doctrine which we profess at first flourished amongst the barbarians; but when, under the glorious reign of Augustus, it took root amongst the nations submitting to your government, it became a source of blessing to your realm." In the time of Christ, the Jew Philo, who was acquainted with Buddha, the *Çramaṇas*, and the Brahmins, in speaking of Alexandria and the whole south-western parts of the Mediterranean, utters these words: "Il y a ici un homme qui s'appelle l'Orient." M. Reinaud, in the "Journal Asiatique," has commented upon the official relations between India and the Roman Empire. It would be a matter of the highest interest to consider this question in all its bearings, and collect all the facts calculated to elucidate the degree of union between East and West. We have reason to believe that a great exchange of ideas took place between India and the West by Alexandria, perhaps also by the Persian Gulf, and the caravans of central Asia. It is certainly astonishing to find Sanskrit in the Catacombs of Rome. In the cemetery of St. Pretextatus, for example, a very curious and well-known painting, reproduced in the great work of Perret, represents the judgment of two Christian women, Vibia and Alcestis. In the middle is a tribunal, upon which are seated two personages; on their left are the two Christians, brought in by the messenger Mercury. On the right are three women, half veiled, and of rigid aspect, having the appellations of *Fata Divina*. Of the two judges seated on the tribunal, one is Diespiter, in the classical attitude of the Olympian Jupiter; the other is not Juno, but *Abracura*. This is a Sanskrit word, which signifies the divinity of the clouds, the Queen of Heaven, the spouse of the Indian Jupiter.

M. E. Burnouf further suggests that the Founder of Christianity intended, not an extension of Judaism to the world, but the re-establishment of the ancient Aryan theory, "Before Abraham was, I am." Christianity holds the Trinity in Unity to be an eternal truth, though only definitely promulgated after the revelation of Christ. The first human and material conception of the Trinity appears to have been in the sun, as the image of divine power, as has been suggested. This produces life upon the earth, the Agni (fire) descends upon the earth from heaven for man's benefit, and the wind sustains the flame and dispels the noxious vapours of the earth. The Agni is the light of the world, and the Holy Spirit accompanies its influence, and pervades all.

In a verse of the Rig Veda, x. 142. 1, says Dr. Muir, the god Agni (Fire) is thus addressed:—"This thy worshipper, O Agni, has been even in thee; O son of strength, he has no other kinship. Excellent is thy triple protection." Here seems an evident expression of the Christian idea as propounded in the Gospel of St. John, and of the later Indian doctrine in the Bhagavad Gita. The fact seems indubitably to be that the gradual accumulation of ideas forms a faith, and that humanity, unable to contemplate the divine in universality, narrows the conception to a power in nature, or to a similitude of a human ruler. Thus, in considering the ways of God to man, though planets, seemingly habitable as our own, roll through space, and though upon our own earth 600,000,000 in India and China have continued in civilisation since the dawn of the history of our side of the world, not containing half that number, we have held that He has only vouchsafed to communicate His will to the ancient Jews, and to our modern civilisations. Though we affirm, therefore, that Christ is eternal, Three in One, that the Holy Spirit, One in the Three, is ever to be prayed to come to us; yet we have been unable to conceive that Holy Spirit, which in the Trinity is Christ, coming before as well as after Him whom we adore.

"In studying the earlier monuments and figures of Christianity," says M. E. Burnouf, "the identity of their metaphysical meanings with the Aryanism of the Vedas, rather than with the Semitic religions, must be perceived, and that the Eastern churches have preserved a doctrinal tendency towards Alexandrian pantheism. When we compare, he observes, the Koran, Bible, and Vêda, we regard the first as the production of a race inferior to our own, we feel in respect to the second that the men it depicts are not of our race, nor of thoughts sympathetic with our own, while in the third all modern science has recognised our ancestry. But we know that in the Aryan migrations the recollection of the ancient country was lost."

It is certain, he remarks, that the Vêda was known in the Greek world before the coming of Jesus Christ, for in the poems published under the name of Orphics are verses translated, word for word, from hymns of the Vêda.

Schlegel, in his "History of Literature," observes that the Greeks recognised in India their own deities, with differences of form and colouring, and the names of the Indian Hercules and the Indian Bacchus afterwards became common among them. He remarks that the Indian doctrine of the transmigration of souls was brought into Greece, through Egypt, by Pythagoras, and that the commercial intercourse between India and Alexandria was of long duration, and, without doubt, attended by considerable flux and reflux of intellectual communication, the Indian trade being of such antiquity that it ascends beyond the historical records of any nation. He says:—

As the Institutes of Manu were composed in verse, so the Greeks of the most ancient period composed their histories, laws, etc., in plain verse. Among the Indians we find a mythology resembling partly that of the Egyptians, partly that of the Greeks, and yet comprehending in it many ideas, both moral and philosophical, which, in spite of all differences in detail, are evidently akin to the doctrines of the Christian religion. There is indeed no reason to doubt that there existed a reciprocal communication of ideas between India and those countries which had the nearest access to the ancient revelation.

Schlegel, as a Catholic Christian, held that the ancient revelation was to the Jews, and in Christ; yet he says, "But the most remarkable point of resemblance between the Indian and Christian doctrines lies in the absolute identity of conception with which both describe the process of regeneration. In the Indian creed, exactly as in our own, so soon as the soul becomes touched with the love of divine things it is supposed to drop at once its life contaminated by sin, and, as the phœnix rises from its ashes, to spring at once into the possession of a new and purified existence—so universal is the prevalence of this idea among the Brahmins, with the same words and same meaning familiar to ourselves—to be new born. From the resemblance between the Indian and Christian religions certain critics have thought that the Brahmins borrowed from us; but he observes, "I think, however, that the prevalence of such notions in India, at a period much more early than this, is proved beyond a doubt by historical evidence." "Perhaps among no other ancient people did the doctrine of the immortality of the soul, and the belief in a future state of existence, ever acquire such a mastery over all principles and all feelings, and exert such influence over all the judgments and all the actions of men, as among the Indians." "The whole poetry of the Indians is full of inward love, tenderness, and elegy . . . the enjoyment of solitude and musing, the delight which is excited by the beauty of nature, above all, by the world of plants." According to their ideas, "whatever is good in the present life is only a foretaste of futurity; whatever evils we encounter are the consequences and punishment of sins committed in some former state of being;" yet "Father and Son[1] are in their innermost being so intimately connected that even death has no power to dissolve the union of their destinies."

[1] See Appendix III.

CHAPTER XXVIII.

Remark of Schlegel's as to the influence of the Oriental systems in early Christianity—Origen a believer in the transmigration of souls—Extract from the Introduction to Dow's translation of Ferishta's History of Hindustan; dialogue between the Divine Wisdom and his son Narud, or Reason—Considerations, again, concerning the name Krishna, the dark one—Whether, as G. Higgins surmised, it is the legendary recollection of a dark race—Archbishop Potter as to black stones erected as idols, from "Antiquities of Greece"—Professor M. Williams as to Christian-like texts in Indian literature having come from Christianity—Number of missionary converts in India.

SCHLEGEL remarked that even in the earliest times of Christianity the influence of the Oriental systems was apparent, and that the mystical sects of the first century consisted, in a great measure, of persons who had embraced different dogmas of the Oriental philosophers, and who endeavoured to blend these, as well as the fictions of altogether inconsistent mythologies, with the doctrines of the new faith. "Even the greatest of the first Christian philosophers, Origen, was a believer in the transmigration of souls, and many other Oriental opinions altogether irreconcilable with Christianity."

In the introduction to the edition of Alexander Dow's History of Hindustan, published in the year 1768, is a remarkable extract from a commentary on what he calls the Bedas, a word which we now transcribe as Vedas. The "Divine Wisdom," he observes, "under the name of Brimha (Brahma) is figuratively represented with one head having four faces, looking to the four quarters, alluding to his seeing all things. Upon the head of this figure is a crown, an emblem of power and dominion. He has four hands, implying the omnipotence of divine wisdom. In his first hand he holds the four Bedas as a symbol of knowledge; in the second a sceptre as a token of authority; and in the third a ring or complete circle as an emblem of eternity. He holds nothing in his fourth hand, which implies that the wisdom of God is always ready to lend his aid to his creatures. He is represented riding upon a goose, the emblem of simplicity among the Hindus."

Here, as throughout the range of Hindu theological literature, we perceive the importance attached to what is considered by them as God's revealed word.

"Narud or Reason—an expression of course suggestive of the Logos, Word or Reason of St. John's Gospel—who is represented as the son of Brimha, desires to be instructed by his father, and, for that purpose, puts the following questions to him"—

Narud. "O father, thou first of God (Brahm, the supreme divinity), thou art said to have created the world, and thy son Narud, astonished at what he beholds, is desirous to be instructed how all these things were made."

Brimha. "Be not deceived, my son; do not imagine that I was the creator of the world, independent of the divine mover, who is the great original essence and creator of all things. Look, therefore, only upon me as the instrument of the great will, and a part of his being, whom he called forth to execute his eternal designs."

Narud. "What shall we think of God?"

Brimha. "Being immaterial, he is above all conception; being invisible, he can have no form; but from what we behold in his works we may conclude that he is eternal, omnipotent, knowing all things, and present everywhere."

Narud. "How did God create the world?"

Brimha. "Affection dwelt with God from all eternity. It was of three different kinds—the creative, the preserving, and the destructive. The first is represented by Brimha (Brahma), the second by Bishen (Vishṇu), and the third by Shibah (Siva). You, O Narud, are taught to worship all the three in various shapes and likenesses, as the creator, the preserver, and the destroyer. The affection of God then produced power, and power, at a proper conjunction of time, and fate, embraced goodness and produced matter. The three qualities, then, acting upon matter, produced the universe in the following manner. From the opposite actions of the creative and destructive quality in matter self-motion first arose. Self-motion was of three kinds—the first inclining to plasticity, the second to discord, and the third to rest. The discordant actions then produced the Akash, which invisible element possessed the quality of conveying sound. It produced air, a palpable element; fire, a visible element; water, a fluid element; earth, a solid element.

"The Akash dispersed itself abroad. Air formed the atmosphere; fire collecting itself blazed forth in the host of heaven; water rose to the surface of the earth, being forced from beneath by the gravity of the latter element. Thus broke forth the world from the veil of darkness in which it was formerly comprehended by God. Order rose over the universe. The seven heavens were formed, and the seven worlds were fixed in their places, there to remain till the great dissolution, when all things shall be absorbed into God.

"God seeing the earth in full bloom, and that vegetation was strong from its seeds, called forth for the first time intellect, which he endowed with various organs and shapes, to form a diversity of animals upon the earth. He endowed the animals with five senses—feeling, seeing, smelling, tasting, and hearing. But to man he gave reflection, to raise him above the beasts of the field.

"The creatures were created male and female, that they might propagate their species upon the earth. Every herb bore the seed of its kind, that the world might be clothed with verdure, and all animals provided with food."

Narud. "What dost thou mean, O father, by intellect?"

Brimha. "It is a portion of the great soul of the universe, breathed into all creatures, to animate them for a certain time."

Narud. "What becomes of it after death?"

Brimha. "It animates other bodies, or returns like a drop into that unbounded ocean from which it first arose."

Narud. "Shall not then the souls of good men receive rewards, nor the souls of the bad meet with punishment?"

Brimha. "The souls of men are distinguished from those of other animals; for the first are endowed with reason, and with a consciousness of right and wrong. If, therefore, man shall adhere to the first, as far as his powers shall extend, his soul, when disengaged from the body by death, shall be absorbed into the divine essence, and shall never more reanimate flesh. But the souls of those that do evil are not, at death, disengaged from all the elements. They are immediately clothed with a body of fire, air, or akash, in which they are for a time punished in hell. After the season of their grief is over, they reanimate other bodies; but till they shall arrive at a state of purity they can never be absorbed into God."

Narud. "What is the nature of that absorbed state which the souls of good men enjoy after death?"

Brimha. "It is a participation of the divine nature, when all passions are utterly unknown, and where consciousness is lost in bliss."

Narud. "Thou sayest, O Father, that unless the soul is perfectly pure it cannot be absorbed into God. Now, as the actions of the generality of men are partly good and partly bad, whither are their spirits sent immediately after death?"

Brimha. "They must atone for their crimes in hell, where they must remain for a space proportioned to the degree of their iniquities; then they rise to heaven to be rewarded for a time for their virtues; and from thence they will return to the world to reanimate other bodies."

Narud. "What is time?"

Brimha. "Time existed from all eternity with God, but it can only be estimated since motion was produced, and only be conceived by the mind from its own constant progress."

Narud. "How long shall this world remain?"

Brimha. "Until the four yugs (ages) shall have revolved. Then Rudder (Rudra), with the ten spirits of dissolution, shall roll a comet under the moon, that shall involve all things in fire, and reduce the world into ashes. God shall then exist alone, for matter will be entirely annihilated."

The Brahmins, Dow observes, have no idea that all the sins which a man can commit, in the short period of his life, can deserve eternal punishment; nor that all the virtues he can exercise can merit perpetual felicity in heaven. The teaching of Krishna, in the Bhagavad Gita, however, appears to point to an eternity of happiness corresponding to that to be enjoyed in the Christian heaven.

Again Narud inquires—

"O thou first of God, who is the greatest of all beings?"

Brimha. "Brihm (Brahm), who is infinite and almighty."

Narud. "Is he exempted from death?"

Brimha. "He is; being eternal and incorporeal."

Narud. "Who created the world?"

Brimha. "God by his power."

Narud. Who is the giver of bliss?"

Brimha. "Krishen (Kṛishṇa), and whosoever worshippeth him shall enjoy heaven."

Narud. "What is his likeness?"

Brimha. "He hath no likeness; but to stamp some idea of him upon the minds of men, who cannot believe in an immaterial being, he is represented under various symbolical forms."

Narud. "What image shall we conceive of him?"

Brimha. "If your imagination cannot rise to devotion without an image, suppose with yourself that his eyes are like the lotos, his complexion like a cloud, his clothing of the lightning of heaven, and that he hath four hands."

After receiving explanation that these symbols exhibit the constant openness of his eyes, the majesty which surrounds him, and his almighty power, and that offerings made to him must be of things which are clean, and offered with a grateful heart, Brimha declares that God requires the free offering of men's substance only as the strongest testimony of their gratitude and inclinations towards him.

Narud. "How is God to be worshipped?"

Brimha. "With no selfish view, but for love of his beauties, gratitude for his favours, and for admiration of his greatness."

After being informed that true wisdom will aid a man to combat his inclinations, but that if they cannot be overcome by reason they must be mortified by penance, Narud inquires concerning the incarnations of Rama and Krishna:—"Thou, O Father, dost mention God as one; yet we are told that Ram, whom we are taught to call God, was born in the house of Jessarit; that Kishen, whom we call God, was born in the house of Basdeo, and many others in the same manner,—in what light are we to take this mystery."

Brimha. "You are to look upon these as particular manifestations of the providence of God for certain great ends."

The above conception of the likeness of Krishna altogether does not seem appropriate to the literal meaning of black as the primary signification of his name, unless it be considered that blackness is suggested in the simile of the cloud. Coincidences of sound and doubleness of meaning have occasioned obliviousness to the original signification of many words. Our master spirit of evil, Satan, the devil, is little contemplated in the Christian world under the aspect of the true meaning of his name, in its derivation, and as he appears in the Book of Job—viz. as the diabolos, the slanderer, accuser or prosecutor. Doubtless our translation of that word by devil causes many persons to consider it as connected in derivation with the word evil. A future Age, either regarding the term itself, in juxtaposition with the word evil, or considering the manner in which Satan has been illustrated in our religious writings and poetry, might certainly conceive its obvious origin to have been deduced from the words do evil, or something of the kind.

The word "downs," in Southdowns, etc., derived from the old Aryan word for hills, is doubtless often popularly imagined to be merely the English word antithetical to ups; the descending instead of the ascending feature being supposed to have suggested the nomenclature.

The Aryans of the north-west of India, little darker than Italians, would scarcely seem likely to have used the word black as a fitting appellation for their divine man, the heroic, graceful, and brilliant Krishna, supposing his story had been a mere poetical invention. As the incarnation of Vishnu, the all-pervading spirit, however, black or dark blue might perhaps have been derived from the deep azure of the firmament. And if Krishna was considered as an incarnation of the divine *Agni*, the epithet *black-backed*, which is applied in the Vedas to *Agni*, on account of the dark material for the fire, might have been bestowed upon him for that reason. Although dark complexions may be considered in India as beautiful as the lighter kind, they undoubtedly seem usually to mark the lower orders of Hindus. Certainly Krishna has so many names, betokening his various spiritual and terrestrial offices, that the meaning of this word might seem to have little importance. But the affinity which the name presents to that of Christ renders its signification more than merely interesting. As Godfrey Higgins suggests, the darkness may be the legendary recollection of the black race which preceded the Aryan, or from which the Aryans emerged, in Hindustan. It would, at all events, appear to indicate that the name is more likely to be traditional than simply invented by the author of the Mahábhárata, or one of the other works which relate to Krishna.

In regard to the connection of this blackness with religious symbolisation in Europe, not only do we find the black bambinos in Christian churches, but it appears that stones which represented the Greek divinities in early times were frequently black.

Stocks and stones in the earliest days of Greece, as in India to the present time, were held worthy of veneration, without regard to their rudeness, if they were endowed with traditional sanctity, or in the absence of finer images. The venerated image in the temple of Jaganatha seems to be a striking instance in India.

Archbishop Potter, in his "Antiquities of Greece," observes that many of the oblong stones erected as idols, and particularly the square stone which represented the god Mars at Petra, in Arabia, were black, "which seems to have been thought in those times the more solemn and becoming colour of things dedicated to religious uses."

If the views of Professor Monier Williams and others are correct, these extracts from the Sanskrit, when they display to us, without possibility of misapprehension, the doctrine of God manifested in the flesh, and in this manifestation giving utterances clearly similar to Christian teaching, ought to be considered as derived from Christianity. They ought to be held to have been introduced into India within our era, and attributed to the success of early Christian missions.

But in accepting this explanation we are confronted with the literary evidence of so many approximating texts in works which seem, on positive testimony, to be of earlier date. And we have to meet the difficulty of conceiving such a fervent welcome of Christian verities that the whole continent became permeated with them in a few centuries, while we now encounter so much obstinacy in the rejection, or at least indifference as to the acceptance, of our doctrines. Of course, it may be explained upon the hypothesis of supernatural assistance accompanying the early missionaries. But, in that case, we ought to consider the believers in Krishna as Christians, who have in course of time forgotten the locality and precise story of the Gospel dispensation; while, in some of their doctrines, they have either altered those which they have received, or else they were differently instructed from ourselves by their apostles; for instance, in the transmigration of souls, which seems, outwardly at all events, not to have been believed in the Christian Church since the time of Origen.

According to modern missionary accounts, claiming 5000 converts per annum, 36,000 years would be required to Christianise the 180,000,000 of India. Allowing for increasing breadth of operations, this, at all events, points to a lengthy period. There are, indeed, numerous Roman Catholics on the western coast, but a large number of these are of Portuguese descent. Not only must the people have become rapidly imbued with the new doctrine, but poems, essays, and legends, illustrative of the religion, must have accumulated with extraordinary rapidity. In fact, a miracle must account for the progress of the Christian ideas; while it is marvellous that no legends should have survived to indicate this adoption of a foreign faith in India, although we possess knowledge of the lives and doctrines of Indian reformers since the time of Christ.

CHAPTER XXIX.

Indian doctrine of the transmigration of souls may be primitive Christian—Christ's references to Gehenna, etc., and our rendering as Hell—Canon Farrar as to the word translated Eternal—As to the Pharisees' use of the word Gehenna—Whether Christ used it metaphorically or actually.

THERE appears to be a mass of evidence, amounting altogether to conviction, that the Christian idea, in a somewhat different form, but approximating to both Protestantism and Roman Catholicism, was revealed to or apprehended by the Hindu inhabitants of the present British India, during a gradual sequence of ideas, extending over many centuries B.C.

The later developments of the idea in India differ from those at present existing in Europe, in proportion as they vary from its earlier promulgations in India. Even in regard to divine punishment, the doctrine of the transmigration of souls, partially accepted amongst early Christians, is combined in India with a conception of purgatorial hells; though not, apparently, of the unending, merciless-seeming hell, which Protestants have ascribed to the necessary justice of the All-merciful God. Our theologians have had to chiefly prove their allegations in respect to this awful, in woe unending future, to which a portion of the human race has been preached and outwardly accredited to have been destined, on Christ's references, in the New Testament, to Gehenna. This was an actual valley near Jerusalem, wherein fires are said to have been constantly burning to consume the corpses of malefactors, etc.; but it is also said to have been applied by the Jews as a synonym for the infernal regions. If thus used figuratively, however, it must have been also used to designate the actual place, and Christ's plain words apply to the actual Gehenna. Better to lose the limb than have the whole body burnt in Gehenna. They have had to assume that, because Dives was said to be in Hades in torment, he was there for a conscious eternity of torture. Our Lord has naturally applied the epithets eternal and unextinguishable to the flames of Gehenna, which are related to have been perpetually burning, and which were likely to be continually in requisition, under their cremation system. Christianity has, therefore, conceived the idea that a body cast into ever-burning flames must be supposed to be constantly burnt in them without being consumed. But the word *αἰωνιον*, which has been translated as eternal, seems, as Canon Farrar has argued, to appear to mean, appertaining to an æon, an age, rather than unlimited time. But, on the other hand, a writer in the "Quarterly Review," in 1878, has argued that there is the word *ἀει* in it, conveying the sense of always. Divine inspiration may have guided preachers of the Word in interpreting Christ's expression to bear the metaphorical signification of a hopeless hell. But He certainly did not say "hell fire," as in our version; while it is doubtful whether he used the word eternal as associated with punishment. If a name may be either employed metaphorically or in regard to the actual place designated, we must, of course, search in the context of the passage for indications of the true meaning. Now, when Christ distinctly depicted the soul of Dives as suffering the torment of flame in hell, He used the classical word Hades. *Primâ facie*, then, His use of the word Gehenna, as coupled with burning in another place, is rather suggestive of the burning in the material flames said to have been constantly, in the ordinary earthly use of the word, burning there. Flames are said to have been continually cremating the bodies, and worms nourishing themselves on the heaps of offal thrown into this defiled valley. It has, however, been argued, in the interests of the doctrine of never-ending punishment, that there is no positive evidence of the valley having been thus used, and that it was simply taken as a metaphor for hell fire, from the old idolatrous sacrificial flames formerly blazing in it. A further metaphorical allusion to awful and unending woe must be acknowledged, therefore, in the introduction of the never-dying worm, though it very naturally applies to the refuse which is cast out in Eastern cities. It certainly appears that we have translated Gehenna as hell because the Pharisees so used the word, according to commentaries upon the schools of Shammai and Hillel. But if Christ is supposed to have employed this metaphor in accordance with their use of it, the eternity is by no means proved, because the schools differed in their views—that of Hillel asserting that, after a time of torture, extinction took place. And the word *αἰωνιον* will again become the test as to whether it signifies for an age or eternity. But, again, it may be urged that it certainly does not appear to be a necessary consequence that any one cast into eternally burning flames must be eternally consumed by them. Moreover, if Christ, like the Jews, used the word Gehenna metaphorically for hell, he may have employed hell itself metaphorically for severe punishment merely. As He distinctly associates the healing of sickness with forgiveness of sins, and does not preach against the prevalent belief in the consequences of sins following in transmigrations of the soul, when the opportunity seems, according to our Holy Writ, to have been afforded Him (St. John ix. 2); we may, with as much propriety, assert that this expression is metaphorical as any other. We must now allow that He did not literally mean that the end of the world was approaching within the lifetimes of some of His disciples, as they conceived from His words. We, in fact, have to explain the Gospels by existing facts; but whether this allusion to Gehenna, the old valley of Hinnom, coupled with the account of the separation of the two classes at the day of judgment, literally teaches the doctrine of eternal woe in a place of punishment, we cannot affirm or deny as a fact. It seems, however, that the assertion that a just Deity creates and condemns His creatures to unending misery, demands more explicit evidence. The ancient doctrine of atonement for sins in the flesh seems certainly prominent in St. Matthew ix. 5, etc.

We have limited the liberalism of Christ's teaching to a third of the more civilised portion of our world's people during the last 1800 years only, and regarded with too much superciliousness those whom we have styled the heathen, though the Greek original of our Testament only terms them the nations (*ἔθνοι*).

CHAPTER XXX.

Our arts and sciences Aryan—The Trinity in Unity only expressed vaguely, if at all, in the Old Testament, or even in the New Testament—Buddhism from India—Krishna and the Cross, as shown in the temple at Mathura—Idea of the Incarnations cannot be entirely posterior to Christ—Sir W. Jones, and story of Krishna—Buddha equivalent to the Logos—Address to Buddha, invoking him as divine—Visits to India of Christians in the second century, etc.

OUR arts and sciences, architecture, literature, and social manners, have undoubtedly descended to us through the two great rivers of Aryan enterprise and civilisation, which we call generically the Classic and Gothic. It would appear that these flowed, not from some fountain in the Bactrian or Caucasian region, but from the watershed of India, supplied by the springs arising from nature's richness in that region. The Semitic origin claimed for our knowledge of the Trinity in Unity of Deity, and of our incarnate Saviour, ought also—while the evidence of ancient literature and existing faiths in the East stands the test of cross-examination—to be referred to this Aryan source. The Trinity in Unity appears vaguely, if at all, in our Old Testament. Even in the New Testament, if the verse 1 John v. 7 be omitted, which is now acknowledged by critical science to be spurious, it is not definitely declared.

In the Buddhism of China, and of the civilisations to the east and north-east of India, we undoubtedly see a religion which originated in India. As a system, it seems to contain much that is in accord with Christianity. As has been remarked, the form of its ecclesiasticism seems as distinctly to resemble that of the Church of Rome as the spiritual products of countries so materially different could possibly resemble one another.

Krishna may have been the actual name of a real ruler, after his death elevated by fervent admirers to the rank of immortal, and finally conceived by the poets as the Almighty on earth. He may have really reigned in Katiawar, and founded a matter-of-fact Dwarka, having taken an important part in the great race or religious wars commemorated in the Mahábhárata.

That the idea of the cross was connected with him seems evidenced by the form of the ancient temple of Mathura, containing a statue of the black Krishna.

It appears generally to have been held impossible by the students of Indian subjects to relegate the whole idea of Krishna and the incarnations to a later period than the time of Christ. Sir W. Jones, whose absolute faith in Christianity was never shaken by his Sanskrit studies, while agreeing with this, thought that the legends of Krishna had received many additions from the West.

With seeming inconsistency he held that these additions were from false as well as true accounts of Christ; though if they are to be considered as invented, surely India, in the course of ages, would be more likely to have invented them than Palestine immediately after the close of the Saviour's career. That ancient stories, related as facts in a distant region, should be ascribed to a real personage of the country in which they reappear, is not by any means contrary to our experience. How many sayings, and even doings, have been imputed to great generals and celebrated wits, etc., in the time of our fathers, and continued to be ascribed to them notwithstanding their own repudiation! These sayings have been sometimes exaggerations or misstatements of their own words; sometimes utterances of others. They certainly demonstrate the ease with which any old legend may be fastened on a new hero. For instance, J. W. Cole, in the "Life and Times of Charles Kean," asserts that he has seen an earlier version of the story attributed to Liston—"Go and see Liston," said an eminent physician to a patient who consulted him as to the best cure for low spirits. "Alas! I am the man," replied the sufferer in a despairing tone. He relates that he has seen it recorded of a celebrated French comedian, who flourished more than a century ago.

Sir W. Jones observed—"That the name of Chrishna and the general outline of his story were long anterior to the birth of our Saviour, and probably to the time of Homer, we know very certainly; yet the celebrated poem called Bhagavat, which contains a prolix account of his life, is filled with narratives of a most extraordinary kind, but strangely variegated and mixed with poetical decorations. The incarnate deity of Sanskrit romance was cradled, as it informs us, amongst herdsmen; but it adds that he was educated amongst them, and passed his youth in playing with a party of milkmaids; a tyrant at the time of his birth ordered all new-born males to be slain, yet this wonderful babe was preserved by biting the breast instead of sucking the poisoned nipple of a nurse commissioned to kill him; he performed amazing but ridiculous miracles in his infancy, and, at the age of seven years, held up a mountain on the tip of his little finger; he saved multitudes, partly by his arms, and partly by his miraculous powers; he raised the dead, by descending for that purpose to the lowest regions; he was the meekest and best-tempered of beings, washed the feet of the Brahmins, and preached very nobly indeed and sublimely, but always in their favour; he was pure and chaste in reality, but exhibited an appearance of excessive libertinism, and had wives and mistresses too numerous to be counted; lastly, he was benevolent and tender, yet fomented and conducted a terrible war. This motley story must induce an opinion that the spurious Gospels which abounded in the first age of Christianity had been brought to India, and the wildest parts of them repeated to the Hindus, who engrafted on them the old fable of Cesava, the Apollo of Greece." Sir W. Jones also remarked that, "The Hindus say that the Deity has appeared innumerable times in many parts of this world and of all worlds for the salvation of his creatures; and though we adore him in one appearance and they in others, yet we adore the same God, to whom our several worships, though different in form, are equally acceptable if they be sincere in substance."

The following description of the poetical Dwarka, Krishna's city, in the Mahábhárata, recalls the heavenly city of the "Revelation of St. John:"—its "walls and pavements glittered with gold, silver, and precious stones; its ramparts were formed of solid gold, and the houses of pure crystal. Vessels of gold adorned the portals of every mansion. The bazaars were decked with splendid stalls; the gardens were shaded with trees of Paradise, and refreshed with the waters of immortality. A multitude of temples raised their towering summits, and the smoke of incense from the altars perfumed the air."

Buddha, or Wisdom, another equivalent really to the Logos, the Reason or Word, seems to have been venerated under an aspect little less consonant with Christianity than the religion of Krishna. In later times, and perhaps from the earlier, Buddhism, like Christianity, has considerably diverged in different countries. The accounts of its line of Buddhas to Gautauma, or Sakya muni, the seventh "Buddha," of the sixth century B.C., or earlier according to Indian accounts, are embellished by various legends. Like the classic Mercury, who was the child of Jupiter and Maia, the mother of Gautauma Buddha was Maia, or Mahā-māyā, spouse of Souta-dama, king of Megaddha, and of the family of Sākya-Sakia. The names of his parents are allegorical, and the appellation of his birthplace may apply to a school of philosophy. H. Thsang, the Chinese pilgrim, when he visited the spots sacred to him, is supposed to have attested his actual birthplace. But in India then, as in Europe now, there seems reasonable probability that legendary saint lore was founded upon pious faith rather than absolutely reliable tradition. The belief of devotees has consecrated with certainty sacred places to the memory of saintly deeds, or miracles which cannot but seem apocryphal to those not numbered amongst the faithful. Till a conventual society recently restored the ruins, a victory of St. Dunstan's over the devil was evidenced by the exhibition at Mayfield in Sussex of the actual tongs with which he had seized the evil one's nose.

The Buddha, or Enlightened, is supposed by some of his votaries to have been conceived without defilement, and born at the foot of a tree. Godfrey Higgins quotes Mons. De Guignes, who, in his "Histoire des Huns," remarks that Fo, or Buddha, was said to have been brought forth from the right side of a virgin, whom a ray of light had visited. The Manichæans held that this was the case with Jesus Christ.

The mother of Buddha seems to be reverenced in China as the Queen of Heaven, and represented above the altars of the Buddhistic temples in similitude of the representations of the Blessed Virgin in Catholic chapels. The prophets and wise men recognised in him the divine, and hailed him as such. Shocked at the miseries which he witnessed in the world, he quitted throne and wife, and abandoned himself to a life of asceticism and teaching; and he endured a temptation in the desert before "declaring the true faith." He was thus addressed in India, where he has been admitted, though not universally, to be an incarnation of Vishnu:—"Thou art the Lord of all things, the deity that overcomest the sins of the Kali Yug" (black or iron age), "the guardian of the universe, the emblem of mercy towards those that serve thee; Om" (a sacred syllable expressive of reverence to the Godhead, to the "I am," somewhat, perhaps, corresponding to our Amen), "the possessor of all things in vital form. Thou art Brahma, Vishnu, and Mahesa; thou art the Lord of the universe; thou art the proper form of all things, movable and immovable; the possessor of the whole; and thus I adore thee. Reverence be unto thee, the bestower of salvation. I adore thee, who art celebrated by a thousand names, and under various forms, in the shape of Buddha, the God of mercy. Be propitious, O most high God."

There is as much room for Brahminism, Buddhism, and faith in the divine Krishna, and in adoring God as Siva, to have co-existed in India at about the time of Christ, as for Roman Catholicism, Lutheranism, Calvinism, and the Anglican and Greek Churches in Europe in the present day.

But notwithstanding the evidence of the existence of these Christian-like ideas in India before the time of Christ, it is not impossible that, in the flux and reflux of thought between East and West, the divine mission of our Lord in Palestine may have produced effects in India. The actual story of His passion, to which in Europe legends from Krishna and Buddha had been added, may have been brought to India, and there adopted and absorbed into their own faiths; for an Indian story is given in the next chapter, which exhibits strange fanciful similitudes to that of the Crucifixion. There appears, at all events, to be no doubt that there were Christian converts in India in the early ages of the Church; though the spread of Christianity there, or the infusion of Christian ideas in the actual age of the Apostles, seems somewhat apocryphal.

Pantænus of Alexandria visited India in A.D. 189, and found St. Matthew's Gospel there. Frumentius, the apostle of

Abyssinia, preached in India within a century or so afterwards; and an Indian primate attended at the Council of Nice A.D. 325, says Wilford; and St. Jerome, in A.D. 420, spoke of St. Thomas' mission to India. Dr. Burton, however, in his "Church History," doubts whether the India of Pantænus is not rather Arabia.

CHAPTER XXXI.

Professor Max Müller's remarks on Wilford—Extracts from Wilford in "Asiatic Researches"—Bible stories in the Sanskrit—Story of Salivahana, or the Crossborne, and of the Brahmin Mand'avyah and his crucifixion.

PROFESSOR MAX MÜLLER, in his "Science of Religion," has discredited Colonel Wilford, who has given us the story, to which allusion has been made in the last chapter, as affording similitudes to the Crucifixion; and which caused Wilford to believe that Christianity had been adopted, in that story, in India. At the commencement of this century, he wrote some very remarkable and very learned, but perhaps, very fanciful essays in the "Asiatic Researches." Professor Max Müller has alluded to certain impositions practised upon him by his Brahman pundit; to which Wilford confesses in vol. viii. of the "Asiatic Researches." Finding that he was anxious to discover legends in India bearing a similarity to our Bible stories, the Brahman interpolated, into Sanskrit MSS., leaves on which biblical stories had been imitated. But Wilford, in a subsequent number of the "Asiatic Researches," apologised for having published these fraudulent writings, and explained the whole matter. And he says that "many of the legends were very correct, except that the name of the country was altered to Egypt or Sweetam." In fact, he asserts that the general character of certain conclusions which he was drawing respecting the existence of biblical narratives in Hindustan was not impaired by these impositions. For instance, he affirms that Noah's history and that of his sons is found in other Puranas than that to which the forgery attributed it. In Canton is to be seen Noah's temple, in which are represented the man, his three sons and their three wives, who were saved from the flood. In this temple are also said to be three figures representing the great God of heaven. These would seem to indicate a passage from India with Buddhism. Whether the Indians took their stories from the Israelites, or whether Moses, according to the relation in the Bible that he was learned in all the wisdom of the Egyptians, adopted Egyptian narratives, which, according to the evidence, were similar to the Indian, is open to question. It would certainly appear more reasonable to suppose that they were produced in a country like India, with a population corresponding to that of Europe, rather than amongst the inhabitants of a territory such as Egypt, which is not likely to have had more than 7,000,000 of inhabitants at any time, as has been observed, and with attributes rather calculated to circumscribe and intensify than to open the imagination. Wilford, in an essay published in the "Asiatic Researches," subsequently to the confession of this Brahminical fraud, and when, therefore, he was likely to have been rendered cautious, produces Indian legends, remarkable in analogy with portions of our Canonical Gospels, and also with passages in the rejected Apocryphal Gospels of Christianity. These legends induced him to believe that they demonstrated the introduction of our religion into India in its apostolic period. It is indubitably remarkable that the two eras in use in India—viz. that of Vicramaditya (Samvat) in the north, and that of Salivahana (Saca) in the south—should nearly coincide with the Christian era. The former commences fifty-six years before our era, and the latter seventy-nine years after it. A continuance of the coincidence exists in the period of the employment of the Sáka era in India. This has been ascribed to about the year 676 A.D.; which date nearly corresponds to the period at which the Christian era began to be adopted in Europe—viz. during the sixth century. Dionysius, a monk of Scythia, and a Roman abbot, first used it about the year 527 A.D. The first recorded instance of its employment in England is in the year 680 A.D. Now it is of this Salivahana, monarch of the Deccan, that is to say the Dakshina, or south of India, that these stories quoted by Wilford, and strangely suggestive of incidents attributed to Christ, are related. His epoch is really contemporaneous with that of Christ, because the one commences from the birth, the other from the death of the founder; and Salivahana lived to the age of eighty-four.

If it can be demonstrated that the employment of the

Christian era in Europe preceded that of Salivahana in India, it would seem reasonable to argue that the story of Christ likewise preceded that of Salivahana in India itself. Christ would, in that case, seem actually to be revered there, though under misapprehensions of His appellation and the locality of His manifestation. The story and the adoption of the era would follow in a natural sequence of Indian importations. Professor Weber, however, states that the astronomer Varáha-Mihira uses the Sáka era, and that he flourished in 504 A.D., or between that and 587 A.D., according to an Indian scholiast. Another astronomer, Brahmagupta, whose date appears to be about the year 664 A.D., reckons by the era of Salivahana, dating it from the year 3179 of the Kali age, and seeming to infer a positive recognition of his story as of occurrence in India.

"According to the Padma and Ganesa Puranas," wrote Colonel Wilford, "a wonderful child was to manifest himself to the world when 3100 years of the Kaliyug had expired, and he was to remove misery from the world, and become 'Saca' the mighty, glorious king."

Wilford appears to have considered the Puranas, in their present form, posterior to our era, though he supposed legends and materials in them to have existed previously. Although he admitted that the idea of the incarnate Deity was known in India before the time of Christ, he seems to have believed this later incarnation in Salivahana to have been suggested by our Gospels; and that an Indian colouring, in the lapse of time, had been imparted to what was in truth Christianity, largely diffused in India.

"In the appendix to the Agni Purana," says Wilford, "it is declared that in the holy and consecrated city of Pratishtana, called Saileya-d'hára, or Saileyam (Salem), firmly seated on a rock, through the mercy of Siva, would appear Salivahana great and mighty, the spirit of righteousness and justice, whose words would be truth itself, free from spite and envy, and whose empire would extend over all the world (or, in other words, that the people would be gathered unto him, the conveyer of souls to places of eternal bliss). A chorus of angels worshipped his mother at his birth, and showers of flowers fell from on high. A miraculous star directed holy men where to find the heavenly child."

It was declared in the Vicrama Charita that the birth of a divine child from a virgin had been foretold 1000 years before it happened.

At the age of five he stood before a most respectable assemblage of doctors of the land, and explained several difficult cases to their admiration or astonishment.

The great Vicramaditya, emperor of India, uneasy at prophecies which he conceived to portend his ruin, and the loss of his empire, sent emissaries to make inquiries respecting him in a year corresponding to the first of the Christian era. He then proceeded, at the head of an army, to destroy the child in his fifth year. Salivahana was the son of a tacshaca or carpenter, but brought up in the house of a potmaker, who used to construct clay figures for the child's amusement. On the approach of Vicramaditya, the child Salivahana endowed with life these clay figures, and formed them into an army. At the head of this supernatural force he defeated the army of Vicramaditya, and cut off the head of the monarch, first granting to him the privilege of retaining his era, which was to be concurrent with his own.

The father of Salivahana, though a carpenter, appears to have been a Brahmin. According to one more mystic account, he was the great carpenter, chief of the tacshacas, a serpentine tribe famous in the Puranas. After his death the mother became pregnant, and, as her brother disowned her, she found refuge in the potmaker's hut. "Salivahana, under the name of Vi-sama-sila, with the triple energy—*i.e.* regarded as an incarnation of Brahma, Siva, and Vishnu—became king of heaven, earth, and hell; all spirits, good and bad, obeyed his orders, his mission, indeed, being the destruction of the demons; his resplendence was like that of the sun, and his fame reached the White Island in the White Sea." He lived eighty-four years, and is supposed not to have died but to have been translated to heaven, disappearing in the year 79 A.D., the first of his era, after having retired for many years into the desert to give himself up to heavenly contemplation. He did not marry, being a mysterious and supernatural being. He is also regarded as a form of Jina or Buddha; Christians being considered as Buddhists, in many parts of India, Wilford remarked.

According to one account, Salivahana, or a king corresponding to him, appears to have been crucified and brought to life again. 145 years after the accession of Vicramaditya to the throne there appeared King Aryya, who was before prime minister of King Jaya Indra, and whose name signifies the lord of victory, or of victorious hosts. It was decreed that he should be wretched and persecuted all his lifetime, and ultimately that he should die upon a cross, and that he would be brought to life again through the assistance of a Phani Canya, or damsel of the Serpentine tribe, and then become a great and powerful monarch. The king, having been deceived by his enemies, threw Sandhi-mati, for such was the name of his prime minister, into a loathsome dungeon. But his enemies were not satisfied, and they informed the king that Saraswati, divine wisdom, or, collectively, those endowed with divine wisdom, had declared that he would be a king. Jaya Indra ordered him immediately to be crucified. He remained on the cross till his flesh dropped off, or was torn off by wild beasts. A certain holy man passed by, and reading his destiny in the Brahmanda, or in his skull, immediately resolved to bring him to life again. For this purpose he performed the pújá (worship), and, after the usual ceremonies and invocations, he rang the bell and was surrounded by a fiery meteor, which announced the presence of the Yoginis, or forms of Devi. Then, arming himself with a scimitar, as usual on such appearances, he proceeded to the forest, where the prime minister had been hung upon the cross. He was forthwith environed by the Yoginis, one of whom, the before-mentioned damsel, arranged the bones together, and the crucified one stood upon his legs; and afterwards ascended the throne, being called, on account of his transcendent virtues, Arya Raja, or the Good King. Having governed righteously for a time, he abandoned his kingdom and the world for an ascetic life.

Sālivāhana, says Wilford, signifies the stake or cross borne, sula or suli meaning a stake, gibbet, or cross; and crucifying being applied to either impaling or extending the arms upon a cross bar. He professed to have submitted the MSS., which he had examined, and from which he had produced these narrations, to the criticism of Sir William Jones, who had pronounced them genuine. Professor Monier Williams, in his "Sanskrit Dictionary," says of Salivahana, that this celebrated monarch is represented as borne on a cross, made of the *Sal* tree or other wood. The word *sûla*, from which Wilford derived the name, with *vah*, to bear, and which has the meaning of a stake for impaling criminals, seems a likely derivation.

According to a story, wrote Wilford, in the Mahábhárata and in the Sadhyádri-Chandra and Scanda Puranas, there appeared in the Deccan a most holy Brahmin, of those called Peishecaras, Tacshacas, or handicraftsmen, whose name was Mandávyah. He proclaimed that he came for the sole purpose of relieving the distressed, and that whatever men claimed his protection, he would readily grant it to them, and even lay down his life for them. Very many of all descriptions came accordingly, and among them a thief, who, being pursued by the officers of justice, claimed his protection, which he readily granted, and was crucified in his place. He then ascended into heaven and took the thief with him. Other relations say that a numerous banditti had taken shelter near the holy man, thinking themselves safe, but the officers of justice arrived, and they were immediately seized and crucified. The holy man was supposed to be a thief, numbered amongst them, and crucified also. He did not open his mouth, but remained absorbed in holy contemplation, inwardly repeating sacred names, with his arms extended and uplifted. Whilst on the cross, the Rishis crowded from all parts of the world, in the shape of birds, to see him and comfort him. A certain thief, who was also covered with leprosy, and, in consequence of it deprived of the use of his limbs, was accidentally dropped at the foot of the cross, wrapped up like a child in his swaddling clothes. This man, after remaining some time, and being divinely irradiated, repented, lived to a good old age, and obtained eternal bliss. A thick darkness overspread the face of the world, and the animated creation was in the greatest distress and consternation. The holy man, being afterwards taken down from the cross, descended into hell, and there encountered and overcame Yama, or Death. Then a general renovation of the world took place under the inspection of Brahma. The holy man, from his having been crucified, was afterwards called Sulastha, or the Cross-borne, which is synonymous with Salivahana.

Wilford further observed that, "if we prefix to this

abstract the legends concerning the infancy of Salivahana, and the era of his manifestation, we shall have the principal circumstances in the life of our Saviour, either from the true or Apocryphal Gospels."

It was decreed that iron should pierce the body of Mandávyah, as well as that of Krishna, because both were accused though guiltless.

The reason alleged for the crucifixion, according to the conception of deeds necessarily producing their consequences, was that the Muni, when an infant, had pierced an insect with a blade of grass. But the Muni, or Rishi, complained that his rigorous repentance, and ascetic severities, ought to have been sufficient penalty, and for unjustly producing the death of a Brahmin, he had power to drive Yama, the monarch of death, out of hell, and, for his injustice, compel him to become incarnate upon the earth for 100 years.

Wilford undoubtedly seems to have believed that, "although they were not the productions of 'crafty Brahmins' of our own time, the originals of these stories were to be found in Palestine, based upon the Gospel narratives; and upon the Apocryphal Gospel of the infancy of Jesus. This Apocryphal Gospel is said to have been received by the Gnostics in the second century; and to have been credited in respect to several of its relations by Eusebius, Athanasius, and other eminent Christians of the early days of the Church.

CHAPTER XXXII.

Accounts of Megasthenes—Colebrooke on the scientific attainments of the inhabitants of ancient India—Hindu astronomy—Considerations as to the antiquity asserted for the Brahminical observations—Signs of the Indian zodiac almost identical with our own—Geometry known to the Indians—Sir R. Phillips on the cultivation of astronomy in India, Egypt, etc.—Trigonometry among the the Hindus, and their knowledge that the earth was spherical, etc.—Observations of the Chinese—Alphabetical writing and playing cards in India.

MEGASTHENES, ambassador of Seleucus at the court of Chandragupta, at Palibothra, in the epoch succeeding the invasion of Alexander the Great, records that the army of Chandragupta consisted of 600,000 infantry, 30,000 cavalry, and 9000 elephants; that the system of the internal government of the country was admirable; that agriculture was fostered; and that the police had orders to provide for the entertainment of strangers and foreigners. He praises the truthfulness, uprightness, honesty, and respect for age, shown amongst the people. Palibothra, Chandragupta's capital, is described as being eight miles in length, and surrounded by walls with 64 gates and 500 towers. And the grandeur and civilisation of his state appears, from the general testimony which bears upon the condition of the Madhyama, and from the tenor of the observations of Megasthenes, to have been of no mushroom growth.

At this period, although the grandeur of Athens was past, the magnificence of Imperial Rome had not yet arisen; while the British Islands were little known to the great civilisations of the world.

In regard to the scientific attainments of the inhabitants of ancient India at a remote period, they had noted the changes in the heavens, eclipses, etc. Colebrooke considered that this people had approximated more closely than Ptolemy to a knowledge of the precession of the equinoxes; and that they had observed the sun and moon with success. Even Bentley, who alleged the Indians to have devised an ingenious system of back calculations, to account for the length of their astronomical periods, allowed that Parasara "by the position of the colures recorded by him lived about 1200 B.C.;" and he considered that their earliest historical period might be held to commence from 2200 B.C. Pritchard has also remarked that "Parasara's work, in the opinion of Mr. Davis, preserves a true account of the solstitial colures in his time, and it was by calculating backwards from this period that the Hindus constructed their hypothetical system, which was long represented to the world as a series of real observations handed down from periods of vast antiquity." Bailly, however, believed Indian astronomy to be founded on observations made 3102 B.C. And in these days, when geology has caused science to take a more extended estimate of the duration both of human and lower life upon our globe than theology has adopted, it seems more reasonable to suppose that observations, allowed by modern astronomy to be applicable to a certain date, should have been really made at that date, unless disconsonant with admitted scientific facts, rather than that they should have been most ingeniously calculated backwards into mythical ages. At all events they must have had extended practice before accomplishing these calculations. Why should the Brahmins, more than other people, have been desirous of asserting for themselves an unreal antiquity? Why should they have supposed that imaginary rather than actual periods gave them more power amongst their own people, or procured for them more respect amongst strangers? On the contrary, they would have been more respected by the English if they had merely produced compact astronomical and other statements in subservience to our own. Surely, moreover, a method of back calculations, if not demonstrated to be utterly nonsensical, must involve exceedingly elaborate scientific processes. But the Brahmins seem to have seen nothing incongruous or absurd in asserting millions of years for the duration of human life in the world of an eternal Spirit. And this may at least show that they had traditional accounts extending to thousands of years. It is curious that they should have undertaken such elaborate hypothetical works.

They had a lunar and mathematical zodiac, and their signs of the zodiac are almost identical with our own, and have been specified in Sanskrit verses. The Ram, Bull, Crab, Lion, and Scorpion are represented by the figures of those five animals respectively. Then the "Pair" are a damsel playing on a vina and a youth wielding a mace. The "Virgin" stands in a boat on water, holding in one hand a lamp and in the other an ear of rice corn. The "Balance" is held by the weigher with the weight in one hand; the bow by an archer whose hinder parts are like a horse. The "Monster" has the face of an antelope. The "Ewer" is a water-pot borne on the shoulders of a man who empties it. The "Fish" are two, with their heads turned to each others' tails.

A certain date is implied by the position of the solstitial points mentioned in a little treatise called the Gyotisha, a date which has been accurately fixed by the Rev. R. Main at 1186 B.C., says Mr. Max Müller.

The Indians divided the circumference of the circle into 360 equal parts, which the Greeks and ourselves have followed. Geometry must have been known to them long before the inditing of their first astronomical treatise, the Surya Sirdhanta, which has been variously ascribed by European critics to periods from 3000 B.C. to the tenth century A.D., but the Brahmins have asserted it to be a divine revelation of 2,164,899 years ago.

Sir Richard Phillips, in his "Facts," observes that "Bailly maintains, from Oriental records, that astronomy was cultivated in Egypt and Chaldea 2800 B.C.; in Persia 3209; in India, 3101; and in China 2952;" that the Indian observations display a perfection of science, of instruments, and of various knowledge, which indicate ages of preparation. He notices that "Indian tables of great antiquity make the tropical year within 1′ 53″ of our best tables (1836 A.D.) Other tables, equally accurate, appear to Bailly, Playfair, and other authorities, to have been constructed 3102 B.C. One of their zodiacs places Aldebaran 40′ before the vernal equinox; which carries it back to 3163 B.C. Other coincidences are astonishing, and prove the length of their observations and the perfection of their instruments. Thus the place of the sun agrees with our best tables within 46′ 54″, and the moon within 37′, yet our tables include various minute anomalies of recent discovery. Their places, etc., of the planets equally agree in the most minute particulars." "The earliest Hindus practised trigonometry and sexagesimal arithmetic. They taught that the earth was spherical, turned on its axis, etc., took latitudes and longitudes, knew the diameter of the earth to be 1600 yojanas, and the moon's distance 51,370, or 32 diameters. In one *yug* they say the Sun, Mercury, and Venus, make 4,320,000 revolutions. They called the Sun *Surya*, Mercury *Budha*, Venus *Sucra*, Mars *Mangala*, Jupiter *Vrihaspati*, Saturn *Sani*, Moon *Chandra*. It certainly seems extraordinary that the Brahmins should have entertained the fancy of evidencing the antiquity of astronomical science, or of illustrating their systems of *yugs*, by laboriously making backward calculations. But, however that may be, it seems clear that their scientific attainments possessed practical value at the time of Moses. According to the Chinese *Shooking*, the periods of the plancts, the Sun and Moon, were well known in the reign of Yao, 2357 B.C. These astronomical observations, therefore, on seemingly valid evidence, introduce us to a scientific civilisation about 3000 years B.C., which must itself have been ancient, unless we conceive these scientific acquisitions to have been obtained by divine revelation.

Playing cards are said to have been introduced into Europe in the fourteenth century of our era. In India they appear to have existed under antique forms at an earlier period, and, from the elaborate and highly emblematic devices on them, taken from the incarnations of Vishnu, etc., to have been there devised.

The origin of alphabetical writing in India seems to disappear into the dim vista of the remote literary commencement. Our European alphabets have been considered to have been derived from the Semitic. On the opposite side of the Madhyama the Chinese possess a system of their own. The Sanskrit alphabet, styled the Devanagari, with its one hundred letters, has been ascribed to imitation of the combined ancient alphabets of the civilisations to the west. As in architecture, art, etc., our Indian cousins have, in this respect also, been held to be copyists. Yet it is strange that our inventive Indo-European Race should have been less able to devise this method of reducing symbolisations of words to convenient compass than the Semitic, which, in other respects, has certainly not displayed superiority in inventive genius. The region of the greatest archaic literary promulgations, taking into consideration Vedas, Vedāntas, Epics, etc., can scarcely be reasonably held to have been urged to these intellectual efforts by an importation from people of smaller literary capacity. Suggestions for letters cannot be discerned in the physical aspect of India as for architectural embellishments. But the people who refine a language and produce extensive literary works in it, and who are recognised as appertaining to the most progressive of the races of the world—who exhibit unquestioned inventive faculties—may be surely supposed capable of inventing an alphabet which we find in use amongst them. Indeed the copiousness of the Devanagari appears to correspond with the dimensions of the Ramáyana and Mahábhárata poems, etc.

Professor Max Müller has said, "To admit, however, the independent invention of a native Indian alphabet is impossible. Alphabets were formed gradually, and purely phonetic alphabets always point back to earlier syllabic or ideographic stages. There are no such traces of the growth of an alphabet on Indian soil." If the remoteness of the scientific Indian civilisation be admitted from the evidences, it may appear reasonable to suppose that the earlier syllabic stages are lost in antiquity, as he allows that the "second Indian alphabet has not been satisfactorily traced to a Semitic prototype." The ancient Indians may have gone through the natural process of forming an alphabet before the Semitic people, and its early stages may have been reflected in western Asia as they progressed. When such comparatively advanced scientific attainments have to be attributed to the eastern Aryans, and when amidst a mass of literature they possess such poems as the Ramáyana and Mahábhárata, even allowing these to be the productions of several authors, one may be excused for being inclined to consider that they must have felt a natural longing for some means of recording their ideas. Their imaginations seem to have been most prolific, and it can hardly be supposed that they remained entirely contented with their system of learning by rote. And if the Institutes of Manu, in their present form, may be referred to about the ninth century B.C., the allusions to reading in them seem distinct, and indicative of settled acquaintance with the art.[1] The word devanagari seems to suggest a divine, and therefore autochthonous, rather than foreign origin.

[1] See Appendix IV.

CHAPTER XXXIII.

Sir R. Phillips on the Phœnician alphabet, etc.—Pickering's remark as to the existence of toleration only in India—The maxim of No history, no war, applied to India—Ourselves and the Mohammedans and Rajpoots in India—Buddhism not shown to be driven forth by wars from India—Sketch of battles with the Mohammedan invaders—Mahmoud and the idols—Brahmins and warriors—Heraldry in India—Arrian upon the Indian valour—Sir J. Malcolm as to Indian originality in stories.

SIR R. PHILLIPS observes amongst his "Facts" that "Taautus or Thoth, the Phœnician, called Hermes or Mercury, is believed only to have modified the older Sanskrit Alphabet, which was brought from the East by the commercial Phœnicians;" that the Sanskrit is probably the parent of most of the Oriental alphabets, even of the Greek; and that "Sanskrit, the basis of Hindoo learning, is said in the East to be the first character;" that "Cadmus the Phœnician introduced the first Greek alphabet into Bœotia, where he settled B.C. 1500; though Diodorus says the Pelasgian letters were prior to the Cadmean. But it is evident that the Cadmean and Pelasgic and Phœnician had the same origin. The Irish alphabet is the Phœnician. Scaliger supposes the Phœnician to have been the original Hebrew character, otherwise the Samaritan, and it is generally supposed to be that which was used by the Jews from the time of Moses to the Captivity."

On almost all topics, both speculative and practical, there appear to exist voluminous essays in the Sanskrit. In history, indeed, it seems to contain little systematic work, or few accounts which can be considered to convey what may be called real historical information, probably because the life of India rolled along for ages with few exceptionally eventful periods to incite historians. Pickering remarked that it would seem that amid the violence with which the earth has been filled, toleration has existed only in India.

The maxim that the country is happy which has no history, because it will indicate that it has had no war, has certainly not been duly applied to India. From the mythological campaign of Rama, and the more realistic-seeming wars of the Mahábhárata, placed by English critics at about 1500 B.C., but by the natives at 3000 B.C.; that is to say, from at least about 1500 B.C. to 1000 A.D., the period of some 2500 years, the inhabitants of Hindustan seem to have been little harassed by wars or invasions. There is related to have been a Persian invasion, which caused some portion of the north-west to become tributary for a time. There was the invasion of Alexander the Great, which was successfully repelled. There may have been wars between north and south, as recorded in the legends of Vicramaditya and Salivahana; and there were other wars and gallant warriors amongst the feudal chieftains and chivalry of Rajpootana; but, as compared with Europe, either in classic, mediæval, or modern times, India seems to have enjoyed by far the larger measure of tranquillity during this comparatively long period. At all events, according to Ferishta's history, the wars were rare in comparison with those of Europe. And the warriors ostensibly were confined to a caste.

We found India partially subdued by the Mohammedans, and still contending for liberty against them. The Rajpoots, whom they had never positively subdued, and the recently risen nation of the Mahrattas, had, towards the close of the eighteenth century, even so far recovered the reverses of the Indian Fatherland as to have secured the Great Mogul, the Emperor of Delhi, in their power. Then the English aided the Mohammedans, and, in a series of wars extending from about 1770 till as recent a date as 1844, gradually lessened the powers of the Rajpoots and Mahrattas, till, for the present, they seem to be virtually extinguished by the British proclamation of empire over the whole land.

It has been asserted that Buddhism was driven from India by a series of wars instigated by the Brahmins. But the evidence for this statement appears merely to have been that the Chevalier Bunsen "surmised" that the Buddhists might have been expelled by war. It might seem that Brahmins and Buddhists in India must have attempted to decide their speculative differences by the sword, like Roman Catholics and Protestants in Europe in the Thirty Years' War of the seventeenth century, etc. But Mr. R. Mitra says that Indian literature has in vain been searched for any indication of such religious wars, between the sixth and tenth centuries of our era, when Buddhism appears to have departed from India, or to have become merged in the existing religions. And the evidence of temples and inscriptions, and the Memoirs of the Chinese traveller, seem to show the two systems abiding side by side, with immunity from warfare as complete as that enjoyed by Protestantism and Roman Catholicism in England in our own day.

Since the tenth century A.D., Patans, Moguls, Portuguese, French, and English, have successively invaded, and partially or completely overcome, the country; but the old Aryavarta fought nobly for its independence, and, if it be dead, died hard.

When Sultan Mahmoud invaded it in 1004 A.D., Jeipal, the Rajah of Lahore, was not vanquished till he was taken prisoner and 5000 of his troops lay dead upon the field. He was afterwards ransomed, and released by the conqueror; but the Mohammedan historian, Ferishta, informs us that "it was in those ages a custom of the Hindus that whatever Rajah was twice worsted by the Mussulman should be, by that disgrace, rendered unfit for further command. Jeipal, in compliance with this custom, having raised his son to the government, ordered a funeral pile to be prepared, upon which he sacrificed himself to the gods."

The Rajah Bachera opposed Mahmoud for four days, and, after immense slaughter on both sides, he turned his sword against his own breast, when just upon the point of being taken prisoner. A fort near Muttra, in the Agra province, garrisoned by Rajpoots, held out for twenty-five days against the assaults of Mahmoud's army. When they found the place no longer tenable, they rushed through the breaches against the enemy, flung themselves from the walls, or burnt themselves in their houses with their wives and children, so that not one of the garrison survived the catastrophe.

In the province of Gundwana a queen, celebrated for her beauty and accomplishments, reigned over a flourishing and peaceful country, stated to have been 300 miles in length by

100 in breadth, and to have contained 70,000 towns and villages. Having repulsed the Mohammedans in a first battle, in which she had encountered them with a powerful army, including 1500 elephants, she was wounded in a second engagement. Finding that the day was lost, and that she must be taken prisoner, she plunged her dagger into her bosom. The garrison of the royal fort slew themselves, with their wives and children, in preference to falling into the hands of the enemy.

At Muttra Mahmoud broke down the idols, and amassed a vast amount of gold and silver, of which materials they were mostly made. Ferishta says that he intended to destroy the temples, but found that the labour exceeded his capacity; "while some say that he was turned from his purpose by the admirable beauty and structure of those edifices." Military oligarchies, and even republics, appear to have existed amongst the Rajpoots and Sikhs at the epoch of Alexander's invasion. The germs of both the Grecian warlike republican oligarchies, as they may be styled, and of the Gothic feudal institutions, seem to have veritably fecundated, if not advanced to maturity, amongst these people. The village communistic system undoubtedly seems in India for ages to have forestalled modern visions of equalised land settlements. But the executive authority, or perhaps, more correctly speaking, the divine right of the sovereign, appears to have been supported by the authority, and under the spiritual guidance, of the Brahmins generally throughout India, conjointly with the existence of the communisms in land. In the time of Alexander, the Brahmins, priests, and warriors, had cities of their own, like the Levites in Israel. These they defended bravely; for a Brahmin, like a Roman Catholic bishop of mediæval days, was not interdicted from using carnal weapons under certain circumstances. And any warrior is held to perform a sacred duty in combating for a just cause. In the Institutes of Manu it is declared that "by a soldier slain in his duty, with brandished weapons, the highest sacrifice is complete." Krishna, when his friend Arjouna expresses compunction at engaging in the slaughter of the army before him, tells him that it is his duty to fight, as belonging to the warrior caste. Buddhism, while abrogating the superior sanctity of the Brahminical caste, does not seem to have interfered with either the land tenure or the kingly office.

Heraldry is found in India, and the lion and eagle appear to have been emblazoned upon the standards of the warriors of the old "noble land," before they were assumed by England and the Powers of Europe. The castle-crowned hills of Rajpootana, fastnesses of the old Rajpoots, recall to the modern traveller the castled crags of the Rhine. The chain-mail of their warrior possessors seems to have been the original form of that worn by our western chivalry at the time of the crusades.

If we take into consideration the allusions in the Institutes of Manu, the Ramáyana, etc., we must altogether admit that the types of almost all the devices of our European mediæval civilisation have been discovered in India, in archaic form.

According to Arrian, Porus, the Maharajah of western India, brought into the field to oppose Alexander 4000 horse, 300 chariots, 200 elephants, and nearly 30,000 foot. Testimony is borne by Arrian to the warlike prowess of the people of the Punjaub, though defeated. He describes them as strong-built and large-limbed. "Even those warlike Persians," he says, "by whose valour Cyrus, the son of Cambyses, deprived the Medes of the empire of Asia, and brought many other nations under subjection, partly by force and partly by voluntary surrender, are by no means to be compared with these Indians."

In regard to Indian originality, as appearing in familiar stories, Sir J. Malcolm says, in his "Sketches of Persia," that "the tales of Boccaccio, etc., which have delighted Europe, and the story of the Jew in the Merchant of Venice, etc., are Mohammedan and Persian, Europe having obtained them through the Saracens; but the Persians have been discovered to have pilfered them from the Hindus, for they are found in Sanskrit, Prakrit, Marhatta, Canarese, Tamil, etc. Almost all ancient tales are taken from the Hitopadêsa and Panchatantra, or five stories, or from the Kathâsaritsagar, or ocean of the stream of narration, compiled about the twelfth century A.D." He remarks that "the warmth of the climate of the East, the ever-teeming abundance of the earth, fosters lively imaginations and strong passions." Many of the Arabian Nights' stories are found to be of Hindu origin; and even our familiar fables.

Æsop may have become acquainted with them during the travels which he is related to have taken into Egypt.

Indubitably, in the ordinary outward aspect of life the Greeks of Alexander's time must, at the least, have been less removed from the Hindus than ourselves. In fact Megasthenes does not appear to have been struck by any great dissimilarity in the outward fashions of the ordinary Greek and Indian life. Proceeding to India from our more northern climate, and under our present civilisation, Indian manners and customs present continually novel aspects to us.

CHAPTER XXXIV.

Colonel Moor as to Sanskrit in Greece—The Ionians, Gnostics, etc.—As to ancient Aryan symbolism—Civilisation of Egypt from India—If Greek names are Sanskrit, Indian origin of Greeks evident—Nomenclature of the Nile—India an epitome of the whole earth—Art of India, Greece, etc.

COLONEL MOOR, one of the noble fraternity of soldier scholars, as a German savan has termed them, which the Anglo-Indian Service has produced, in his work entitled "Oriental Fragments," has afforded some very suggestive hints as to the course of civilisation. He distinctly indicates its progress from India itself to Greece, and not from the north-west of the Hindu Koosh; flowing, as has been supposed, in divergent streams, eastwards and westwards. He instances what he terms Kallicisms in Greece, *i.e.* names evidently derived from Kali, the spouse of Siva, and deity especially presiding over mountains, and sacred clefts in mountains, such as Callidia on Mount Parnassus, and the poetical fount of Calliroe; and he traces the farther progress of Indian emigration to the extreme north-west of Europe. He assigns to Caledonia the signification of black mountains, from the meaning of black in *Kali*, and from *dun*, which expresses a hill or height in both the Gothic and Celtic languages. This certainly seems to evidence an Indian connection with ancient Scotland as clearly as the word New York exhibits English influence in America.

The meaning of Heliconda he considers to be hill of the sun, and Mount Tricala refers to time in the Sanskrit, seeing the past, present, and future. A lofty and snow-crowned mountain in Greece bears the appellation of Malashivo, which, in the Sanskrit form of Mala-Siva, would signify the garland or wreath of Siva (mālā). Then he adduces the ancient name of the Ionians, as derived from the Indian symbol of Kali or Parvati—passive nature, which she represents, though she is, at the same time, the active energy of Siva, and both father and mother of all things. Natural clefts in the rock, wells, tanks, etc., are *Ioni* or *Yoni*. These ancient Greeks would seem to have been of the Yoni sect of India, the adorers of passive nature in Kali.

Lemprière follows Greek authors, in his Classical Dictionary, who cared not to seek for any origin for their nation which was not autochthonous, in merely deriving the appellation of Ionians from Ion, grandson of Erechtheus, sixth king of Athens, who built the city of Helice; of which Calisto was an inhabitant. She it was who was changed into the constellation of the Great Bear, but she also seems to have been called Helice herself. She was one of Diana's attendants, and was thus metamorphosed by the jealous Juno, who discovered that Jupiter had fallen in love with her.

In the Vedas the road to the dwelling of Yama (death) is represented as guarded by two four-eyed, brindled, terrific dogs, which suggest Pluto's Cerberus.

Colonel Moor, besides classical affinities, found the derivation of the sect of Gnostics, against whose heresies the Gospel of St. John is thought to have been written, in the Hindu Nastikas, mystics in practice (unbelievers). He remarked that, as Moses was said to have been learned in all the wisdom of the Egyptians, he was virtually learned in the wisdom of the Hindus, which may be believed to have been much the same, 1570 B.C., as now; and that the loves of Yusuf (Joseph) and Zuleika is a very common Eastern story. He observed that the sun and moon are all in all with Hindu theologians; the sun being the ark from which all have come, to which all must return. The Hindus, he wrote, except in the case of the privileged classes, are interdicted still more strictly than the Papists from reading the more sacred Scriptures. Similarly Pococke, in "Greece in India," brings the Pelasgi into Greece from Pelasa, an ancient name of Bahar, and finds Sanskrit derivations in a large number of otherwise untranslatable Greek appellations. Not only did Colonel Moor discern Indian names and Sanskrit words in Greece, as well as customs and symbols, but largely dispersed in Europe, and even Africa. The funereal obsequies and cake belonged to both Hindus and Greeks, he remarked, and may be further perceived in masses for the dead and the Irish wake. Feasting at funerals was a custom of the days of Homer, in whom we also find mention of funeral pyres; the Greeks, like the Hindus, both burning and interring their dead. He traces an affinity between the threefold leaves of the lotos and the shamrock; but the nomenclature of Irish places would seem to indicate an Indian descent with almost absolute certainty. The cross, he also showed, is seen as a mystical figure long anterior to Christianity, such as ♀ ♁ ♁; the circle representing the creator and preserver of the world, and the T the wisdom derived from him. ⊙ ✠ ± are signs of the supreme wisdom; Ψ, the trisula of Siva, is recognised in Neptune's trident. Vishnu is the descending or aqueous element symbolised as ∇. Siva, or Fire, is represented in the pyramid Δ, and this may be the esoteric meaning of the pyramids of Egypt. Mighty truths, Colonel Moor remarks, are hidden under the series of incarnations of Vishnu, which have been quoted in rhythmical form in a former chapter. Godfrey Higgins affirmed that there is not a particle of proof, from any historical records which he could discover, that any colony ever passed from Egypt to India; but that there is direct, positive, practical evidence of the Indians having come to Africa. He cites Eusebius, Herodotus, and Philostratus, the last of whom says, "The gymnosophists of Ethiopia, who settled near the sources of the Nile, descended from the Brahmins of India, having been driven thence for the murder of their king."

If the derivation of the word Nile from the Sanskrit *nîla*, black or dark blue, be admitted, it would seem as evident that Indians were concerned in the civilisation of Egypt, as Dutchmen or Englishmen in South Africa; as shown by the nomenclature of Orange River. The Hebrews called the Nile *Sihor*, the Black.

In fact the civilisations of Egypt and Babylonia, and the people of Greece, Rome, and modern Europe, are apparently the products of the north-westerly emigrations of the old Aryan race. The modern Aryans are still continuing this western course, for the same obvious reason which before influenced them, viz. that it is the principal way open to them. But then, as now, there were migrations to the south-east. And the hardier inhabitants of the more northern regions seem constantly to have returned to conquer those who had remained in the voluptuous south; when their growing populations, or spirit of enterprise, aided by increasing knowledge, has urged them forth to conquer the old enriched regions from which they had originally emanated. Macedon and Rome subdued vast territories, and, in their turn, gave way to the Goths. Russia seems progressing surely southwards. Britain, in her marvellous conquest of India, is the most exalted example; for her influence was established at a time when communication between victors and vanquished was only effected in voyages of over four months' duration.

India has been styled "an epitome of the whole earth." China has, however, been more absolutely self-contained. It had not fertile and agreeable territories, so accessible as the borders of the Mediterranean to India. The Chinese and Indians respectively prevented extensive colonisation of their races to the east and west of the fertile districts in which they were multiplying their populations, and improving their civilisation, at the period in which our theologians have placed the destruction of the world by an universal flood—viz. the year 2348 B.C.

As names in ancient Greece and modern Europe can be translated into Sanskrit, and otherwise are not to be explained, it is, of course, as evident that we must admit them to have been named by colonists from India, as that we must allow the presence of the Dutch, French, Spanish, and English to be shown in the nomenclature of American localities.

But in regard to the connection to be proved between India and Greece, or the descent to be traced, besides language, legends, and symbols, there are evidences which appear to have been little considered. We are, perhaps, too much disposed to picture Greece from the remains of temples in the elegant harmonies of the four architectural orders, and from the art exhibited in such statues as the Apollo Belvidere and the Venus de Medici. Graceful, but severely rather than elaborately fanciful, has been our estimate of Greek taste. It was repugnant to many artistic minds to discover that the Greeks painted their marble edifices and tinted their statues. The general aspect of the life of Greece is, of course, no more to be absolutely imagined from a contemplation of the Elgin marbles, or the temples at Pæstum, than that of England from Gothic cathedrals and ancient castles. A study of the general antiquities of Greece displays a manner of life full of the enthusiastic, the fantastic, and even what we might now consider, in religious observances, etc., the ridiculous. And it must be remembered that the freedom of Greece was only known by the citizens, while the numerous slaves were as arbitrarily retained in their servile condition as the pariahs in their outcast state by the old caste laws of India.

CHAPTER XXXV.

Old Greek aspects of life suggested in those of modern native Bombay—Also of Jewish and other ancient civilisations—Slight impression made by foreigners upon the Hindus—India conservative of fashions anterior to the famous days of Greece—Classic art observable in Bombay, also old English forms in house architecture in the native streets—Costume, etc., of Hindu and Parsi women, and comparison with the description of the daughters of Zion in Isaiah—Calcutta Baboos—Little temples in Bombay—Potter's wheel, etc.—Indian devotees and their rosaries—Hindu mode of tying the hair suggestive of our last century style, just as the wigs of Elephanta suggest those of the first half of that century—Pure warrior and merchant castes said to have left India—Possibly to be found in ourselves, etc.—Brahmanical edicts against emigration proving its prevalence—Instance of migration across a continent in the inhabitants of the Halligs—Aryan emigration in ancient as in modern times—The Druids Brahminical—The Germanic languages displaying affinities with the Pali—The Buddhistic form of Sanskrit—Priestly spirit more prominent in the south—Greeks could easily have come from the Bombay district—Successive steps of human culture easily discerned in India, with its rich plains, sylvan regions, rivers, and sea-coast.

Our old prejudices may be offended by the observation that the aspect of life in the native streets of Bombay resembles that of old Greece. Making allowances for differences of climate and vegetation, and for the blackness of the sunburnt lower orders of India, it would seem not to be more dissimilar than that of modern America to modern Europe. As the India of the Hindus does not appear to have materially altered since the time of Alexander the Great, the western side of India, if placed in juxtaposition with Greece at that period, would have presented to it as close a resemblance as existence in a town of the United States to that of an old English, German, or Spanish town in the present day, according to whether we are taking north or south. The Greeks found many things old in India, but new to themselves; so does the American in Italy. The old centre land still presents us with the aspects of ancient civilisations. Suggestions not only of Greek, but of Assyrian,

Babylonish, Egyptian, and Jewish scenes are to be taken from it. It must be remembered that the lower orders of these people must have been dark, even of the Greeks. The Portuguese and English have been settled in Bombay for about three centuries. There are also the Mohammedan and Parsi settlers, the latter of whom are much anglicised, and even play at cricket with enthusiasm; while the former gaze on us with apathetic, though sometimes rather scowling indifference, as they smoke their hookahs in the stalls of their special quarter. It must be allowed that during the seven centuries of Mohammedan influence in India the Hindus have become to a certain extent affected by their fashions. The Hindu women in the especially Mohammedan districts appear to be retained in greater seclusion than is required under the Hindu laws or customs. Of course, Europeans cannot have been in such positions of importance in the country for some three centuries without the native life being affected by that also. But the impression is so slight that, away from the great British capitals, or cantonments in up-country stations, scarcely a trace of anything European can be seen; and even in the Presidency towns, the life preserves its indigenous aspect very completely. The autochthonous appearance of the people is especially open to observation in the island of Bombay. The bulk of its population of 647,000, according to the estimate of 1872, are Hindus, who remain as purely consistent in their own manners and customs as if the foreigners had only just made their appearance amongst them. The Mohammedans are conservative also, and appear to present in India much the same aspect as they afford in Mecca, and which they doubtless exhibited in the age succeeding that of their Prophet. They are autochthonous as to their fashions of life, and these are totally dissimilar to those of classic, mediæval, or modern Europe, though they have in Constantinople assumed a commercial gloss of European civilisation. But the Hindus, while so essentially preserving their peculiar style in religion, literature, art, etc., exhibit affinities to classic and mediæval Europe as close as could possibly be, considering the diversities of climate. They retain all their seeming originality of aspect, and are evidently the archaic commencement, not the result of the ancient civilisations. England retains old systems and fashions, and ancient edifices, not to be found in America or

Australia, and may retain many of them after America and Australia have considerably changed their present aspect. So India conserves things which were in existence before the famous days of Greece, and which have outlived its transformation from the Greece of Pericles to that of King George I.

Birmingham hardware goods are to be seen in the stalls of the Bombay bazaars, and Manchester cotton stuffs are bought by the people; but they are worn after their own fashion, and the wearers are no more anglicised by their use than English are orientalised by wearing Cashmere shawls or Delhi jewellery. They take advantage of our railways, and of the tramway cars which ply between the fort and native town; and they acquire the English language when they find it will be useful to them, and they have no objection to availing themselves of English educational advantages. But their life remains in its entirety their own. It has grown up amongst themselves in the course of thousands of years, as testified by the literature and art remains. It no more occurs to them to alter it than to Londoners to adopt the habits of their Indian visitors. There may, of course, be exceptional instances of anglicised Hindus amongst the wealthier classes, but the ordinary Hindu life of Bombay retains all the ancient characteristics.

The Fort of Bombay, the old business quarter of the thickly populated island, exhibits large and heavy houses, suggestive of the Portuguese who formerly held it. They are what may be termed classical perhaps in form, but they certainly display little application of classic art either in stone or wooden ornamentation or of mural paintings. Within the last few years noble edifices, both in the classic and Gothic styles, have been erected, but too recently to have afforded any suggestions for the styles observable in the more purely native parts of the place. The English bungalows at Mazagon, and on Malabar Hill, are picturesque rambling structures, with verandahs and sloping roofs, and occasionally classical columns are employed in porches, or for divisions in the interiors. But the classical forms introduced are certainly not sufficiently prominent to have produced much, if any, effect upon the minds even of an imitative people. Yet the native streets of Bombay exhibit a frequent use of classical façades, and pilasters of inferior types of the so-called Corinthian and Doric orders, while, as has been remarked, the native houses are often painted in panels, with broad contrasts of colour in their borders, and with figures or foliage in the centre. These decorations cannot be compared, in beauty and artistic effect, with those which may be seen in the finer style of Pompeian houses, but they may certainly be compared with those which, arguing by analogy, probably diversified the ruder and humbler dwellings of the Pompeian neighbours and predecessors. And not only is this observable in Bombay, but in those villages in the vicinity, in which the houses rise to architectural superiority beyond the mere mud huts, with palm-leaf thatch, of most Indian villages. That these may be relegated for models to their own ancient architecture, the mention of two-storied houses, balconies, porticoes, triumphal arches, gilding and decorating, etc., in the Epics, seems reliable evidence. Allusions are also made in these to temples, and to the stone steps of tanks. Caryatides, like those of Greece and Egypt, abound in the Tamulian structures of southern India. And Mr. R. Mitra has compared Orissan art with the Dædalian and Æginetan of 500 B.C., and with the Etruscan, Egyptian, and Assyrian schools. The Orissan figures are light, life-like, and graceful, though there is an inferiority in the sculpture of muscles. This may not unreasonably be held due to the inferior development of the human figure in the climate of that district. Besides the red earthen pots and others of the classic form which we are accustomed to contemplate in our art museums, the Pompeian cooking pots and utensils to be seen at Naples precisely resemble those still in use amongst the Hindus. While, in the embroidered robe or veil, the Hindu women, above the coolie or labouring class, resemble our pictures of Greeks, in their profusion of golden ornaments, and in the flower-wreaths adorning their radiant locks, braided closely to their small heads, they seem to suggest Greek, Assyrian, or Jewish ladies—in fact, the ladies of the old world. The feet are usually bare, as are frequently represented those of the Greeks, especially when engaged in religious ceremonies. They wear rings on the toes, and sometimes bunches of little silver bells on the anklets; but there are Hindus of both sexes who wear sandals of the exact description of some represented on Greek sculptures. In the nose-ring, often of pearl, the symbol of marriage, the Hindus retain an ornament which the better taste of the Greeks seems to have abrogated or never adopted. But this appears in the graphic picture of the daughters of Zion in Isaiah iii. 16, which is curiously applicable to Hindus in the present day. Neither the Hindus nor the Parsis conceal the countenance in Bombay, though the Mohammedan women are there so closely veiled that not even their eyes are permitted to be visible. These last, and the Parsi women, in their brightly-tinted silken robes, which are passed over the back of the head, and the close white cap, wear slippers, so that the bare feet of the Hindu women are again autochthonous.

The Scotch lasses seem to affect bare feet to a far greater extent than can be explained by poverty.

But for the great red or coloured Mahratta turban the men might look classical in their loose white garments; and the Greek pileum, or skull-cap made of felt, may be seen on the heads of the Bombay fishermen, of almost the identical shape observable in ancient Greek illustrations, and also suggesting those of the Neapolitan fishermen. These skull-caps may be made wholesale now in England and exported to India. But "felting," in Smith's "Dictionary of Antiquities," is said to have come from the East to Greece, so that this is no argument against their having originated in India.

The Calcutta Baboos, now perhaps more frequently adopting European costume, have presented, till late years at all events, very approximate pictures of the gentlemen of old Greece and Rome, in their flowing white robes, with their heads only covered by their close-cut hair—their legs bare, only their feet being modernised perhaps in European shoes—their robes more voluminous than the Greek pallium in aspect, and less so than the Roman toga, but suggestive of both.

The little temples in Bombay have usually the porch or nave, supported by wooden pillars, in a form resembling that which the meaner Greek temples must have assumed, judging from the more splendid specimens which have descended to us. At the upper end the images are placed on altars or tables, in close shrines, such as those which the earlier Greek temples contained. The pyramidal spire, however, or dome, of appearance dissimilar to the Mohammedan dome, which surmounts the shrine, does not seem to obtain any similitude in old Greece.

But we find these perpetuated in the Gothic spire, and in the Byzantine and Italian domes. Where, in the native Bombay edifices we do not see the classic façade and wall paintings, we have profuse carvings of beams, porches, and galleries, imparting, for instance, to the part of the Kalbadevi Road principally occupied by the opium dealers, and other thoroughfares, a resemblance to the most picturesque of old English, German, or French streets.

It may be by a succession of coincidences that these resemblances have come; or it may be that the ephemeral presence of the Greeks some eighteen hundred years ago left an impression curiously deep upon a people now so slow in adopting foreign manners. It may be that English or Portuguese architects or artists in India have taught the natives, less impregnable in these than in the other concerns of life, to build and decorate after these ancient classic and Gothic modes. It may be that the potter's wheel, which again seems to be an Indian invention, automatously produces vases of the old classical shape; and that the older Grecian gold and silver work greatly resembles the Hindu jewellery on account of the natural accordance of the instinctive productions of archaic jewellers. It may be that the feminine costume of both peoples has been induced by instinct also, without any descent of tastes or fashions from the one to the other. But when we also find the classic and Gothic styles suggested in the excavated temples, in which personages of aspect seeming at least coeval with the old Assyrian monarchies are represented, the origin of these things in India, even without the literary evidence, seems reasonably surmised. If Elephanta be delusive in its aspect of decay, and really appertaining to our own era, and susceptible therefore of the imputation of Egyptian or Greek influence, it must, at least, be confessed that Karli was not due to Gothic examples.

Dr. G. Birdwood, in a paper read before the Society of Arts in February 1879, observed, "The potter's art is of the highest antiquity in India, and the unglazed water-vessels made in every Hindu village are still thrown from the wheel in the same antique forms represented on the ancient Buddhistic sculpture and paintings. The correlation of his forms, colours, and details of ornamentation is perfect, as if his work were rather a creation of nature. He maintains inviolate the integrity and form and harmony of colouring, and the perfect unity of purpose and homogeneity of effect, in all his work. The mystery of his consummate work is a dead tradition now; he understands only the application of its processes; but none the less must it have been inspired, in its origin, by the subtlest interpretation of nature. Some of this primitive pottery is identical in character with the vases found in the tombs of Etruria, dating from about 1000 B.C.

"The Indian potter's wheel is of the simplest and rudest kind."

According to Lemprière, later Greek authors attributed the potter's wheel to Anacharsis, a Scythian philosopher of 592 B.C., who came to Athens. Scythia appears to have designated Tartary the region to the north of the Hindu Koosh. So an Indian origin is here suggested for it. Certainly the aspect of the Indian pottery is autochthonous.

The Grecian philosophers are represented as going bareheaded and barefooted, clad only in one rugged garment. In Bombay Hindu devotees or philosophers may be even seen in that garb amidst the busy commercial throng of that business centre of modern times. The rosaries of Roman Catholic Christendom may be frequently noticed upon genuine Hindus, who bear upon them all the marks of their sects, unaffected by Catholic or Anglo-Catholic missionary zeal. Over the usually white garment, which corresponds to the European coat, the respectable Hindu wears the scarf or stole, which is retained as one of the most sacred vestments of the above-mentioned communions. It is his napkin and pocket-handkerchief. His tonsure is not at the top of his head, like that of the Roman Catholic priests, but at the sides and back, somewhat as the Normans seem to have worn it. As in the sculptures at Elephanta are seen head-dresses bearing a remarkable resemblance to our wigs of the last century and modern legal fashions, so, at the backs of the heads of modern Hindus are, curiously, to be seen long locks, tied in almost the precise style which was affected by the beaux towards the end of the eighteenth century, after wigs were partially disused. It is not absolutely impossible that these have been copied from the English of Warren Hastings' time. But the wigs of Elephanta, even according to Mr. Fergusson's most recent date for the place, cannot have been imitated from the wigs of Clive's, the preceding period.

The division of the Indians into the four great castes of Brahmins, warriors, merchants, and cultivators, seems to have been modified, even in Alexander's time. Megasthenes divides them into castes or classes, as follows:—1, Philosophers; 2, Agriculturists; 3, Herdsmen; 4, Handicraftsmen and artisans; 5, Warriors; 6, Public inspectors; 7, Royal councillors.

As the pure warrior and merchant castes are said by the Hindus to have disappeared from the greater part of their land, and only the Brahmins and Sudras, or cultivators, of the four great castes to remain, besides the numerous tradesmen and handicraftsmen, who constitute species of castes, it may certainly be reasonably concluded that the increase of Brahminical influence, and the attractions afforded by more temperate climates to energetic souls, caused the gradual abandonment of the country to the priesthoods and conservative agriculturists; with the exodus occasioned by wars. That the descendants of the warriors and merchants of the old Arya varta, in ancient and modern Europe, after an abortive attempt under Alexander of Greece, 2000 years ago, have returned and proclaimed empire over the whole of their original fatherland, under Victoria of England, seems an established fact. We have returned rather than set out to assume dominion in the original home of our race; from which the Brahminical power occasioned our departure during various periods, from 1500 to 4000 years ago. If this does not convey to us any more abstract right to rule the country than the descent from Europe would give to Americans to conquer our continent, it at least seems a retributive course for events to have taken. Ancient Brahminical interdicts against emigration demonstrate the prevalence of it. The abstention from strong meats and drinks which they inculcated, probably with similarly benevolent motives to those which actuate our vegetarian and temperance societies in England, may have increased the suavity of the people but diminished that ferocity which seems necessary to the preservation of independence in a world in which might has as yet been right. The early colonists may in part have been a kind of pilgrim fathers; more primitive in their political or religious exile than those who abandoned England for America at the period of our great civil and religious war, two centuries and a quarter ago.

The inhabitants of the Halligs, small islands on the western coast of Sleswig, afford a remarkable instance of emigration from an extreme south-east to an extreme north-west point of a continent. They are said to trace their descent from the Greeks. The women wear, or wore a few years ago, a sort of Oriental dress, their faces partially concealed, and the hair wound in plaits around a Greek fez. This seems to correspond to an emigration from southern India to Asia Minor.

The Aryan population of Europe, when approximating to 200,000,000, about the eighteenth century A.D., has established its colonies to the West, in America. These have retained the languages and general manners of the old continent—viz. the Anglo-Saxon Teutonic tongue in the north, and the Spanish Latin language in the south. Usually, however, they have modified the existing order of most European states, and abrogated their ancient forms of government in respect to monarchy and state churches.

At about the eighteenth century B.C. India seems likely to have been sending forth emigrants, who retained in Europe the language derived from the form of language preceding the Sanskrit, with which we are acquainted, and the general manners and traditions of the old country. The real motive of the Mahábhárata war has been surmised to have been a contest between those powers which supported the Brahmins and those who advocated the religious liberty, and abolition of caste—the mainspring of the early Buddhists. The Brahminical party seems to have obtained the supremacy in the end. As in Europe, various other causes may have influenced emigrations. In Europe not only did exiled Puritans find their way to the new settlements, but also oppressed cavaliers at another epoch; and numerous adventurers of all classes, in search of gold, or of a stirring life, or simply of a sufficient livelihood. As the Latin and Teutonic races, from the south and north of Europe respectively, have colonised the south and north of America, so from India it appears that a similar course has been taken. The Buddhists of the north have proceeded to northern Europe, mingled with Brahmins, who may have found the country too hot for them during periods of the early Buddhistic supremacy, or who may have found their class too numerous, or may perhaps have been infected with a missionary spirit. At all events, the Druids seem to present an aspect, both in their office and doctrine, distinctly Brahminical. The Germanic languages display affinities with the Pali, the form of the Sanskrit in Bahar—the sacred language of Buddhism. Although the connection between the Teutonic and Indian divinities has been lately denied, the evidence seems to preponderate in favour of the identity of Woden and Buddha—not of the Gautauma or Sakya Buddha of the modern Ceylonese, etc., but a more ancient Buddha. Emigration seems likely to have continued in the same direction from about 1500 B.C. to the period when the rise of the Mohammedan power in Western Asia seems to have partially closed the communication between East and West. The warlike element seems to have pressed towards, or necessarily been more developed in, the north of Europe, while the priestly or literary and commercial spirit sought the softer south and its shores, tempting to commerce. The priestly spirit still seems especially to cling to the south; though in England we have lately witnessed a renaissance of it. But perhaps our great commercial empire, and our tropical dependencies, have lately constituted us more of a southern than a northern power, notwithstanding our latitude. Germany and Russia now seem the advancing northern powers.

Besides the Pelasgic there appear also to have been colonists in Greece from the districts of India more to the southwards, the language, subsequent to their departure, assuming the forms of classical Sanskrit in India, and Greek in Europe. These, from the Bombay or Surat district, could have easily coasted round the Arabian Sea and ascended the Red Sea, and finally crossed from Egypt or Phœnicia into Greece. In the former, at all events, they must have found little space for settlement.

If the astronomical, literary, legal, and architectural evidence of India be admitted to indicate some thousands of years of civilisation before the Christian era, the avoidance of over-population there is thus explained, together with the problem of the progress of the arts and sciences. Instead of the mountainous Bactrian region for the birthplace of the Aryans, and Babylon and Egypt for the mystic cradles of the sciences which the Aryans of Europe now cultivate most extensively, let us acknowledge India, with its rich plains, sylvan districts, rivers, and sea-coast, and the exuberant tropical islands to the south, to be the source from which we, the leading race of the world, and our arts have proceeded; having arrived at our wisdom there by the promptings of Providence in luxuriant nature. We shall, at all events, then be able to trace the successive steps in culture more easily than from those suggestions which we perceive in the races which are still nomads in the deserts, or savages in the tropical islands. We shall discern natural reasons for settled institutions and labour protected by law.

CHAPTER XXXVI.

Archbishop Potter on the Pelasgi, etc.—Brahminism apparent in Egypt—Sanskrit at the Eleusinian Mysteries—Quotations from the Vedas in the Orphic hymns, etc.—Bacchus, Osiris, and Siva—Symbol of the Fish used by the Christians in the Catacombs of Rome—The "Fish" avatar, from the Ode of Jayadeva—Christian idea appearing, by much evidence, to have been manifested to the Hindus—Instances of similarities in Greek and Indian festivals, marriages, etc.—Infanticide amongst the Hindus and Greeks—Buckle upon the influence of the Indian scenery, etc., in producing their art conceptions, or imagery of the Divine.

"THE PELASGI," observes Dr. Boyd, in a note on Archbishop Potter, "are acknowledged by the concurrent voice of all antiquity to have brought with them into Greece a peculiar and distinct system of religion. They are acknowledged, moreover, to have been the founders of the theology of the Greeks. They established an oracle at Dodona; they instituted the mysteries of the Cabiri; and there is every reason to believe that those of Eleusis were of similar origin. In a word, everything connected with them tends strongly to confirm the belief that they were a sacerdotal race, a caste of priests." . . . "The earliest monuments which the geography, the antiquities, the mythology, the architecture, and the religious systems of the most remote times afford, clearly indicate that, in a very distant period, colonies of priests from northern India, with the worship of Buddha, spread themselves over the countries along the Phasis, on the Euxine, in Thrace, along the Danube, over many parts of western Europe, and even through the whole of Greece. The Pelasgi evidently were a colony or race of this kind, and their very name, *Raseni* or *Tyrseni*, especially the two last syllables, *seni*, connects them in a manner with the *Sindi* or people of India."

Egypt and Babylon would naturally have been colonised by, or civilised by a certain mixture of settlers from, the outgrowth of the population of the western side of India at an earlier period than Greece, for the obvious reason that the valley of the Nile and the plains of the Euphrates are the nearest attractive districts on that side. In the pyramids we probably behold sacred edifices, not merely tombs, but symbolisms of the Divinity called in India Siva. Brahminism, *i.e.* the sacerdotal caste, somewhat, however, conjoined with the military, and the Brahminical divinities, seem to be clearly apparent in the Egyptian mythology. The preservation of bodies in mummies appears to be an original idea of the Egyptians, being probably connected with belief in the soul regaining and revivifying its old body at the day of judgment. This belief is evidently represented in the Egyptian paintings. "The Egyptians received their rudiments of civilisation from Meroe in Ethiopia, the seat of a sacerdotal caste or royal priesthood. Did Meroe then also civilise India, or India Meroe? From various circumstances it would appear that the priority is to be assigned unto India," says Dr. Boyd.

It would rather seem, from the fact of the priestly functions being assumed by the kings and chieftains in Greece, and from the priesthood never becoming a separate caste, or even distinct class corresponding to our modern priesthoods, that the Pelasgi were of the warrior caste of India rather than the "sacerdotal race." Even under the Brahminical system in India the warrior caste participated in some of its sacred privileges, and Brahmins, as has been observed, might, on the other hand, assume arms. But the Buddhists from whom the Greeks descended were such merely in antagonism to Brahmins. They had not yet abrogated the blood sacrifices of the Vedas, for Homer even relates that Achilles slaughtered twelve Trojan captives at the funeral of Patroclus.

Archbishop Potter observes that among the primitive Greeks all things were carried on with a great show of piety and devotion, and that it was a common opinion among them that their prayers were more successful when offered in a barbarous and unknown language. The Romish Church still considers it correct to utter the petitions of the more solemn, or mystic, services of the Church in a tongue unknown to the mass of the people. As that unknown tongue is the parent language of the more especially Catholic nations, so is it probable that the unknown tongue of the Greek religionists was the parent Indian language of Bharata Land, or Hindustan. At all events, these mystic words *κὸγξ ὄμπαξ*, with which the initiated were dismissed at the conclusion of the Eleusinian mysteries, have been reduced to meaning in the Sanskrit, whereas none appears to be forthcoming for them in the Greek language. The mystic syllable om, with which the second word commences, is at least indubitably similar to the sacred syllable of the Indians. Κογξ has been thought to signify an object of ardent wishes, *πὰξ* a change of fortune. Quotations from the Vedas have been discovered in the Orphic hymns, as has been remarked. Although the Eleusinian mysteries were mentioned with reprobation by the Fathers of the Church, as having been partly celebrated with obscene rites, and as having given occasion to many excesses, the Pagan philosophers, especially of the Platonic school, speak of them with high encomiums. Cicero, in allusion to the advantages to be derived from them, said that, in them, " not only do we learn a method of living in joy, but also of dying in the enjoyment of a better hope."

The worship of Bacchus, who is fabled to have made an expedition of conquest to India, is evidently of Indian origin, and this divinity is also considered identical with Osiris of Egypt. " Bacchus and Osiris both float upon the waters in a chest or ark, and they have both for one of their symbols the head of a bull, etc. etc.; and hence Bacchus is styled Bougenes by Plutarch," says Dr. Boyd, who continues :—" It is equally impossible not to recognise in Bacchus the Shiva (Siva) of India, as well as the Lingam, his symbol;" and " If we wish to call etymology to our aid, we shall be struck with the resemblance which Dionysus (Διόνυσος), the Greek name of Bacchus, bears to Dionichi (Deva Nicha), a surname of Shiva. One of the symbols of Bacchus is an equilateral triangle; this is also one of Shiva's, who is represented in the Hindu mythology as assuming the form of a lion during the great battle of the gods. He seizes the monster that attacks him, and assails him with his teeth and fangs, while Dourga (Parvati or Kali) pierces him with a lance. The same exploit is attributed, in the Grecian mythology, to Bacchus, under the same form, against the giant Rhœtus. Bacchus being the son of Jupiter by his union with a mortal maiden, is, in effect, an incarnation of the Divine, narrated in a materialistic manner. His mother, Semele, like the virgin mother of Christ, received divine honours after her death. Bacchus seems to have been identified with Apollo by the followers of Orpheus. The manner in which the worship of Bacchus came into Greece, probably by means of several successive migrations, through regions widely remote, will ever remain an enigma of difficult solution. The Greeks, indeed, made Thebes the birthplace of this deity, but that proves nothing for his origin. Thebes in Bœotia was the centre of the Cadmean Asiatic mythology: a god whose worship came to the rest of Greece out of Thebes, was for them a deity born in Thebes, and hence arose the legend of the Theban origin of Bacchus."

In the I.H.S. which appears amongst our Christian symbolism has been perceived the monogram of Bacchus. Originally *ies*, with the long Greek *η* Latinised, it has been rendered as expressing Jesus hominum Salvator. The fish was a symbol in the adoration of Bacchus, which also appears in the Catacombs of Rome amongst the Christian inscriptions.

The Greek letters in the word fish, IXΘUΣ, represent the initial letters of the sentences in Greek, Jesus Christ, Son of God, Saviour; and this has been supposed to have been the meaning of the adoption of the symbol. It might equally apply to Bacchus, or Iacchus, the Chrest, or benignant, as to Jesus, the Christ, or anointed. It would hardly appear probable that the Christians should have adopted such a recondite method of expressing their faith, unless they had attributed sanctity to the symbol. Of course it may have been merely a curious coincidence, or they may have considered it expedient to veil their religion under an old symbol. But it not unnaturally suggests a connection of ideas. Strict Protestantism, fearing the idolatrous use of the Cross, has rejoiced in observing that, instead of it, the Fish has been discovered to have been adopted by the early Christians. But Protestantism probably did not consider that the Fish might be recognised as a sign of the possible origin of the religion from what have been termed Pagan sources. The Fish also represents the first incarnation of Vishnu for the benefit of mankind; this avatar being for the purpose of rescuing the Scriptures from the deep.

In the ode of Jayadeva, an Indian lyric poet, it is thus described:—"Thou recoverest the Veda in the water of the ocean of destruction, placing it joyfully in the bosom of an ark fabricated by thee, O Cesava, assuming the body of a fish. Be victorious, O Heri, lord of the universe."

The pre-manifestation of the Christian idea to the Hindus appears to be evidenced by such a body of testimony that if one of its heads, like the Hydra's, is destroyed, another immediately arises in its place. It may be allowed that the strange stories of Salivahana and Mandávyah are the reflex of Christianity, and that the Bhagavad Gita was suggested by the teaching of the Gospel of St. John; yet the life and doctrine of Krishna remain as the seeming originals of much of the story of Christ. If it even can be demonstrated that Krishna, and the other incarnations of Vishnu, were unknown in India before His time, we yet find the Christian idea in the teaching of the real or apocryphal Buddha, whose era, or the era of whose supposed manifestation, is placed at some centuries B.C. at the latest. Then the idea of the incarnation in Manu leads up to the materialistic form of it in Rama, which by a natural transition suggests Krishna.

From what comparatively scanty materials the imagination of Shakspeare evolved Hamlet, Romeo and Juliet, and all his wonderful volume of plays! Rama, like Hamlet, was probably in real or imaginary existence before the poet of the Ramáyana elaborated him into the present object of adoration as the incarnate divinity.

Indian doctrinal points naturally assume a rather different dress of words from that in which they are clothed in the West; but they do not appear to differ so considerably as the material clothes which cover the body in the two parts of the world.

In a paper published by Mr. C. Bruce an ancient Homeric hymn to the earth is shown to resemble strikingly a hymn in the Atharva Veda.

As with matters of religious teaching, so with those which afford suggestiveness of the Greek manner of life, they appear to be too numerous to be mere coincidences, or to have been all adopted in India from the Grecian kingdom in the north-west. The similarities of the Sanskrit, Greek, and other Aryan languages, might of course be explained on the hypothesis which Professor Max Müller and others have put forward, viz. that the race arose in some primitive home to the north-west of the Hindu Koosh, or elsewhere. But we also find classical altars, ancient excavations of evidently Indian design, containing architectural ornamentation in the Greek or Etruscan character; and temples, such as those of Manipuri, constructed in crucial form, with decorated ceilings, doorways, and colonnades of classical construction, found amongst immense varieties of more distinct Indian types. We have a Pantheon of divinities presenting remarkable parallels to those of Greece, and yet of absolutely autochthonous aspect, and illustrated by a voluminous literature; and we acknowledge that the Greek divinities are, for the most part, not autochthonous. When we add to these evidences the testimony of language, we must surely recognise the probability of the Greeks having been not merely colonists from Asia Minor or Egypt, or from some Aryan cradle, the traces of which have become obliterated in the lapse of time, but from the actual, existing mother country India, seemingly so unchangeable in its essentials that it is reasonable to regard them as idiosyncratic. If we contemplate the performances at Hindu festivals, and read in Archbishop Potter's "Antiquities of Greece" the accounts of those of the Greeks, they seem curiously similar in character, while the European carnival is a legitimate successor in the line of both. We read of the festival of torches in Greece—of another in which the youth beat one another with sea onions. It is related of a sacred festival in Laconia that "the boys, having their coats girt about them, play sometimes upon the harp, sometimes upon the flute, sometimes strike at once upon all their strings, and sing hymns in honour of the god Apollo in anapæstic numbers, and shrill acute sounds. Dances performed by a circular chorus, processions carrying boughs, etc., or uttering exclamations or lamentations, dancing, singing, beating brazen kettles, etc.—all these notions of sacred festivity are eminently in accordance with what may still be seen in the island of Bombay, under the shadow of Bible societies, missionaries of all denominations of Christianity, cotton manufactories, railroads and tramway cars. In the festivals of Bacchus the worshippers assumed fawn-skins and mitres, carried drums, pipes, flutes, and rattles, and crowned themselves with garlands, while some made exhibitions of antics in comical costumes. Persons of both sexes ran about, dancing in ridiculous postures, yelling, making hideous noises, and simulating frenzy. In one Argive fête the men and women changed garments. In an anniversary at Athens, the skins of beasts sacrificed to Jupiter were worn. In a festival in honour of Minerva, her statue was undressed and washed, a process constantly applied to Hindu images. No one who has witnessed an Indian marriage procession by night can fail to be reminded of it by the following description of a Greek nuptial ceremonial, taken from Smith's "Dictionary of Antiquities:"—"It was accompanied by a number of persons, some of whom carried the nuptial torches. Both bride and bridegroom (the former veiled) were decked out in their best attire, with chaplets on their heads, and the doors of their houses were hung with festoons of ivy and bay. As the bridal procession moved along, the hymeneal song was sung to the accompaniment of Lydian flutes, even in olden times." After entering the bridegroom's house, it was customary to shower sweetmeats upon them, as emblems of plenty and prosperity. At the marriage feast women were invited as well as men; but they seem to have sat at a separate table, with the bride, still veiled, amongst them. Both the married persons and their attendants were richly adorned and decked with garlands. The bride was usually conducted from her father's house in the evening, in a chariot, with her husband sitting beside her; and, besides the accompaniment of torches and music, singing and dancing were sometimes added.

The above description is perfectly applicable to an Indian wedding, notably in the article of sweetmeats, which are held to be very essential. The nuptial march is accompanied by a variety of discordant—at all events, to English ears—instruments of music, a flaring of torches, a glittering of golden "joys" and jewelled ornaments from a clump of women resplendent in richly tinted and embroidered silken attire. A train of the presents which have been bestowed upon the married pair forms part of the procession, with a numerous array of the male friends in their best apparel, and "the bride in a covered chair." There is the slight difference that the Indian bridegroom is usually on horseback. Both are so "swathed round with garlands as hardly to be seen," as Bishop Heber expressed it. The horse will be gorgeously caparisoned, to match the bridegroom's splendour; and over the latter's head is borne the umbrella which, as has been observed, has become a token of the Pope's dignity in Rome.

The fondness for garlands which so constantly appears in the classic idea of ceremonial or festive adornment, is essentially Indian. An English guest at a native entertainment in Bombay will probably find a wreath of flowers hung around his neck after he has taken his seat to see the dancing. During the marriage solemnity the Grecian company are said to have diverted themselves, and honoured the gods of marriage, with music and dancing; and the guests at a Hindu wedding, in the present day, will be similarly entertained.

The European ceremonial is not dissimilar in general character, and probably a similarity of the nuptial festivity may be discovered in all countries with any pretensions to civilisation. But the Greek and Indian customs seem definitely in agreement. Probably Australian weddings will bear an equally close resemblance to British.

"Presents," says Bishop Potter, "were made to the Greek bride and bridegroom, which were carried in great state to the house by women." "The married couple being shut up together in the chamber, the laws of Athens obliged them to eat a quince, by which was intimated that their first conversation ought to be pleasing and agreeable." "At this time the young men and maids stood without the door, dancing and singing songs, and making a great noise by shouting and stamping their feet." In England less delicacy appears to have been observed towards the newly-married pair than at present, even in the eighteenth century. Roderick Random, in Smollett's works, describes himself and bride as remaining for the night in the house from which they had been married. They are aroused by drums beaten beneath their window in the morning. Roderick's uncle knocks at their chamber door, and tells him to "turn out, as he has had a long spell." At breakfast his wife receives the compliments of the company on her appearance, which, they said, was, if possible, improved by matrimony.

The Hindu practice of widows immolating themselves upon the pyres of their husbands seems to be an expression of the same idea which led, amongst the old Greeks, to the consumption of slaves, captives, animals, and precious things in the funereal flames of men of quality. This ancient Aryan idea of the cremation of the dead, from India, Greece, etc., has come to us in these modern times. The Parsi manner of exposing the bodies to be devoured by vultures seems to be the strangest mode of burying adopted by our race. But the story of Krishna's suspension on a tree, to be the prey of vultures, would seem to indicate its Aryan antiquity. As amongst the Hindus it is the habit of the women to eat apart from the men, so, according to the Greek custom, men and women were not invited to banquets together, though subsequently in Rome women were allowed more freedom. Veiling the face when abroad seems to have been practised both by ancient Hindu, Greek women, and earlier Romans, but not with the total exclusiveness enforced among the Mohammedans. The Hindus were by no means deficient in treating the sex with due honour, as has been set forth in literary quotations, and in recognising the claims of woman to a certain education; while the laws in the Institutes of Manu very distinctly propound her rights to the possession of property. In Greece women seem to have had certainly no greater amount of privileges, undoubtedly not having attained to the position enjoyed in later times by Roman matrons, much less to that which is their birthright in modern Europe. Under the ancient Grecian laws it was forbidden to women and slaves to study or practise medicine; but free women were subsequently permitted to undertake the avocation of accoucheur. As in India, so the ladies of pleasure in Greece were distinguished by a peculiar dress. The remotest part of the house was assigned for the women's apartments, and here their most constant employments were spinning, weaving, and doing all sorts of embroidery and needlework. The provision of all necessaries indoors was usually committed to them. Beef, after being offered in sacrifice at all events, was eaten by the old Hindus as by the Greeks, and there was no prohibition of pork as amongst the Jews and Mohammedans.

Infanticide, which has been the custom amongst certain Hindu tribes, was also legally practised by the Lacedæmonians and other Greeks.

The Greeks of Homer's Iliad, like the Indians of Vyasa's Mahábhárata, fought in chariots. Elephants were transported from India and employed in Grecian warfare after the invasion of Alexander, which shows a readiness in the Greeks to adopt foreign methods; for, bearing in mind the passage respecting fire weapons in the Rámáyana, the mysterious Greek fire may have come from the same source. The long bow was Indian, Greek, and English. The old Greeks hurled great stones as missiles, Diomedes laying Æneas prostrate with a ponderous one. So do the satyr or monkey-warriors of King Hanuman, in the Ramáyana, strive against the weapons of Ravanna's giants, by hurling rocks at them, and trees torn up by the roots.

The old Hindu tales, like Hindu art, seem to have a Grecian semblance in their essential forms, but to be accompanied with exaggeration which offends our taste, and with fancifulness which seems distortion. But each style of literature, as of art, is the offspring of the characteristics of its country. The sombre slopes and rugged peaks of the Ghauts; the forests, dense with an infinite variety of fantastic foliage, from the plume-like palm and huge-leaved plantain to the trees of more European aspect, with the picturesque varieties of creepers; the dangers which lurk in them from tigers and venomous serpents; the sublimity and fierceness of the forces of nature in storms and the heat of the sun; the profusion of the rainfall in ordinary years, and the occasional droughts and their accompanying famines and pestilences;—all combine to excuse the inhabitants from having made images of Siva or Kali repulsive in horror. Thousands in India die from one fell stroke of nature's arm. From such promptings seem naturally to have proceeded works which appear to us gross or grotesque, in exaggeration of detail or eccentricity of form. Buckle commented upon this feature. But they also produced that which must be allowed to be noble and elegant; while the remains of their ancient structures also exhibit great massiveness in the stonework; while the largest bricks in the world have been assigned to India, as has been observed.

Comparing Indian scenes again with those of northern Europe, the art and architecture of the former seem naturally to glide into those of the latter. There also architecture advanced from solidity and comparative simplicity to the more fantastic style. With the revival of classical learning it assumed the classical dignity of form, but our own age has witnessed a renaissance of the fanciful mediæval styles. Under the later grandeur of the Roman Empire pomposity and elaboration reigned. The Hindus have gone through similar transitions, with a corresponding chain of connection running through them.

CHAPTER XXXVII.

Indian and Greek temples and images—Village temple and village church in England compared—Brahmins and English clergy, etc.—Sequence of ideas traced in the Aryan race different from the patriarchal model of the Semitic nations.

At the entrance of the Greek temples was usually placed a vessel of stone or brass filled with holy water, in order that "those who entered to pray or offer sacrifices might first purify themselves," as is observed in Smith's "Dictionary of Antiquities." In this matter, at all events, the antiquity of the Catholic practice seems evident.

Professor M. Williams has observed that "It is curious that the Hindu notion of the restless state of the soul until the funereal s'rādda is performed, agrees with the ancient classical superstition that the ghosts of the dead wandered about so long as their bodies remained unburied, and were not suffered to mingle with those of the other dead." This superstition may be found in England; ghosts being sometimes attributed to the want of burial in consecrated ground.

The character of the early Greek temples was dark and mysterious. They had no windows, and received light only through the door, which was large, or from lamps burning in them. They were divided into the vestibule, treasury, and holy place in which stood the altar and images. "The idol," says Archbishop Potter, "was at first a rude stock. In Achaia there were kept, very religiously, thirty square stones, on which were engraven the names of so many gods, but without any picture or effigy. A very ancient statue of Venus at Delos had only a square stone instead of feet. Plutarch and Pausanias inform us that, amongst the ancient Greeks, statues were generally of wood. Themistius has told us that, before the time of Dædalus, all the Grecian images were unformed, of one piece, and without separate feet. In after ages they changed the rude lumps into figures resembling living creatures, generally men, and then an image was called *βρέτας διὰ τὸ βροτῷ ἐοικέναι*, because it was like a man. In the more refined ages such of the unformed images as were preserved were reverenced for their antiquity and preferred to the most curious pieces of modern art. Sometimes they were made not only of common but also of precious stone, and of gold, silver, brass, and all other metals." The position of the statues was in the middle of the temple, at the opposite end to the entrance, where they stood upon pedestals, raised above the height of the altar; the subterranean or infernal deities having, instead of altars, little ditches or trenches. Before temples were in use, altars were erected in groves or other places. Altars were various in shape, some being adorned with horns.

So in the Bombay temples the front part is usually open, and at the farther end is the shrine, lighted only through the door, and by the faint beams of little lamps burning before the images placed on a sort of table or altar. The above description of the Greek temples and images, etc., is absolutely applicable to the little Hindu temples or pagodas, while, as has been remarked, the horned altars are to be seen in the neighbouring villages.

At Elephanta it would seem that the great three-headed bust may have been veiled, in its recess, by a screen or curtain,—from indications on the walls.

Sometimes the outer portions or naves of the Bombay temples are closed around, sometimes they are mere porches. Only a railing sometimes separates the inner temple, leaving the images quite exposed to the view of the outer world. One little pagoda standing in a frequented thoroughfare consists simply of a shrine with three gaudily bedizened images on a table. These are usually uncouth in all the temples, and they are not rendered more venerable in aspect by bundles of tawdry clothing and ornaments. Still the images of Madonnas in the chapels of Roman Catholic Europe have often appeared in equally tawdry attire. A little bell is rung when a worshipper approaches to utter his prayers, or lay his gift before the image. This is said to be done in order to call the deity's attention to his adorer's approach. In Catholicism bells were said to be rung to scare the demons from the churches.

The pyramidal tower of the pagoda rising amongst the palms, plantains, mango groves, or tamarinds of the Hindu village, seems to bear comparison with the spire of the English village church rising amongst the oaks, hazel, beech groves, or elms. In the vicinity of the former, the font of the Protestant Church, or holy water basin of the Roman Catholics, appears in its archaic dimensions in the form of a sheet of water.

The early Christians went down into the water to be baptized.

Supposing Hinduism to have been derived from Christianity, or Christianity from Hinduism, the expansion of the font into a sheet of water, or the contraction of the latter into the former, might be not unreasonably expected as a consequence of climate.

The lectern for the Scriptures is also to be seen in the Hindu places of worship.

The collective body of clergy and lawyers in England virtually constitute a caste not altogether dissimilar to the Brahminical caste of India. The hereditary element does not exist by compulsion; but English professional circles will nevertheless be found to be contained in a circumference by no means indefinite. The schools, colleges, etc., which have opened the way to the learned professions have maintained considerable exclusiveness; and, as in old India, there has been some alliance between the Brahminical and Kshatrya or warrior caste; *i.e.* the Church has family connections in the peerage, landed gentry, and army. Till recently the Vaisya or merchant caste has been separate, and enjoyed but little political power; while the Sudras or cultivators have been distinct again. The barriers of class have not been defined; but a marriage with one of a different caste is usually regarded with aversion and distrust.

As in England, so in Greece and India were the houses of the divinity endowed with lands for their support.

In the Ramáyana the Brahmins in a procession are described as white robed, not apparently alluding to sacrificial vestments, or those required by ritual, but to their ordinary garb. White appears, then as now, to have been usually worn by all classes of Hindus. Black is at present the predominating costume of ceremony in Europe, and the especial attire of the priest when not occupied in his sacred functions, or of the lawyer when professionally engaged. White is retained in the performance of the ritual of our Church, but has been abrogated by the Lutheran as well as the Calvinistic and Presbyterian Churches.

A black deerskin was ordered to be the garb of a Brahminical student. A black chlamys is related to have been at one time the academical costume of an Athenian student, subsequently altered to white.

In all these matters, the sequence of ideas in successive generations of the Aryan race, from its south-eastern point in India to its north-western in England, can be traced; different from the patriarchal model with which we are familiar amongst the Semitic nations.

Yet in the united families of the Hindus we may see the patriarchal group, which preceded the village communism of the Aryans. They became Aryans when they had learnt systematically to cultivate the soil.

CHAPTER XXXVIII.

Professor Max Müller and the Indo-European race from Bactrian region — Arguments as to the Aryan race originating in India instead of their attaining civilisation in a district which they entirely abandoned—Central American civilisations—Max Müller as to the pastoral pursuits of the early Aryans—M. Oscar Peschel as to the Aryan race from the Caucasus—Comparison of Hindustan and the Caucasus.

PROFESSOR MAX MÜLLER has advanced the theory of the growth of the Indo-European race in civilisation in some part of Asia which it has now quite deserted. He has promulgated the notion of its separation, and, in several series of emigrations, at different epochs, discovering new and more convenient or agreeable abodes. One great branch he has supposed to have travelled eastwards and become the Aryan Hindus; the other, having proceeded westwards, to have matured into the present Aryan nations of Europe. He has said that the Sanskrit is the most ancient type of the English of the present day—that "the Sanskrit and English are but varieties of one and the same language—that we are by nature Aryan, Indo-European, not Semitic—our spiritual kith and kin are to be found in India, Persia, Greece, Italy, Germany, not in Mesopotamia, Egypt, or Palestine;" but he ascribes the origin of our civilisation to a region very different from those in which it has been prolonged. He does not appear to have assigned value to the living record of ancient days in the life of India under its autochthonous aspect. Our history has been continued in fertile and well-watered districts, more or less adjacent to that great incentive or aid to progress in arts and commerce, the sea. But, according to the view adopted by him, it commenced in the mere pastoral life of the comparatively arid uplands of what has been called Central Asia, in a district which the race has entirely abandoned. Can any historical evidence, however, be produced of a race totally deserting the region in which anything deserving of the name of civilisation, or national life, has grown up? Would not such a proceeding be, on the contrary, totally repugnant to the ordinary home love of the human kind? Babylon has become a heap of desolation. The district in which it was situated has been abandoned after its desolation by conquest; but it was originally only rendered habitable by human ingenuity and labour. It was rather, as has been argued, a commercial centre, in a country producing food by elaborate culture, than a city brought to its grandeur by those natural influences, which create the capital of a territory in which man has increased and multiplied under its natural advantages such as the greater part of India. Apart from the divine curse seeming to have been uttered upon it, according to our Holy Writ, its circumstances appear to have precluded its rising from the overthrow of conquest. And Bagdad takes its place in modern times. Even Iceland, having obtained a national life, has not been relinquished for the fair fields which America might have been thought to have offered to its inhabitants, cultivating and inhabiting their bleak volcanic island with extreme difficulty. The Goths descended from their forests upon southern Europe and settled there; but they did not altogether abandon their northern seats. The Turks have possessed themselves of the luxuriant capital of the old Eastern Roman or Greek Empire; but their ethnological kindred still remain in their ancient Asian wildernesses of Turkestan. Greece has direly suffered from foreign conquest and oppression; but its people have remained, retained their ancient language and character with the mere modifications of time, and nobly regained their old independence. Nations have been expatriated, and they have largely emigrated; but there have been remnants which remained in the ancient home. Greeks of the old Empire have still clung to their seat of power in Constantinople. No tradition has indicated that it was conquest which compelled the archaic Aryans—the powerful race which east and west has obtained empire of the world—to abandon entirely an original home; and that, in consequence, they immediately conquered new abodes for themselves in India. The Ghebers or Parsis have found in Surat and Bombay a refuge from the Mohammedan invaders of Persia. But they do not appear, as political refugees, to have obtained their new settlements by force of arms; and their monuments remain in their old country, which they did not entirely desert. If it was as the peaceful pioneers of civilisation that the Aryans entered India, their remains of peaceful arts would surely be discoverable in their original abode. But in the course of time, in the vast wildernesses of the geographically-central Asia, the traces of the ancient houses and other evidences of settled civilisation, to which their literary remains bear testimony, may be discovered. Yet, considering the relative aspects of India and the central Asian region, it might still be a question as to whether the ruins of old cities in the latter ought not to be regarded as the seats of colonial rather than of autochthonous Aryan civilisation. It is easy to conceive the abandonment of a settlement of civilisation on account of its advantages being found in course of time not to compensate for the difficulties of its situation, or on account of surrounding hostile barbarians becoming too powerful. But, for civilisation to grow by its own strength and impulses, would seem to require conditions which would prevent the desertion of the country in which it had sprung up. People flourish according to the amenities of their land in natural products or advantages of situation; they do not arrive at a full civilisation and then look for territory adapted to it. Nature is the parent, not the adopted child, of autochthonous culture. The ancient mounds of the valley of the Ohio, containing the relics of a settled agricultural population, which had made considerable progress in the arts of life, as Sir Charles Lyell says in his description of them in the "Antiquity of Man," may be cited as affording evidence of the abandonment of a naturally advantageous situation. But it may be reasonably affirmed that these were colonial rather than autochthonous. As it seems to be admitted that the Central American civilisations came from Asia, these might have been the first settlements effected by the adventurers; subsequently deserted in favour of the more southern seats, perhaps on account of the Red man's inroads; or they may, more probably, have emanated as settlements from the Mexican or Toltecan people after their firm establishment in the country; to which races they have been thought to have belonged from the form of skulls dug out of their burial-places. They may have either been destroyed by the Red man after a time, or, as belonging to the milder, by the more ferocious of these people. Sir C. Lyell adduces evidence to show that they had commercial intercourse with the natives of distant regions.

When we read of the ferocity with which the English fought in the civil wars of the Roses, only four hundred years ago, of the number slain in the battles, and of the sanguinary reprisals after them, by people who professed to believe in the religion of love taught by Jesus, we need not be amazed at whole populations having been put to death amongst some of these ancient races. The Bible, indeed, distinctly represents such wholesale destructions as having been consonant with the Divine will when the chosen people were winning their way to their heritage in Canaan. It was not once only that they "utterly destroyed all that was in the city, both man and woman, young and old, and ox, and sheep, and ass, with the edge of the sword (Joshua vi. 21). There is, at all events, no evidence to show that the civilisation of these cities was autochthonous; while a variety of testimony seems to indicate an Asian origin for the Central American States, with which they were connected apparently.

It may be contended that, after the various emigrations had taken place, which the Professor indicates, an Aryan remnant was left in the ancient home, which remnant was utterly destroyed by the Turanian or other people. But surely traditions must have survived of the demolition of our fountain head. The emigrants cannot have been so completely callous to those left in the ancient home as to have treated them with such indifference as never to have enquired into their fate; to have allowed their destruction to lapse into complete oblivion. The common emotions of humanity seem to negative such an idea. Professor Max Müller, indeed, and others who have advocated the birth of our race on or about what has been styled the "Roof of the World," have made no contention of this kind. He speaks of the Hindu as being the last to leave his common home, having seen his brothers all depart towards the setting sun, and that, then, turning towards the south and the east, he started alone in search of a new world. Even this name, "Roof of the World," seems to indicate an unlikely birthplace.

As has been suggested, if the Vedic Sanskrit could change

to the classical, and the classical to the Prakrits in India itself, the pre-Vedic language from which all the Aryan dialects, including perhaps these Prakrits, have been derived, may have preceded the Vedic Sanskrit in India also. In fact the Sanskrit altogether affords the aspect of being the direct descendant of such a language, still abiding in the old family home. As Professor Max Müller has observed, "No other language has carried off so large a share of the common Aryan heirloom—whether roots, grammar, words, myths, or legends ; it is natural to suppose that, though perhaps the eldest brother, the Hindu was the last to leave the central home of the Aryan family."

Instead of having been the last to leave, it seems more in accordance with human nature, and the experience of human affections for places as well as persons, to consider him as still in the original home. The Brahminical, warlike, mercantile, and cultivating classes of the Hindus under their modern aspect, and the inferences to be derived from the Institutes of Manu as to the prevalent feeling amongst the ancient Hindus, would certainly appear to display an indigenous race ; and to show in India the spring from which the Aryan streams have irrigated the world. Is it correct to conceive the spring of such mighty streams dried up? It would surely seem more reasonable to suppose that it possessed sufficient volume to survive, with its grandly-flowing rivers ; that it did not send them forth, and then disappear ; while these in their new regions were gathering strength from fresh sources, having become parted from the old reservoir.

In the Vedic hymns frost is not the enemy, but drought, observes Mrs. Manning.

Peacocks, parrots, quails, and partridges inhabit the woods of the Vedic world ; and elephants trampled them down. Hymns describe rivers as rushing to the great water ; which would seem to signify the ocean, when considered in conjunction with the allusions to merchants, etc.

They allude to the snowy mountains, but the Himalayas can be seen as far to the south as Meerut. Their imagery of the rains seems engendered in the region of the monsoons. They go southwards rather than northwards in their metaphors, while in the Punjab apparently uttering their verses.[1]

[1] See Appendix XII.

When the Aswins are praised for sweeping away the Dasyu with the thunderbolt to create great light for the Arya, this has been interpreted to allude to aborigines who were being driven out or subdued. Yet Dasyu means a thief, and therefore may more reasonably be held to allude to the robbers who, then as now in the civilised world, preyed upon the labours of honest folk.

The Dasyu skins were darker, and it is still the case in India that the more aristocratic classes are widely lighter in colour than those of the lower orders.

The Professor has observed that Burnouf first considered the Zend more primitive than the Sanskrit, but subsequently altered that opinion; and "that the Zoroastrians and their ancestors started from India during the Vaidik period can be proved as distinctly as that the inhabitants of Massilia started from Greece; but that we have no evidence to bear us out in making the same assertion of the nations of Persia and Media in general." Here then might be recognised our original stock. Balkh has been called the mother of cities, and the capital of Persia in the ages of fable, and, in or near Balkh, may be conceived to have remained the remnant of the Aryan race; developing into the Persians, after these western and eastern emigrations, and subsequently infected with the Zoroastrian system from India. But Balkh seems to have owed its ancient consequence and wealth rather to its advantageous position for commerce than to its innate resources. It is physically more probable that India colonised Balkh than that Balkh colonised India. Balkh may have been the mother of Persian cities. Persia, like Balkh with its vicinity, seems never to have been endowed by nature with those special attributes which appear to afford in India the opportunities for the developments of all the Aryan tribes. India contains sufficient diversity of aspect amongst its inhabitants to evince the probability of its sending forth our various nations in old times; but Persia seems to have contained a distinct division or branch of our race rather than the germs of the whole; and the Persian nation rises into prominence in western Asia at a period modern in comparison with that at which great kingdoms were flourishing in civilisation in India. Altogether the Aryans of the original home must be supposed to have disappeared in the mists of time, unless that home is admitted to be the present British India.

Professor Max Müller, in arguing his case, has shown from the historical evidence of their language that the early Aryans were simply a pastoral people, and that they had not seen the sea before their separation; as evidenced by the difference of its name in the Sanskrit and other derivatives of the original language. He argues the pastoral commencement of the people in the similarity of the terms applied in the various branches of the family to the matters of pastoral significance. The word, for instance, from which daughter is derived signifies milkmaid. M. Oscar Peschel has observed, on the other hand, that the derivation of the word for camel from the Arabic is decisive against Bactria as the original Aryan home.

And nothing could possibly be adduced more indicative of what must have been the earliest sign of Aryan civilisation in Hindustan itself than the pastoral terms. On the vast pastures of various parts of India a wealth of cattle must have been the predominant feature before the cultivation of cereals was brought into common use upon its fertile plains, or at least contemporaneously with agriculture. The value of the cow, as has been observed, has been recognised from all known ages in India by the sanctity attributed to that animal. What can be more reasonable than the supposition that in India itself the duty and name of the milkmaid should have been bestowed upon the archaic daughter of the race? The legends of Krishna again exhibit the veneration bestowed upon what must have seemed, to the inhabitants of this region—when they emerged from barbarism—the invaluable cattle. M. Oscar Peschel, however, whose authority has just been quoted as antagonistic to the placing of the Aryan cradle in Bactria, has equally objected to its being assigned to the country in which the lion and tiger were inhabitants, as the Sanskrit appellations for those animals have not been preserved in the Aryan languages. The names for the cereals, moreover, are dissimilar; and he has pronounced in favour of the Caucasus as the original centre of our race. But surely, in the lapse of centuries, the names of these animals might have been forgotten by the Aryans, when we consider the number of words which have dropped out of our own employment since the time of Shakspeare, though applied to matters of familiar use. The tiger would have been absolutely a foreigner to Greece, and the lion, if more familiar, would seem to have been of somewhat different species east and west. And barley seems, at first, to have been the only cereal cultivated by the Greeks, upon which some word, suggested by, or previously existing in the country, might surely have been easily applied. The name in use amongst the Finnic or other tribes, whom the Aryans appear to have gradually displaced, may have become adopted. The European colonists in America are already employing some new names for things known in England by an old settled nomenclature, while they have retained expressions which have fallen out of English speech. At all events the points noted seem slight evidence to outweigh the testimony of the general form of languages, of kindred mythologies, and the clear traces of similarities in art, architecture, manners, and customs. In regard to the word camel, however, its appellation may appear to be of considerable importance in this historical investigation. The camel must have been the means of the Aryans transporting themselves from a Bactrian home, and they would have found it exceedingly useful as they descended from the region watered by the five tributaries of the Indus towards Delhi. Camels are employed to great extent upon the plains of North-Western India, which, for months in the year previously to the rains, seem parched and sandy deserts. Egypt almost becomes realised in much of the scenery of the North-Western Provinces as strings of camels cross the yellow plains, though the annual rains convert those plains into verdant landscapes so rapidly as to seem the work of enchantment. But these plains are only deserts in similitude, for the grass-cutter will bring provender from a field which has no appearance of verdure.

The Aryans could scarcely have forgotten the name of their old useful animal, or altogether ceased to use him, if they had descended southwards; but if they had ascended to the northern plains of the Indus they might have only become acquainted with him by intercourse with the nomad tribes beyond the mountains. It is difficult to conceive the Aryans, as either conquerors or colonists, entering India, not as mere warriors, but accompanied by their wives and children so as to propagate their race in the country, with only the assistance of the horse.

The social condition of the Hindus, moreover, as reflected in the hymns of the Rig Veda, exhibits the civilisation of a people long educated in those districts of the earth in which settled abodes are suggested by the surrounding circumstances of nature. Allusions are found therein to towns and cities, to mighty kings and their prodigious wealth, to golden ornaments, and armour of gold and iron, to the needle, and to musical instruments, and to the fabricating of cars; also to medicine and astronomy, to gamblers, courtesans, thieves, and to the law of inheritance, etc.

If the race had developed its earlier civilisation in the Caucasus, according to M. Oscar Peschel's view, it would appear geographically improbable that it should have traversed Persia, crossed the sandy deserts of Caubul and Bokharia, and penetrated the passes of the mountain barrier of India, before spreading along the inviting shores of the Mediterranean into Greece and Italy, and thence into all southern and central Europe. India must, in that case, have been a later refuge of the race. But it is in India that the ancient literary monuments are found upon which these philological arguments are based. If the influences of India caused this earlier development of literature, why should it not be admitted that it occasioned the growth of the race altogether—the tropical gardens to the south affording that home for its birth and infancy which is wanting in the case of the Caucasus? Like those of Bactria, the fertile valleys of that comparatively small region appear to contain nothing to suggest the commencement of the great eastern and western religious, literary, commercial and art-loving polities. And barbarous tribes appear to have inhabited it in the classical times of Greece and Rome. When we compare Hindustan and the Caucasus, as to natural products, dimensions, and centres of population, taking into consideration the autochthonous civilisation of China, it seems impossible to deny to the former the possession of superior incentives to the attainment of civilisation.

CHAPTER XXXIX.

Professor Max Müller as to the Aryans "before their separation" not having known the sea—Argument that this might have happened on the plains of the Ganges and Jumna, or North-Western Provinces—Caspian Sea—Quotation from the Rig Veda as to sea-voyaging—Berosus and tradition of foreigners arriving by sea at Babylon—Probability of early Indian voyaging—Salt-pans—Diversity of English terms used in hunting and for weapons—Pickering's observation that the races of men that occur in cold climates can be traced, in continuity, to the Tropics—The three anthropoid orangs allotted to Borneo, Sumatra, and Western Africa respectively.

PROFESSOR MAX MÜLLER has argued that the difference of the name for the sea in Sanskrit and its sister languages indicates that the Aryan race had not seen the sea before its "separation." This would refute M. Oscar Peschel's view. But in regard to India it must be remembered that the plains of the Upper Ganges and Jumna afford a district of some 120,000 square miles, without approaching within 300 miles of the coast, yet without coming closely to the Himalaya mountains on the north or the deserts on the west. The extent of British India is difficult to realise when we consider it as a country and not as a continent. The sea-girt England and Wales only contain 57,785 square miles, but it is not improbable that, in the eighteenth century, many persons in the Midland Counties had never seen the sea, even if there are none to be discovered in the nineteenth century. The ancient Ayodhya was situated at about 450 miles from the nearest sea-coast. Canouge was still more distant. The plains of the five tributaries of the Indus are equally remote, with the sandy desert of Sinde between them and the sea, with which they only communicate by a river full of shifting sandbanks and difficult to navigate.

Moreover, our Aryan progenitors, if in the Bactrian region, could not have been materially farther from the Caspian Sea than from the Arabian Sea in the North-Western Provinces of Hindustan. They would have been as likely to have conferred a distinct appellation upon that inland sea as upon the Arabian Sea or Bay of Bengal.

The Caspian, however, in respect to emigrations by sea, or maritime expeditions, would not seem to have offered, like the Arabian Sea, temptations to trade. It presented no highway to shores whereon the products of rising civilisation would find a ready mart. It possessed no pearl fisheries. It was not within the zone of the monsoons or constant winds. Yet it would appear to be an expanse of often storm-tossed waters, an object of nature sufficiently striking to suggest a particular name for it. And in later times, at all events, the Caspian filled an important place in the highway of commerce between east and west. In fact, even if it could be demonstrated from the Vedas that the early pastoral Aryans were absolutely unacquainted with the sea, their civilisation might still have more feasibly arisen on the plains of the Ganges and its multitudinous tributaries, and on the five rivers of the Punjāb, than in the valley of the Oxus; unless the geographical aspect of these districts has entirely changed within the Vedic period, of which there seems to be no evidence.

And if this had been an inland people merely, who had passed from the Bactrian district to North-Western India, instead of being connections of the inhabitants of the Rajpoot districts and of Gujerat, it is remarkable that they should have obtained such a practical acquaintance with the sea by the time the hymns of the Vedas were composed, as to allude to its commercial aspect.

There exists positive evidence in a hymn of the Rig Veda that the sea was familiar in its period. In the volume of the "Calcutta Review" for 1868, it is observed that in *Ashtaka* (book) 1, *Anuvarka* (chapter) 10, *Varga* (section) 21, the 6th Sukta, or hymn, distinctly alludes to the ocean and its phenomena; and merchants are depicted as pressing earnestly on board ship for the sake of gain. In the same book (chap. xvii., sec. 8) mention is made of a naval expedition, and of a vessel foundering in a gale. This vessel is described as *Sataritram-navam*, a 100-oared ship. "The Rig Veda, moreover," continues the reviewer, "bears testimony to considerable progress in the art of shipbuilding. The Phœnicians have had the credit of having been the first to build sea-going ships; but in this, as in so many other matters, history or legend does not appear to have gone sufficiently far to the eastward.

Berosus, the learned Chaldæan and Babylonian of the time of Alexander, adduces the tradition of foreigners arriving by sea and imparting to Babylonia certain arts and civilisation. A foreign nation is related to have come up the Erythræan Sea (Persian Gulf) and instructed the Chaldæans in letters and arts, which nation could not have been the Egyptian. Taken into consideration with the extract which has been quoted from the Veda, these may be reasonably conjectured to have been Indians.[1]

Sea ventures seem indeed to be a point of connection between the ancient Aryans of east and west. The people of the Madhyama appear to have been naturally likely to have improved the art of shipbuilding.

Undoubtedly it is more humanly probable that people should have constructed vessels from the timber of wooded sea-shores, such as those on the western coast of India, than from those bordering on the northern Arabian Sea. They are more likely to have gradually enlarged their maritime enterprises westwards from the vicinity of Bombay, than eastwards from the mouths of the Red Sea or Persian Gulf. The natives on that side of India must have taken to canoes as naturally as the South Sea islanders. And the presence of much European shipping in the harbour of Bombay, during these last 200 years, has not occasioned alterations in the peculiar style of the native craft. Their light fabrics, sharp prows, and one immense latteen sail, present indeed similarities to the feluccas of the Mediterranean; but if they have formerly imitated those, why have they not, in modern times, taken example by our vessels?

A mere difference in the appellation applied to the sea by the Aryan nations scarcely seems sufficient evidence in itself to demonstrate that, before the emigrants who became the Greeks, etc., parted from the people who developed into those of the Vedic Sanskrit period, the Aryans had not made acquaintance with the sea.

[1] See Appendix XI.

Corresponding to the Greek ὕδωρ and Latin *unda*, we have the Sanskrit *udaka* and *udan;* and therefore Sanskrit terms for water were continued by the western Aryans, in the sense of wave or billow. The Sanskrit word *vāri*, water, is adopted for the sea in the Latin *mare* and the Russian *more*. The early Aryans may have simply styled the sea the water; for such will probably be found to be the present rustic nomenclature for any large river or lake in a rural district. The word may subsequently have become stereotyped for sea amongst the tribes of the western Aryans. Different appellations might be expected to have been eventually bestowed upon the blue ocean, the green Arabian and Oman's seas, and the blue but tideless, landgirt, island-studded Mediterranean; just as we have employed the two words ocean and sea. The Arabian Sea and Bay of Bengal present very different aspects, in respect to colour, tides, periodical instead of variable winds, etc., to the Mediterranean and Ægean seas; and the nomenclature of the former might not have been transferred to the latter, supposing the Indian seas to have obtained specific appellations, before the compilation of the Vedas.

The fact that the western words for ship, oar, and rudder are Sanskrit, seems valid evidence, in conjunction with other testimony, in favour of the Aryan race developing its civilisation partly by the sea. Then the Sanskrit *sara* appears to signify salt extracted from sea water, though Professor Max Müller has doubted this meaning. It is, however, indubitably a fact that salt-pans have been in common use on the sea-coast of India; and it is to be regretted that the English impost of the salt-tax has recently increased the price of salt to such an extent that they no longer pay for the working. Three pennyworth of salt has been raised in value, by the duty, to about 4s. 6d. Tons of fish are said to have rotted down the sea-coast, because salt could not be procured by the impoverished natives to assist in their drying; and therefore this valuable and constant article of food amongst large classes of the people seems to have been rendered extensively unavailable. But, as has been remarked, the archaic pastoral Aryans on the plains of the Punjab or Upper Ganges, might have composed or sung most of the Vedic hymns, with scarcely a definite acquaintance with the sea. The desert of Sinde on the one side, with the mountains of Rajpootana, Malwar, and the Western Ghauts, and, on the other, the swampy and pestilential delta of the Ganges, present imposing obstacles to approaching it. Orissa seems not to have been mentioned in the epics, though the temple of Juggernaut must mark an ancient sea-side resort. The peninsula of Gujerat on the western coast, and the western and southern shores, seem principally to have been in the cognisance of Valmiki and Vyasa. In prehistorical as in historical times, the greater enterprise of man seems naturally to have been directed towards the setting than the rising sun.

While in the employment of war chariots, and in other respects the modes of warfare in the epic periods of India and Greece present similarities, Professor Max Müller has observed that the terms for war and the chase mostly differ in the Aryan dialects. This appears to militate against the theory of the descent of the warriors of the latter from the former; still the argument seems to lose its weight when we consider the extreme technicality of much of the nomenclature of the crafts of war and hunting. In the copiousness of Sanskrit these may have become as diversified in that language as in English. The old science of venery had quite a language of its own 300 years ago, which is certainly no longer popularly comprehended. Military terms have greatly altered in the same period, even when the thing expressed has remained virtually the same. The nomenclature of weapons, for instance, has varied with the slightest alterations in their form. A sword has been styled a falchion, glave, rapier, escroc (a small stabbing sword), a bilbo, a sabre, a cutlass. A spear with a battle-axe head has been a halberd, partisan, glaire, and spontoon, according to small variations. A gun has been termed an harquebuss, caliver, fuzil, musket, rifle, carbine, and blunderbuss, for differences which the archæologist of days when soldiers may fight with nitro-glycerine hand-engines, or something of the kind, will comprehend with difficulty. In fact, a comparison of the English literature of Queen Elizabeth's days and of the American of Victoria's would not afford the same appellations for small firearms.

A modern adjutant would probably stare if his commanding officer, being a Shakspearian student, told him to darraign the regiment. And names were bestowed upon horses formerly which are rarely if ever used now, such as palfrey. Domestic articles and animals do not appear in old or modern times to have obtained such copious vocabularies for slight variations. The observable affinities between the ancient Indians and Teutons seem to outweigh these occasional points of difficulty. So the indications of Sanskrit in the Celtic languages, together with the ascertained features of Druidical rule, point to India as the Celtic birthplace. Comparing the physiognomies of the people of northern and southern India with those of northern and southern Europe, there would appear to be general suggestiveness of the Celtic in southern as of the Teutonic in northern India. The Scotch Highlanders' ancestry seems to be indicated in Afghanistan and amongst the Himalayas; where also a people of aspect and manners, suggestive of the Swiss, seems to be found.

"All the races," remarks Pickering in his "Races of Men," "that occur in cold climates, can be traced in continuity to the tropics." To carry the history farther back, he observes that "Oriental tradition, in placing the origin of man in Ceylon, reconciles in many respects the requirements of zoology;" and that "of the three orangs which, of all animals, in physical conformation and even in moral temperament, make the nearest approach to humanity, one has been allotted to Borneo, another to Sumatra, and the third to western Africa." Three races, originally only a degree above the apes, may have become more or less endowed with divine wisdom, and become humanity in the three great divisions of Eastern Asia, Western Asia and Europe, and Africa.

CHAPTER XL.

Miss C. G. Cumming's "Hebrides to Himalayas"—Scotch and Swiss affinities amongst the people of the Himalayas—Buddhism, its prayer-wheels, arks, etc., resembling that of the Israelites—"Merry-go-rounds" in India—and Biblical stories.

MISS CONSTANCE GORDON CUMMING, in her book entitled "The Hebrides to the Himalayas," has made some curious observations as to the Caledonian and Swiss affinities noticeable amongst the Himalaya mountains. She describes the general appearance of the houses of the Himalayan Highlanders as resembling the Swiss; while she considers the costume of the Paharis as very similar to that of the lowland Scotch. The men are dressed in warm blouses and trousers of grey homespun, with a plaid over the shoulders, and a cap of thick "woollen material, not unlike a Scotch bonnet; and the women are dressed in bright striped woollen material, with a long petticoat and plaid, sometimes in one piece like the old Scotch dress; while the poorest girl fastens her plaid with a large brass brooch of precisely the old Celtic pattern." She again observes that "it is curious that the Celts of Scotland, the Khabyles of Algeria, and these Paharis of the far east, should fasten the identical striped woollen material with the same very peculiar brooch." She also notices a passionate love of home amongst these Highlanders of the Himalayas, and a custom of sitting round the fire of pine or cedar wood to tell wild stories, like the Highlanders of Scotland. There exists amongst them, she says, a curious prejudice against naming husband and wife, similar to that which makes our Highland wife speak of her husband as "himsel'." She says that, as in the Highlands of Scotland, so the old custom is to be found in the Himalayas of walking sunwise round people, cattle, houses, or chapels, from superstitious motives; while the houses, with their projecting roofs and balconies and profuse carving, bear much resemblance to those of Switzerland.

She remarks that the general arrangements of the Buddhist chapels, in the mountainous regions which she visited, greatly resemble those of Roman Catholics. She saw priests habited in scarlet, with scarlet caps like a low mitre, divers small altars with images of saints, vases of flowers and incense burning before each image; and before the grand image of Buddha was a low table, whereon were set cups of water, tea, flour, milk, butter, etc. She found relics, offerings, sacred trumpets, etc., and everywhere was engraved the mystic sentence, *Aum mani padmi*—Om, the jewel, the lotus. And the logical termination of ceremonial worship seems to have been reached in the Buddhist prayer-wheel, in which the sacred sentence may be made constantly to revolve to the comfort of the worshipper, seemingly similar to that which attends upon the due repetition of *Aves* on a rosary. In the prayer-wheel Buddhists seem to have carried formal devotion to a ridiculous point. The Roman Catholic missionaries found them in possession of chaunted litanies, a form of baptism, incense, tho laying on of hands, processions carrying banners, the use of holy water, confessions, adoration of relics, ringing a small bell during the service, and shaven crowns with the priestly robes; monastic celibacy, with orders of nuns as well as monks, ascetic separation from the world in life-long penances worked out in lonely cells by hermits, ritualistic altars with images, generally of some female saint, crowned with a halo of glory; matins and vespers, with the choir standing right and left; rosaries of black beads, etc.; joss-sticks instead of the Romish tapers, and the great scarlet umbrella as the mark of Buddha's sovereignty. Their ceremonials therefore had remained parallel with those of Rome and those revived by modern Anglican Ritualists, up to the point of a prayer-wheel. She observes that the village deity lives in a sort of ark, which is fastened to long poles and taken out daily. "On the solemn festivals they sing and dance about the ark, with beating of tomtoms and sounding of trumpet-shells, making processions suggestive of those in which David danced about the ark." She says that, "I think that we must admit that the trumpery, tawdry ark, wherein the poor Pahari reverences a presence which he desires to honour, has, to say the least of it, some curious affinities to that glorious tabernacle of the Israelites, even the coincidence in size is very remarkable. The name of the Himalayan ark, and the accompanying ceremonies, are found in the Abyssinian Church."

She found "merry-go-rounds" among the Himalayas, spinning done by the men as they walked along, like the Welsh girls; and, as in Scotland, she says that the villagers collect their flocks into one great herd, and go slowly round the village, following the course of the sun. Certainly all these customs are not due to the presence of Europeans amongst them, for they have scarcely been visited, except by a few sportsmen, and still fewer travellers. It is difficult to conceive that they adopted their ark from the Israelites, for, if they had thus obtained it, why should they have imitated them in this respect alone? It would rather appear that the arks in the Himalayas and in Palestine are descendants of an ancient custom, probably in existence amongst the Egyptians, brought, with other customs, from the Indians. It is not extraordinary, apart from the divine interposition, that Moses should have ordered his sacred things to be carried in the old fashion. The ark would really seem to be merely a highland form of the "idol car" of the lowlands of India. It would also be adapted to the wanderings in the desert. In Switzerland travellers are conveyed in chairs, where carriages on wheels are unable to pass. On the other hand, it may be imagined that these Himalayan highlanders are the descendants of the lost ten tribes of Israel. But such a conjecture would appear to be supported by no evidence beyond this identity of arks.

The lost ten tribes have also been conceived to have been our own ancestors; but there appears to be no accurate testimony in favour of the idea, which depends principally on the belief that we have been especially favoured by the Almighty.

This authoress quotes the following discoveries of biblical stories in India. They may, of course, have travelled thither; but the prolific genius for story-telling exhibited amongst the Hindus may induce those who do not credit the absolute verbal inspiration of the Bible to think them probably autochthonous amongst them.

In building the great temple at Anaragapoora in Ceylon, it was commanded, as in building the temple of Solomon in Jerusalem, that every stone should be duly chiselled and polished in its own quarry, that no sound of hammer or axe, or any tool of iron, might disturb the solemn silence. A Cingalese king, bringing back captives from India, smote the waters of the sea, so that they parted, and he and his army marched through dry. The miracles of Elijah and Elisha, the chariot of fire, the judgment of Solomon, etc., are related as traditions of the Cingalese kings and prophets; with a sort of version of the narrative of the widow of Zarephath and the barrel of meal that wasted not. A race of itinerant fishermen in Borneo are related to perform an annual offering to the god of evil by launching a small bark, loaded with all the sins and misfortunes of the nation, which are imagined to fall on the unlucky crew that may be so unfortunate as to meet with it. This looks like a version of the Israelitish idea of the scapegoat, coming from one common centre.

From the Himalayas we have descended, in these remarks, to the extreme south of India and the islands. It may be maintained that the old commercial or other intercourse conveyed these stories to India or Ceylon. Considering, however, that the narratives are not in themselves in accordance with our human experience, and that we have rejected similar miracles when related of mediæval or modern saints, they may have been ancient traditions either of India or Palestine. Faith may hold them to have been actual occurrences, duly recorded in the annals of the Jewish nation, and attested with the same accuracy as proceedings in our journals of the Houses of Parliament; or they may be believed to have been divinely revealed, as facts which have occurred, to the "inspired" historian. Otherwise, if we compare India with Palestine, and the voluminous imaginative literature of the one with the literature of the other, the originals of stories appearing in both would seem more likely to have been Indian.

CHAPTER XLI.

M. L. Jacolliot's version of the Indian story of Adam and Eve, and Paradise in Ceylon—Mohammed's version—Adam's Peak—Temple of Ramisseram—C. Gordon Cumming's stories of Krishna—The heavenly city promised to his followers—His cursing a patch of ground—Christ as represented in the Catacombs of Rome—The Vedas and the future life—Chess invented by an Indian queen—Mesmeric cure—Almost miraculous power.

THE origin of man in Ceylon, according to the old Eastern tradition to which Pickering alludes, is illustrated by a mountain in that island bearing the appellation of Adam's Peak. The line of rocks connecting it with the mainland is styled Adam's Bridge. M. Louis Jacolliot, Judge in the French settlement of Chandernagore, has recently produced a version of the story of the fall of our first parents in the work entitled "Le Bible dans l'Inde," which recounts the manner of, and reason for, the expulsion from that Eden, in an analogous manner, yet differing in an important point from that of the biblical story. Professor Max Müller, in his publication on the "Science of Religion," has thrown doubts on the authenticity of this story, but he does not seem to have brought forward any positive evidence to contravene it. He merely suggests that it may have been invented by some crafty Brahmin, to gratify, or stultify, M. Jacolliot. It may also be conceived to have been invented to debase the Christian and Jewish faiths in the Mosaic story of the Fall. He suggests that, as one Brahmin deceived Wilford, so may another have recently practised on the credulity of M. Jacolliot. The greatest industry in Sanskrit research, however, and the most rapid comprehension cannot be confident of having read all religious or traditionary literature existing in the MSS. of India, or of having become acquainted with all its legendary lore; and M. L. Jacolliot may have discovered a genuine old story. The numerous colleges of Brahmins have evinced reticence in keeping their sacred literature from European investigation, rather than alacrity or pride in producing it. While the placing of the parents of the human race in Ceylon seems to epitomise the view of its tropical origin, the transference of the idea to some garden-like valley, such as that of Cashmere, seems naturally to have followed.

M. Jacolliot's Indian version narrates that "Adima and Héva, the first man, and that which 'completes' life," were placed in the fruitful island of Ceylon, and ordered by God to unite and produce humanity. The Prince of the Rakshasos, or evil spirits, inspired Adima with discontent. Tempting him to the shore opposite the mainland of India, he displayed before him a beautiful prospect thereon, with a bridge of rocks inviting access to it. Adima, impatient at being confined within the boundaries of even the lovely Ceylon, was eager to pass over to this tempting region; but Héva endeavoured to dissuade him from deserting the home assigned to them by the Almighty, and in which they had been ordered to remain. On Adima refusing to be restrained, she declared her intention of accompanying him, notwithstanding her regrets and compunction, as she felt it to be her duty as his wife. They accordingly traversed the rocks; but, on arriving at the opposite shore, the fascinating prospect proved delusive. They found a mere barren waste of sands and rocks; while the half of those rocks, which had composed their bridge, sinking into the sea, rendered return impracticable.

A voice from heaven proclaimed that, as they had abandoned the abode which had been appointed for them, they must, in the future, toil for their livelihood, but added, "Woman, thou hast only sinned from love to thy husband, and thou hast hoped in me. I pardon him for thy sake. But you may no more return to the abode of delight which I created for your happiness. Through your disobedience to my commands, the Spirit of Evil has obtained possession of the earth. Your children, reduced to labour and to suffer by your fault, will become corrupt, and forget me. But I will send Vishnu, who shall incarnate himself in the womb of a woman, and shall bring to all the hope and the means of recompense in another life, praying to me to soften their ills."

This speech may be a mere paraphrase of our sacred history, emanating from the imagination of M. Jacolliot, or from the craft of some Brahmin at Chandernagore; or it may be a legendary narrative arising out of the story of the garden of Eden, with that of the redemption of man, conveyed to India by Christian missionaries, and engrafted on the incarnation of Vishnu, the Preserving Power in Krishna. The appellations of Adam's Peak and Adam's Bridge may be thought to have been bestowed upon the mountain and line of rocks, which may be seen marked in ordinary maps, simply from the account of Adam's fall in the Koran. Mohammed placed the paradise of Adam and Eve in the seventh heaven. From this they were cast down to earth, after they had been tempted by Satan to eat of the fruit of the forbidden tree. Adam descended to Ceylon, and Eve to Arabia, where Adam, 200 years after, found her, and retired with her to Ceylon. Here they continued to propagate their species.

But unless there had been some ancient legend concerning it, why should Mohammed, in western Asia, have brought Adam to this distant southern and tropical isle? Our Holy Scriptures say nothing to suggest it. The whole story, as related in the Koran, looks like a compromise between the biblical and some Eastern version.

Adam's Peak is also held sacred to Buddha. The footprint, ascribed to Adam, is by the Buddhists supposed to be that of Gautauma Buddha. By the Hindus the line of rocks is connected with the invasion of Ceylon by the army of Rama, as related in the Ramáyana; and temples of extraordinary size and remarkable architecture occupy the island of Ramisseram, which is situated in the straits between Ceylon and the continent.

In Hamilton's "East Indian Gazetteer" it is said that "Ramisseram is an island of great sanctity, and possesses a celebrated pagoda, the entrance to which is through a lofty gateway, about 100 feet in height, covered with carved work to the summit. The door is about forty feet high, and composed of single stones, placed perpendicularly, with others crossing over—the massiveness of the workmanship resembling the Egyptian style of architecture. The square of the whole is about 600 feet, and it is probably one of the finest pieces of architecture in India."

The dimensions of India, and the number and diversity of its religious legends, may be easily conceived able to afford room for a story of the fall of man in connection with Ceylon and this line of rocks, as well as that of Rama, which has occasioned the sanctity of the island and the construction of this temple.

It is a fact that great difficulty has been found in ascribing the site of the garden of Eden to the north of the plains of Shinar, to which part of the world the biblical narrative appears to point, from the mention of the river Euphrates. The description of the rivers of Eden does not seem to apply aptly to the Euphrates and Tigris, with the Araxes or Phasis; near the sources of which the garden has been posited by our theologians. If we abandon the exoterical signification of the account in the Bible, and suppose that the Almighty, instead of forming man in his completeness, intellectual and physical, from the dust of the ground, endowed with reason a being who, in natural progression, had arisen above the highest apes which we now behold; in those forms which present the aspect of being crude attempts at the human, its exoterical meaning seems perfectly in accord with natural history. The Indian version, as narrated by M. Louis Jacolliot, is another pointed epitome of our early history, more applicable to the Aryan than to the Semitic races.

Subsequently the Spirit of God, taking flesh, or man rising to knowledge of the divine, led humanity in India, as since in Europe, as previously perhaps in the other worlds, which we contemplate in the distance as stars, to appreciation of holiness.

M. L. Jacolliot's story certainly suits our modern notions of woman's mission in life better than the Jewish version of the Fall, though the latter may accord with certain cynical notions concerning her. And, as has been observed, the position of woman in the ancient Aryan civilisation of India was similar to that which she takes in our own, rather than to that in which she has been retained in the Semitic civilisations. Her influence was constantly and reverentially regarded as beneficent by the old Aryans, though their literature shows that they had recognised her capacity for becoming coquettish or shrewish. It is said in Manu that "day and night must women be held by their protectors in a state of dependence;" but the general context of the Institutes shows that the dependence rather corresponded to that in which the European ladies are held, as to chaperones, escorts, and etiquette, than to that in which Mohammedanism keeps them in the Zenana. Woman's province was undoubtedly held to be the domestic, and it may be considered that a position of degradation was assigned to them in the eating after, instead of with, the men. But the Greeks had corresponding customs with regard to them; and in England we have, at all events, a great number of dining societies—legal, municipal, masonic, and military—at which women are excluded, besides the modern clubs.

Professor Weber, in commenting on the Sutras of the Veda, remarks—"We must at any rate assume among the Brahmins of this (the Vedic) period a very stirring intellectual life, in which even the women took an active part. We have here a faithful copy of the scholastic period of the Middle Ages: Sovereigns whose courts form the centres of intellectual life; Brahmins who with lively emulation carry on their enquiries into the highest questions the human mind can propound; women who with enthusiastic ardour plunge into the mysteries of speculation, impressing and astonishing men by the depth and loftiness of their opinions, and who—while in a state which, judging from descriptions, seems to have been a kind of somnambulism—solve the questions proposed to them on sacred subjects."

By copy of the Middle Ages of course the Professor means picture, as this period upon which he is commenting is admittedly more ancient than the Christian era.

This account of the sort of condition of clairvoyance, into which the women seem to have been plunged, is suggestive of what has been seen in connection with spiritualism, etc., in our modern times.

Miss C. Gordon Cumming has also adduced fragments of the stories and religions of Krishna and Buddha, which present some of these similitudes to those of Christ; which, from the time of the missionary Ward's book, at the commencement of this century, have been combated or maintained in European thought.

Krishna, she remarks, is now adored in Muttra (Mathura), where once twenty convents, occupied by 3000 monks, were sacred to Buddha; and where seven great towers surmounted the shrines, wherein lamps burnt day and night over his relics. Probably the fanciful stories related of Krishna seem no more preposterous to the Hindu than the turning of water into wine at the wedding-feast appears to us as narrated of Christ. Not only are anecdotes of our Lord but of the classic Apollo and Orpheus found in Krishna's career, as if the earlier history of Krishna or Cesava had travelled to Greece before the diviner aspect of the Bhagavad Gita, etc., had been imparted to him.

At the sound of Krishna's flute the stones and trees became animated, and he frolicked with and sang to wood-nymphs and milkmaids. Pilgrims at Muttra still hang linen rags as votive offerings on the branches of the tree whereon he caused the garments of a number of bathing milkmaids to be suspended, leaving them abashed and garmentless in the water. He strangled the huge black water-serpent which had poisoned the sacred river; crushing the head of the serpent beneath his foot after it had bitten his heel. So did Apollo and the Egyptian Horus slay serpents which had terrified their mothers. Under his sacred and Christian-like aspect, Krishna, "standing on a certain hill, healing people who thronged around him, made them whole whether their disease was mental or bodily." "He taught the people that he was at once their creator, their refuge, and their friend; their sacrifice and the road of the good; their counsellor and their teacher; and that they who knew and trusted in him also knew and trusted in Brahma the Supreme." His performance with the milkmaids' garments has been attributed to the desire of seeing them naked, but is more reverentially ascribed to the inculcating of a lesson for modesty of demeanour, or a rebuke for their manner of bathing.

The heaven promised to his followers is a vast golden city, with mansions, palaces, arches, pillars, etc., built of precious stones, gems, etc. Rivers of crystal flow through it; and there are lakes with the red, blue, and white lotus, with himself reposing in the midst on a throne, floating on the water.

He once cursed a patch of ground, which is narrated to have remained barren to this day. It has been observed that Christ, in the early pictures in the Catacombs at Rome, was painted as a good shepherd amongst flocks, with the pastoral pipe, like Krishna. Sometimes an ideal youth, sometimes a bearded man, sometimes as Orpheus surrounded by wild beasts, enraptured by the melody of his lyre. By the close of the fourth century we get the present type of countenance, which may be seen again as attributed to the Egyptian Serapis.

In some verses of the Vedas, observes Miss C. Gordon Cumming, Vishnu only appears as one of the Adityas—twelve characters of the Sun, corresponding to the twelve signs of the Zodiac.

She graphically remarks that the Vedas are full of the future life, telling how Yama was monarch of the world till sin entered, and with it sorrow, disease, and death; but Yama, passing through the grave and gate of death to the land of immortality, obtained a kingdom for himself, and now seeks to guide men thither. Death is recognised in the Vedas as only a heavenly birth. Agni is besought, in chaunts round the funereal pyre, to kindle the unborn part and convey it to the world of the righteous, "crossing the dark valley;" "the feet of him stained with sin to be washed," etc. The dead is adjured to clothe himself in "a shining form, a new and glorious body, that he may meet the Lord of death with the ancient ones—who, through mediation, through laying down their lives for others and bestowing their goods on the poor, have obtained the victory and gone to heaven."

Buddha, like Christ and Krishna, is also related to have delivered discourses on a hill. She relates that chess is said to have been invented by an Indian queen, by name Wandodaree, wife of Ravanna, king of Ceylon, the demon monarch of the Ramáyana. It is said to have been common for 4000 years in Hindustan, whence it went into Persia and Arabia, Spain and western Europe. Its ancient Sanskrit name was Caturanga, or Four Parts, and two persons originally played against two. The word rook is derived from the Sanskrit *rudh*, to check. Pawn accords with *peon*, an attendant. And again:—"It is impossible to walk through any Hindu ecclesiastical bazaar without recalling the descriptions of all the vessels of the (Jewish) Temple—cauldrons, pots, and bowls, shovels, snuffers, spoons, censers, basons, lamps, candlesticks, etc."

She records a curious instance of mesmeric cure, or power exercised by the imagination, in the case of her own moonshee's, who simply prayed over a woman almost in convulsions from a scorpion-bite in the foot, and rubbed the wound, and she recovered; and another of a man endowed with almost miraculous power in curing snake-bites, waving a dagger over the apparently dying patient, in part of his process.

A remark of hers charmingly illustrates the sanctifying and softening influence of distance of time. She says :—"I have often marvelled to see English ladies returning from church, where they had been paying devout homage to the memories of saintly Syrian Jews (the tradesmen of 1900 years ago), yet shrinking with contemptuous aversion from contact with their own servants, men differing in colour by but a few shades."

CHAPTER XLII.

Genesis not contradicted by placing the Eden of the human race in Ceylon—Rivers of Eden corresponding to the rivers of India and the Euphrates—Author of "Vestiges of the Natural History of Creation" on the origin of man in India—Is pristine purity shown in Genesis?—History showing that the world has altogether advanced in culture—Dow as to the Brahminical origin of Abraham—Considerations as to the Aryan element in the Jews, formerly classed with ourselves as Caucasian—Jews and Parsis compared—Possibility of a common ancestry of Jews and Affghans.

It does not seem that the account of the fall of man in Genesis is contradicted by placing the Eden of the human race in the tropical districts of Asia. The description of the garden of bliss and its rivers is inapplicable, in a definite way, to any existing region; but in a general, or metaphorical sense, it applies to India, or to Cashmere in a particular sense, more definitely than to any other part of the world. The conception of the Eastern origin of the legend seems to obtain consistency from the derivation of the word Adam from the Sanskrit rather than the Hebrew. In the latter language the name has been held to signify "red earth." In the former, Ādima means first, primitive, or original. This certainly appears to be a probable derivation of the word Adam, applied to the first man. The Sanskrit *ava, desiring, loving*—from *av*, to satisfy, fill, love, help, obey, embrace—looks very suggestive of a derivation for Eve. The word cherubim has been attributed to an Aryan origin. In fact, a general indication of the East appears throughout the biblical narrative, from Adam to Abraham. The expression in Genesis ii. 8, "And the Lord God planted a garden eastward in Eden," seems to point to India. The vague word eastward would surely have not been applied to Armenia or Babylonia by a writer in Canaan. In England we do not speak of countries nearer than Egypt or the Turkish empire under the appellation of the East. It suggests a general idea in the mind of the writer that man had commenced his history in some region to the eastward of the part of the world with which he was acquainted—viz. the Egyptian, Syrian, and Babylonian territories. It can scarcely be supposed that he had no knowledge of the vast inhabited countries beyond, considering the evidence of ancient commercial intercourse which has been adduced; especially as, in the account of Babel, the tower-builders are said to have journeyed from the East. He may have had a general impression that garden-like realms lay there from which man had been compelled to wander forth. Travelling traders must surely have transmitted accounts of the superior luxuriance in verdure and general wealth of the regions to the eastward. The rivers of Eden accord sufficiently with a poetical, legendary, or metaphorical account of man's origin, or the rise of civilisation in or about the really central part of the Eastern Hemisphere—viz. India.

The Pison (Genesis ii. 11), "which compasseth the whole land of Havilah, where there is gold," applies aptly to the Brahmaputra, which takes a great circuit through the mountains of Thibet and Assam before it returns to propinquity with the Ganges in Bengal. Assam has yielded a considerable quantity of gold. The word Havilah again, like that of Euphrates, may be considered of Aryan origin, as Professor Max Müller has said.

"The Gihon, which compasseth the whole land of Ethiopia," or Cush, may be understood to mean the Ganges; for it can hardly be supposed that the historian of the Bible intended the Nile, which flows in the land which we have called Ethiopia. He could not have imagined, living within cognisance of the two rivers, that the Euphrates and Nile, running in different directions, both flowed out of the same source. It appears that, in the Homeric period, Eastern Ethiopians were held to exist, who may be assigned to India. The geography of those periods was vague; but the author of the Bible, putting aside the question of Divine inspiration, must have possessed some definite knowledge concerning the two great rivers in his own part of the world.

The third river, "which goeth towards the east of Assyria," or eastward to Assyria, may be vaguely intended for the Indus, as well as any other existing river; while the Euphrates is named as the fourth. The Indian rivers might, by the biblical author, writing in western Asia, be conceived to have the same source as the Euphrates. The latter seems remote from the Indus; but the confounding together of the Caucasus and Hindu Kush does not seem so particularly absurd in studying the geographical knowledge of the ancients. Hesiod supposed the Ocean Stream to surround the earth, and knew little of the countries removed from the Mediterranean; and even Herodotus placed a bald race to the north-east, watching and gathering gold on the Hyperborean mountains. The rivers are given as distinct streams, but flowing from the four heads into which the river of Eden had been parted.

Four rivers have been fabled to flow from the Olympus of the Hindus. Four sacred rivers are said to issue from the lake called Manasarood, in the Himalayas—viz. the Brahmaputra, Ganges, Indus, and Sita, according to a tradition amongst the divines of Thibet. In fact, the biblical account appears to be in general accordance with the legends of the East, and to correspond especially with the tradition which has assigned the valley of Cashmere as the site of the garden. At all events, these four rivers seem to agree with the general tenor of the Bible narrative.

Bishop Butler remarks that Allahabad is venerated amongst the Indians as the traditional residence of the first parents of mankind. In India, as in Europe, diverse opinions have prevailed concerning the site.

The valley of Cashmere, however, seems most naturally to have been regarded as Paradise, on account of its loveliness, and the manner in which it is fenced around by the mountains.

By the Persians Cashmere was called the "unequalled." By the Indians it has been considered as holy land. The description of its charms has become familiar to us in Moore's exquisite story of its Feast of Roses, etc., in the Lalla Rookh. The three first of these rivers have their sources amongst the snow-clad mountains which environ it, and the Jhylum river in the valley itself answers to the biblical story. The whole of Cashmere is said to represent a garden in perpetual spring. Violets, roses, narcissuses, and innumerable other flowers grow wild in it, and the temperature of its atmosphere is not less celebrated than the romantic beauty of its situation and the fertility of its soil. In 700 places carved figures of snakes exist, according to Hamilton's "East India Gazetteer," which are said to be adored by the Hindus, and which again seem to have a weird correspondence with the biblical story. The truth surely is, that instead of having been adored they were represented here and elsewhere as enemies to man overcome by the Divine power.

The author of "Vestiges of the Natural History of Creation" wrote:—"Assuming that the human race is one, we are most called upon to inquire in what part of the world it may most probably be supposed to have originated. One obvious mode of approximating to a solution of this question is to trace backwards the lines in which the principal tribes appear to have emigrated, and to see if these converge nearly to a point. It is very remarkable that the lines do converge, and are concentrated about the region of Hindustan. The language, religion, modes of reckoning time, and some other peculiar ideas of the Americans, are now (1844) believed to refer their origin to north-eastern Asia. Trace them farther back in the same direction, and we come to the north of India. The history of the Celts and Teutones represent them as coming from the east, the one after the other, successive waves of a tide of population flowing towards the north-west of Europe. This line, being also traced back, rests at the same place."

This author then produces evidence for the origin of the Iranian, Malay, and Mongolian populations, and also the Syrian and Egyptian, from the same centre; but he shows that the negro is more probably of independent origin. He remarks that there is a tradition amongst the Hindus which places the cradle of the human family in Thibet; and that another makes Ceylon the residence of the first man. He observes that "we may expect man to have originated where the highest specimens of the quadrumana are to be found. Now these are unquestionably found in the Indian Archipelago." Undoubtedly much of the uncivilised humanity upon the earth seems only a big degree above the most advanced quadrumana, who seem themselves above the four-footed animals.

Is "pristine God-derived purity," as the author of a work entitled "Homo *versus* Darwin" has styled it, shown in Genesis? It is said in the biblical cosmogony that God blessed the man and woman, and saw that every thing which He had made was good; but man fell directly he was tempted. Then God is related to have cursed the serpent, and said that man should eat out of the ground in sorrow. Cain, his first-born offspring, committed murder, and received the reprobation of the Almighty in the first narrative given us concerning him. Noah, the second father of the human race, according to the biblical account, the chosen one of God, became drunken when he was tempted with wine. Surely these stories accord with a conception of natural proneness to err—to be corrected by knowledge learnt in suffering—taught by the incarnate Spirit, rather than with the notion of a fall from Godlike purity. If M. L. Jacolliot's version be a correct transcript of an ancient Hindu legend, it is virtually in accord with the biblical narrative; though in the one case man's discontent, and in the other woman's curiosity, are represented as the cause of the sin. But can we actually believe that progress in the world, or the pursuit of knowledge, is really sinful, though knowledge brings the sense of sin?

History testifies that the world has advanced, taking it altogether, in civilisation and knowledge, though occasionally retrograding. Why should we scorn an ancestry amongst the highest of those we call the lower animals? All animals, from mollusk to man, are parts of an harmonious whole; or an inharmonious, as it sometimes seems, when creatures, from man downwards, prey upon one another. Man is the ruling power, but so tyrannical and capricious, that he even slays the feebler animals for mere amusement. Protestant Christianity asserts that a great portion of humanity is so abominable that a just God can only condemn it to eternal torture, or at least death. Now the animals seem to fulfil their allotted walks in life with constancy and regularity, according to their natures. Man's intellect since the endowment with, or arrival at, reason and reflection, has ranged from the divine to what is termed the diabolical, and seems to exhibit rather a nature adapted for moral amelioration than one originally created in divine purity, because this erring nature appears from the first in Adam.

Taking chapter iii. verse 8 of Genesis again, in which it is said that God "was walking in the garden in the cool of the day," it would seem that the making of man in God's image, as described in chapter i. verse 26, was intended by the writer to refer to a material likeness. God is contemplated as a man in Genesis, as appears distinctly in this chapter iii. Eastward, again, appears to be the origin not only of the legends of the early history of humanity, but of the Jewish patriarchs (x. 30).

Dow, in the preface to his history, makes some curious remarks as to the origin of Abraham, of whose antecedents the Bible simply records that he was ninth in descent from Shem, the son of Noah, and that he was the son of Terah, the place of whose nativity was Ur of the Chaldees.

He undoubtedly appears to have regarded himself as a foreigner amongst the people of the region in which he was wandering, according to the biblical narrative.

The year 1996 B.C. has been assigned by Bishop Usher's chronology for the birth of Abraham, at which period, according to the literary and scientific evidence of India and China, those countries were enjoying civilisation too considerable to be recent. Egypt, on the testimony of its monuments, could then claim to have possessed it for 3000 years.

In the Koran Abram's father is styled Azer, who is considered by some of the Mohammedans as the son of Terah. Abraham is related to have been an idolater in his youth, brought to the knowledge of the true God. According to the Mohammedan legend he is not only supposed to have taught the true religion, but the arts and sciences. He also made inquiries as to the resurrection from the dead, and finally bequeathed the religion of Islam to his children, with its heaven and hell, etc.

In the account in Genesis we read of no aspirations for the future life, but merely of the heritage promised to his descendants. But as the narrative especially related to the descent of the Israelites from him, this may have naturally become the most prominent point. And the account was written by Moses, who introduced no after-life into his system of laws, unlike that of Manu, as has been observed.

Ur of the Chaldees has been assigned by orthodoxy to Chaldæa, in Armenia, which contained the sources of the Euphrates and Tigris. In the Book of Joshua, xxiv. 2, it is said: "Your fathers dwelt on the other side of the flood in old times, even Terah the father of Abram, and the father of Nahor, and they served other gods." It would appear, therefore, that little or nothing is said concerning India, and that the ancestry of Abram are left in sufficient vagueness. As no information except the names between Shem and Terah is given, any extraneous evidence may be justifiably brought to bear upon the original seat of his parentage. Dow observes that "whether the Hindus possess any true history of greater antiquity than other nations, must altogether rest upon the authority of the Brahmins till we shall become better acquainted with the records. Their pretensions, however, are very high, and they confidently affirm that the Jewish and Mohammedan religions are heresies, from what is contained in the Vedas. They give a very particular account of the origin of the Jewish religion in records of undoubted antiquity. Raja Tura, say they, who is placed in the first ages of the Kal Jug, had a son who apostatised from the Hindu faith, for which he was banished by his father to the west. The apostate fixed his residence in a country called Mohgod, and propagated the Jewish religion, which the impostor Mohammed further corrupted. The Kal Jug (Kali Yug) commenced about 4885 years ago; and whether the whole story may not relate to Terah and his son Abraham is a point which we will leave to others to determine."

The syllable 'bram, in the original name of Abram, may be certainly taken as corroborative of this assignment of a Brahminical descent to the Israelitish and Mohammedan patriarch. It is, at least, a curious coincidence, that this syllable in his name should be similar in sound to the appellation of the great spirit, Brahm, of the Brahmins. Abram is represented in the Bible as an emigrant from his own country, by the Lord's command, seeking a land in which his descendants shall become a great nation. In the Gospel of St. Luke, iii. 34, his father is styled Thara, and, "according to Suidas and others, Terah was a maker of images." But Dow's Indian story differs from the biblical, in that Terah is himself the emigrant to the west. This, however, does not seem in itself a sufficient variation to outweigh all other evidence. Even the biblical narratives of Christ have had to be reconciled in some discrepancies by theological students. Abraham is described as being very rich in cattle, in silver and in gold. This is suggestive of emigration from India, not from poverty, but, as Dow's story relates, from religious motives; still the wealth may have been made by successful sales of his pastoral wealth in Egypt, as Dean Milman surmises in his "History of the Jews." It seems not unreasonable to suppose that the polytheistic system of the Vedas, even although its divinities are merely supposed to be emanations from the One Supreme Spirit, may have been as repugnant to a Protestant mind in those days as the saints of Roman Catholic Christendom to our modern reformers. Abraham may be regarded, without contravening our Holy Writ, as a great original dissenter; not merely from the political assumptions of the Brahmins, as would seem to have been the case with the early Buddhists, but from a mode of worship which he considered derogatory to the dignity of the One true God. The Hebrews have now adopted the Aryan tongues, when settlers in Aryan lands, and only retained the Hebrew as a sacred and learned language. So may they formerly have adopted the Semitic speech of that part of Asia to which they had proceeded, and have abandoned their old Indian language with its polytheism. This notion receives corroboration from the Hebrew language having been thought to be less copious than the Arabic; which seems to be an older form of the Semitic than the Hebrew, so far as we can become acquainted with it.

In contemplating the modern Parsis in Western India, they seem to afford a distinct parallel to the Jews in Europe in general appearance, in their success in commercial pursuits, and in their adherence to their ancient religion, and to their ancient speech only as the language of religion. Their faiths present broad similarities when regarded from an outside point of view. The Hebrew religion has been found to have been infected by the Persian during the captivity in Babylon.

The Aryan races have usually retained language and characteristics in their colonisations. Yet it does not appear impossible that we may claim kindred with those whom we have so long regarded as the once chosen but lately abandoned people of God. They may have a descent from north-western India; having adopted the Semitic language because they found themselves amongst people of more settled civilisation than that found by Aryans in Europe amongst the old inhabitants. Of these the Aryans seem to have occasioned the gradual extermination in Europe, as, in modern times, in America and Australia. The European races, in those countries, are continuing their mother tongues. But if a number of our settlers permanently took up their abodes in China or Thibet, they might find themselves compelled to use the language of their adopted country. They might, however, like the Jews, still retain the religion which they had brought from their parent country, if the people, amongst whom they had settled, did not interfere with their profession of it.

In the course of many generations these emigrants, amongst a totally foreign race, might become exclusive in their faith, and stereotyped in their spiritual ordinances. Their unitarianism, combined with the peculiar customs which they have maintained in ages of habitation amongst foreigners, keeps them, perhaps, still distinct amongst races really of their own kindred.

Abraham seems to have retained the old Aryan altars, though refusing to recognise the Vedic sub-deities. So has the Church of England preserved the Catholic altars, but rejected the intercession of saints.

The Jews may thus be a branch of the Aryan race, or a race between the Aryan and Semitic, which were formerly classed together as Caucasian, till the intrinsic differences of the languages were observed. But it is not denied that these may have diverged from a parent language in the remote past. In fact it would seem that, instead of the Affghans being descended from the Israelites, it is possible that Israelites and Affghans, who have been considered Aryan, may be descended from the same parent stock inhabiting the regions about Caubul. The Jews may be commercial descendants of the same ancestors as the Affghans, still retaining amid their wealthy European settlements some of their old ideas of the freedom of the mountains. We Europeans scarcely regard the Jews as merely a religious sect, but as a race of foreigners settled within our borders, and, although adopting our country for the convenience of the time, prepared to return to Palestine, or migrate elsewhere, with their property, should advantages offer. The Parsis similarly retain their distinct aspect in India.

The Affghans, like the Jews, are Unitarians, idol and image

haters under the dispensation of Mohammed, as the Jews under the dispensation of Moses.

This view is certainly in accordance with the general tenor of the account in Genesis of the origin of the patriarchs, who came of a race which inhabited the earth eastwards. Abraham would seem to have travelled westwards, thus following the example of those who built Babylon of bricks, which, humanly speaking, they had learned to make in the civilisation of the continent of India.

The Jewish religion, after the return from Babylon, is thought to have been infected by the Persian system. Here the Aryan religion had assumed the aspect styled the dualistic, as exhibiting the antagonism, or, more correctly speaking, the alternating effects of Powers of Good and Evil, Light and Darkness. But here, as in India, the Supreme Spirit seems to have been all in all, from whom these creative and destructive powers had come; the personification of Evil, Ahriman, equivalent to Satan, being a conception of the later phase of the religion.

CHAPTER XLIII.

Schlegel on the doctrine of the transmigration of souls in India and Egypt—The Trinity in Egypt—Eusebius as to the Creative agent, etc.—Osiris the judge before whom souls are taken—Aryan traditions amongst the Jews—The metempsychosis expressed in a question to Christ—Elias in John the Baptist—Josephus as to the doctrines of the Pharisees and of the Essenes—G. Higgins on the metempsychosis in the Early Christian Church and amongst other nations.

THE Book of Genesis affords us no indication of any doctrines held by Abraham and his immediate descendants as to the rewards or punishments of a life beyond the grave. The Aryan doctrine of the transmigration of the soul, and its progress through successive bodies, with its hope of eventual reunion with the supreme and universal Spirit, seems to have been held in Egypt; but Moses, educated in its wisdom, is not related to have promulgated it to the Israelites, nor is there any mention in his books of the Christian heaven and hell. As has been remarked, Schlegel said that "the doctrine of the transmigration of souls through various bodies of animals or other forms of existence, and even through more than one repetition of human life (whether such migrations were intended as the punishment of souls for their viciousness and impiety, or as trials for their further purification and amendment),—this doctrine, which has been and still is so prevalent in India, was held likewise by the ancient Egyptians—even in the minutest particulars on the course of migration allotted to souls, and on the stated periods and cycles of that migration the coincidence is often perfectly exact."

The author of a Treatise on Egypt, published by the Religious Tract Society in 1841, wrote of the Egyptian religion that "its divinity recognises the doctrine of a Trinity, and the hope of a future incarnation of God. Its ethics rest upon the tenet of the immortality of the soul of man, upon his responsibility to his Maker for his deeds on earth, and upon his appearance after death at the judgment seat—that God's favour is everlasting life, and His wrath is death eternal." The embalming and preservation of the body would seem to infer that the Egyptians anticipated the resurrection of the actual body, and hoped for its resuscitation for the future life of the soul, rather than for the passage of the soul into another body.

According to Eusebius, from the monad Amoun issued an egg, which produced Ptha, the Greek Hephæstus, who was the creative agent of the universe, the divine intelligence (corresponding apparently to the Logos, the Word or Reason of the Almighty) sent by the Supreme to create all things from the beginning. Ptha is divinely incarnated in Horus, who is connected in idea with the moon, and descends to Hades as Hermes or Thoth, the conductor of souls. In his final incarnation he taught mankind the arts, etc. Thoth ascends again to heaven, through wisdom, light, and splendour, again to be absorbed in God, as the sun or wisdom of God. Osiris is the judge, before whom the souls are taken, and thence they are conveyed to Paradise, if good. They bathe in the pure river of the water of life, but the wicked are sent back to earth to transmigrate into animals, or transported to the regions of eternal darkness for torments.

Although no similitude of these doctrines appears in the books of Moses, in the institution of the Levites he seems to have appointed an ecclesiastical hierarchy, corresponding to the priesthood of Egypt or Brahminical caste of India. According to the Pharisees, moreover, he left many doctrines which were preserved only in tradition, and these seem to have partaken of the Indian character. Doctrines and ritualistic practices, not ordained in the laws of Moses, were held to have been duly transmuted from the promulgation of the law on Sinai. Amongst these was the doctrine of the transmigration of souls, the existence of which is certainly demonstrated in the question put to Christ, "Has this man sinned, or his parents, that he was born blind?" to which it was replied that it was in order that the glory of God might be manifested in him, as He afterwards said of the sickness of Lazarus (St. John xi. 4). The purport of the question is more correctly apprehended on reference to Indian law, which affirms a man born blind to be under a curse, and incapable of inheriting property, on account of grievous sins in a previous existence. Our Lord did not rebuke the doctrine according to our version, although He declared this case of blindness to be only designed for the manifestation of the Divine glory.

In an edition of the Greek Testament, published in 1826, and dedicated to the Bishop of Norwich, it is observed amongst the notes, which are stated to have been chiefly taken from those of the then late Bishop of Calcutta, that "the Jews believed at this time in the transmigration of souls, or metempsychosis. And they were taught to believe that a soul which had sinned in one body might afterwards be punished in a more imperfect one. To this effect is that saying of the author of the Wisdom of Solomon, that 'being good, he came into a body undefiled' (viii. 20). The disciples of our Lord seem to have adopted this philosophical doctrine, and to have asked him whether the sins of this man, in his pre-existent state, or those of his parents, were the cause of his calamity."

Again, in a note on Matt. xvi. 14, it is said that "these popular opinions concerning Jesus, whom they knew to have been born and brought up amongst themselves, manifestly presuppose the doctrine of the transmigration as being pretty general amongst the Jews. It was the expectation of the Jews that Elias or Elijah should come again to prepare the way of the Messiah. And they had a notion that Jeremiah should at some time appear to recover the ark of the covenant which he had hidden" (2 Macc. ii. 5).

Christ, when disclaiming to be Elias himself, distinctly asserts that He is come in John the Baptist, His forerunner (Matt. xi. 14); and again in Matt. xvii. 12, 13; while the apprehension of the doctrine by the disciples is shown by its being related that they understood that He spake to them of John the Baptist. It is remarked in a note of the above-mentioned edition of the Greek Testament that "the similitude between Elijah and John was striking—both zealous, singular in wild attire, fond of solitude, austere, undaunted enemies to vice, which they openly rebuked."

According to Josephus ("Antiq. of Jews," xviii. 2), "The Pharisees attribute all things unto Fate, and yet they take not an assent of will from man, supposing that God tempereth all things in such sort that, by His ordinance and man's will, all things are performed, good and evil. They believe also that the souls of men are immortal, and that after death they receive their reward, according as they have addicted themselves to virtue or vice in their lifetimes; the one to lie in perpetual prison, the other to rise again very shortly." "The chief article of the Pharisees' belief," he again writes in the "Book of the Wars," ii., "is that all things are to be attributed to God and Fate, yet that every man may, in many things, of his own power, do good or ill, though Destiny may help much therein; and that the souls of men are incorruptible; but only the souls of good men go into other bodies, and the souls of wicked men are sent into everlasting pain." And in the oration at Jotapata it is said—"Unto those souls who are obedient unto their Creator when He calls them He gives a holy and sacred mansion in heaven, from whence, after a revolution of the heavens, they are again remanded to animate bodies as pure as themselves. And that, on the contrary, they that cause their own death go into dark hell."

Whereas, according to the Brahminical and Buddhistic doctrines, a condition of heavenly repose—of bliss in tranquillity more or less merging in absolute extinction of self—seems to be held forth as the result of purity of life, while continual transmigrations are the consequence of desires of this world, this expression by Josephus of the pharisaical ideas would seem to present renewed existence as the reward of good and extinction the punishment of evil. But the passage which has been quoted from the Wisdom of Solomon, and other evidence, would, altogether, appear to indicate that the prevalent belief of the period in Palestine was that the fleshly habitation of the soul in continuing lives would vary according to previous existences for good or ill, and that an imperfect body was the consequence of ill-doing. Christ indubitably seems to represent disease as the result of sin when He says in St. Matthew ix. 6, "But that ye may know that the Son of man hath power on earth to forgive sins (then saith He to the sick of the palsy), Arise, take up thy bed, and go unto thy house."

The doctrine of eternal reward or punishment, in a condition of continued bliss or torment, may seem to have also been inculcated in the monastic sect of the Essenes of Palestine; as in the Elysian fields and Tartarus of the Classics; and in the Pythagorean and Platonic systems the metempsychosis was taught. Josephus says of the Essenes that "it is an opinion amongst them that the body is mortal and corruptible, but the souls remain immortal; and being of a most pure and ethereal substance, wrap themselves in bodies as in prisons, being drawn thereto by some natural inclination. But when they are delivered out of these carnal bodies, they presently, as freed from a long bondage, joyfully mount into the air. And of the good souls they say, as did the Grecians, that they live beyond the ocean in a place of pleasure, where they are never molested with rain nor snow nor heat, but have always a sweet and pleasant air. But the wicked souls, as they say, go into a place very tempestuous, where there is always winter weather, always lamentations of those who are for ever to be punished. For I judge that the Greeks are of this opinion when they say there is an isle for the virtuous, whom they call Heroes and Half-Gods; and that the souls of the wicked go to a place in hell, where it is feigned that some are tormented, as Sisyphus, Tantalus, Ixion. Another sort of Essenes allow moderate marriage."

The drawing of the souls to bodies by natural inclination, however, seems suggestive of pre-existence as an individuality, which trenches again upon transmigration before this relegation to the pleasant or tempestuous place. Godfrey Higgins observed in the "Anacalypsis" that "many of the early fathers of the Christians held the doctrine of the metempsychosis, which they defended on several texts of the New Testament. It was an opinion which had a very general circulation both in the East and in the West. It was held by the Pharisees amongst the Jews, and among the Christians by Origen, Chalcidius (if he were a Christian), Synesius, and by the Simonians, Basilidians, Valentinians, Marcionites, and Gnostics in general. It was held by the Chinese, and amongst the most learned of the Greeks by Plato and Pythagoras. Thus this doctrine was believed by nearly all the great and good of every religion and every nation and age."

He considered that the Pharisees had intermingled Magian notions (acquired during the Captivity in Babylon) with the law of Moses.

CHAPTER XLIV.

Dean Milman's sketch of the Essenes and their doctrines—Suggestions of the rules of Indian ascetics in the Essenes—Erskine on the separateness of the Jews—The Gipsies—Resemblance in sacred histories, east and west—Besides Abraham, Melchizedek at least had divine truth—Quotation from Max Müller as to studying man's natural growth in the Veda.

DEAN MILMAN remarks that the Pharisees "believed in the immortality of the soul and the existence of angels, though their creed on both these subjects was strongly tinged with Orientalism." Of the tenets of the Essenes, whom he defines as the monastic orders of the Jews, Dean Milman says that they "seem evidently grounded on that wide-spread Oriental philosophy, which, supposing matter either the creation of the Evil Being, or itself the Evil Being, considered all the appetites and propensities of the material body in themselves evil, and therefore esteemed the most severe mortification the perfection of virtue. The reverence for the names of the angels points to the same source, and there is one ambiguous expression in the account of Josephus, which, taken literally, would imply that they worshipped the sun."—"Among groves of palm trees, of which, according to the picturesque expression of Pliny," he writes, "they were the companions, and amid fertile fields won from the barren wilderness, they (the Essenes) passed their rigid and ascetic lives. They avoided populous cities, not from hatred of mankind, but from dread of their vices. In general no woman was admitted within their domains, and they were recruited by voluntary proselytes, or by children whom they adopted when very young and educated in their discipline. Among the Essenes all pleasure was forbidden as sin; the entire extinction of the passions of the body was the only real virtue. An absolute community of goods was established in their settlements; but for charity, or for the assistance of the poor or the stranger, they might draw as largely as they would on this general revenue. They were all clothed alike in white garments; they rose before the sun, and devoted all the time to break of day in offering up certain ancient prayers. After this they received their orders from the superior, and went to work at the labour or craft in which they were skilled; but their artisans might only work the articles used in peace, though they carried arms when they travelled to defend themselves against robbers. Having worked till the fifth hour, eleven o'clock, they assembled for refreshment. First, however, they washed and put on a linen garment, and entered the common refectory as if it were a sacred place; there in silence waited till grace was said, then each received, from the baker and the cook, his portion of bread, salt, and hyssop. They observed the Sabbath with the strictest precision; they all met in their synagogues, where the elders interpreted the sacred writings, explaining them chiefly by parables. Though they sent their gifts to the Temple, they offered no sacrifices there. They were strict predestinarians. They believed that the body was mortal, the soul immortal. They believed, with the Greeks, in a delightful region beyond the ocean, in which the souls of the good dwelt for ever. There rain and snow and parching heat were unknown, but the air was continually refreshed with balmy and gentle breezes from the sea. The souls of the wicked were doomed to a cold and gloomy place of everlasting punishment. They were great students of their sacred books, and especially of the prophetic writings; many were endowed, according to Josephus, with that gift. They studied likewise the nature and cure of diseases, and the medicinal properties of herbs and minerals. They were bound by solemn vows to worship God and to be just to men; to keep inviolable faith; if entrusted with authority to abstain from all wrong and from splendid apparel; to love truth and hate liars; to communicate only to members of the society the tenets of the sect. They abstained from all oaths, considering an oath as bad as perjury. They abhorred slavery as an infringement of the natural equality of men. In their civil constitution they were all equal, as regards their rights, but divided into four classes, of which the superior looked down so much on those beneath them, that, if touched by one of the lower order, they were defiled, and washed themselves. No man was admitted into the society without the strictest probation; the proselyte received a small pickaxe, linen garments, and a white dress, and so commenced his year of noviciate. Whoever was guilty of any great crime was expelled the society; having sworn that he would receive no food from any but his own sect, the outcast fed like a beast on the grass of the field, till at length he perished with hunger. The Essenes were cruelly persecuted by the Romans, who probably entered their country after the capture of Jericho. They were tortured, racked, had their bones broken on the wheel, in order to compel them to blaspheme their lawgiver or eat forbidden meats. They did not attempt to appease their tormentors; they uttered no cry; they shed no tear; and even smiled in the worst agony of torment, and, in stedfast reliance on the immortality of their souls, departed rejoicing from life."

It is incontestable that suggestions are, in this account of the Essenes by Dean Milman, contained, on the one hand, of the rules for Brahminical students and ascetics in the Institutes of Manu, and, on the other, of the general tenor of the teaching and ordinances of apostolic Christianity. The Therapeutæ, or "contemplative" sect of Jews in Egypt, seems to afford a still nearer resemblance to the Hindus. The pure following of Moses seems to have abided in the Sadducees, who trusted only in his written law,—"which say that there is no resurrection," in the words of St. Matthew, and who rejected all these traditions and mysticism of the Pharisees. These last appear to have constituted the more popular sect. Christ seems to upbraid them for their hypocrisy and devotion to mere ceremonial rather than for their essential doctrines.

The castes and sects of India, for generation after generation, have retained their religious and social positions virtually unalloyed. After contemplating, as a special place of example, the continued exclusiveness of English, Protestant and Catholic —Portuguese Catholics, Parsis, Mohammedans, and Hindus, with their subdivision of Jains, in Bombay, the separateness of the Jews in Europe and the rest of the world altogether bears far less of a miraculous aspect than formerly. Erskine, counsel for the prosecution, on the indictment of the publisher of Paine's

"Age of Reason," in the year 1797, alluded to it as powerful evidence for the actual truth of Christianity; but the Jewish position loses its uniqueness as we widen our sphere of vision; the Parsis, as has been observed, presenting a similar phenomenon since the conquest of their country by the Mohammedans. And there are also the Gipsies, who have evidently come from a wandering Indian people, probably of the Pariah or outcast tribes. Europe at first styled them Bohemians, not being able to look far eastwards for their origin. Classes in India have preserved their exclusiveness in religion and social intercourse for ages.

The Jews may have proceeded from a commercial caste of the north-western borders of India, or Abraham may have been the emigrant son of a chieftain, as related in Dow's disquisition on his origin, or he may have dissented from his image-making father's views, and so wandered westwards in search of a home, with his family, servants, and cattle.

He has been assigned to about the same period as Zoroaster, and it has been thought that personal intercourse may have taken place between them. But there would appear to have been ample space for both in the Asian regions to the north and west of Caubul. The Bible, at all events, seems to offer no suggestions, unless the Iranian prophet could be referred to the divine Melchizedek. But he is assigned to Canaan, while Abraham and Zoroaster have been thought to have possibly met in Haran or Arran, whence Abraham went forth to seek the Promised Land.

The points of resemblance between the sacred books of the Jews and the Persians, as of their present aspect and position in the world, seem to exhibit a similar degree of similitude to those noticed as existing between the Ramáyana and Iliad, and in the legends of Krishna and the Gospels. There is the obvious explanation of ancient Aryan origin, except to those who insist upon the religious necessity of our believing that God extended his first favours only to Abraham and his descendants, and that civilisation first arose on the plains of the Euphrates. The most orthodox, however, must at least admit that the divine light had irradiated the mysterious Melchizedek, King of Salem, "the priest of the most high God" (Genesis xiv. 18), who was "made like unto the Son of God" (Hebrews

vii. 3). He, at all events, according to the Bible, must have been a standard of divine truth in the age of the patriarchs, showing that they did not alone possess it. The authors of Genesis (Moses) and of the Zendavesta (Zoroaster) may have been alike acquainted with old legends, which had been originally born in India. The Madhyama was prolific of meditation and imagination for the reasons which have been given, as evidenced by the enormous bulk of its religious and romantic literature and art, fanciful in every variety of form.

Professor Max Müller has admirably said that when we "study man's natural growth" in the Veda, "we see him blest with the choicest gifts of the earth, under a glowing and transparent sky, surrounded by all the grandeur and all the riches of nature." He has "a language capable of giving soul to the objects of sense, and body to the abstractions of metaphysics."

In every respect this description seems to apply to India; and there we find this Veda; while the country remains in its ancient and apparently autochthonous culture to this our day of British rule in it. The religion of the Vedas, Buddhism, Krishnaism, the faith of the Jains, and Sivaism, must all be allowed to have originated in India; but the Osiris of Egypt may be thought to have influenced the latter, just as the purer and more Christian-like aspect of the Krishna religion may be held to be actually owing to Christianity. But if the Vedic expressions of devotion to Agni, etc., are denied any influence conducing to the formation of our Western religion, they must at least be supposed to have affected the faith of Krishna. And the inhabitants of the Indian continent, virtually of the size of Europe, have originated so much, that it seems more reasonable to admit that the gradual association of ideas in the course of thousands of years formed all those faiths which we find there. The Aryans thus claim to have received them by divine inspiration. We Aryans of the West, ignorant of our cousinship in the East, have thought the divine inspiration Semitic. We knew it to be older than ourselves. The personifications of the Sun, Wind, and Fire in the north-west; the dome-shaped emblem of creative power in the south, became merged in the adoration of deified humanity. Under the appellation of Buddhism, or enlightenment, a system of monasticism arose. Jainism was another aspect of it, and

Mahadeva (great god) was the personification of deity, under which this chiefly came, as apparently shown by the adaptation of the lingam to the dhagob, subsequently surmounted by the umbrella of honour, and converted into a relic shrine, like the altars of Roman Catholicism. The warriors of Rajpootana and the north-west naturally were disposed to adore the divine in the chivalrous Krishna, who lived in the world of aristocracy, rather than in the ascetic Gautauma, who contended that rank was of no benefit, and that the abnegation of earthly honours was the highest privilege of man. Krishnaism and Buddhism might seem to have gradually arisen to those expositions found in the Mahábhárata, and in the Buddhist canon of Scripture, during the thousand years B.C. The Apollo of Greece was a descendant of earlier aspects of Krishna, from the incarnation of Vishnu, considered as the Sun. Sakya-Buddha, if he actually lived at the epoch which we have assigned to him on the faith of the Ceylonese chronicles, introduced a stricter meditative asceticism into the Buddhist system, which was really the adoration of the divine in perfected humanity. Christ may have been the fulfilment of all. If the Bhagavad Gita was founded on His words, at all events the imagery of the Agni was before His time, and strangely foreshadowed the story of His life. There is plenty of space in the respective districts of Mathura and Magadha to allow of both Indian systems growing up independently. And the dialects of the two countries were different.

Brahminism naturally came into existence amongst the warlike people of the north-west as a counterfoil to the military power; just as the strength of Roman Catholicism placed its foot upon the necks of the haughty warriors of Europe for a time. In claiming class barriers for themselves, the Brahmins —*i.e.* the literary, learned, or thinking society of the period— had naturally to order them for the other ranks of men. Krishna was claimed as the divine incarnate in a warrior, for their support. Buddha, Christ, and His possible copy in Salivahana, came for the people, without consideration of rank.

CHAPTER XLV.

Mr. Fergusson on Indian architecture—Considerations as to the origin of art in India, Egypt, Greece, etc.—Pickering as to the cultivated plants of Egypt—Commencement of our architecture at the Tower of Babel, according to the Bible—Quotation from the "Pioneer" of Allahabad as to a modern Hindu temple—Central American civilisations from Asia—Arts and sciences proceeding from India, evolved out of the suggestions there of Nature.

MR. FERGUSSON, in his History of Indian Architecture, seems to represent that both the Babylonians and the Greeks arrived at the arts of building and sculpture in stone before the Hindus. He considers that the Dravidian races of the south of India commenced a very active period of temple-building in about the seventh or eighth century of our era, or at the earliest, the fifth century. These races he conceives to have been descended from or allied to the Accadians, or ancient inhabitants of Babylonia. At this comparatively recent epoch they began to imitate their ancestors, or elder cousins, of the plains of Shinar; or perhaps, in their architectural efforts, subjectively followed the instincts of their race. He thinks that the Hindus took example by the Greeks, during their temporary establishments in the north-west of Hindustan, and emulated the stone architecture in which these had lately become so excellent. He attributes to the Hindus a strong imitative faculty or instinct.

As the origin of Greek art has been referred back to Egypt, and prototypes of the earlier Greek style are found in the excavations of Nubia, we are again, therefore, relegated to these wonderful settlements on the Euphrates and the Nile—these artificial oases, or comparatively small districts of fertile meadows amongst vast arid tracts, for the original fountains of the arts. The minds of men must again be referred to heaven-sent inspirations, or inexplicable intuitions of genius, for their art conceptions. Pickering has said that "it is no new remark that the cultivated plants of Egypt have all been derived from abroad." But, according to this opinion, though nature in Egypt had to be supplemented, the arts sprang in original conception from the soil. They, at least, were not borrowed or introduced. It would seem that in thus assigning the rise of stone architecture to Egypt and Assyria, Mr. Fergusson contradicts his own theory of the derivation of stone from wooden architecture. The Assyrian and Dravidian styles may not display the wooden forms, and he may therefore mean that these arose spontaneously in stone; but surely the builders must be held to have first seen architecture in timber, and the styles arising out of it, before they boldly cut and adapted stones to their purpose, or made bricks in imitation of cut stones.

According to this view, the Aryan race in Greece acquired from the Egyptians the rudiments of a style of art and architecture, which it has since cultivated partially in India, and continuously in the Roman Empire and modern Europe. In the south of India the Dravidian race is thus considered to have adopted from its kindred in Babylonia architecture and art, which has long survived the extinction of the parent city or empire which created the style. The destruction and continued desolation of Babylon may be assigned to the fulfilment of the Divine prophecies recorded in the Bible. Still it is strange that the architectural style of this artificial settlement should have taken root and flourished with such tenacity among the millions of southern India, amongst whom it has so indigenous an aspect.

Why people devised in Egypt or Nubia, or the Accadians in Assyria, certain architecture rather than in India, can only be answered by the assertion that the Word of God informs us that architecture commenced with the building of the Tower of Babel on the plains of Shinar, and therefore that the priority must be assigned to that part of the world. As, however, we have modified our conceptions of the meaning of many biblical passages since becoming acquainted with astronomy and other sciences, we may surely explain this portion of its records also in the light of other history.

The Hindus can imitate accurately, and have doubtless imitated, Greeks, Portuguese, English, etc.; but, on the whole, the aggregate of peoples in India, as bounded by the Himalayas and the ocean, continue in their peculiar fashions. Many temples have been lately erected in all the completeness of the Indian mode; not merely in districts little likely to have been affected by European influence, but even in the midst of English commerce. In the little island of Bombay, one may be seen with a tramway running past it. Within the year 1875, to quote from a Bombay correspondent of the "Pioneer" of Allahabad, a "Hindu temple has been lately finished, which occupies a conspicuous position in the frontage of the Kalbadevi road, not far from the establishment of the Bible Society. It is remarkable as exhibiting the complete characteristics of the Hindu style, unaffected by the western civilisation in its vicinity. It is constructed of stone, profusely carved and decorated with coloured images of dancing girls, exuberant monkeys, ascetics, and youthful Indian Apollos piping to light blue cattle who listen in rapt and intelligent attention. This is the first view of a Hindu place of worship which the Prince (of Wales) will obtain on the road from the Fort to Byculla and Parell, and it will serve as an apt introduction to the novel architectural scenes which he will behold in India. An inscription announces it to be the gift of Soonderdass, son of Thucker Mooljee Jetha, and dedicated to God Dwakanathajee, Sumvant 1921; and from this point he will see little evidence of European life till Byculla again brings it on the scene."

In comparing other races with the Aryan, we see that the Africans have advanced but never reached the high order of civilisation. The Mongolians have progressed somewhat, still have remained more or less barbarous. The Chinese race has produced a most systematic materialistic civilisation, owing to the natural advantages of their fertile and well-watered country. We do not find, in the present day, that the comparatively desert tracts stimulate to invention of arts to counteract the sterility of nature. On the contrary, we see the inhabitants leading simple and inartificial lives. The inhabitants of more naturally favoured districts introduce the arts of civilisation amongst them if they obtain them. To America it would seem that the Mongols, or tribes allied to them, made their way by Behring's Straits or the Aleutian Archipelago, and became the Red man. From India humanity spread over the world to the north and north-west by the various routes open; and its people, or its civilisation even, probably reached the north of America by the westerly winds and currents prevailing across the North Pacific, and founded the Central American civilisations.

Pickering has stated that, within a few years of his writing, a Japanese vessel had drifted to the American coast near the mouth of the Columbia river.

In India our world-ruling race may be held to have evolved the arts and sciences out of the suggestions of Nature; upon evidence nowhere in the world besides to be found to admit such an inference.

Mr. Fergusson has shown from wooden forms came the first stone architecture; but seemingly at some thousands rather than a few hundred years B.C. Gradually the wooden forms, in some of their architectural styles, became merged entirely in the application of others suitable only to stone, by the natural procession of ideas in small steps. Thence to Egypt by the oared galleys which appear to have been used, up the Red Sea to Assyria and the Euphrates, by the Persian Gulf to Greece and northern Europe, by the Red Sea and Egypt, or through Asia Minor and by the Hindu Koosh and Caucasus, proceeded the inhabitants of the central land which had grown into the broad divisions of Aryan and Dravidian, with their arts. These were improved upon and stereotyped according to the national styles, naturally occasioned by the scenes in which the people became domiciled. Such—to recapitulate—rather than a radiation from the site of the Tower of Babel, would seem suggested by geography, by the remains of ancient cultivation of art and literature in India, and by the fact that it preserves, in the aspects of its people and their manner of life, pictures of the pre-Christian civilisations of the earth, besides suggesting those of mediæval Europe. If this aspect had been derived from imitating the various ancient peoples, it would seem reasonable to suppose that the modern Europeans, settled amongst them for more than two centuries, would have been also more or less universally copied.

CHAPTER XLVI.

Colonisation and art going from India to Egypt, etc., Greece, etc.—Art in India suggested by the exuberance of Nature—The cotton-pod—Indian flowers, etc. —Value of the cocoa-nut palm in dawning civilisation—Sir R. Phillips as to manufactures in cotton, etc., commencing in India—Note of Megasthenes.

OF course structural temples now in existence in India might be universally shown to have been erected since the fifth century A.D., or so, without impugning the probability of their being the successors of similar edifices. We know in England that many bits of Saxon ecclesiastical architecture, which seems to have been of similar character to that which we term Norman, are hidden in the later additions of churches. The conduct of the Hindus in the present day, in respect to conservatism in their style of sacred architecture, would certainly induce the belief that structures of ten centuries ago, suggesting classic or Assyrian art, were descendants of a long line of gradually improved autochthonous architectural attempts rather than imitations of foreign designs. From this fruitful soil the superabundant inhabitants pressed outwards rather than poured inwards, as from Europe in the present day towards the New World. There were doubtless famines, pestilences, and wars to keep down the Indian populations in old times as at present. But emigration must also account for the overflow of population produced on that prolific soil and climate during the 3000 years B.C. in which the Institutes of Manu suggest the existence of an orderly, agricultural, commercial community, with only one of the four chief castes devoted to warfare. As has been observed, their immense old works for storing water show the attention anciently paid to the obviating of famines by irrigation. In the richness of variety, the combination of the stupendous and fanciful, of Indian scenes, art assumed surprising varieties of shape. Art designs kept pace with the multitude of nature's suggestions in a region which embraces throughout its well-defined length and breadth the vegetation of both tropical and temperate climes. Amid the marble mountains of Greece, overlooking the blue Mediterranean, this art, inspired originally by the fulness of nature, became tempered to more simplicity and acquired truer nobility. In Egypt and Assyria the absence of timber occasioned the settling of the styles of architecture in the granite or brick work of those countries respectively. The forests of northern Europe subsequently modified those Gothic forms, the prototypes of which may be seen in the excavations of Karli and Salsette. The inhabitants of the old Madhyama imitated; but it was Nature who taught them in mountain and forest scenery, and in the luxuriance of that vegetable life on which our animal life is founded, which in the cosmogony of Genesis is created before animals and man. Dress has been an important consideration in the history of civilisation. Like the fashions of our houses, elegance and eccentricity in costume have by turns prevailed. For the commencement of that art which has culminated in luxuriance in modern Paris, again in India the first hints for fashions may be discerned, devised, and exhibited by Nature. From sewing the fig leaves together to make aprons, as recorded in Genesis iii. 7, to the weaving of cotton into raiment, and adorning it with the flower patterns, seems the evident commencement of civilisation in this respect. Cotton is not considered indigenous to the district of the Tigris and Euphrates.

The Hindu ladies, in their Greek-like robes, and the Bombay fisherwomen with their single pieces of cloth wrapped gracefully around their figures from neck to knees, leaving head, arms, and legs bare, with merely little gay cotton jackets in addition, have been totally unaffected by crinolines and the various European modes which have passed before their eyes during the last 200 years in this island. It is scarcely probable that the Hindus copied the Greek women of Bactria, or the temporary Greek settlements of north-western India. But if we consider the flowers of the Indian woods, and the cotton-pod, allowed to be indigenous in India, exhibiting its useful product, it seems evident that in Nature the ancestresses of these women may have found their models. These inhabitants of India, who still sit upon the ground, or rather upon their ankles, in something very like the original monkey fashion, whose appreciation of their floral world is seen in their constant employment of its blossoms in chaplets, and in the passages of admiration in their poems, etc., may be most reasonably conceived to have been taught by the great milliner Nature herself. A wealth of Nature's loveliest ornaments is theirs for imitation, combined with other influences which have caused the civilisation of their land to soar above that of the aborigines of the tropical islands. Was it not natural to imitate in the fabricated cotton the beautiful tints of the great flower bells, which hang in fascinating profusion and picturesque suggestiveness of the feminine robe? To quote from the "Modern Traveller," of the year 1828, a few passages illustrative of the Indian floral wealth:—"Among the Indian trees and shrubs remarkable for their beauty the *Hibiscus ficulneus* is distinguished by its magnitude and the profusion of its elegant blossoms; it is also of peculiar value in a tropical climate, as hardly any insects are found under its shade. The cotton tree rises, with a thorny trunk eighteen feet in circumference, to the height of fifty feet, without a branch; it then throws out numerous boughs which are adorned in the rainy season with large purple blossoms; these are succeeded by the capsule containing the cotton. The *Nyctanthes hirsuta* (or *Sambac*) and the *Jasminum grandiflorum* (*Kadtumaligu*) boast the most fragrant blossoms of the Indian flora; the former perfuming the night, the latter giving forth its scent by day. The *Gloriosa superba* and the Indian vine form by their union bowers worthy of paradise. The *Butea superba*, a small tree, by the striking contrast of its green leaves, black flower-stalks, and large scarlet papilionaceous blossoms, attracts the admiration of the most incurious. Among the trees which diffuse their fragrance over the forests of Hindustan, while they adorn them with their splendid blossoms, is the *Pandanus odoratissima*, together with various species of *Bigonia*. The elegant *Atimucta* (*Banisteria bengalensis*); the *Tchambaga*, used by the Indians for adorning their hair and perfuming their clothes; the

Mussoenda, which displays in fine contrast its white leaves and blood-red flowers; the *Ixora*, which, from boughs six feet in height, exhibits its scarlet and yellow tufts of flowers 'like so many bright flames enlivening the foliage of the woods;' the *Sindrimal*, which opens its flowers at four in the afternoon, and closes them at four in the morning; and the *Nagatalli*, or *Pergularia tormentosa*, a parasitical plant poisonous to the serpent tribe;—may also be mentioned among the more curious and remarkable varieties in Indian botany. The sensitive plant is said to grow spontaneously in the Amran district of Goojerat. The fine white rose called the koondja scents the vales of Delhi and Serinagur; and the rose plantations of Cashmere yield the highly valued attar," etc. etc.

Besides the life-sustaining plantain, the mango, held by many to be more delicious than the peach, and the fruits of both tropical and temperate regions, India, like the tropical islands, possesses in the cocoa-nut that which must have been one of the first aids to, or suggestions for, the commencement of utensils for food and drink, in addition to its other numerous benefits. The gourd may have suggested the larger description of domestic vessels, but the cocoa-nut requires only to be broken in half to afford a most convenient cup. Its contents offer both meat and drink, its fibres yield rope or matting, and the big leaf of the tree is obviously available as thatch for roofing.

While European savans have been seemingly reluctant to admit the higher originality of the Hindus in our prevailing forms of religion, art, architecture, political conceptions, poetry, etc., they seem at least to have admitted their priority in the spinning and weaving of cotton, silk, and wool. Sir R. Phillips observes that "Hindu manufactures are generally imitated in Europe, and even retain their names. Calicoes, cossacks, jaconets, boncks, chintzes, mulls, japans, ballusores, bandanas, pullcates, ginghams, etc., are all Indian names and mere imitations;" and that the Hindus have the priority even in the minute circumstances of package, salvage, fringe, marks, etc. etc. Megasthenes even affirmed that famines had never visited India, the people gathering in their two harvests annually, with their double rainfall, and never losing both harvests. In his observations as to their truthfulness, good faith in dealings with one another, rare resorts to lawsuits, etc., combined with this view of their immunity from famine, he certainly represents them thus as a people, inhabiting a country with incitements to civilisation. Grain harvests mean property, and property demands order in the State and the aid of religion. Babylonia was prolific in grain, but not adjacent to the gardens in which nature could support primeval man till his transition to culture.

CHAPTER XLVII.

Sanskrit and Tamulian languages, etc.—Longer periods to be allowed, 15,000 years or 450 generations being no really excessive period for the growth of civilisation, etc.—The Indian castes all credited with the same origin in their cosmogonies—Reality of religion in India—The old warrior and merchant castes may be now in Europe—Codification of laws—Distinctness of nationality possible between Indians of North and South, as between Teutons and Celts, yet of same family, language, etc.

ALTHOUGH the languages of the Aryan and Semitic races, formerly classed together as the Indo-Caucasian, seem to show no clear community of derivation, it appears to be not impossible that they may be referred to some common origin in the remote past. So, in regard to the Dravidian, or Tamulian, or Telingan races of India, although the obvious Sanskrit words existing in their dialects are considered to have been introduced in comparatively modern times, it would nevertheless seem in accordance with the philological evidence that the Sanskrit and Tamulian languages branched off from the archaic tongue and dialects of the people of the earlier pre-Vedic Indian civilisation. In fact affinities seem to be traceable between the Semitic, Turanian, and Indo-European families of speech, as if they had been originally allied.

On comparing the aspects of Teutons and Celts in Europe, that of Aryans and so-called Dravidians in India seems suggestive of a parallel. Pickering has remarked that no distinction between the white and Telingan race is recognised by the people of India themselves. He observed coincidences between the Greeks and Indians of the island of Celebes, which seem due to a common source in India as a whole. He adduces spears, shields, swords, altars, sacrifices, auguries from entrails of victims and flights of birds, while he notices that the Indian proa resembles the Mediterranean galley. He states that Æsop's Fables are found amongst the Malays. If we admit

India, as the central region, to be the original model from which these fashions came, this seems no marvel; but otherwise we can hardly conceive it possible that positive Greek influence was felt in this remote Eastern island. If the Vedas exhibit the Sanskrit of between 1500 B.C. and 3000 B.C., which changed to the classical Sanskrit, and again diverged into the various dialects of India, considered to have been derived from it, surely there may have been, some 10,000 years previously, a language in existence, or group of languages, from which Sanskrit, the Semitic tongues, and the Tamil of southern India, may have alike proceeded. Civilisation may have been then commencing in India in the pastoral and cereal-cultivating forms, and in the more arid portions of Asia in the nomadic, while the Finnish people may have been pressing or pressed towards northern Europe from Tartary. This period of 10,000, combined with the semi-historical 5000 years, or more completely historical 4000, only makes 15,000, no lengthy duration of time as compared with astronomical periods required for light to travel from the fixed stars to ourselves, etc. etc., not to mention eternity. In fact, 15,000 years, to return to the computation of three generations per century, only afford us 450 generations, no great number for the realisation of steam and electricity by mortals, which, even if known, as the religious world may suppose, to Adam, the divinely educated father of the human race, had certainly been forgotten since his fall.

Mr. Fergusson appears to assert that the position of the Aryans as a conquering race is shown by the Brahminical caste system; the subdued races being placed in inferior castes. But this theory is not at all supported by the account of the origin of castes and the general remarks concerning them in the Institutes of Manu. And he has written, "It is remarked that, in their buildings, a community of thought and inspiration is displayed, which could not have resulted unless the Tamulians and Aryans have drawn from one common source," which seems contradictory to this opinion concerning the Aryans as conquerors. According to the account in the cosmogony of Manu, the four pure castes alike proceeded from Brahm, the eternal and absolute spirit; the Brahmins being produced metaphorically from the most honourable part of the figure, the seat of intellect.

In fact, the Brahmins are not represented as a ruling race, but as a class set apart for the service of God, in regard to religion, law, the constant perusal of the holy scriptures, etc. They are to act as guides or advisers to the kingly and warrior and other castes; but the powers allotted to them rather resemble those exercised in England by the clerical and legal fraternities than those assumed by the old Norman military conquerors. And although much moral authority is allotted to them, it is only to be theirs on condition of their leading most self-denying lives. Their self-negation is indeed ordered to extend to almost every act of their existences; and the doctrine is carefully inculcated that Brahmins are nearest to God, and to the hopes of future blessedness. They are taught that failure to continue in purity of life will occasion the loss of their superiority to other men. It must be remembered that, according to the doctrine of the transmigration of souls, distinctly promulgated, in a systematic form, in these Institutes, those born in lower castes may aspire to become Brahmins in a future life, and thence to rise to life in the Eternal. And a misbehaving Brahmin is to be punished by degradation to a lower caste in a next life, while men may, by gross or sensual habits, sink so low as to become the meanest animal or even vegetable existences; which all have the spirit of life within them. It is related, in Indian legend, that a Brahmin, who desired to become a sovereign with the purest intentions, was reborn as a monarch, and became a most virtuous and excellent ruler. Divine sanction is attributed to the kingly authority, but again, not as apart from the general caste system, but in subservience to the Brahminical moral authority. The Institutes of Manu, allowed by modern science to have been the production of the epoch succeeding that which produced the hymns of the Vedas, thus demonstrate that the priestly and learned caste were aiming at the possession of power, and the preservation of their class purity, but that, professedly at least, and, to judge from the Institutes, to all appearance sincerely, this class desired to serve the Supreme Spirit of Holiness faithfully, and to employ their power in harmony with the interests of the other castes, for the benefit of mankind in general. It is impossible to contemplate the excess, the superstitious zeal of religious devotion, which characterises, and has historically characterised, the Hindus as a people, without believing that devotion, rather than hypocrisy, was the mainspring of their conduct. Death may come to them suddenly in so many ways, from the savage animals in the forests, or snakes in the grass, in addition to the methods of destruction which menace Europeans, that from this, combined with the enthusiasm in asceticism amongst them, it must be conceded that, while we believe religion to be reality upon earth, it has here obtained a likely home. There is sense of humour and plenty of gaiety amongst the Hindus, but their old literature seems to show a serious people. Ayodhya and Palibothra can scarcely have been so gay as Paris, or as devoted to practical work as London. Christians, with narrowed gifts of charity, have characterised the Brahmins as crafty and hypocritical. If they can lead lives of seeming self-negation only for the moderate recompense in worldly goods which they obtain, and some veneration of the multitude, who can be confident that our comfortably situated Rectors and Deans and lordly Bishops are entirely devoid of self-seeking motives?

The religious exercises and retirement into the forests for the contemplative hermit life, advocated in these Institutes, seem to have become very prevalent. And the Christian virtues of temperance and docility have reigned amongst the masses of the people. The old hard-drinking, hard-fighting set—the original warrior caste—certainly seems to be chiefly recognisable, mingled with the merchant caste, in Europe, though still existing in parts of India.

The position and history of the Brahmins and of the other castes altogether suggests a condition of society evolved in indigenous growth, rather than a combination of conquering and conquered races. Mr. Fergusson has indeed recognised the absence of any assertion of difference of nationality for the superior castes in the Institutes. But he seems to regard these as a comparatively modern conception of jurisprudence, not as a compilation of ancient laws, legends, etc. They clearly, however, appear to be a codification of ancient traditions concerning the studies and devotions of the Brahminical class, and, for the castes in general, of the rights of property, and justness of conduct in the concerns of marriage, commerce, war, etc. etc. In our Blackstone's Commentaries the Normans are exhibited as conquerors in the remarks on the feudal system, and in those upon the customs of our ancient English tenures, such as descend upon the modern Manor. In the Institutes of Manu no such claim is advanced to the possession of the land by a class; and the system of ownership would certainly seem to have been due to the gradual arrangement in settled order of rights of property which had arisen out of the cultivation of the soil.

The four castes of the Aryans may therefore be held to have been permanently ordered to remain separate under this legal system, arising in the north of India. These Aryans, who so arranged their polity in regard to their commencement as a people, might have been originally akin to the Dravidians or Telingans of the south. It would appear that the inhabitants of northern and southern India might have grown out of the same stock; yet, as they settled into civilisation, they might have lived for ages without intercommunication beyond that of mere travellers from one to the other. The chains of the Vindhya mountains, the Nerbudda river, the savage jungles of Orissa, and the rugged sylvan and mountainous districts of Berar and Gundwana, rendered the plains of the Ganges decidedly distant from the banks of the Krishna. These rivers are, in fact, about 600 miles apart, an important distance before these days of railways. If it can be demonstrated that no affinity can be discerned between the essential components of the Aryan and Dravidian or Tamulian forms of speech in India, it can only be evidence of the separate growth of their civilisations and languages. It cannot militate against this theory of the Aryan origin in sub-tropical and luxuriant India rather than upon the more barren uplands of central Asia, and of mankind in general from the tropical regions of Asia rather than from the plains of the Euphrates. If the Aryans had developed in the Bactrian or Caucasian districts, they would still have been near people speaking a different class of language. If, therefore, Sanskrit and the older Tamulian speech cannot be brought into a family like German and Latin, taking other evidences into consideration, it ought only to be held to show that in the earlier history of Aryan civilisation much absolute invention was bestowed upon our language to separate it so entirely from the Turanian forms. The curious intermingling in the excavated temples of Ellora, of the different styles of Karli and Elephanta, may not only indicate conjunction between the religions of the north and south, but also between their civilisations; or it may show that the countries became politically united. So in northern Italy the classical art of southern Italy and Greece, and the Gothic style of the north, have coalesced. But the Latin and Teutonic unity of race has only become recognised in modern times.

CHAPTER XLVIII.

Considerations as to the origin of the Aryan race in propinquity to those styled Tamulian—London and Rome—Idioms of the Deccan, etc.—Pritchard as to an element in India like that which produced the Gothic tongues in Europe—The higher castes may have more easily developed in India itself—Quotation from Pritchard as to tradition giving the origin of mankind as one Race—Natural sequence of agriculturists and warriors preying upon the peaceful people, and Brahmins by education and religion restraining them—The Catholic priesthood in Europe—Quotation from the Ode of Jayadeva as to Vishnu, incarnate and bathing in the blood of Kshatryas—Difference of appearance between the classes and peoples of India not greater than between those of Europe—Buddhism a reaction against class assumptions—Early civilisation of the Tamulians—Natural reasons for the commencement of architecture, etc.

It appears that the early Tamulian literature exhibits Sanskritic derivations in its terms of philosophical import, etc. This would seem to indicate that when the north and south of India intermingled, after each had singly advanced in its own characteristics and civilisation, the south brought exuberant fancy in art and the north science and literature to the general improvement. A similar phenomenon appears to be observable in southern and northern Europe. Since the epoch of the Roman Empire Art and Music seem especially to have found their schools in the former, philosophy and science in the latter. In the days of the Roman Empire the Aryan race was widely different in north and south in respect to the amelioration of manners and education, if the accounts which have come to us are correct. But the north with its barbarism contained certain manly virtues and a love of liberty, which have resulted in our own civilisation. London has advanced in its commercial influence throughout the world beyond Rome.

"The most celebrated Indian grammarians," says Pritchard in his "Researches into the Physical History of Mankind," "who have written in Sanskrit, regarded the Tamul and all the other dialects of the Dekhan as Prakrits, or as dialects entirely formed on the basis of the Sanskrit, and derived from that language with more or less of popular corruption." And this opinion he observes to have been at one time universal amongst Anglo-Indian scholars. But more accurate research has fully proved, he continues, that the idioms of the Dekhan form a distinct family of languages, which borrow much from the Sanskrit in literary compositions, but have in reality no essential connection with that ancient idiom. "Late writers have thought that they perceived traces of a further affinity between the dialects of the Indian peninsula and the popular idiom of Hindustan—that there is much that springs from a common original in the Telugu, Kannádi, and Tamil, and in the popular dialect of northern India. Apart from the words of Sanskrit derivation, or from the Persian and Arabic introduced after the Mohammedan invasion, there are words apparently common to the two classes of language. In the methods of conjugating verbs and declining nouns, in respect to the use of auxiliaries in the first and the smaller number of cases in the second, the characteristics seem in accordance. There must, therefore, in India," says Pritchard, "have been some element, like the Gothic and other Germanic tongues in Europe, though much less influential, to produce this modification of languages, the greater part of whose vocables are Sanskrit; but where will either history or tradition allow us to look for any such modifying cause, except in an aboriginal language, following a different course in this respect from the Sanskrit?" He draws a conclusion that if it should become established that the modern language of Hindustan is derived from the native idiom of the barbarous aborigines of India, we shall be obliged to suppose that the Sanskrit was the idiom of the higher classes, and the barbarous tongue that of the lower orders at the same time; just as Norman-French in England was spoken by the higher class, while Anglo-Saxon prevailed among the lower people. He observes that four great tribes are represented in the poems, *sastras*, and cosmogonies of the Hindus, as coeval in origin; the Brahmans springing from the head of Brahm, the kingly and warrior caste from his arms, the merchants from his thighs, and the Sudras from his feet. But all of these, or the three first at least, he thinks may have entered

India in one body and reduced to a life of labour the aborigines, including perhaps the fourth caste, the Sudras or cultivators of the soil.

But again it must be urged that it is in accordance with both natural and political history rather to conceive these higher castes as developing, under the advantages offered by India itself, and in its ample space. It is also in accordance with the rights in the soil claimed by the peasantry under Hinduism in India. The language which they there elaborated may there have arisen with greater probability than elsewhere. In north-western India the warrior and learned classes became defined aristocracies, and the latter fenced their order by exclusiveness, and the bulwark of religion; eventually extending throughout the peninsula this stereotyping in caste of the natural order of men.

And Pritchard also makes an observation which corroborates this view. "Among the Buddhists," he says, "a separate tradition or myth has been handed down respecting the origin of mankind; and this explicitly declares that Brahmans, Xatriyas, and all the other castes, are of one race. In the extracts from the 'Atthakatha,' published by Mr. Turnour, we find a legend importing that mankind, after their corruption by guilt, found it needful to have a punisher of crimes. They chose from the common stock the most beautiful for their sovereign. The choice fell upon a Khattiyo, that is a Xatrya, who became accordingly ancestor of the warrior tribe, and himself a Rajah. It is added, 'Thus it was, descendant of Wasitho, that in the race of Khattyo the illustrious name descended as his original appellation; they are descendants of the same, and not of different races of mankind.' This is a strong testimony that no difference of race was known, as a matter of fact, among the ancient people of Hindustan."

There seems to be no reason why the aristocratic classes of India should not have arisen to power from amongst the masses by a natural process. First, the physically strongest would sway the rest. Then the intellectual would endeavour to keep down the tendency to tyranny in the strong by the engine of religion or superstition.

The aspect of the Brahmins, from their picture as presented in the Institutes of Manu to that afforded by them in our own time, is so evidently that of a class endeavouring to obtain influence by intelligence, and at least the profession of virtue, that it would seem to have been by arts, not by arms, that, from the north-west of India itself, not from the more barren realms beyond, they gradually grew into power over the whole country. Not only the race, but the Brahminical idea, or the Brahminical idea alone, may have spread from north to south.

When man had become acquainted with agriculture, according to the cruel predatory habits which we see in him in common with the wilder animals, a warrior class would naturally have begun to prey upon the peaceful industrious cultivators, or pastoral owners of wealth in flocks and herds. Then the rising Brahmins, for the benefit of themselves and the community at large, may have probably brought these warriors into the subjection of intelligence, just as the Roman Catholic priesthood, in later days, subdued the savage soldiers of northern Europe. Some great warrior who espoused their views may have occasioned, in the remote past, the origin of the idea of the personal incarnation of the Preserving Spirit of deity in the sixth great incarnation of Vishnu, in the first of the three Ramas. This is related in the Ode of Jayadeva :—"Thou bathest in pure water, consisting of the blood of Kshatryas, the world, whose offences are removed, and who are relieved of the pain of other births, O Cesava, assuming the form of Parasu Rama; be victorious, O Heri, lord of the universe." This is the seventh incarnation in the rhymed account of the chief incarnations of Vishnu, which has been quoted.

The difference in appearance between the aristocratical and other classes in the various States in India does not seem to be greater, on the whole, than may be observed between them in Europe. As in Europe, so in India, the people of the south are darker than those of the north; and the skins of those who labour with their hands, and are exposed to the sun, are darker and coarser than those of the Brahmins, etc. Some of the latter have complexions of complete purity. But these are evidently due to the abstinence of the class for ages from coarse aliments and manual toil, and from marriages which we term mésalliances. Between the inhabitants of northern and southern India, and between the Sikh and Bengalee, there are differences of corresponding distinctness, though of course different in character, from those which distinguish the German from the Italian.

The so-called Aborigines, found in a rude condition amongst the hills, etc., have either not advanced or they have retrograded from their situation, or from the caste system—our gipsies also seeming to have come from Indian outcast tribes. Even if their race is held to differ, as the Siamese from the Malayans, there is room for them and the superior races to have originated in India as for the latter in Asia to the eastwards and its islands.

Climates and natural conditions widely vary in India, intercourse between districts being often naturally difficult. That man should have commenced the pastoral and agricultural life, impelled by the necessities of existence, and claimed the right of property in the land which he had cultivated; that the strong and ruffianly, becoming especially skilled in the use of weapons, to which they had particularly devoted themselves, should have plundered the peaceful property-holders; seems the obvious history of the beginning of civilisation. Then arose an intellectual class, observing the heavens, meditating on man's nature, etc., by whom religion was apprehended and divine terrors invoked in aid of the security of peaceful folk. The fear of heavenly castigation, in the lightning blast or whirlwind, was impressed upon the minds of the tyrants and marauders, and this intellectual or priestly class naturally protected itself with caste restrictions to preserve its purity and power. This progress of events seems more consonant with probability than the notion of a whole race rising to civilisation yet entirely deserting a region which had been so favourable as to suffer them to quit the nomad existence for settled homes. The love of home seems to be a constant emotion in human nature; and the philological evidence appears to indicate that the Aryan race had settled abodes before its western branches were separated from the eastern. Wherever the Aryan race originated in Asia, it must have been in the vicinage of some people, Turanian or Semitic, using a language belonging to another family, and exhibiting different characteristics from the Aryan. India, with its more luxuriant soil and climate, its propinquity to rich tropical regions, etc., would seem to have afforded a home more conducive to lingual and political progress than the regions beyond the Hindu Koosh. The inhabitants of the south of India appear to present undoubtedly more affinity to the Aryans of the north than the people of Turkestan or Tartary. It would not seem improbable, on the other hand, that the Aryans, or their progenitors, multiplying on their fruitful Indian soil, before they commenced the voyaging which resulted in the civilisations of Babylon and Egypt, should have penetrated the mountains to their north-west, and settled more or less permanently in the fertile valleys. These would offer sufficiently strong temptations for cultivation to those who were acquainted with agriculture, but can surely not have possessed the same incentives or suggestions to commence it, as the fertile river plains of the sub-tropical Ganges, and the five rivers of the Punjab. It would seem in accordance with the development of artificial contrivances to aid existence as they are required, as early astronomical observations show a northern latitude, if the science of astronomy should have naturally received an impetus when the Aryans found themselves amongst the more barren regions of Asia; whereon the observation of the stars becomes a matter of practical importance. The Aryan race has most fully utilised the science of navigation, steam, and electricity, now that it has settled in our island at the north-western extremity of Europe; from which it has returned to subjugate its ancient ancestral land, the older and original, but now feebler branch of our family.

In considering Pritchard's comparison of the Sanskrit and more barbarous idiom of India with the co-existing Norman-French and Anglo-Saxon in England, it must be remembered that the conquest of England by the Normans corresponds to the over-running of Bengal by the aristocracy of Oude, not to an irruption of foreigners from beyond the Indus. Normans and Saxons are both Aryans.

The inventive faculty of our race, which has in these later days produced so many scientific and mechanical discoveries and inventions, appears, in its early history, to have given birth to the Sanskrit language, which has been so much lauded by philologists for its grammatical structures, harmony, and capacity. It certainly seems reasonable to suppose that the language arose in the country in which we find the literature by which we are acquainted with it. Certainly the arts of the southern Indians display in them neighbours more susceptible of civilisation, and more in harmony with the Aryans of the north, than the tribes which, in historical times, have inhabited the mountainous regions or wild steppes of Northern Asia.

Investigations into the civilisation of the most ancient Tamulians of India are said to have brought to light towns, temples, the arts of weaving and dyeing, etc., but not literature, painting, or the fine arts. Temples, however, would be sufficient to evince the dawn of art. That sculpture in wood is natural to uncivilised man in tropical regions is shown by the wood carvings to be found amongst the islanders of the eastern seas, as has been remarked. In the mountainous and rocky districts of Southern India, the transition to stone seems natural. These temples and towns may be reasonably conceived to have displayed this species of ornamentation. The fulness of this may perhaps still be seen in the wonderful excavations of Ellora, made after Brahminism had descended southwards, and religion had begun to be illustrated in sculptured representations of the human forms of deity, and when its symbolisations had begun to be elaborated into systems.

Physical reasons would urge the construction of houses and temples in the south of India, of an order superior to those naturally demanded by man rising to mechanical knowledge in South Sea islands. Not only are the rainy seasons usually heavy, but the heat, tempered by no sea breezes inland, and the scorching dust of the dry weather, render interiors from which the glare of the sunshine and the dust may be excluded, most obviously welcome. The long hours of enforced cessation from active exertion in the heat of the day would naturally afford, or even suggest, opportunity for careful and assiduous attention to such an art as carving—commencing in wood and continuing in stone.

CHAPTER XLIX.

Considerations as to the prototypes of the Gothic style at Karli, etc.—Greek style at Beni Hassan, but the Tuscan column common in the wooden form in India—Ionic style at Persepolis—Mohammedan conquest of India as to destruction of Temples—Southern India more likely to have suggested Temples than Assyria—Temples in Cambodia—Treatises on architecture in the Sanskrit—Excavated rocks at Mahabalipuram—As to the lion in India—So-called Græco-Buddhistic figures found in the north-west of India—May not they and the capitals in Corinthian style attributed to the Greeks be Indian, as Corinthian style only in vogue in Greece from about Alexander's period?—Temple of Chilamburam—Tanjore, and works of irrigation—Correspondence between Christian era and that of Salivahana.

CONTEMPLATING the Hindus collectively throughout India, there would certainly not appear to be more difference between those of the north and south than between the inhabitants of northern and southern Europe; and their arts and manners of life vary in the same proportion. Indeed there would seem to be no greater variation than between the English and the Irish-speaking population of Ireland;—that is to say, they represent two great branches of the family tree.

Two different styles of art, architecture, and life in general, grew up in southern and northern Europe. In the case of the Classical nations, their art conceptions have not been supposed to be autochthonous. Egypt has the credit of their origin. The excavations of Beni Hassan in Nubia have been allowed to exhibit the prototypes of the Doric style, formed before the fifteenth century B.C., or thereabouts.

For Gothic art a prototype has not been acknowledged amongst another race; but in India, at Karli, etc., are as distinct models for the Gothic style as the columns at Beni Hassan for Greek architecture.

In India there exist specimens which may also be recognised as the prototypes of those at Beni Hassan. In fact, it appears that both the Doric style and another totally divergent, and suggesting the general type of what is termed the Gothic, which styles have been so extensively affected by our Indo-European races, are to be found in our seemingly original country. We have not only improved upon them but invented them. The prototype of the Tuscan column is to be commonly seen in its wooden form in India—the probably direct descendant of the first efforts at architecture.

The Ionic style has been noticed in the ruins of Persepolis. Taking into consideration the Oriental rather than Grecian aspect of these remains in general, and the certainty that the Zend-speaking people came from the east rather than the west, and were closely allied to those who spoke the Sanskrit; considering also the infinitely greater probability of art relations existing between Persepolis and India than between Persepolis and Greece; it altogether seems reasonable to surmise that India rather than Greece afforded the model. There appears to be nothing in the history or surroundings of Persepolis itself to argue the probability of its having been the original fountain of the style.

The Mohammedan conquests doubtless occasioned the destruction of temples and many great architectural works in the north. As the style exhibited in the cave temples of Karli, Salsette, etc., has been considered Buddhistic, and seems evidently to be either Buddhistic or early Brahminical, and as both Brahminism and Buddhism appear to have arisen in the northern division of India, and the style of architecture is likely to have descended southwards with the Brahminical or Buddhistic power, it seems probable that we see in these a northern style of architecture, originally produced in timber. This style has been reproduced in northern Europe. The German language has been thought to display especial affinity to the dialect of the Buddhistic Bahar. Language and architecture therefore seem to accord in constructing the history of the progress of our race from northern India to northern Europe.

Southern India still exhibits in actual use those magnificent and marvellously-fanciful temples, which are more likely to have preceded than followed those resembling them in Assyria; if Nature, ever varying in forms of vegetable life, be admitted to be more likely to suggest art than when she assumes her more barren aspect. Here may the cradle of infant art be more reasonably supposed to have existed than in any other part of the world, because the greater number of educational incitements to art efforts were here offered, combined with climatic inducements to improve upon the shelter afforded by nature.

The noble temples in Cambodia, and the extensive remains of Hindu religious edifices in Java, attest the extension of art from the Indian centre, eastwards as well as westwards.

Thirty-two treatises on architecture have been computed to exist in Sanskrit literature, which would appear to corroborate the view that the extraordinary varieties of architectural embellishments to be seen in India have not been due merely to accident or imitation, but that they have been carefully premeditated. Mr. Fergusson seems to suggest the inference that the Indians worked by curious instincts, like ants or bees, for he talks of the excavators of the mythological cave temples as a "rock-cutting race."

The ancient divinities, emanations from the Supreme Being, who had their abode on Mount Merou, seem to have been carried in the Greek imagination to Mount Olympus. After this Vedic system, the Sivaic and Buddhistic forms of faith, and the later adoration of Deity incarnate in Krishna, seem all to have followed with accompanying architecture, and have been continued with adaptations to circumstances by the active Aryan mind in more temperate climates.

It is difficult to believe that the curious excavated rocks at Mahabalipuram, near Madras, belong to an age within our era, as seems to have been recently thought possible, notwithstanding their cogent signs of remote antiquity. They appear, at all events, to exhibit an elaboration and antiquity of style in their sculptures; such as may be conceived to have descended from a long cultivation of autochthonous art.

They are situated on the sea-coast, and styled the Seven Pagodas, though that number does not exist. A lofty rock is so thickly covered with sculptures and works of imagery, as to have been thought to resemble a petrified town. Facing the sea there is a pagoda, estimated at 26 feet in height, cut out of a single rock, with exterior sculptures in bas-relief representing the heroes of the Mahâbhârata. The top part is arched like a roof. Near this temple are columns in an excavation carved in resemblance of the Egyptian style, and of that seen in Elephanta; and the surface of the rock to about 90 feet in extent and 20 in height is covered with sculptured figures, amongst which are gigantic representations of Krishna and his favourite Arjouna. A corroded and defaced sculptured group is said to represent Krishna attending the herds of Ananda.

Bishop Heber observed that "the real city of Mahabalipoor, whose ruins stand amongst the cliffs at the distance of a short half-mile inland, has really been a place of considerable importance as a metropolis of the ancient kings of the race of Pandion; and its rocks, which in themselves are pretty and picturesque, are carved out into porticoes, temples, bas-reliefs, etc., on a much smaller scale indeed than Elephanta or Kennery, but some of them very beautifully executed."

Amidst the sculptured rocks an excavated temple contains at one end a gigantic figure of Vishnu, sleeping on an enormous hooded snake with several heads, which form a canopy over the deity. At the opposite end is an eight-armed goddess, mounted on a lion, rescuing a figure who is suspended with the head downwards from a buffalo-headed demon. The figure and action of the goddess are executed in very spirited style. The stone of which these sculptures are formed is a species of granite extremely hard, according to "The Modern Traveller."

Mrs. Graham states that copper plates were dug up, containing grants of land for the maintenance of the temples, dated above a thousand years ago, and these refer to the sculptured rocks as of unknown origin.

The whole of the sculptures have been conceived to present the appearance of having been wrecked by some convulsion of nature, before they were finished. On rocks washed by the sea are sculptures, indicating that they were once out of it; and it is asserted that the surf breaks over the ruins of a large and magnificent city. "There are really," says Bishop Heber, some small remains of architecture which rise from amid the waves, among which a tall pillar is conspicuous.

Besides the elephant, monkey, etc., the lion appears amongst the sculptures. As the lion has been thought not to be a native of the south of India, here may perhaps be discerned an argument for assigning these sculptures to some Assyrian artist. But the designs of the sculptures in general seem to be essentially Hindu in character. And it is not by any means impossible that some Indian, voyaging in accordance with the evidence which has been cited, had seen a lion. But indeed there is testimony from ancient Indian records to show that the lion (singh) was formerly found in most parts of India. Lions are sculptured at Elephanta.

A figure in Greek-like art is held sufficient for ascribing Indian sculptures to Grecian artists, though the portions considered foreign appear amongst other and varied work of indubitably indigenous aspect. This seems particularly to be the case with the specimens labelled as Græco-Buddhistic in the Indian Museum at South Kensington, which have been recently exhumed by General Cunningham in his archæological survey in the vicinity of the ancient Grecian kingdom of Bactria. In the midst of architectural ornamentation of essentially Indian and Buddhistic character are life-like figures. Such figures are found amongst the more fantastic Indian sculptures in many parts of the country. Yet it is asserted that this people, which could produce the Ramáyana and Mahábhárata poems in a language, elegant and similar in construction to the Greeks, could not have made some simple and correct autochthonous art efforts at representing the human form. One sitting figure is labelled in the museum as Græco-Buddhistic, which rather presents the characteristics of the effigy of some mediæval monarch in a Gothic cathedral than of the Greek school. The attitude, with the legs akimbo, and the style of the head are very suggestive of our mediæval art. It ought to be ascribed to some adventurous European of the crusading days, rather than to the Greeks; if it must needs be relegated to an exotic origin. Corinthian capitals of archaic and half developed appearance are here assigned to the Greeks, though they occur amidst architectural ornamentation of Indian character. But, as the Corinthian capital is only historically related to have been introduced into Greece at about the time of Alexander's invasion, and the prototype of the Doric order is admitted to exist outside Greece, it might rather appear that the prototypes of the Corinthian order are here. They may have travelled from India to Greece in the communication which had come into existence just before Alexander's invasion. The form of the Corinthian capital is related to have been imitated from the leaves curling over a basket, but this well-known story does not appear to depend upon evidence which will stand the test of cross-examination.

As a specimen of the southern art of this Indian people styled imitative, here is a description from the before-mentioned "Modern Traveller" of the Chilamburam Pagodas, situated on the coast, three miles south of Portonovo (half-way between Cuddalore and Tanjore). These "are held in high veneration from their supposed antiquity, and are visited by numerous pilgrims. They are encircled by a high wall of blue stone. The chief of the four pagodas is on the same plan with that of Juggernaut, though on a smaller scale, and is esteemed a masterpiece of architecture. Each of the three gates is surmounted with a pyramid nearly 200 feet in height, built with large stones about 40 feet long and more than 5 broad, all covered with plates of copper adorned with figures. The whole structure extends 1332 feet in one direction and 936 in another. In the area of the temple there is a large tank, skirted on three sides with a beautiful gallery supported by columns. On the fourth is a magnificent hall, ornamented with 999 columns of blue granite, covered with sculptures." According to Bradshaw it is still attended by 3000 priests.

As a picture of a part of India which has escaped the sufferings of Mohammedan conquests, and which has exhibited, within our time, a specimen of Hindu rule, the principality of Tanjore may be cited. Here may be seen the advantage of carrying on the care of the old rulers in providing for irrigation. Great works for storing water against rainless years "fertilise a tract of country from Devicotta to Point Calymere,—which would otherwise remain a barren sand," as is said in Hamilton's "Gazetteer." "For the purposes of irrigation prodigious mounds have been raised at Coilady, to prevent the waters of the Cavery from rejoining those of the Coleroon after they have separated near Trichinopoly. From this southern branch of the river canals are conducted in all directions, which, by means of embankments and reservoirs, are diverted into every field." In Tanjore, says the "Modern Traveller," "almost every village has its pagoda, with a lofty gateway of massive architecture, where a great many Brahmins are maintained; and in all the great roads to the sacred places are *choultries* for the accommodation of pilgrims." The pyramidal tower of the temple in the city of Tanjore, considered the largest in India, is 200 feet in height, profusely sculptured, and was described by Lord Valentia as "a very beautiful piece of architecture." Behind the Rajah's palace and temples, says the "Gazetteer," a rich country is seen, covered with rice-fields and clumps of trees, and beyond all a chain of lofty mountains. "In remote ages this was the great seat of learning in the south of India, and here the almanacs were formed, according to which the year 1800 of the Christian era corresponds with the year 1722 of Salivahanam, and the 4901 of the Cali Yug."

CHAPTER L.

Buddhist art in the north-west—General Cunningham's explorations—Buddhist monks not likely to have copied Greeks—Arguments for assigning to Cashmere, rather than Nubia, the priority in the Doric column—Chronicles of the Kings of Cashmere—Philostratus related by Wilford to allude to statues by Greek artists in the Punjab—Art remains in Orissa—Colonel Moor as to Indian sculptures not much surpassed in Greece—Mr. Broadley on freedom of design in Buddhistic remains in Bahar—Lieutenant Pullan's discovery of a small temple of "exquisite" design in the jungle, at the foot of the Himalayas—Stones joined by iron clamps in ruins of old cities—Greeks conceiving that the Indians worshipped Bacchus and Hercules—Pictures of the primitive apostolic preachers to be seen amongst Hindus, as described by Professor M. Williams—Architecture commencing in wood, in regions rich in timber—Comparison of English architecture—Indian statues of women looking out of form to us, on account of their carrying their infants astride of their hips.

TAKING into consideration the extensive, peculiar, and varied remains of Buddhist art in the north, it is difficult to conceive, from what we see in the present day in the east, the Buddhist monks as having recourse to Greek artists for the adornment of their monasteries. The remains of these, lately unearthed by General Cunningham on the borders of the old Greek kingdoms, seem to present all the peculiar characteristics of the Indian Buddhistic style. But in figures and the capitals of pilasters, etc., are suggestions of Greek art.

Greek coins have been discovered in the territories occupied by these Greek kingdoms, and Greek sculptures may be expected to be also found there. About the year 1787, however, a pot of Roman gold coins, to which allusion has been made in Chapter XXIV., principally of the reigns of Trajan and Antoninus Pius, was found under the remains of a small Hindu temple at Nellore. This place is at about 100 miles from Madras, and the coins, in this instance at all events, show communication with, not necessarily influence of, Rome. It is possible that the discovery of Greek coins in north-western India may have occasioned too much credence to have been given to the idea of Greek influence prevailing in the arts, etc. It would seem reasonable to suppose that these figures and architectural ornamentations, in the midst of work of Indian aspect, may be accepted only as additional instances of the affinities presented between the Aryans of India and Greece. It would not appear unreasonable to surmise that, instead of the Buddhists seeking the assistance of the Greeks, an occasional artist or sculptor accompanying the armies, or an adventurer before the invasion of Alexander, carried back to Greece sketches of Indian edifices, etc. This has, at all events, occurred in our later European invasions. The Greeks are not unlikely to have adopted such a suggestion as the Corinthian capital from India, if the original Doric column is to be attributed to Nubia. Modern Europeans have occasionally employed the modern Oriental style. The discovery of Greek art and architecture may be anticipated, in this seat of their government for two or three centuries. But it seems improbable that ancient Buddhist monks should have resorted to Greek artists or Greek models, when modern Indians do not imitate the English in their religious edifices. The Buddhist monks seem to have been a fraternity like the Roman Catholic monks, keeping themselves essentially distinct. It does not appear that they invoke the aid of European artists, or even imitate European forms to any appreciable extent in the present day. The prototype rather than the copy of the Corinthian column may have been discovered.

Mr. Fergusson has remarked that " nowhere in Cashmere do we find any trace of the bracket capital of the Hindus, while the Doric or *quasi* Doric column is found everywhere throughout the valley, in temples dating from the eighth to the twelfth century." These may be sequent to archaic fanes.

Now this Doric or *quasi* Doric form of the excavations at Beni-Hassan is considered anterior to the Greek. No reason would appear why, in the Vale of Cashmere, naturally so superior in beauty, and with ancient records which profess to extend backwards to thousands of years B.C., the simple Doric column should not have equally come within the range of man's invention. In fact, the arguments which have been advanced would assign to Cashmere rather than to Nubia the originality. The style may have found its way thence down the Indus, and to Greece by the Nile; or from Cashmere to Egypt by the Indus, and to Greece across Asia by the Caucasus. Even supposing the *Radja Taringini*, or Chronicles of the Kings of Cashmere, whose first author is alleged to have written about 1148 B.C., to be a comparatively modern compilation by some Brahmin, tradition must, at least, be allowed to indicate a pre-Christian civilisation for this garden-like valley. Yet, in the vicinity of the varied India and the Himalayas;—in which, upon both plains and mountains, discursive, fanciful, and massive styles of architecture, in timber and stone, are found,—a *quasi* Doric column must needs be assigned to the influence of the Greek invaders, although the Greeks themselves are supposed to have adopted it from the Egyptians. In fact, the question travels always in the circle, to be argued upon the issue of the priority of Egyptian and Indian civilisation.

The Greeks are allowed to have copied. India, from considerations of the aspect of the country, its literary remains, and the race inhabiting it akin to our own in Europe, is more likely than Egypt to have invented the originals.

European architects have been occasionally employed by Indian princes in these later days. The Taj Mahal at Agra is related to have been erected by an Italian. This beautiful structure, however, is a work of the foreign, conquering, Mohammedan race; and the Italian architect absolutely imitated the style which has so distinguished the Mohammedans, who, like the Hindus and Jains, have adhered to their own art conceptions for their sacred buildings.

Philostratus is related by Wilford to allude to statues made by Greek artists in the Punjab. It would seem extremely probable that Greek sculptors should have found their way thither and have made statues; but those discovered amongst the ruins of Buddhistic monasteries, surrounded by all the attributes of work evidently Indian, need not be necessarily Greek because they bear resemblance to the later Greek style. The earlier Greek sculptures present more of the crudity usually observable in Indian forms. The Greek sculptors may not only have made statues, but studied and taken models of an Indian style. Perfection, rather than craving for originality, seems to characterise Greek art. Remains in Orissa and other parts, where there is no geographical reason for suspecting Greek influence, appear to show that the Indians, like the Greeks, advanced to a period of grandeur and grace in art, from which they declined under the influence of foreign conquest or other reason. The evidences afforded by the art remains in various parts of India would appear sufficient to show that the art of the country became polished as it advanced, in parallel lines with its language and literature. We have been astonished at discovering the similarities in the construction of the languages of ancient Greece and ancient India. We ought not to be again astonished at finding that their arts were anciently as nearly related. Affinities between ancient India and Greece have been set forth in Chapters XXXV.–XXXVII.

Northern India at the time of the Grecian establishment in Bactria, as evidenced by Megasthenes and Arrian, displayed its marked differences to Greece in its Brahminical system and its fervour in asceticism, in living on vegetable food, early marriages, painting the face with the sectarial marks, etc.

But, as has been shown, the Indians have by no means wholly abstained from flesh and strong potations. There seems to be no reason why their art should not have become as classic as their language. When the resemblances between the Sanskrit and Greek languages were first observed, some European scholars ascribed the former to a clever imitation of the latter by the Brahmins. The arts of ancient India and Greece seem to have corresponded like their languages.

Colonel Moor observed that "it may be doubted if the sculptors of Greece have much surpassed those of India." In Canara, about 400 miles below Bombay on the western coast, and about as far from the old Greek kingdoms as London from the Balkan mountains, is a colossal statue 70 feet in height. This is carved in the solid stone, and represents a young man with wreaths of laurel around him. It is smoothly polished and finely carved, with the nose aquiline and the under lip prominent. India abounds with elaborate sculpture of all sizes and most diverse forms. Amongst these it exhibits classic correctness occasionally.

A rather rude Corinthian pilaster, of the description lately unearthed in the Punjab, by no means looks beyond Indian ingenuity. There is much work in this region in which over-fancifulness has degenerated into the grotesque or uncouth. But exuberant imaginations often refuse to be restrained by the nice rules of perfectly harmonious taste. Even our Shakspeare affords an example of the most sublime of imaginations occasionally descending from grand conceptions to trifle with quaint conceits, in a manner sometimes overburdened with quibbles. In his disregard for the stricter dramatic "unities" he certainly exhibits a spice of Indian irregularity, for the same reason, viz. that genius in archaic art ages is less fettered by rules. Certainly Greek art, like the best form of Indian, lost its perfection under foreign conquest, or from some inherent cause of decline.

In an article on "Buddhistic remains in Bihar," Mr. A. M. Broadley has remarked that many of them exhibit great freedom of design. Amongst sculptured figures he discerned one which appeared to be costumed in a tight jacket with ornamental facings, pantaloons and boots, and a girdle with sword. He describes one sculpture as representing a chariot drawn by seven horses.

In 1867 Lieutenant A. Pullan, surveying in the forest at the foot of the Himalayas between Garhwal and Rohilcund, found in the dense jungle a small temple "of exquisite carving and design;" the figures on the frieze alto-relievo, with groups of wrestlers, Ganesh with his elephant's head, etc. At the four corners were women's heads and busts, a lion and a ram, reminding him of the gargoyles of Gothic cathedrals. He then came upon other ruins, slabs—one being square, beautifully carved and adorned with a three-headed divinity, and a female head, etc. He further found two square miles covered, under the "tall tiger grass and tangled bamboos, with heaps of small oblong bricks, interspersed with carved slabs of stone; on one slab was a mailed figure resembling an ancient Gothic knight.

In central India cities and temples are found of remote date, with the massive stones of which they are constructed joined together by iron clamps.

As the Greeks conceived that the Indians were worshipping Bacchus and Hercules, in Krishna, or Bala Rama, and in Siva, and from the general tenor of those of their remarks which have descended to us, it may be reasonably inferred that they saw in India architecture of a character homogeneous with their own. That temples were in existence in India at that time can be shown from allusions to them in the Ramáyana epic and Institutes of Manu.

The Greeks have noticed certain peculiarities of the Hindus, but it must be evident that the aspect of the Hindus would not altogether have differed so greatly from their own as that of the modern English. There must have been the same general similarity between the appearance of the Greeks and Hindus at that epoch as between English and Italians in the present day. In fact the Indian fashions were then nearer those of the civilised world of Europe and western Asia. And they alone have remained constant. If we would contemplate living pictures of our Lord's apostles, as He sent them forth (St. Matthew x. 10), we must look for the nearest approach to them in the conservative India. In the "Fortnightly Review" of December 1878, Professor Monier Williams has given a description of the clergy belonging to one of the reformed sects of the adorers of Krishna, whom he saw at the Temple of Wartal, near the Baroda railway. They certainly seem to present an aspect considerably nearer that of the primitive preachers of Christianity than our Anglican clergy or dissenting ministers. He saw them in their lodgings near the temple —small cells just sufficient for the most parsimonious shelter. "They travel on foot, undergoing many privations and hardships, taking nothing with them but a staff, the clothes on their backs, their daily food, their water jar, and their book of instructions. They may be seen here and there in the ordinary coarse salmon-coloured dress of ascetics, striving to win disciples by personal example and persuasion, rather than by controversy. Some other proselytising societies might learn something of their method."

Our Lord, indeed, even sent out His disciples without staff or bread, but He is related in Luke xxii. 35 to have rescinded that order.

To return from the aspect of Indian life to its ancient architecture. In the regions rich in forest timber houses of course continued to be constructed in wood; and in the religious excavations, and occasional stone structures, the style which was prevalent and had reached grandeur was naturally employed. In the north-western plains, however, and in other parts, the comparative scarcity of wood and the presence of stone would have rendered an earlier adoption of the latter necessary, when few but mean edifices had been raised in timber, the supply not being sufficient for extensive structures. There being, therefore, no fine models in wood, human ingenuity devised a style suitable to stone or brick. But a general impetus to architecture had first been given in the timber structures of districts which may be considered to have been within probable knowledge. The so-called Indo-Corinthian capitals, and the peculiar pyramidal spires of Indian architecture, are evidently suggested by Indian vegetable forms. Similarly in England we find well-built stone villages, amongst the Cotswold Hills for instance, extending back to the time of James I., but ancient timber cottages amongst the Sussex forests. Constant construction in stone must cause wooden forms to be gradually merged. In Cheshire and Lancashire we see mansions in timber; and London houses, even those of the nobility, seem to have been largely constructed of wood till 200 years ago.

Amongst the diverse styles of woodwork in which the timber fronts of the Bombay houses, in the native town, are constructed, suggestions of the Greek Orders certainly appear. They seem naturally there, amongst the generally autochthonous aspects of the streets and their life. In the interior of the new Temple, however, in the Kalbadevi Road, to which allusion has been made, and of which the exterior presents marked Hindu characteristics, the interior has such an aspect of classic proportion, that here Greek or modern influence might seem to have been exerted. Yet the interiors of older and less regularly constructed temples lead up to it as naturally as any European interior in Bombay; and it is difficult to conceive that they should desert their own architectural traditions for the interior only of the building.

Under the theory of Art suggested by Nature, the gradual transition from the extremely fanciful styles of southern India to the plainer, more classical, fashion of the north, seems undoubtedly in harmony with the gradually changing aspects of Nature; as from the fantastic variety of the vegetable forms of the tropics we ascend to the foliage of our European type.

The fierce sunshine of northern India would render the colonnade an obviously desirable addition to an edifice. The columns naturally assumed as many varieties in India as the trees from which they were shaped. And the bracket, and crude Classic styles, and that seen in the excavations of Karli, etc., were applied in stone in due course.

Much of the eccentricity of the aspect of Indian sculpture, as it seems to us, is due to the difference of the figures and attitudes of humanity there to those which we see in Europe. That torrid climate does not develop the muscular system to its finest form. In the North-West Provinces, where these so-called Greek examples occur, humanity assumes a far nobler bearing than in the southern districts. The difference between the figure of the average Sikh and Bengalee is immense. Then the quaint contracted aspect sometimes observable in the sculptures of women, may be ascribed to the custom of the living models in bearing their children seated astride upon their hips. The accounts of the Mohammedan destruction of art in north-western India leave room for the possibility of a deal of ancient work of classic character having been in existence. In India after the Mohammedan conquest, as in Europe after the destruction of the Roman Empire, there seems to have been a decadence of art, which could not revive where national liberty was lost.

We have been putting the cart before the horse in argument. Finding classic art in India, Egypt, and Greece, we have made the sequences—Egypt, Greece, India, instead of India, Egypt, Greece, as it ought to have been apparently.

The Babel builders, in their acquaintance with brick, display its ancient employment in their "east," *i.e.* the Indian west. This again may account for the decay of ancient edifices. Brick has been extensively employed in Amritsir, Lahore, etc.

CHAPTER LI.

Turanian aspect of ancient statues of Buddha may indicate the existence of Buddhism in pre-Vedic times—Human thought may have conceived a man approaching the Divine before apprehending the Divine in man, and before Brahminism arose—Religion of Buddha extensively adopted by Turanian people—Sakya muni the seventh Buddha—Christ's admission of divine revelations before Him in the Prophets—Civilisation arising amongst Aryans of northern India and Dravidians of south on account of tillage of the soil necessary and comparatively easy, etc.—Man spreading in the world after learning to light fire—Return to primeval bliss in idleness in the West Indian Islands.

THE Turanian aspect of the ancient statues of Buddha in India may indicate the existence of Buddhism—before even the age of Vedic Sanskrit—amongst the archaic race to which allusion has been made. The esoteric meaning of Buddhism, prior to its position as opposed to Brahminism on the point of hereditary caste sanctity, and prior to the incarnation theory, seems to be the veneration of a man as teaching the way to godliness, instead of reverence for the Deity under some symbolical form. The ancient statues of Buddha are suggestive of some of those of the Egyptian divinities. It seems a natural process of human thought to conceive a man approaching to the divine before actually cognising the divine incarnate in man; and before the patriarchal government in religion had been modified by the assumptions of a class to superior sacred knowledge, and the right of instructing in religion. Out of such a conception the later Indian and Egyptian mythological expressions would seem naturally to have arisen. The regents of the elements might be adored, and yet a Buddha, a perfection of human wisdom, be set up as the model for the imitation of humanity. There seems to be an affinity between the divinely instructed lawgiver Manu, and Buddha. The first name, derived from a root signifying thinking, is not opposed to the second, which means wisdom.

The Pali, the sacred language of Buddhism, is akin to the Sanskrit; and Professor Max Müller describes it as "once the popular dialect of the country where Buddhism took its origin," *i.e.* the ancient Magaddha, the modern Bahar. The religion of Gautauma Buddha, or Sakya muni, has been largely adopted by Turanian people. This demonstrates that they supplied the deficiencies of their own spiritual ideas with those of our Aryan race; the leading people of the world in enterprise and intellectual advancement in the present day, and in those old times in which we have given Egyptians and Assyrians credit for so much original genius. At all events, they were then most advanced in literature, which we now esteem so important an element of civilisation, and which we nowhere find existing without art and science. Buddhism in India, 500 B.C., was probably no more an entire novelty than the religion of Christian Protestantism in Europe 1500 A.D.

Though the previous Buddhas, who constitute Sakya muni the seventh in succession, seem to be shadowy or mythical beings, they show that an ancient origin was claimed for the religion. It was not proclaimed as his absolute revelation. Christ admitted the divine revelations before Him in the law and the prophets. Buddha, like Him, claimed to come for reformation. The entire aspect of Buddhism in India, and its monasteries, would seem to exhibit little probability of any borrowing of foreign art for architectural ornamentation.

Greek arts and inventions may have made some way in India, but apparently as corresponding to the influence of those of the United States of America on Europe. For instance, we have adopted the revolving pistol from America, but a small firearm, some centuries old, on the revolving-chamber principle, is to be seen in the Armoury of the Tower of London. So the Greeks may have improved what the Indians originally invented.

Egyptian and Assyrian civilisations may have emanated from the south-western parts of India; the Celts, later, from the same quarter; the Greeks and Romans from the west; the Persians, Teutons, and Slavs from the north-west, with the waves of their emigrations rising in the central or even eastern districts, and differing as the peoples of the Madhyama differ. These have all continued, and sometimes improved upon, the original arts and sciences of the mother country. Our Anglo-Saxon has at present culminated in the inventive progress and culture of England and its colonies, and America. We have forgotten our Indian origin ; but in a few generations colonists in the South Sea Islands may be aware that they have proceeded from America, but oblivious of the former European descent.

The Aryans in the north of India and the Dravidians in the south, and the two conjoined, after religion and art had assumed definite forms in each, have invented, because they were in the region of the world most suggestive of imitating nature in art. Their civilisations arose because the tillage of the ground had become necessary to their increase, and labour induced attention to order and the rights of property in the fruits of the soil. Our race thought of cultivating the wild cereals, or of rendering the seeds of the coarse grasses more capable of sustaining life, just as it has since devised the application of steam and electricity. There is no need for conceiving a submerged southern continent, or more than slightly altered face of nature in that region. The allusions to the rainy season in the Ramáyana, and the suggestions of heat in the descriptions, seem to show that the climate was not materially different in those days of strong meats and drinks, and old-English-like faith in the long bow. The existing islands, with India, the Chinese peninsula and China, seem sufficient to allow of man's discerning the first great artificial requirements of educated life. Being formed to walk upright, when he had acquired the art of lighting fire, and had adopted clothing, he was in the way of obtaining all his present acquaintance with the forces of nature and laws of the universe; and of feeling a reverential desire to comprehend his obligations to the Almighty Spirit, and the meaning of his own individually-felt existence. In heat and moisture life begins. As it tends towards colder climates fewer animal species exist, and human aids to life become more requisite, till our life ends geographically with the Esquimaux. These scarcely dare to remove the thick clothing of skins which retain the warmth in their bodies. Neither in the polar regions, nor in the small oases in the midst of sun-baked deserts, in the more or less completely rainless districts of the earth, could man have arisen, unless it be maintained that he was literally created out of the dust.

Instead of making vague conjectures as to the situation of our Scriptural garden in the vicinity of the sources of the Euphrates and Tigris, if we allow that it was "eastward," as is said in Genesis, we may practically recognise it in the tropical Asiatic islands, notably in Ceylon, as south of the regions peopled by the leading race of the world. But a general suggestion of the Valley of Cashmere might seem to exist in the narrative of the Bible, to which the abode of primeval bliss might very naturally have been transferred, as has been observed. From the islands man may have passed to the mainland, and learned to labour and to light fire. The inventor of this seems to have been the first and most useful of inventors, for he enabled our heat-requiring, tropically-born bodies to spread throughout the world.

A modern instance may be observed in which man has returned, in some measure, to his original garden. The West Indian negroes, on many of the islands, freed from the enforced toil of slavery, have simply taken to subsisting in careless tranquillity on the bounty of nature. They work, perhaps, half a day in the week to secure some luxuries, but nature affords them all that they require for existence. They are said to look sleek and contented, and they will not be moved to work. It has been told us, under our religion, that *laborare est orare;* but while thus teaching devotion in toil, it also is said to inform us that labour was God's curse upon us because our first parents partook of the tree of knowledge. If governments and missionaries will only leave these negroes alone, they may return to primeval bliss in ignorance as well as idleness.

CHAPTER LII.

Civilisation originating in India and China, but principally in the former, as demonstrated from the spirit of Brahminism, showing itself in aristocracies, guilds, etc., and in Buddhism, or the spirit of Liberalism, competing with it, both being undoubtedly of Indian origin—The plains of the Euphrates and Nile enjoying a pre-eminence in history of the world not deserved—Chinese more self-contained and less enterprising in expansion than the Aryans of India—Roman and British Empires emerging from India—A spiritual conception of the Almighty arising in the Madhyama—Hindustan and the United Kingdom compared geographically—Changefulness of the history of England —Christian doctrines and practice undoubtedly inculcated in ancient India.

THUS, then, the history of our culture may be conceived to have progressed in streams flowing from a great reservoir fed by natural sources, the tropical and sub-tropical India. These have supplied our western world with populations, and carried with them knowledge of the original efforts at attaining those artificial aids to existence, which have enabled our comparatively small islands of Great Britain and Ireland to support a population of some 34,000,000, and hold the sovereignty of an empire extending in continents and islands around the world. The Turanian streams are turgid in comparison with the Aryan, and the great Chinese lake has been replenished, at all events in the important matter of its popular religion, from the Aryan in India. African life never seems to have attained a polity deserving of the name of civilisation, except when traced to the Asiatic source. Emerging originally from the tropical realms at the south-east of Asia, with the exception of the negro, man has developed, according to the exigencies or amenities of his situation, into the pastoral, nomadic, or commercial life. The priests and warriors have contended, or sometimes united, for power to rule those engaged in the actual food-rearing processes. Spirit or intellect has finally obtained the mastery over mere physical force. Under Brahminical, that is to say caste or class organisation, it gained great influence. But this has been largely superseded by the liberal spirit which offers power to the intelligent and strong irrespective of birth. This is the essential principle of Buddhism, whether in politics or religion. But even Buddhism has organised its religious brotherhood, bound in the ties of definite rules. In fact, the history of the political economy of the world seems to show that man speedily recognised, and has continually acted upon the motto that union creates force. The spirit of Brahminism in the old Aryan civilisation became extended to every trade or mechanical employment. All united themselves in petty castes, which have been followed in Europe by our guilds, professions fenced by rules or etiquette, and trade unions. But the spirit of Buddhism has abolished birth trammels. These have, however, been jealously retained by the aristocracies of Europe, and undoubtedly prevail amongst all classes to considerable extent; because it is natural that the son should follow the father's calling, and find advantages in matrimonial alliance with his own class, in most instances. India especially became the great reservoir, because it was the most central country in the world for all the purposes of civilisation, and contained within itself natural advantages calculated to suggest to humanity the means of supplying its wants as it multiplied its numbers and enlarged its borders. Europe and America have been admirably adapted for continuing and improving upon the artificial life which the sub-tropical India commenced.

The plains of the Euphrates and Nile, the district of the Oxus, and the valleys of the Caucasus, seem to have enjoyed a pre-eminence in the history of the world which cannot be sustained by a comparison of their natural advantages with those of the land of the Ganges. China, from its larger proportion of territory, from its less central position, and perhaps from some radical difference in the spirit or capacity of its original inhabitants, has been self-contained rather than enterprising in expansion. Its people have had no Europe to invite the more energetic to colonisation. Possibly, however, it may be open to conjecture as to whether the old American civilisations issued from China or the Indo-Chinese peninsula. The Chinese seem to exhibit considerable activity in settling upon the islands to their south. And Chinese emigration in general seems to be largely continuing in the present day.

Apart from an hereditary emperor, China has adopted the Buddhistic or non-hereditary principles, both in religion and politics. Europe has partially relinquished the hereditary or caste system in political life. The Church of Rome constituted the only means by which the barriers of birth could be overleaped in mediæval times. The warrior caste, not the Brahminical, was uppermost. In the present age, in England, while the Brahminical caste seems to have been renewing its efforts at the acquisition of power, and while the Kshatrya or aristocratical and warrior caste has never quite relinquished it, the merchant caste has been steadily obtaining preponderance; which seems natural, as the country has held the commercial empire of the world for the century leading up to 1879; when the world seems to be disputing it.

It was to the north of the mountains and forests of central India, in the region enclosed by nature,—on the west with desert, on the east with dense jungle and the Brahmaputra and its tributaries, on the north by the grand mountain chain of the Himalayas, in the district watered by the Ganges and the Indus,—that humanity seems to have founded the original civilisation in religion and science, arts and arms. From this, through many windings and temporary settlements, have emerged the Roman Empire, and the British, computed in the "Statesman's Year-book" to be sixteen times as large as that of ancient Rome, and to be, in fact, the most colossal empire in the year 1879 which the world has historically known. Its history has been changeful. About four centuries ago the English monarch ruled a great part of France. A century ago he still swayed the destinies of America. In 1877 proclamation has been made of Empire in India, while the colonies are continually growing in importance. In the eighteenth century we seemed more especially allied with northern Europe. In the nineteenth we appear to have become an Asiatic power.

A spiritual conception of the Almighty, the Vedic hymns, literature in philosophy, poetry, and science, and a language considered by philologists most admirable in its volume and grammatical regularity, arose in the Arya Varta or Madhyama. Brahminism and Buddhism, systematised there, seem to be the prototypes of the religions and political constitutions of the cultured world.

Hindustan may be roughly estimated as containing some 270,000 square miles within the above-mentioned boundaries, in the plains irrigated by the Ganges and its numerous confluent streams, and 90,000 in the district of the five rivers which unite in the Indus. This excludes mountains and deserts. The United Kingdom of Great Britain and Ireland is estimated at about 122,000; so that this Indian region affords an enclosed space of about three times the extent without approaching the sea. This is, however, conveniently adjacent, and is likely to have induced great extension of the arts of civilisation by tempting to commercial enterprises. The spirit of the north, descending southwards with advancement in culture, combined with physical strength, must surely have been calculated to give an impetus to the sea adventures of the naturally more effeminate southern people who had lived upon its borders.

Lastly, of prominent forms of faith, in this prolific country or continent, the race with which science now admits our cousinship undoubtedly became acquainted with the doctrine of a Trinity in Unity, and incarnate Saviour leading to a future of bliss; after passing through many more or less materialistic conceptions of this great Christian doctrine of the Divine dealing with the human. And the doctrine of Christian charity has been not only largely and liberally inculcated in their sacred literature, but put into practice, as widely as consistent with a world, in which what is called evil seems always necessarily mingled with good.

CHAPTER LIII.

Christ's doctrine not really disconsonant with the Hindu tenet and practice that all religions teach men to be good—Indian doctrine of the purification of a soul for divine life, through successive births, more in agreement with Christ's teaching than purgatory, or hopeless punishment in hell—Renewed arguments as to *aionion* (eternal) punishment—That we are regaining the original Scriptures of our Aryan race—Arguments as to Christ preaching the ancient Aryan doctrine of transmigration, as shown in the New Testament—Considerations as to St. Paul's doctrine in respect to Scripture—As to whether St. Paul would have condemned the Hindu Scriptures—Krishna as the prototype of Christ—Considerations as to St. John's Gospel.

IT is difficult to quote any words, of those which have descended to us as Christ's, disconsonant to the following observation of Colonel Moor's upon the Indian faith, viz. that "it seems a tenet of practice as well as of doctrine with the Hindus that all religions teach men to be good. They even say that those of other faiths than that of Krishna, who adore the Divine with honesty of heart, unconsciously worship Him in Krishna." If we admit this of those who, in old times, and in regions not now acquainted with, or able to comprehend the purport of the name of Christ, are devoutly and charitably disposed, and have faith in the Eternal Goodness, though they do not worship Him under the same name as ourselves—we do not destroy but enlarge the sphere of the benefits of the Divine Spirit in Christianity.

The Indian doctrine of the purification for the divine life of a human soul, through successive births, may not seem less in agreement with His teaching than the Romish purgatory, at all events. As to the endlessness of torment in hell, again it must be observed that Protestants have to assume that this Gehenna in which earthy bodies were burnt was intended to refer to a spiritual hell; and that He implied damnation in this use of the word κρίσις, which may more reasonably be rendered separation—separation from the divine, in accordance with the Indian doctrine; or it may refer to the judicial investigation which, according to the Egyptians, was undergone by the soul before it was relegated to a new transmigration. The judgment passed after death, in the palace of Osiris, decided whether the soul was purified, or whether it must return to the earth. Certainly the word indicates an act of judging rather than of passing condemnation.

The Indo-European race, from which we are descended, had expressed the doctrine of the soul's immortality, for many centuries before the time of Christ, in the sacred writings of the old Madhyama. We have adopted as inspired Scriptures, leading up to our Christian faith, the old records of the Jewish nation, in which it is difficult to find the doctrine even obscurely hinted. We have adopted them because they were the sacred books of the people amongst whom we have supposed the great and divine promulgation of our religion only to have taken place. But it appears that, in the fulness of time, we are regaining the original Scriptures of our ancient Aryan civilisation, wide as that of modern Europe in its scope, from which, through Egypt and Persia, may have come the higher education of the Jews. In the better understanding of the ideas entertained—previously to this teaching—by the congregations which listened to Christ, we may the more truly comprehend the meaning of His words.

Protestantism asserts that the Saviour did not employ the words in a literal sense, when He said of the bread in the Last Supper, "This is my body." Many of His expressions, besides those in evident parables, have been interpreted as figurative —as not to be taken, at all events, in their absolutely literal sense, such as those referring to the seemingly immediate end of the world. The word Gehenna, to return to a former argument, may of course have been used figuratively for a place of eternal spiritual burning; just as the word "body," in reference to the bread, may have been uttered in a mystic sense only. But the use of it certainly corresponds literally to saying, in the present day, that it is better to lose a limb than the life by being hanged at the Old Bailey, or, in the last century, at Tyburn. To have the body burnt in the valley of Gehenna seems to have indicated a disgraceful end, like losing life at

Tyburn. And, as the Gospels represent Christ as assigning sin as the cause of bodily disease, the disgraceful destruction of the material body in Gehenna would further seem to have been naturally and obviously adduced as the penalty of sin. Taking text with context in our history of Christ's life and teaching, and His employment of an Indian expression when He preaches the doctrine of Regeneration, it would seem more consonant with a general view of the evidence afforded in the Gospels that He was declaring deliverance from this world, the power of Death, and the continued miserable consequences of misdoing, rather than from an eternal hell of actual or metaphorical flames, designated under this simile. He was preaching to persons of whom many, apparently, must have known the doctrine of rewards and punishments in successive births, with continued life as the result of purity; for the Pharisees are related to have been accepted as the teachers of the people, who are likely, therefore, to have been acquainted with this belief of theirs. He was, moreover, frequently addressing the Pharisees themselves. It seems, in truth, that He was offering the hope of final union with God, through faith in Himself, in accordance with the doctrine of our Aryan race, which was, at all events, approximate to the Pharisaical doctrine.

It may be urged that, in the answer to the materialistic Sadducees, who demanded whose wife she was to become in the resurrection who had successively married seven brothers, in accordance with the Mosaic law, Christ ignores any but a spiritual revivifying of the soul. But it may be presumed that He answered the question as applied to the spiritual resurrection which He was teaching, responding indirectly, as when asked respecting the payment of tribute to Cæsar, or in regard to the authority by which He was preaching (Luke xx. 3). The Sadducees had probably inquired with thoughts in their minds of the theory existing amongst the transmigration doctrines that a loving husband and wife might hope to be re-united in another life; which idea seems likely to have originated the Hindu practice of the widow sacrificing herself upon her husband's pyre. And they applied this idea to the spiritual resurrection which our Lord was proclaiming. A close consideration, moreover, of His words seems to remove any appearance in them of antagonism to this ancient Aryan doctrine, which may seem more consonant with the idea of divine love than the condemnation of eternity for the sins of a period.[1] According to St. Luke xx. 35 *et seq.*, Christ said, "But they which shall be accounted worthy to obtain that world and the resurrection from the dead, neither marry nor are given in marriage; neither can they die any more, for they are equal unto the angels."

The expression "to obtain that world" might seem to be spoken in contradiction to obtaining merely a resurrection in this world again. Nothing is said respecting the possibility, according to the Catholic doctrines, of one or more of the brothers being revived for condemnation. And the words in St. Mark xii. 25, "*εκ νεκρῶν αναστῶσιν*;" and in St. Luke, "*της αναστάσεως τῆς ἐκ νεκρῶν*," seem to suggest a rising up from out of the dead, or, as *νεκρὸς* is also held to signify "morally or spiritually dead," from out of those who are dead in sins, and liable to their continued consequences. "Neither can they die any more" (*ἔτι*), which may mean that they cannot be subject again to birth and death. It may be remarked that the word translated as "world" in St. Luke xx. 35 is *αἰῶν* (aiōn) twice repeated. It is the adjective derived from this word thus translated as "world," viz. *αἰώνιος* (aiōnios), which we have rendered as eternal, and upon which, as has been remarked, we have based our belief in an eternity of torment in hell.

Of course the parable of Dives and Lazarus actually introduces Hades (not Gehenna) as a place of flame. But if this parable be accepted as teaching an eternal duration of the sinner's punishment in the flames of hell, we must literally suppose that there is a great gulf (Luke xvi. 26) between a material heaven and hell, and that the saints can converse with the condemned. And if these words of Christ's had a literal signification, it must again be urged that so must those have borne it concerning the portents before the end of the world, which were to happen in the lifetime of those with whom He was talking. But these last evidently had not such a signification; neither may the others have possessed it.

Christ frequently rebuked the Pharisees for their practices, but He is not related to have impugned their doctrines.

[1] See Appendix XIII.

This must be good *negative* evidence that He admitted them. Two thousand years hence, published sermons of divines of our Church of England may be in existence, containing moral discourses and assurances of the hopes of heavenly happiness through the intercession of a Saviour. No allusion to the eternal punishment in hell may be found in them, but a reference to the doctrines of the Church of England will be a guide to the belief held by the preacher upon that point. If he did not actually contravene the established doctrine of the church, it would be correct to infer that he, as one of its ministers, admitted its teaching in that as in other respects. So, if Christ uttered no protest against the doctrine of the metempsychosis then in existence amongst the Jews, while by keeping His passover in the Temple and reading in the synagogue on the Sabbath He demonstrated His adherence to their religion, it must be reasonably inferred that He admitted it. There was no need for the doctrine of the transmigration of souls to be preached, because it was already believed. It would seem to have been the consummation in the divine life which He was teaching. By faith in His doctrine the seven brothers and the wife whom they had successively espoused, in order that they might raise up seed to the childless brother, might hope to awake to the resurrection of eternal life, where they would neither marry nor be given in marriage (Matt. xxii. 23-33).

To understand the full doctrines of a divine of the present day from a few of his discourses, it will be necessary to the student of the future to investigate the general belief of the Church. We seem to have been contented in Christ's teaching to accept what was held in that branch of the Church subsequently to the epoch of Origen, which had come to be considered orthodox, *i.e.* more than 200 years after the death of its Founder. It is not even contrary to the letter of the Scriptures, which we consider holy, to allow that the divine light may have irradiated the writers of scriptures which our Aryan ancestors or cousins and other nations have esteemed sacred. It must be remembered that St. Paul's text, 2 Timothy iii. 16, "All Scripture has been given by inspiration," etc., and which has been held to refer to those writings only which are contained within our precise canon of Scripture, may reasonably bear a wider application. It was uttered when not all of the books which we now hold under the orthodox view to be canonical were written, and when evidence indicates a valid possibility of others being in circulation in the church which have been pronounced apocryphal, such as the Epistle of Barnabas, the companion of St. Paul. It may therefore be argued that St. Paul rather referred to all thoughtful writings, which in all ages have exercised what human wisdom has deemed a salutary influence, and which mankind has adopted as sacred. In the three years which he informs us in Galatians i. 17, 18, he passed in Arabia, returning to preach in Damascus (Acts ix.), he must surely have perused many writings which have not descended to us, or at least conversed with the ascetics of the desert about them. Without saying that they influenced his divinely-inspired ideas, he may at all events have recognised their value. Moreover, the fact of his miraculous conversion and his faith in the resurrection of Jesus need not have caused him to contemn all his old Pharisaical learning. His Epistles do not seem to indicate such a view. In an age when comparatively few men wrote he may have been naturally disposed to assign a higher value to writings, and consider those of moral worth inspired by the Spirit of God, not merely human in conception, or under the inspiration of the devil. His words at all events are "all Scripture." The Greek word which we translate as Scripture certainly did not bear that distinctive meaning which we now attribute to the term as compared with writing. Timothy must have supposed that St. Paul's words (2 Timothy iii. 15) referred to more scriptures than those included in our Old Testament canon, which closes with the prophet Malachi about 420 B.C. The scriptures, which he had known from his childhood, would seem likely to have extended over a wider literary field. Of course in his childhood none of the New Testament Scriptures had been written, and not all, according to orthodox dates, when St. Paul wrote to him. St. Paul's Second Epistle to Timothy has been usually assigned by theologians to 65 or 66 A.D. The Gospel of St. John has not been considered at the earliest date to have been written before 68 A.D., while it is generally ascribed to 97 A.D.; so we have to hold that St. Paul referred to that Gospel prophetically, also to the Revelation of St. John. Our canon of Scripture was only settled in councils of the church many years after.

St. Paul would doubtless have condemned the superstitious practices of the Hindus, and perhaps protested against their images; although that branch of the Church of Christ which admits the use of images would probably deny this last allegation. But he utilises the Athenian altar, and quotes from the Grecian books (Acts xvii. 28). It would seem that he would have been disposed to have selected the good matter from the Sanskrit writings if his apostolic journeyings had extended to India, and that he would have recognised any scintillation of Christian doctrine amongst them. Our missionaries appear to have been inclined to regard Krishna principally from the point of view obtained in the more fanciful stories of the mass of literature concerning him, and especially to dwell upon his licentiousness, without considering the differences in Eastern and Western ideas, and between Brahminism and Buddhism, or even in Brahminism itself, upon the question of marriage.

Krishna, as a prototype of Christ, might be presented in either a truly Christian or so-called heathen guise, by producing or suppressing sayings, stories, and the general accumulation of legendary and fanciful lore which has centred around him during the course of some 5000 years according to the Hindus, and some 3500 according to our own calculations. His words, as have been shown, also point to a spiritual resurrection. In the case of our Lord, the fanciful stories which may be seen in what are called the Apocryphal Gospels, have been suppressed. Humanly speaking, the Gospel of St. John having been written sixty years after the death of Christ, when the author was about ninety years of age, and in the midst of the philosophisings of the Alexandrian school, it is natural to expect that a different colour should have been imparted therein to the mission, and variations to the words, of the Saviour. That His life should, even in the fifty years, have received additional supernatural appendages is not surprising, when the facility is observed with which miracles are credited, both amongst the votaries of Catholicism and spiritualism in the present day, and when the inevitable growth of personal anecdotes and accretions of words and incidents are noticed, even in the lifetimes of influential men. If within fifty years of our Saviour's death we find incidents attributed to his life which we discover to have been previously assigned to Krishna, our faith in the great essential doctrines, taught in love and universal charity by Christ, surely need not be thereby annulled.

CHAPTER LIV.

The astronomer Parasara's observations—Colebrooke's discoveries as to the Indian knowledge of the solstitial points, etc.—Considerations as to the Ramáyana in connection with the invading of the South—As to the periods assigned to Buddhism under King Piyudasi, etc.—Early Greek history obscured —Inspired Jewish history terminating, according to our system, 420 B.C.—Reasons for the absence of regular history in India—Buckle's observation that the discrepancies in the European notions concerning Indian historical points show their great antiquity—M. Klaproth on the Vale of Cashmere's early history—Assistance of Divine personages recorded in our sacred histories for the peopling of the world—Series of Cashmere monarchs—If the Vedic hymns, etc., not due to long periods of intellectual growth, they ought to be referred to Divine inspiration.

According to a summary in Pritchard's "Physical History of Mankind," Vyãsa, the reputed author of the account in the Mahábhárata epic of Krishna's doings, and also the compiler of the Vedas, has been recognised as the son of the astronomer Parasara, who, as mentioned above, has been admitted by Anglo-Indian criticism to have recorded the observations of the positions of the Colures in about the fourteenth century B.C. Mr. Colebrooke has observed, says Pritchard, that the Jyotish, or calendar of months and seasons, adjusted to the different religious ceremonies ordained in the Vedas, contains adequate means for determining the period at which this adjustment was laid down, and in which period it would appear that the Vedas were compiled. Hence he inferred that they were compiled about the fourteenth century B.C. He discovered that the places of the solstitial points and equinoxes, at the time when this calendar was formed, are clearly pointed out in several passages.[1] Vyasa, whose epoch has thus been determined upon the authority of his father's records in astronomical science, is said to have been contemporary with the heroes whom he has celebrated; but modern criticism seems only to allow to

[1] See Appendix IX.

Vyasa a portion of his colossal poem. Parasara is related to have been the grandson of Vanisht'ha, an astronomer and a legislator, who was the preceptor of Rama, king of Ayodhya, or Oude, the hero of the first great epic of the Hindus; which records, says Pritchard, also the first invasion of the Deccan by the sovereigns of northern Hindústan.

As has been suggested, however, the perusal of the Ramáyana scarcely corroborates the idea that this poem was intended by the author to actually commemorate this event. So far from invading the south, Rama, in the epic, proceeds thither, solitary and despairing, and obtains the aid of the sylvan monarch in recovering his bride from the power of the demon. It might more reasonably be held to narrate very figuratively a conquest of Ceylon. According to this attempt at assigning definite epochs within what we have considered sensible periods, the Hindus are supposed to have commenced their career of power in India at about 2200 B.C. Rama and Krishna, since affirmed to have been successive incarnations of the all-pervading, preserving Spirit, became engaged in great wars, and the Vedas were compiled within the next 700 years. Buddhism, under Asoka's influence, became the prevailing religion of the country at about the year 300 B.C.; that monarch being identified with Piyudasi, whose name appears in inscriptions upon a number of remarkable pillars. But Sir William Jones, in attempting to fix the dates of Indian chronology from the lists of sovereigns in different books, etc., computed the commencement of the kingdom of Ayodhya, where Rama afterwards reigned, at 3500 B.C.

It seems at least to be affirmed with certainty that the compilation of the Vedas, and the epochs of Rama, Krishna, etc., cannot have been less remote than 1300 B.C.; and that the institution of Buddhism occurred by 500 B.C. at the latest. Greek history, before the former period, is, as Lemprière observes, darkened with fabulous accounts and traditions. The exodus of the Israelites from Egypt has been assigned, by orthodox chronology, to 1491 B.C., while Solomon succeeded David on the throne of the "chosen people" in 1015 B.C. Those portions of the Jewish history which we have pronounced to be inspired terminate at 420 B.C. According to our system, purporting to be founded upon the Bible, the universal deluge occurred in 2348 B.C.; to about which age, as has been shown, Indian and Chinese astronomical observations have been discovered to extend at the least. It would seem that, if we allow the later dates to be correct which have been assigned by European critics to the vague Indian literary and political standpoints, the antiquity of Eastern culture, in science, etc., as displayed in its literary remains, is still higher than any of which we have any historical knowledge in our Western and Scriptural worlds. They indicate a previous growth from barbarism transcending in its duration the most remote dates assigned to the monuments of Egypt, and apparently leading up to them as well as to the Indian remains themselves.

If Vyasa, or the author of the Mahábhárata, whoever he may have been, wrote that poem in its general entirety in the thirteenth century B.C., or thereabouts, the miracles, etc., recorded in it would seem to indicate that the poet had adopted existing legends. The story of Krishna would, therefore, be relegated to nearer the period assigned for it by the Hindus, 3000 B.C. If, however, the miraculous portions, like the didactic, are held to have been interpolations, its original author may have simply narrated the events of the war, with not much more colouring than may be found in the contemporary accounts of a newspaper correspondent at the seat of a modern campaign. In the first case the name of Krishna might have a legendary signification. In the second it would probably be the actual appellation of the hero. His superhuman qualifications might have been attributed to him during the next few centuries. But it certainly does not seem reasonable to suppose that a mere poem created a religion. And if the miracles and didactic discourses be removed from the character of Krishna, it would seem that he is less prominent in the poem than the Pandu princes. In fact, the whole poem has the aspect of being a compilation of existing stories, if not by one hand, at all events in accordance with one design. And its general tenor would seem to suggest the history of a traditional hero, about whose person divine attributes and honours had centred. This, however, might easily happen in a century or two.

The records of modern spiritualism may even be thought

to testify to the distinct possibility of miracles being imputed to an individual in his lifetime, even in such a scientific age as our own.

Wonder has been expressed that such a voluminous and comprehensive body of literature should have been discovered in the Sanskrit, this language considered to have been no longer living as popular speech since the time of Christ, though once generally spoken, at all events among the higher classes,—yet that nothing worthy of being dignified with the name of history should have come to light. But it may be urged that the literary personages of an archaic and autochthonous civilisation were scarcely likely to have thought of carefully recording passing events for the benefit of future civilisations, when they knew of no past civilisation to excite their interest in previous ages, and suggest the compilation of records for the benefit of posterity. If the Brahminical and higher castes had actually invaded India through the difficult mountain-passes on the north-west, it might have been expected that some poetic or legendary story would have remained of the event, if it had occurred at so comparatively recent a period as 2200 B.C., or even 3000 B.C.; which have been the dates assigned for the event by European criticism.

Our modern histories seem to be mostly undertaken to enunciate a political theory or to serve a Party. Ancient chronicles were recorded to glorify the absolute rulers of those old days; and if there were no great national movements, magnificent conquests, or special acts of benevolence to narrate, it naturally occurred to no one to make an accurate notation of the ordinary events of life. These, in the primitive pastoral and agricultural civilisations, may have continued for generation after generation without any important war or other event sufficiently notable or extraordinary to engage an historian—to initiate, in fact, a purely original literary character. They are not likely to have had political parties to encourage historical partisans. The inhabitants of Bharata, however, became engaged apparently in this great war of the Mahábhárata, and it found an historian, or series of historians or poets, who, having collected the legends concerning it, or, from personal knowledge, celebrated it in an epic poem, exceeding in length the great epic poems of the Christian world put together, viz. the before-mentioned 120,000 epic verses. If British commentators, instead of lamenting the absence of regular Indian histories, could have induced the Anglo-Indian Government to procure an entire translation of this stupendous work, the British masters of Hindustan would have had a poetical view of Indian thought almost equivalent to history. Portions not considered consistent with modern notions of delicacy might have been surely subdued in their details.

Men seem, in these old Indian days, as now, to have written for the instruction of their fellows. They recorded their notions on philosophy, medicine, music, morals, and even architecture. They indited a code of laws. They had apparently commenced their literary career by collecting their sacred hymns and recording the regulations for their religious ritual and sacrificial formularies. Having probably no political parties to serve in writing histories, it did not occur to them to note in careful annals the ordinary passing occurrences, or to dive into past events which had no special significance for them. When they have recorded astronomical observations or lists of their successive monarchs, with some apparent ingratitude, we have usually set to work to curtail their epochs to the dimensions of our good old Archbishop Usher's chronology. We have styled the writers crafty Brahmins endeavouring to obtain importance by claims to descent from what we have considered preposterous periods of time.

The Brahmins—the literary class of old Indians—appear to have become so influential as to have been able to afford to despise the labour of celebrating kings or warriors. They probably rather desired to glorify themselves, or extend their æsthetical ideas on various topics in the philosophical or scientific essays which have descended to us in the Sanskrit. The great epics seem to be records of the manifestations of God to man in the incarnate Preserver, and incitements to devotion, and belief in Brahminical excellence, rather than epithalamia of deified monarchs. Certainly the Ramáyana, notwithstanding some professions of contemporaneousness in the poet, bears the aspect of being composed at a period when the hero whom it commemorates belonged to the almost legendary past. In regard to the lists of monarchs, and other data, from which modern science has endeavoured to construct definite historical processes, it may again be observed, with Buckle, that the discrepancies, and general uncertainty pervading them, and the differences in the conclusions culled from them by European commentators, are sufficient to indicate their great antiquity. The first part of the Raja Tarinjini is asserted to have been written about B.C. 1148. The Vale of Cashmere is therein related to have been reclaimed from a vast lake by the holy Casyapa, son of Marishi, son of Brahma, who accomplished this task by opening a passage through the mountains, through which the waters escaped.

M. Klaproth observed that it is not improbable that the valley was originally a large reservoir, and that, as Bernier supposes, a convulsion of nature opened the mountain-barrier which closed it on all sides, and gave vent to the waters, which then flowed into the plains of the Punjab. The territory thus recovered by Casyapa was related to have been peopled by that holy man, with the assistance of certain gods whom he brought down from heaven for that purpose. This took place at the commencement of the seventh *manwantara*, or the age in which we are now, according to the Hindu chronology.

It may be parenthetically recalled to mind that the assistance of divine personages is also recorded in our Holy Scriptures as concerned in the peopling of our earth. We are not informed whether their offspring proved to be moral or the reverse, though the latter appears to have been the case, as we have accounts of the parentage and ancestral line of Noah, who was descended from Seth the son of Adam, and all mankind beyond his family are related or inferred, both in the Old and New Testaments, to have been destroyed. It is said in Genesis, chapter vi. verse 1 *et seq.*—"And it came to pass, when men began to multiply on the face of the earth, and daughters were born unto them, that the sons of God saw the daughters of men that they were fair; and they took them wives of all that they chose. And the Lord said, My spirit shall not always strive with man, for that he also is flesh; yet his days shall be an hundred and twenty years. There were giants in the earth in those days; and also after that, when the sons of God came in unto the daughters of men, and they bare children to them, the same became mighty men which were of old, men of renown."

From the epoch of the first divinely-born colony of Cashmere down to the reign of Gonerda I., the first prince whose name is mentioned by Kalhana, the reputed author, Cashmere is stated to have been governed by a series of fifty-two monarchs, whose reigns collectively form a period of 1266 years. As Gonerda I., who succeeds these sovereigns, the contemporary of Krishna, appertains, according to Hindu notions, to about the year 2000 B.C., the commencement of Cashmerian history, by the authority of this chronological document, is placed at 4000 B.C. But the princes who reigned, after the draining of the valley, by the miraculous conversion of Casyapa, are related to have been undeserving of mention, on account of their contempt for the precepts of the Vedas. The Vedas, therefore, are supposed to have been then in existence. In fact, the inhabitants of India appear universally to have predicated an antiquity for their civilisation, vast as compared with the Christian chronology founded on the Mosaic records, though not unduly extensive when considered in relation to geological conceptions of the shortest time scientifically likely to have been occupied in the present formation of the earth. At all events, the admitted compilation of the Vedas in their present shape, in about the fourteenth century B.C., with the systematised forms of ritual which accompany them, must, humanly speaking, presuppose a growth in religious ideas which would relegate their commencement to many thousand years B.C. From the civilisation dawning in apprehension of the divine to the advanced spiritual conceptions of the Vedas, unless they are allowed to have been transcendently delivered by superhuman wisdom, a long interval seems to have been required for the successive stages of thought. Putting aside the Biblical statement that Moses was learned in all the wisdom of the Egyptians, as not indicating any probability of his employing that learning in arranging his system for the guidance of the Israelites, our Church appears to maintain that he was, in actual fact, divinely instructed before delivering his laws and ordinances. If the Vedic hymns and ordinances occupied no long period in gradual formation, but were devised with similar suddenness, they would similarly seem to have required the Divine interposition; unless, indeed, they should be ascribed by the piety of Christendom to promptings of the devil.

CHAPTER LV.

Sir R. Phillips' remarks as to the culture of the Britons—The Celts accompanied by Brahminical institutions—Phœnicia the starting-point from Asia to Europe —Ourselves continuing the westward progress to America—Restrictions against emigration in the ancient Hindu laws sufficient to show its prevalence—Pritchard's observations as to the speech of the first German tribes in Europe allied to the Zend and Sanskrit, etc.—Poetry amongst the Servians and Russians—Ancient religion of the Slavs, etc.—Celtic belief in the transmigration of souls—Accounts from Diodorus, Strabo, and Cæsar, concerning them—The Druids—Feudal constitutions in Gaul, according to Pritchard—Personal adornment of the warriors—Their divinities—Human sacrifices amongst the Gauls; and slaves, friends, etc., burned upon the chieftains' funereal pyres—Sequences of ideas observable in comparing Rajpoots and Goths—Favourite wives of deceased Thracians immolated with their husbands—Pausanias and fire temples in Lydia, where the priests repeated litanies out of a book in a barbarous tongue, which may have been Sanskrit—Northern European legends and snowy mountains consistent with the Hindu deities on the Himalayas.

Sir Richard Phillips remarks that the Britons had arts, agriculture, towns, religion, and even colleges of learning. They had annual meetings, where laws were made, and justice administered, and heinous crimes punished by burning in wicker baskets in the presence of the people.

The Celts seem, indeed, to have been accompanied by Brahminical institutions; and their settlements in Europe present appearances of having proceeded from long-continued sea transits. To the Phœnicians has been ascribed the origin, but to Phœnicia the points of embarkation should rather have been assigned. As well might the colonisation of America be held to have entirely resulted from a people autochthonous in England, or those western points of Europe from which the American settlers have taken their departure. Between the continents of India and Europe the ports of Phœnicia appear, on the maps, to be the obvious starting-places for a progress westwards by sea. Between 700 B.C. and 2000 B.C.—which has been considered the epoch of Phœnician grandeur, through Phœnicia to the Mediterranean, and by the north-western routes overland, at about the same time, seem to have been proceeding the great streams of Aryan emigration which have resulted in Teutons and Celts. So, in the present day, are northern and southern Europeans respectively continuing their migrations to Northern and Southern America, in the routes first opened by the valour and adventurous spirit of Columbus and Cabot, followed by Francis Drake and Raleigh.

An extension of time beyond our old historical limits accounts for forgetfulness of, or carelessness respecting, the Asian origin. Only of late years have we English inquired backwards for our birthplace beyond the European regions from which we last emanated. If it be admitted that the cradle of the Aryan, or Caucasian, or Indo-European race is to be discerned in Asia, Bactria or Persia may be easily conceived to have been the last place to which Teutonic traditions or recollections would go, supposing India to have been the original starting-point. The part of India from which these northern emigrants by land would have emerged, would have been a region of rugged mountains and vast sunburnt plains, swept by the hot winds of the deserts on the east before the annual rainfall. The intervening deserts and mountains in the case of the northern migrations, and the settlements in Egypt and Asia Minor in the case of the southern, would occasion the memories of the original fatherland to lapse. In the present day our emigrants are chiefly taken from the least literary of our classes. They are, in themselves, unlikely to indite positive records of their progresses. But the immense growth of historical literature will probably prevent the Americans and Australians of two thousand years hence from forgetting their original homes.

As has been observed, the restrictions against emigration, in Indian laws ascribed to about 1000 B.C., are sufficient to show that it largely prevailed. Customs, traditions, language, Sanskritic literature, and the names of places in Europe and even Africa, combine to afford the evidences for ascribing to India itself the origin both of our mediæval chivalrous and superstitious, and of our modern mercantile and scientific civilisations.

Pritchard observed, "That the original speech of the first German tribes who entered Europe, and of all the branches of the same stock, is allied to the Zend and Sanscrit, nobody can for the future doubt."

"The affinity of the Slavonic and the Sanskrit is very obvious," he further remarked; and that "some students of the Celtic language have fancied a near relation between the Celtic and the Slavonian." Also that "poetry appears to have been cultivated by the Servians and by the Russians even in Pagan times;" and "the literature of the Slavi is, from its very commencement, monastic." "The assertion that the Slavonic nations, notwithstanding their polytheism and the worship paid by them to inferior divinities, believed in the existence of one supreme God, under whom all the rest acted as subordinate angels, is confirmed by Helmoldus." "The religion of the Slavi contained the dualism of the Iranian nations, and the opposition of the good and evil principles; the former identified with light, the latter with darkness." The Prussian priesthood "were governed by a supreme pontiff called the Griwe, that is, Graue, senator, graf, who was at the same time legislator, supreme judge, and high priest. His station has been compared with that of the Great Lama of Tibet. The ancient Prussians, Prutheni or Pruzii, are said to have worshipped, besides other objects, a triad or three principal deities." The first was the god of the firmament and of thunder; before whose sacred oak a perpetual fire was maintained. The second had the form of a young man crowned with spikes of corn, who was the god of fecundity; young children were sacrificed to him, and a sacred serpent kept in honour of him. The third was the divinity of death and evil, symbolised by three skulls. "It is a fact, though a very surprising one, that the language of the ancient Prussians and Letts was strongly allied to the sacred and classical dialect of Hindustan."

"The Celts believed in a future state and in the transmigration of souls. The opinion of Pythagoras," says Diodorus, "prevails amongst them, that the souls of men are immortal, and live again, after a certain time, in other bodies. This belief," he says, "is supposed to excite greatly to valour and contempt of death." The dogma of the Druids was that of the metempsychosis; which was connected with that of cycles and renovations of the series of events. Strabo says that they taught, in common with many other ancient nations, that the soul is indestructible as well as the world itself, and that fire and water are destined at periods to prevail. "They dispute much," says Cæsar, "concerning the heavenly bodies and their motions, and the magnitude of the world and of regions, concerning the nature of things, and the power and dominion of the immortal gods." Cæsar also informs us that throughout all Gaul there were two dignified orders—the sacerdotal or Druids, and the knights or military caste. "These alone," he says, "are held in any respect; the common people are regarded nearly in the light of slaves, nor are they admitted to councils. The Druids manage all the affairs of religion, public and private sacrifices, and are the interpreters of all divine things. They are held in great respect as the educators of youth. It is their business to settle all disputes, public and private. In controversies respecting boundaries or succession to property, and in criminal accusations, they are judges and appoint punishments."

The sanctity of the banyan tree was transferred to the oak, which bears a general resemblance to it, except in respect to the strange tendrils drooping to the ground which mark the Indian tree.

"Gaul," says Pritchard, "seems to have had a sort of feudal constitution, in which the influence of clanship and alliances between kindred tribes was a very prominent feature; and the Veneti were skilful in shipbuilding and in maritime affairs before the intercourse between them and the Romans began." Amongst the Gauls, Strabo says that three classes of men are held in great esteem, the Bards, Vates, and Druids; the former of whom are singers and poets, the second perform sacred rites and study the doctrine of nature, and the latter, in addition to natural philosophy, devote themselves also to the study of ethics.

The people seem to have lived in huts thatched with straw, and to have been more or less naked, resembling in these points the poorer natives of Hindustan. Shaven heads, and moustaches only allowed to grow upon the face, add to the likeness. War chariots seem to have been used by them, as by the ancient Orientals and Greeks of the time of Homer.

We learn from Strabo that women sometimes took part in the performances of the Druids; and that in an island near the mouth of the Loire ceremonies were performed similar to the orgies of Bacchus, in which females were alone employed. He says that the men are fonder of war than of agriculture, still that they cultivate the soil so that there is no waste land, and that they keep large herds of oxen and swine, their food being especially composed of the flesh of the latter. Those who are in office have robes dyed and embroidered in gold; and men as well as women ornamented their necks and arms with a profusion of golden chains, and rings, and bracelets; and the warriors of ancient Gaul were celebrated for their flowing locks, which they kept tied in tufts behind their heads. The whole nation are said to have been remarkable for personal cleanliness. Their arms were battle-axes and swords; the chariots were armed with scythes for battle. Five of their divinities were identified with Mercury, Apollo, Mars, Jupiter, and Minerva. The Celtic god considered similar to Mars appears to have been Hesus, mentioned by Lactantius. A statue of a deity bearing the name of Esus was formerly discovered underground in Paris. He wears a crown of boughs, and holds in his left hand a branch which he is about to cut off, with an axe brandished in his right hand. He is only attired in a covering round the loins and a loose garment over the left shoulder.

Cæsar informs us that it was a prevalent opinion amongst the Gauls and Britons that nothing but the life of a man could atone for the life of a man; inasmuch that they had established even public sacrifices of that kind. They preferred for victims such as had been convicted of theft, robbery, or other crimes; but when real criminals were wanting the innocent were made to suffer. Strabo says that some were shot with sacred arrows, or hung upon crosses; and, a colossus being made of rushes fastened with wood, sheep and beasts of every kind, and men, were burned together. The funerals of the Gauls, according to Cæsar, were magnificent; the favourite animals of the deceased, and even his slaves and dependants, were offered upon his funereal pyre; and friends and dependants are even said to have burned themselves with the deceased, in order that they might live with him in a future state. The Scandinavian legend of the Asus attacked by the Powers of darkness seems a descendant of the Indian similar story of the Asuras.

The above considerations seem, coordinately with the language, to point distinctly to an Indian descent, suggesting the immolation of Indian widows, etc. They curiously lead up to the Christian idea of the atonement, in which Christ is not merely represented as the incarnate deity, teaching us the way to godliness, and exhibiting the highest example of courage, constancy, and self-sacrifice in his death, but as necessarily offered to God—Himself to Himself under the conception of Trinity in Unity—as a blood sacrifice; accepted in satisfaction of the sins of the world, and in lieu of the blood sacrifices of the old dispensation.

Sequences of ideas seem evident in comparing the feudal and warlike institutions of the Rajpoots and Goths, the blood sacrifices of the earlier Aryan religions, the dominant religious classes of the Indians and Celts and their doctrines; as in the later Hindu religion of preservation by faith in the incarnate divine spirit and the Christian hope in salvation by the name of our Lord.

The Etruscans, by uniform ancient tradition, were regarded as not indigenous to Italy. Their proficiency in agriculture, manufactures, literature, science, art, and their system of elaborate religious ceremonial in the hands of priests, combined with their doctrines as to the cycles and revolutions of time, and the general aspect of the figures graven on their sarcophagi, etc. etc., display, with little room for doubting, their Oriental and probably actual Indian origin. Lydia was the last station within their national memory. The ruder Pelasgi of Greece are likely to have been earlier emigrants, who naturally settled on the nearer shores of Greece, while the Etruscans had to extend their explorations or settlements farther. They were apparently to some extent connected with or derived from the Pelasgi.

The favourite wives of deceased Thracian chieftains, splendidly dressed, are said to have been immolated on the tombs of their husbands, whose funerals were celebrated with great festivity, accompanied with loud lamentations. This people are said to have smoked hemp. It can scarcely be contended that the rude hookahs and cigarettes of the lower Indian classes are derived from European example; and an affinity may be discerned upon this point. The Brahmins object to the use of tobacco for smoking, and it is also interdicted to the Parsis.

Englishmen, in the rough life of the back woods of America

and Australia, seem to have retrograded in intellectual culture, and grown rougher in their general manners than all but the lowest classes in the old country; who also lead rough lives. So do the Indians seem, in their progressions to the north-west, to have become ruder in their ideas and habits of life.

Magianism and the reverence of fire, after the Persian manner, appear to have been spread throughout Asia Minor. Pausanias has described fire temples in Lydia, where the priests, after arranging the wood, repeated litanies out of a book in a barbarous tongue. The discovery of the *Swastika* at the site of Troy adds testimony of fact to the theory that this may have been an ancient Indian as easily as a more recent Persian rite, as is demonstrated by the descriptions in M. E. Burnouf's "Science des Religions;" and the barbarous tongue may either have been the Sanskrit or the language of the Zendavesta, introduced after the age of Cyrus. While the Lydians are related by Herodotus to have resembled the Greeks, "many traits may be collected in the history of the nations of Asia Minor, remarks Pritchard, which seem to connect them with the Iranian and other Eastern nations."

If it be urged that the northern European legends celebrate snow-clad mountains rather than sun-dried regions, it must be remembered that the abodes of the Hindu deities have been placed above the snowy peaks of the Himalayas. Mahadeo sits enthroned amid everlasting snows, at the source of the most sacred branch of the Ganges. Our actual Anglo-Saxon traditions merely seem to extend to Hengist and Horsa, said to have been greatgrandsons of the god Woden; and our British legends of King Arthur and his chivalry only demand for scenery our own forests. Like all the others of the Aryan family, we have remained content with acknowledging bare emigrations or warlike transits from the last previous settlements of our tribes, and have only entered upon these more distant investigations within the last scientific generation or two.

Mitford commented upon the strong resemblance between the Heroic account of Greece and that of our Teutonic ancestors.

CHAPTER LVI.

Professor Maine on the Village Communities in East and West — This system still remaining in India and Russia—Our land law traced to the Manor by our text-books; but, according to Von Maurer and Nasse, this part of our legal history requires reviewing—Conquest or leadership in battle giving a pre-eminence amongst the western tribes — The Indian system of property and tenure closely resembling the ancient proprietary system of the Teutonic Races—Landmarks traced from the Village group to the Manorial to be found in India—Political liberty and rights of the masses apprehended in the East.

PROFESSOR MAINE of Oxford, formerly law member of the Supreme Government of India, and author of "Ancient Law," in his publication entitled "Village Communities in the East and West," has produced such parallels in the early land settlements of Europe and India as to render, in conjunction with the evidences of parallels in other concerns of life, the theory of a community of origin seemingly unanswerable.

Again, it may be urged that the ideas respecting the land settlements in east and west are traceable to the dawning civilisation in the Bactrian region. The patriarchal system of the nomad tribes may have developed in the Bactrian region into the form of the community of the Indian village or European township. But the growth of the institution in India itself, where it still remains, and, in the emigrations from that country, its continuance by the early Aryan colonists of Europe, appear to be more consonant with probability; when the evidence is taken into consideration which has been adduced concerning the language, architectural forms of ancient excavations, old habits as displayed in the Mahábhárata epic, etc. The warlike habits of the Europeans subsequently occasioned its modification.

The necessarily nomad life of the Arabs caused the archaic patriarchal form of community to continue amongst them as more convenient. Tribes or families wandering amongst the occasional oases in the deserts required no careful division of land, which was speedily exhausted in its scanty supplies in each temporary resting-place. Encampments were their homes instead of villages. But Abraham was seeking a settlement—or was promised a settlement—for his descendants. He was not a true nomad.

Professor Maine states:—"It does not appear to me a hazardous proposition that the Indian and the ancient European systems of enjoyment and tillage by men grouped in village communities are, in all essential points, identical.—The assumption which the English first made in India was one which they inherited from their Mohammedan predecessors. It was that all the soil belonged in absolute property to the sovereign, and that all private property in land existed by his sufferance.—If very general language were employed, the description of the Teutonic or Scandinavian village communities might actually serve as a description of the same institution in India. There is the arable mark, divided into separate lots, but cultivated according to minute customary rules, binding on all. Wherever the climate admits of the finer grass crops, there are the reserved meadows, lying generally on the verge of the arable mark. There is the waste or common land, out of which the arable mark has been cut, enjoyed as a pasture by all the community *pro indiviso*. There is the village, consisting of habitations each ruled by a despotic paterfamilias. And there is constantly a council of government to determine disputes as to custom." Professor Maine further affirms that "the description given by Maurer of the Teutonic mark of the township, as his researches have shown it to him, might here again pass for an account, so far as it goes, of an Indian village. The separate households, each despotically governed by its family chief, and never trespassed upon by the footsteps of any person of different blood, are all to be found there in practice." He remarks that the council of elders in the Indian village communities appear actually to legislate, although they only profess to expound the existing customary law under which the community is considered to exist. The villages "include a nearly complete establishment of occupations and trades for enabling them to continue their collective life without assistance from any person or body external to them.

Besides the headman, or council exercising quasi-judicial, quasi-legislative power, they contain a village police. They include several families of hereditary traders; the blacksmith, the harness-maker, the shoemaker. The Brahmin is also found for the performance of ceremonies, and even the dancing-girl for attendance at festivities. There is invariably a village accountant. But the person practising any one of these hereditary employments is really a servant of the community, as well as one of its component members. He is sometimes paid by an allowance in grain, more generally by the allotment to his family of a piece of cultivated land in hereditary possession. Whatever else he may demand for the wares he produces is limited by a customary standard of price, very rarely departed from. It is the assignment of a definite lot in the cultivated area to particular trades which allows us to suspect that the early Teutonic groups were similarly self-sufficing. There are several English parishes in which certain pieces of land in the common field have from time immemorial been known by the name of a particular trade; and there is often a popular belief that nobody not following the trade can legally be the owner of the lot associated with it. And it is possible that we here have a key to the plentifulness and persistence of certain names of trades as surnames among us."

Professor Maine observes that the ordinary text-books of our law practically " trace our land law to the customs of the manor, and assume the manor to have been a complete novelty introduced into the world during the process which is called the feudalisation of Europe. But the writings of Von Maurer, and of another learned German who has followed him, Nasse of Bonn, afford strong reason for thinking that this account of our legal history should be reviewed. The mark has through a great part of Germany stamped itself plainly on land law, on agricultural custom, and on the territorial distribution of landed property. Nasse has called attention to the vestiges of it which are still discoverable in England."

The mark, or township, was "an organised, self-acting group of Teutonic families, exercising a common proprietorship over a definite tract of land, its mark; cultivating its domain on a common system, and sustaining itself by the produce. It is well known to have been the proprietary, and even the political unit of the earliest English society; it is allowed to have existed amongst the Scandinavian races, and it survived at so late a date in the Orkney and Shetland Islands as to have attracted the personal notice of Sir Walter Scott. In our own country it became absorbed in larger territorial aggregations."

In fact, it appears that conquest, or the leadership in battle, gave to individuals or families in the warlike western communities a pre-eminence in the community which at length resolved itself into absolute ownership, or the links of the feudal system; while in the more peaceful, or more conservative, general community of India these causes did not operate, and the village community remained, in its democratic completeness, till we commenced to tamper with it. The Mohammedans, though claiming as conquerors the lordship of the soil, by the teaching of the Prophet, under whom they professed so to own it, interfered not with the ordinary cultivators of the land, so long as they paid the required tribute. There appear in parts of India to be chiefs corresponding to the chieftains of our Celtic clans; and hereditary headmen, who approximate to our lords of manors in a very distant degree. India, under its ancient constitutions, while acknowledging the authority of the executive in the sovereign, and the superior sanctity and learning of the Brahmins, conserved a free and democratic possession of the soil. Professor Weber conceives that the prince styled Vispati in Vedic literature was probably elective. This title, he remarks, is still preserved in Lithuanian. The redistribution of land, ordained under the Mosaic law, again corresponds to what appears anciently to have been an Indian practice. The East, which we have held to be only the slave of despotism, seems to have preserved an element of liberty which Europe has, or had, largely lost.

Professor Maine observes again that the East is certainly full of fragments of ancient society; of which the most instructive, because the most open to sustained observation, are to be found in India. He thinks that the Indian evidence gives colour to the theory of the origin of a great part of law in the Patriarchal Family. The Patriarchal Family, when occupied with those agricultural pursuits which are the exclusive employment of many millions of men in India, is generally found as the unit of a larger natural group, the Village Community. The Indian system of property and tenure, closely resembling that which Maurer believes to be the ancient proprietary system of the Teutonic races, has occasionally, though not universally, undergone changes which bring it into something like harmony with European feudalism. India is the great repository of veritable phenomena of ancient usage and ancient juridical thought. He remarked that the English dominion of India at first placed the natives of the country under a less advanced regimen of civil law than they would have had if they had been left to themselves: during many centuries the Hindus had preserved a great body of unwritten custom, differing locally in detail, but connected by common general features, and he deprecates the common European view of the extreme influence of caste throughout India. He affirms that the real India contains one priestly caste, and some princely houses, tribes, village communities, and guilds, which advance a claim to belong to the second and third of the old Brahminical castes, but that otherwise caste is merely a name for trade or occupation; and the sole tangible effect of the Brahminical theory is that it creates a religious sanction for what is really a primitive and natural distribution of classes. The true view of India is that, as a whole, it is divided into a vast number of independent, self-acting, organised social groups—trading, manufacturing, cultivating. These Indian customs became suddenly of wholly new importance, by the startling coincidence found to exist between them and those of the Teutonic and Scandinavian countries, in which a primitive village system was shown to have existed; and by the fact that the primitive European tenures, and primitive European tillage, constitute the actual working system of the Indian village communities.

A person aggrieved in an Indian village community complains not of an individual wrong, but of the disturbance of the order of the entire little society. The rights of Teutonic families over the common Mark were controlled or modified by the rights of every other family. Of all the landmarks on the line of movement traced by German and English scholars from the village group to the manorial group, there is not one which may not be met with in India, saving always the extreme points at either end. Again the Aryan race, as from India to Europe, so in its migrations to America, continued the ancient custom; for the earliest English emigrants to North America—who belonged principally to the class of yeomanry—organised themselves at first in village communities for purposes of cultivation. The land was first held by the company as property in common. House lots were assigned, and then tracts of meadow land, and in some cases mineral land. Pasture and woodland remained in common as the property of the company, but a law of the "General Court" in 1660 provided that "hereafter no cottage or dwelling-house be admitted to the privilege of commonage for wood, timber, or herbage, but such as are already in being, or shall be erected with the consent of the town." From that time, observes Professor Maine, "the commoners appear as a kind of aristocracy, and the commons were gradually divided up. This is not only a tolerably exact account of the ancient European and existing Indian village community, but it is also a history of its natural development, when the causes which turn it into a manorial group are absent."

If the Aryan race thoroughly arrived at the principles of political liberty in the West, it undoubtedly seems to have apprehended, and conserved in the East, those of the general rights of the masses to possess a beneficial property in the soil; which rights, in the west, were largely swallowed up by the greed of the great warriors who obtained power, from whom our territorial nobility are, as a class, descended.

To add another to the list of concordances between Indian and Greek civilisation, as indicating the birth of the latter from the former, the village system was also the early state of legendary Greece. Grote, after describing a Greek village in a fashion whigh might serve almost without alteration for one in India, quotes Mills' description of an Indian village community as a parallel to that depicted in his text, observes Mr. John Bruce Norton in "Topics for Indian Statesmen."

CHAPTER LVII.

Considerations as to the periods of the world's history—Observation of M. E. Burnouf as to the freedom of Brahminism from dogma—Church of England has acknowledged the privileges of the regal and military class, to which it was rendered subservient—Before the rise of Brahminical assumptions in India, M. E. Burnouf remarks that each father of a family was priest—Establishments of priests and choirs for the Vedic system—Jaganatha, the "hope" of the people—Buddhism ordained to its disciples to "go forth among all races, and to all countries, and preach the righteousness which passeth knowledge" —E. Senart's idea that the history of northern Buddhism only showed a number of Hindu legends created about a possibly ideal being—Buddhism inculcating universal love.

ALLOWING that Almighty Power has worked by constant laws, we have to consider the lapse of time during which our globe may have revolved in its orbit, in a condition approximating to the present, *i.e.* capable of sustaining vegetable and animal life upon it. We have to allow time for these forgotten migrations of our race, for the previous rise of their religious and other cultured ideas in the East, and for the possible transmutation of animals from the saurians, etc., revealed by geological investigations, to the present species. The several thousand years which have elapsed since some of existing species were preserved as mummies in Egypt, appear to have effected no change. But when we contemplate even 10,000 years as relatively a long period, are we not somewhat in the natural state of error in which the mind of an ephemeral summer's day's insect might fall, if able to reflect and form estimates of time from the duration of its own existence? Living for one day, after its rise from the chrysalis, it might conceive sixty days a long period for the life of the man who can crush it, just as we, able to live towards a century, have allowed about sixty centuries only for the duration of humanity upon the earth. The insect might fancy the statement wickedly preposterous, if informed that our existences might extend to some 20,000 times the duration of its day. As a simile, it does not seem an irrational, proportionate comparison by "rule of three" to say that, as the insect's one day is to the 25,550 days of man, so may the human 70 years be to 1,788,500 years for the life of the world, past and future, after the completion of its primary formations. If we allow about a fourth of these for the past changes of species, viz. 400,000 years, and about the thirtieth part, viz. 50,000 years, for man's growth from infancy, from crude civilisation to our present state of scientific culture, the computation seems reasonable in the light of scientific facts. It is at all events more consonant with them than our old dogmatic chronology. The Brahmins have been larger in their ideas, and nearer modern scientific approximate chronology, than our own theologians.

Brahminism, observes M. E. Burnouf, is what Christianity ought to be, free of dogma—"Si quelque Brâhmane acquiert avec les années une autorité qui manque à d'autres, il la doit à sa science et non à une superiorité de fonction." "Cette égalité hierarchique des prêtres a pour conséquence la liberté dans les doctrines: s'il y a eu dans l'Inde une orthodoxie ce n'est pas l'autorité d'un chef ou d'une réunion quelconque de brâhmanes qui l'a fixée, c'est uniquement sa conformité avec le Veda, c'est a dire, avec la sainte écriture." But while thus admitting the liberty of thought, the ability of each individual to approach the Supreme Spirit—an admission which seems in absolute consonance with the plain letter of Christ's teaching, in our Holy Writ, the Brahmins have set up the barriers of hereditary class-ship. Buddhism, throwing down these barriers, has established in their place an ecclesiastical hierarchy, and proclaimed an orthodoxy of faith in ecclesiastical councils.

The Church of Rome has claimed to be above all earthly hereditary honours, but the Church of England, as established by Henry VIII., Elizabeth, and James I., has distinctly acknowledged the privileges of the regal and military caste, to which it was rendered subservient. In fact, the Reformation in England was, in its political aspect, a protest against the claims of the Buddhistic hierarchy of Rome; which, although still a democratic institution when amongst aristocracies, had established too severe a spiritual despotism for the aspirations of British liberty, political and intellectual. Its overthrow in England tended to enhance the power of the regal and noble caste. A Wolsey became henceforth impossible. But the merchants have gradually acquired authority, though the Brahminical class, in its combination of the professions of divinity and law, has obtained or retained extensive influence.

Before the rise of Brahminical assumptions in India, remarks M. E. Burnouf, each father of a family was priest while he fulfilled the sacred functions; then the priesthood, as we find in the Iliad, became settled, like the royal and military power, in certain families. For the sacrifices of the Vedic period, establishments, numerous priests, and species of choirs, had come into existence. Not only did Buddhism abrogate the claims to superior sanctity of the hereditary sacerdotal class, but in the incarnations of Vishnu, as in the teaching of Christ, union with the divine is freely offered to all. Jaganatha is like Christ the Hope of the People, and his apostles similarly preach the sacrament of the holy food, rice sanctified, offered, and eaten. In his temple high and low partake of the sacred sustenance together, and even priest and peasant become equal before his shrine. At Puri, rice purified by presentation to Vishnu may be taken from a Christian's hand. As has been shown in a somewhat different form of the quotation, Krishna, the incarnate Vishnu, had also beautifully inculcated the great point of Christian practice when he said, "Let the honest man suffer the blows of the wicked, as the sandal tree that's felled by the woodman's stroke perfumes the axe that wounds it." Ramanuja, as has been observed, in an age remarkably closely antecedent to that of our European reformers, viz. about the year 1150 A.D., selected ten disciples from despised castes, and wandered through India, preaching one God to be worshipped in spirit and truth. He proclaimed the unity of God under the name of Vishnu, the all-pervading spirit, cause and creator of all, and equality of caste before him.

Buddhism had ordained to its disciples to "go forth among all races, and to all countries, and preach the righteousness which passeth knowledge." E. Senart considered that he found, in the northern Buddhistic life of the founder of that faith, not history but an assemblage of Hindu legends centred about a being whose existence may be called in question, his mother Mayà being the impersonation of a philosophic idea. In his life, the incarnation, miraculous conception, miraculous nativity, and renunciation of the world after marriage, through intensity of feeling for its woes, may certainly be the impersonation of an idea or assemblage of ideas. Man personifies to realise; and the idolatry which mentally depicts a human embodiment of the divine is an advance upon the idolatry which requires a realistic image to satisfy its imagination. Perhaps both are necessary, in the stages of advancing human thought, to the apprehension of the divine; which must find for us its most vivid expression or representation in the human image or thought. Buddhism reprobated the sacrifices of the Vedas, and inculcated universal love with the theory of a gradual intellectual or religious perfection.

CHAPTER LVIII.

Sir Charles Lyell on the Indian and Egyptian Schools of Philosophy—As to the grandeur and absurdities of the conceptions in the Institutes of Manu—Their asserted revelation based upon astronomical theories—Sir C. Lyell as to former convulsions on our planet—He concedes some foundation of observed facts to the theories of the Brahmins—He observes that the doctrines of Pythagoras as learnt in the East are extremely curious and instructive—Our race in the old centre land has obtained glimpses of many matters of modern science—As it was said that Christianity depended on the admission of the infallibility of the Romish Church, so now the literal inspiration of every text in the Bible is depended upon by Protestants—The liberality of Buddhism displayed in a promulgation by King Piyudasi—Under the ancient Aryan system, so long as the soul retains desires of the flesh, so long will it continue to be re-born—The necessary sequences in pain and pleasure succeed one another as inevitably as night and day—Quotation from the Hitopadesa as to pleasure and trouble—In exhibiting his contempt for the body the Hindu hopes his soul will return to the divine—St. Simon Stylites still suggested in India—As it was in the time of Alexander the Great, so in the days of Victoria, Empress of India.

SIR CHARLES LYELL, in his "Principles of Geology," observes that "the earliest doctrines of the Indian and Egyptian schools of philosophy agreed in ascribing the first creation of the world to an omnipotent and infinite Being. They concurred also in representing this Being, who had existed from all eternity, as having repeatedly destroyed and reproduced the world and all its inhabitants." "The compilation of the ordinances of Manu was not all the work of one author nor of one period, and to this circumstance some of its remarkable inequalities are probably attributable. There are many passages wherein the attributes and acts of the 'infinite and incomprehensible Being' are spoken of with much grandeur of conception and sublimity of diction. There are at the same time such puerile conceits and monstrous absurdities in its cosmogony, that some may be disposed to impute to mere accident any slight approximation to truth or apparent coincidence between the Oriental dogmas and observed facts." In the cosmogony, however, the expression occurs equivalent to the text in the Jewish scripture which says that the Spirit of God moved on the face of the water.—"This pretended revelation was not purely an effort of the unassisted imagination, nor invented without regard to the opinions and observations of naturalists. There are introduced into it certain astronomical theories, evidently derived from observation and reasoning. Thus, for instance, it is declared that at the North Pole the year was divided into a long day and night, and that their long day was the northern and their night the southern course of the sun; and to the inhabitants of the moon it is said one day is equal in length to one month of mortals. If such statements cannot be resolved into mere conjectures, we have no right to refer to mere chance the prevailing notion that the earth and its inhabitants had formerly undergone a succession of revolutions and catastrophes interrupted by long intervals of tranquillity."

Sir Charles Lyell then proceeds to comment on the obvious marks of former convulsions on every part of the surface of our planet. He considers that some foundation of observed facts may be conceded for the theories of the Brahmins, that they may have been acquainted with the existence of fossil remains in the strata, but that the doctrine may originally have been handed down from a ruder state of society.

The doctrines which Pythagoras had learnt in the East are, says Sir Charles Lyell, "extremely curious and instructive" in regard to the illustrations derived from natural events; "for we here find a comprehensive and masterly summary of almost all the great causes of change now in activity on the globe, and these adduced in confirmation of a principle of perpetual and gradual revolution inherent in the nature of our terrestrial system. These doctrines, it is true, are not directly applied to the explanation of geological phenomena. Had this been the case, we might have been called upon to admire so extraordinary an anticipation with no less interest than astronomers, when they endeavour to divine by what means the Samian philosopher came to the knowledge of the Copernican system."

The system of Pythagoras certainly seems to be Buddhistical and his knowledge Indian. He is related to have spent some twenty years in the East—partly in Egypt and perhaps in India—before he founded his sect at Crotona, in which he promulgated his theorems in mathematics and natural philosophy, combined with the doctrine of the metempsychosis. In proof of this he claimed the acquaintance with previous existences of his own.

Our Race in the old Centre Land evidently managed to obtain considerable glimpses of many matters of science into which we have acquired such apparently clear insight during the nineteenth century in Europe. The Brahminical priesthood seems to have entertained no apprehensions lest the promulgation of scientific truths should be injurious to religion. They seem to have allowed that ascertained facts could only add to the true knowledge of God's works, and, although they strictly held the Vedas to have been divinely revealed, they do not appear to have thought it necessary to fight over the literal interpretation of texts. In Christendom each new science has had to surmount the orthodox opposition. Three centuries ago it was said that if the infallibility of the Church was destroyed Christianity must perish with it. Now it is urged in Protestantism that to deny the literal inspiration of every text in the Bible is fraught with danger, if not absolute destruction, to our religion. This discovery of the essentials of Christianity in India may be considered subversive of Christ's doctrines. But it need be held to be no more antagonistic to them, in their large sense and comprehensiveness of truth, than the teaching of astronomy and geology. We must credit our minds with capacity to comprehend facts. We cannot otherwise know anything of the Supreme Spirit, working in the material. Here are facts, and we simply must admit them, and alter our preconceived notions in accordance; as we have been compelled to alter them several times since the establishment of Christianity, as science has progressed.

The following publication of regal sentiments in Buddhism seems more consonant with the spirit of Christ's gospel than many Papal bulls, or decrees of Protestant Synods. Why need we doubt that it appeared in Buddhism, the religion of "wisdom" or "enlightenment," by the teaching of the Divine Spirit of all space and all time? It is a promulgation by King Piyudasi:—"The king beloved of the gods desires that the ascetics of all creeds might reside in all places. All these ascetics profess alike the command which people should exercise over themselves, and the purity of the soul. But people have different opinions and different inclinations. A man ought to honour his own faith only; but he should never abuse the faith of any body. There are even circumstances when the religion of others ought to be honoured. And, in acting thus, a man fortifies his own faith, and assists the faith of others. He who acts otherwise diminishes his own faith and hurts the faith of others."

Too many Christians appear likely to conceive, however, that this is far from exhibiting the teaching of the divine; because they seem to consider an attitude of antagonism towards, and even abuse of, the faith of others a demonstration of goodly Christian zeal.

Under the ancient Aryan system the undying principle of life and light within us may lose consciousness, or, according to some schools, preserve it, in blissful return to the universal divine Spirit from which it emanated. But so long as it retains desires of the flesh, so long will it be reborn, compelled to suffer those ills to which the flesh is heir. Spirit cognises itself in matter. The Deity becomes manifested in humanity. Our good or bad, that is to say our actions in or out of harmony with the eternal laws of the universe, continually produce their necessary sequences in what we call pain and pleasure. These succeed one another as constantly and inevitably as night and day. Knowledge is only to be obtained in suffering. And as it is said in the Hitopadesa, as translated by Wilkins :—"When pleasure is arrived it is worthy of attention; when trouble presenteth itself the same. Pains and pleasures have their revolutions like a wheel."

Good and that which we call evil, but which is requisite to produce the good, alike proceed from the divine Spirit, which is all in all.

It is supposed in Brahminism to be possible to recall to the mind former existences; as professed by Pythagoras, who asserted actually that he recognised himself as having been Euphorbus, slain at the siege of Troy, and as professed also by Gautauma Buddha, when "enlightened," according to the Buddhists. After periods of reward or punishment in heaven or hell the soul is also held, in Buddhism as in Brahminism, to return to the earthly life, as evidenced in the last words of the Chinese pilgrim, Hiouen Thsang. Professor Max Müller, in "Chips from a German Workshop," has reprinted a letter to the "Times," in which he states that "he tried to show in his articles on the Buddhist pilgrims that Nirvana signified 'utter annihilation.'" But he quotes these words of Hiouen Thsang's, which at least must be taken to signify that the annihilation might be indefinitely postponed:—"I desire," said the Chinese pilgrim before his death, "that whatever merits I have gained by good works may fall upon other people. May I be born again with them in the heaven of the blessed, be admitted to the family of Mi-le, and serve the Buddha of the future, who is full of kindness and affection. When I descend again upon earth, to pass through other forms of existence, I desire, at every new birth, to fulfil my duties towards Buddha, and arrive at the last at the highest and most perfect intelligence."

The Roman Catholic doctrine of works of supererogation appears to be here displayed; whereby it is said that those good works of the sainted, which are beyond those required for their own salvation, may be imputed unto others.

By exhibiting his contempt for the body the Hindu devotee hopes that his soul will depart from it in absolute purity and return to the divine. It would seem certainly that a self-consciousness in heavenly repose is amongst their hopes of the future, as in those of Christendom. Their intense asceticism certainly suggests a hope of consciousness of bliss in reward. It is of course logical, if once asceticism be admitted to be a preparation for a higher life, to practise the utmost excess of it. The celebrated St. Simon Stylites, who dwelt on the summit of a pillar for thirty years, not only is to be found in prototype in the literary remains of India, but he is to be seen there in the present day, performing penances of perhaps equal severity and eccentricity. Asceticism appears to be somewhat on the wane in Catholic Europe, though it has recently been mildly revived in Anglo-Catholic England. Egypt and Syria witness a different form of it in Mohammedanism. But in India it still reigns in all or a great part of its ancient rigour. As it was in the time of Alexander the Great, its invader more than 2000 years ago, so it is in the days of Victoria, in 1879 Queen of Britain and Empress of India, the old Arya varta.

CHAPTER LIX.

Considerations suggested by Professor Weber's "History of Indian Literature."

PROFESSOR WEBER of Berlin, in his "History of Indian Literature," recently republished and translated into English, affirms, as has been observed, that the Mahábhárata epic did not assume its present shape till some centuries after the commencement of our era; and those parts of it which afford the Christian aspect, therefore, to which allusion has been made, and from which quotations have been taken, may be actually due to Christian influence. He holds that those portions in the Ramáyana in which Rama is represented as an incarnation of Vishnu are later additions to the poem. In fact, he represents that the purer and more sublime passages in the adoration of Krishna as the Supreme Being incarnate upon earth for our salvation, may be due to Christianity, as Professor Monier Williams has also conceived possible.

If, then, this be really truth, the ancient Aryan literature of India and Persia still affords us a most valuable key to unlock the history of the preparation of the human mind for the reception of the grand mystery of an Incarnate Saviour, as revealed in Palestine. We clearly find in it types of the Christian idea, which certainly seem to foreshadow it more definitely than any in our Old Testament previously to the prophecies of Isaiah. To renew instances, the Professor observes, quoting from Roth, that "in the Persian Veda the Avesta, 'the contest' (*i.e.* the celestial contest between light and darkness) descends from heaven to earth from the province of natural phenomena into the moral sphere. The champion is a son, born to his father, and given as a saviour to earth, as a reward for the pious exercise of the Soma worship. The dragon slain by him is a creation of the power of Evil, armed with demoniacal might, for the destruction of purity in the world." He remarks of Agni, the divinity of fire, that the songs dedicated to him in the Rig Veda are the most numerous of all. "He is the messenger from men to the gods, the mediator between them, who, with his far-shining flame, summons the gods to the sacrifice." Agni, says Professor Weber, with the divinities of the Sun and Wind, gradually obtained precedence over all the other gods, and "speculation presses on and seeks to establish the relative position of these three deities, and to arrive at unity for the Supreme Being." "The Sun-god seems, in the first instance, to have been promoted to this honour."

As the conception of God with us (Emmanuel) first distinctly appears in the prophet Isaiah, at or before the period of the Jewish captivity in Persia, and as there is a possibility of his having derived the idea from the Persians, it may, on the other hand, perhaps be also contended that he communicated it to them; and that it became adopted in their sacred books from the prophetic Jewish inspiration instead of an Aryan source. If this idea of the incarnation, as apparent under a general conception in the Institutes of Manu, and the undoubted pre-Christian sacred literature of India, and also of Persia, has led to no further autochthonous development in India itself, it must be accepted as prototypical of the Christianity which was subsequently to be embraced by the western Aryan race; after being revealed amongst the Semitic people of Palestine.

Providence, according to the view of the promulgation of divine truth in Palestine only, bestowed upon the Eastern Aryans remarkable prototypes of the great doctrine which was subsequently to illumine the Western Aryans. The Aryans of India, however, though as a people, or assemblage of peoples, refusing to acknowledge the Deity as incarnate in Christ Jesus of Nazareth, must have eagerly grasped the doctrines delivered by Him, and also portions of His history. These, as related in the comparatively scanty records of our Gospels and the writings of St. Paul, they appropriated. Within the first centuries of our era they interspersed them through their epic poem, the Mahábhárata, bringing it, with a brilliant display of imaginative power, in elaborating Christian incidents and words, up to the stupendous bulk of 120,000 epic verses. They rendered their

Krishna Christ, in respect to his miracles, doctrines, and declaration of divine fulness upon earth, though retaining many legends which have been considered to impart a worldly, or even licentious, aspect to his character, according to our western notions. They then must have conceived the idea, unless this be admitted amongst the prototypes, of the all-pervading spirit of Deity present with us; not in one incarnation only, appealing to a portion of the human race for the first nineteen centuries after the revelation, but in many incarnations, in this and other worlds, in all ages and under all forms. On Rama they again especially bestowed attributes of Christ. The Buddhists seem to be allowed by Professor Weber to have compiled their sacred scriptures before the commencement of our era; yet they again may, he surmises, have also transferred legends of Christ to the history of their founder. Alluding to Beal's "Romantic Legend of Sakya Buddha," the Professor remarks:—"The special points of relation here found to Christian legends are very striking. The question which party was the borrower, Beal properly leaves undetermined; yet, in all likelihood, we have here simply a similar case to that of the appropriation of Christian legends by the worshippers of Krishna." As much of the moral teaching of Buddhism undoubtedly resembles that of Christianity, it would again appear that the Christian idea prevails in the more remote Turanian world as in the eastern Aryan, having been incorporated also into their older faith. However the sequence of ideas, or prevalence of prototypes, be arranged, it seems evident that, as in acknowledged Christianity there are the three great divisions of the Roman, Greek, and Protestant Churches, so, in the civilisation of the world, there are three great religions which now contain the Christian idea—viz. the Brahminical, Buddhistic, and our own. A Buddhist certainly does not seem to differ doctrinally more from a Papist than the latter from an Unitarian, who still professes to be within the pale of Christianity; while in his ritual he approximates much more closely. According to the analogies of human reasoning and history, the sequence of ideas from the conception of the Agni—the Deity on earth in fire—to Krishna, Buddha, Christ, and Salivahana, seems probable. If the actual revelation of the divine only in Christ is to be held, not only do these Eastern notions afford pertinent prototypes, but the eastern extent of the adoption of Christian ideas might really seem to argue Divine assistance. If these ideas are enveloped in superstitions, so are those of Papists, according to Protestants. Indeed some Protestants even seem to deny that they can be truly called Christians; and *vice versâ* as to the other side.

While Professor Weber thinks legends and doctrines of Krishna or Buddha may be derived from Christ, he says in respect to the ceremonial aspects of Buddhism and Christianity:—"Now this relic-worship, the building of steeples,—traceable perhaps to the topes (stúpas), which owe their origin to this relic-worship—the system of monachism, the use of bells and rosaries, and many other details, offer such numerous features of resemblance to Christian ritual, that the question whether Christianity may not perhaps have been here the borrowing party, is by no means to be summarily negatived, particularly as it is known that Buddhist missionaries penetrated at an early period, possibly even in the two centuries preceding our era, into western countries as far as Asia Minor."

A writer with the army at Jellalabad in 1879 has remarked that the frescoes of Buddhist caves in that neighbourhood suggest Christian art. He inquires, "Was the Christian halo or glory derived from Buddhistic paintings of Buddha?" As he preceded Christ, his halo may be not unreasonably esteemed the prior.

In a note, however, Professor Weber adjoins that "neither is the contrary supposition—namely, that Christian influences may have affected the growth of Buddhist ritual and worship, as they did that of the Buddhist legends—by any means to be dismissed out of hand. Indeed, quite apart from the oft-ventilated question as to the significance of such influences in the further development of Krishna-worship, there are legends connected with the Siva cult also, as to which it is not at all a far-fetched hypothesis that they have reference to scattered Christian missionaries."

That the Buddhists, like the Brahmins, should have also interpolated the stories and doctrines of Christ amongst their own, is undoubtedly exceedingly wonderful. Divine interposition would again seem to have almost been required to effect it. Their adoption of ancient western ceremonial appears incomprehensible when we contemplate their present continuance in their own usages.

In the literature which Professor Weber classifies as the Vedic, and which he ascribes, in the main, to pre-Christian and remote ages, though he considers that it may have been enlarged to modern times, the religious conceptions of Christianity seem often apparent. These may possibly, perhaps, be interpolations, in which case it must again be remarked how closely the Aryan mind in India approached the divine truth in sublimity; while its appreciation of the Christian verity was evidenced by its adopting these actual portions of Christian revelation as soon as they were presented to it. Human intellect, amongst our Aryan cousins in the East, would seem, according to this view, to have pursued profound and lengthened investigations into the nature of deity, and the relations of the human soul towards it. But the actual comprehension of divine truth was denied to them, and only revealed to the "chosen people;" whose previous Scriptures certainly appear to present God, as David, for example, has powerfully and beautifully depicted Him (Psalm iii. etc.), as rather the Protector of his suppliants from temporal ills than the Eternal Spirit of the Law and Order of the universe, in whom the soul exists to eternity. To this holy people we have held the divine revelation alone to have been vouchsafed; who, under Moses and Joshua, had escaped from Egypt, to form settlements, after much bloodshed amongst the previous inhabitants, between the shores of the Mediterranean and the deserts of Syria—Palestine being of about the size of our counties of York and Westmoreland, according to Bishop Butler's computation in his Geography. It would appear, according to this idea, that emanations from the revelation of the Old Testament were incorporated into the older Sanskrit literature, and from the New Testament into the later Sanskrit writings. Yet still the reflection returns that Moses is said in the Bible to have been learned in all the wisdom of the Egyptians. Humanly speaking, still in accordance with our sacred Scripture, Egyptian learning may have afforded a foundation for the history of Eden and the Fall of man, etc., and for the laws attributed to him; or they may have been partly Chaldæan traditions surviving amongst the Hebrews. We are relegated to the old question of the priority of Egyptian and

Chaldæan or Indian civilisation and knowledge. The question is again left in vagueness as to what occasioned man's intellectual growth, for, as has been observed, no divine revelation is recorded in the Bible to have been bestowed upon these. Was it, then, in India, a continent approximating to the dimensions of Europe, surpassing in all nature's bounties, able to contain a population of 200,000,000; or was it in Egypt, a river plain between deserts, with some 7,000,000 of inhabitants, a cultivated garden rather than a primeval Eden, that man arose to those arts which we find illustrated in the rock-cut temples and tombs of the two countries? In Egypt we must allow their origin to remain in mystery. In India we trace it to the imitation of Nature's gifts. To open a way to the comprehension of the dependence of early Art upon Nature's promptings, seems to be the work of a golden key. It may only reveal some chimera of the understanding; but it seems in accordance with the analogies afforded by acknowledged scientific facts. The actual revelations of God to man, as claimed by European Aryans on behalf of the ancient Hebrews, by Indian Aryans on behalf of their own ancestors, and by the Mohammedans for their Prophet—revelations in the voice from the clouds, and in the vision—seem dependent upon faith rather than evidence which would satisfy a court of justice in temporal concerns. If childlike faith be a sign of divine knowledge, that of the Hindus is as childlike, amongst the people, as our own amongst the various sects of Christendom, and not more closely associated with the veneration of images. The early chapters of Genesis may have been actually revealed by God to Moses, but the only evidence is assertion; and a similar claim is made for the cosmogony in the Institutes of Manu.

Ideas continually, even in the Vedic literature of pre-Christian India, foreshadow or correspond to our own religious receptions from the Old and New Testament. A lord of evil is assumed to exist—a human and a universal sacrifice are mentioned. Fishermen play a part in the stories—legends of the deluge and rescue of Vaivasvata occur; in fact, it is evident, from Professor Weber's exposition of profound and exhaustive scholarship in the Sanskrit, as from Indian commentators in general, that our Biblical revelations are also to be found in the more voluminous Indian scriptures. Indian records do not seem to ascribe to Manu any possibility of foreign education, such as the Jewish Scriptures distinctly assign to Moses. Indian traditions may be vague; they may seem to us sometimes grotesque; but are the biblical stories of Balaam, Jonah, and Samson less so, if accepted literally? The Indian chronology, preposterously extended as we have considered it, seems, at all events, to accord with the teachings of geological science more approximately than the period of about 6000 years; which we have been taught, in the universities and schools of the Church of England, to allow for the history of the world. The criticism applied to the chronology of these Indian sacred books, if transferred to the Bible, might certainly impugn the data of Christian orthodoxy as powerfully as of Brahminism. Our Old Testament, in its present form, would be attributed to Ezra, after the return from the captivity in Babylon. Ancient writings may be admitted to have existed from the age of Moses; but interpolations must have been as probable amongst the Hebrews, at about the epoch of Ezra, as amongst the Brahmins at the Christian era. Internal evidence has been held indubitably to disassociate the Gospel of St. John from his Revelation. Many arguments have indeed been found for assigning the Gospel to another hand, and later period than the end of the first century. The method of criticism which ascribes the divine song of the Hindus to plagiarism from the Gospel of St. John, may deny the authorship of the apostle to the Gospel; and, reversing the allegation, refer its contents to suggestions from the avowedly Aryan production. St. Paul's Epistles have been alleged to have been due to different hands.

At about the period when the Indians became amenable to Christian influences, they were, according to Professor Weber, considerably infected with the Greek spirit. He refers to it that portion of the Ramáyana which presents a similarity to the Homeric story. But, as has been argued, there appears to be so little reciprocity between the epics of Valmiki and Homer, that the incidents of the abduction of Sita and Helen would rather seem to have been founded upon a story known independently to both authors. And the Indian author and Milton have also, in common, the assent of the Deity to descend upon earth for man's benefit. This may have been suggested by the Christian story to both; but it seems to arise naturally out of

Vedic ideas, and may be easily conceived to have been produced by the Indian poet's imagination. The only foundation for Milton's conception in the New Testament is the simple statement that "the Word was made flesh" in St. John, and the account of the miraculous conception in the two of the Synoptical Gospels.

The Professor observes also that "it was, however, Greek influence that first infused a real life into Indian astronomy." Now the first amongst the Greeks who acquired knowledge in this science approaching that of our modern times, is narrated to have been Pythagoras, who is said to have obtained his learning during many years' travel in Egypt and Chaldæa, and possibly in India. As the older Indian astronomy is ascribed by Professor Weber to Chaldæan influence, we are once more relegated, in the old circle, to these two mysterious settlements on the Nile and Euphrates for the commencement of culture. Thales, said to have been the first who calculated with accuracy a solar eclipse, is previously related to have studied geometry, astronomy, and philosophy, under the priests of Memphis. But the Professor allows that the Hindus independently attained a high degree of proficiency in algebra and arithmetic, and that we owe to them the invention of the numerical symbols.

To music and medicine and anatomy, as practised in a scientific manner, he certainly seems to admit an autochthonous origin amongst the Hindus. As they seem, indeed, to have had acquaintance with most modern scientific attainments, they must be allowed to have evolved some out of their inner consciousnesses, or the suggestions of the outer world. But, whenever the same ideas simultaneously existed amongst them and other nations, the Indians seem to be pronounced by the Professor the copyists; although the people whom they are considered to have imitated are themselves supposed to have acquired their ideas from foreign sources. Notwithstanding the autochthonous aspect of the Indian zodiac, as quoted in Chapter XXXII., he asserts the Hindus to have "unquestionably borrowed it from the Greeks."[1] When it is mentioned in what he classes as Vedic literature in a work of evidently vague antiquity, though appertaining to the "epic period" rather than that of

[1] See Appendix X.

the older Vedic writings, he simply ascribes the book to the age when Greek influence may have been felt. Yet he says that the Indian astronomical science sprang out of astrology. And the signs of the zodiac are associated with astrology, and not unlikely to have been invented amongst those who practised it. The reciprocity of intercourse between Greece and India, and afterwards the Roman Empire, at about the commencement of our era, certainly seems to have produced a mutual interchange of ideas. But, as has been urged, the progress of thought can be so distinctly traced in India, and the remains in literature, art, and science, are so vast and varied, that there is no necessity for attributing the higher developments of astronomy, or of the Incarnation theory, to foreign sources; though, of course, suggestions may have been received. In fact, the Professor says that, after the Greek influence had enabled the Hindus to cultivate astronomy in a scientific spirit, they continued "even, it would seem in some points independently, advancing astronomical science farther than the Greeks themselves did."

Their learning and scientific capacity is thus admitted, but in advocating the theory of the inspiration of the Indian imagination from the promptings of Nature, such a question as that concerning the authorship of the zodiac seems of importance. Certainly the people who conceived the ten avatars of Vishnu, with their apparently esoteric significations, may be reasonably imagined to have devised the signs of the zodiac. The fish, tortoise, etc., of the one series seem in concord with the fish, bull, crab, etc., of the other. No suspicion has been entertained that these avatars are other than indigenous. An esoteric meaning may be discerned in the zodiacal figures, apart from astronomical considerations, which seems to evidence their birth also in India. The fish, ram, bull, crab, lion, and scorpion, half of the signs, represent the prominent classes of lower animal life; while the "Pair," with the mace and vina, depict the courage of the man and pleasurable accomplishments of his partner. The weigher with the balance may stand for commerce, while the man emptying the water-pot may be taken for a representative of the menial caste, his emptying of the water being naturally emblematical of the fertilising Indian rainfall, or of the advantages of irrigation in its absence. The

"Archer" and "Monster" signify the military class in the one case, and possibly the wilder neighbouring tribes in the other. The boat in which the Virgin stands, with her lamp and ear of rice corn, has a distinct meaning in Indian symbolisation. And a reason may be perceived for the two fishes, in the fact that a single fish might be supposed to represent the avatar of Vishnu. It has, in fact, been remarked that the Indian zodiac has a mythological significance. The avatars and zodiacal signs in no way clash, for, in the first, it is as the lion-king or man-lion, not as the lion only, that Vishnu descends in the fourth incarnation. It might have appeared probable that the elephant would have been represented in an Indian series of this description. But it must be remembered that the Deity of Prudence was endowed with an elephant's head. The serpent also was occupied in their symbolism. The Gemini, which we have adopted, do not seem to be so expressive as the original "Pair;" especially as associated with the month of May. Capricorn, as we have also Aries, seems less meaning than the Indian "Monster" with the head of an antelope. Altogether the closeness of signification, as applicable to the country, remains with the Indian signs. They undoubtedly have the appearance of originality.

It must, of course, be presumed that these signs of the zodiac were not devised upon some sudden freak, without intention of meaning attached to the figures. The constellations, which have now deserted their signs in the revolution of the heavens, can hardly have entirely suggested the names by the position of the stars.

If they had been invented in Chaldæa, a camel might have been expected amongst them. Though the study of the stars seems perhaps less likely to have been so sedulously pursued in India as amongst the regions, more or less rainless, of western Asia, yet it is evidently to our Aryan race, not to the Semitic Arabs, that our great astronomical discoveries are due. And the unclouded brilliant skies, with the moonlit and starlit halves of the months regularly succeeding, which are enjoyed for some eight months out of the twelve in India, seem there also suggestive of astronomical observations; especially as the nights, after the heats of the day, are often balmy and tempting to watchfulness.

The finding of signs of the zodiac amongst the Chinese and Japanese, of parallel though different nomenclature, may afford another argument for their having been due to central India. At all events the Buddhism of these people is allowed to have originated there. And, in regard to their not having been designed in Greece, the following evidence seems to be potent, viz. that they appear on the porticoes of the temples of Denderah and Esne in Egypt. M. Dupuis, in his "Origine des Cultes," has arrived at the conclusion that the earliest of these temples dates from 4000 B.C. Upon this point he has been attacked by M. Fourier, and defended by MM. Ideler and Biot; but, whatever the date of these temples may be, it seems evident that the authorship must be debated between Egypt and India, not with Greece. The concurrent arguments would certainly seem to consign them to India. It is not contended that they appear in Greece at an approximation to this ancient date. According to Letronne's investigations, as quoted by Professor Weber, the completion of the zodiac did not take place amongst the Greeks before the first century A.D.

The Professor has adduced the zodiacal signs as an argument for referring the Jyotisha, or Vedic calendar, to a period within our era, instead of allowing it the antiquity which has been attributed to it. He has also produced them in opposition to the asserted age of other treatises. Greek words appear in Hindu astronomical writings; but in regarding the mass of evidence concerning Indian science, the acceptance of this fact as a testimony to the importance of Greek influence seems like contending that French cookery has been largely affected by English example, because the word *biftek* has been adopted into their culinary vocabulary. The term Yavanas appears to have been applied to the Greeks and afterwards to the Mohammedans, and upon this, dates attributed to the epics, and the notion of Greek influence therein, have been partially based by commentators. But the name may undoubtedly have been applied to the Greeks, or any other western people, during the old commercial and other intercourse, which had evidently existed between East and West for centuries before the expedition of Alexander. It cannot be held to have been firstly and solely bestowed upon the Greeks of that period, as it has been subsequently employed to designate a different people. Communication between India and the Western world had not been non-existent till Alexander reached the Indus; as between the old Central American civilisations and Europe before Columbus crossed the Atlantic. Altogether, in comparing the conservative India, with its extensive and varied remains of human culture, with Greece and the region of the seven churches of Christendom, the contention that the former borrowed from the latter might infer the possibility of a scientific conception in the remote future, when America may be peopled by 200,000,000, that political economy and Protestantism were introduced into Europe from the States of Massachusetts and Pennsylvania.

No art in India may have approached in artistic perfection the Greek statuary, no architecture have rivalled theirs, and the most sacred expression in the Indian faiths may not equal the simple sanctity of Christianity. But a review of the history and circumstances of the two regions seems to point to India as the natural source from which, in India itself, perfection was, humanly speaking, nearly attained, to be achieved absolutely, perhaps, on the shores of the Mediterranean. So may Massachusetts have studied political economy to certainty, and Pennsylvania have produced what may seem the purest of Christian churches to an age 2000 years hence. At that period the dates attributed to Sir Dudley North and Hume, to Wycliffe and Luther, may be shown, on the internal evidence of literary works, to be unsound. Messrs. Sankey and Moody, on the testimony of their hymns, may be demonstrated to have protestantised the Church of Christendom. While attributing the origin and growth of astronomical science, however, to the Aryan India, the situation of Babylon certainly must be regarded as likely to have occasioned the bestowing of much attention there upon this science. And the scientific acquirements of Pythagoras, obtained in the East, according to our accounts, must have fructified on the Mediterranean. But from East to West, following the course of the sun, was the progress of the sciences. Rays of the Western light may have flecked the East, on which the radiance had dawned, before the sun of the science of the Greek Empire sank into the waves of warlike semi-barbarism; to return upon our own day.

As has been contended, the long conservatism of India and its physical advantages, with its art remains in every pattern, argue autochthonity for this continent, rather than for the small territories of Greece, or the river plains of Babylon and Egypt. And the district of the Indus, not that of the Oxus, affords the most probable home for the rise of Aryanism as displayed in the Vedas. Perfection may have been attained in the respective arts of the Western peoples, and there was reciprocity doubtless between the West and the more originally fertile East, as there is at the present day. But the Indians as a group of nations were probably no more affected by Greek example then, than by English example now. The ancient Greeks after the time of Alexander may have had some effect upon them, just as the English in the present day. But the actual aspect of the country and its arts were no more changed under the visit of the Greeks than they have been under the sway of the English. The commercial capital of Bombay, insular and inhabited by Europeans for two centuries, seems, as has been argued, sufficient living proof of the conservatism of the Hindus. Possibly, under the influence of the colleges, art schools, etc., which we are establishing, and the efforts of missionaries, we may be beginning to effect more changes amongst them. The position of the Greek kingdoms would seem to have been more analogous to our own under the East India Company than to our present Empire.

The question of the antiquity of the two great Indian epics in their completed form, in so far as they contain, that is to say, the Christian-like conceptions, is certainly very important. That the text may have become corrupted in parts, or that emendations or additions may have been made, seems demonstrated; but that a systematic series of interpolations should have been effected, with a view to increasing the sanctity of the incarnations of Vishnu by the addition of Christian incidents and doctrine, is at least surprising. If passages in the life and teaching of Christ were so acceptable to the Hindus, the difficulty constantly recurs as to why they did not, in accordance with the theory which they have adopted of the divine manifesting itself in many human aspects, accept Christianity altogether. If, in its first ages, they imperfectly comprehended the Christian story in its totality, though they apprehended and gladly accepted fragments of it, why do they not, it may again be asked, more eagerly and generally adopt our actual New

Testament and its narratives? They must have more opportunities of becoming acquainted with it than they formerly could have possessed. They then could scarcely, without a miracle, have obtained even portions of its teaching so easily as they could now secure the whole by the presence of our missionaries and the dissemination of the Testament in print. Yet the Brahmins, many of whom understand English perfectly, and whose class is supposed so readily, eighteen hundred years ago, to have transferred Christianity to Krishna, now appear to treat foreign religions with indifference. If they adopted miracles and texts from the New Testament then, they might be expected to revise and add to their faiths from the fuller exposition of our religion which they can obtain now. But as a body they appear to be undisturbed by our modern opinions and systems.

Both in the Vedic literature and ritual there seem to be conceptions and practices naturally leading to those of more modern Hinduism and Buddhism. It must be remembered that the Roman Catholic missionaries found the latter in force, so that if adopted from Christianity it must have been in the early ages of the Church. But Protestantism asserts that this ritual in the Church of Christ is not a divine or necessary ordinance. It styles certain Romish doctrine a "fond thing, vainly invented." Instead of having been invented, it may have been copied from Eastern sources with its concomitant practices, set forth in Article XXII. of our Church.

The stories of the Ramáyana and Mahábhárata indubitably appear, upon their internal evidence, to be autochthonous—in harmony with the whole tone of Indian thought. Greek or Christian influences seem less likely to have affected them than passages in the Vedic literature, which seem sufficiently to suggest or lead up to their contents. We may be confident that their authors had some acquaintance with the Vedas, but their having been amenable to Greek or Christian influence is simply conjectural. If their archaic aspect is merely due to the genius of the authors—the Sir Walter Scott and Harrison Ainsworth of their epochs—we must highly respect the talents of those authors; but certainly the traditions of a people, in assigning works of the kind to a remote age, must surely be as worthy of consideration, in the absence of positive evidence, as our own conjectures. There seems, indeed, to be positive testimony to the existence of these poems before the time of Christ, but, as is not unnatural at a period 2000 years ago, it is open to cross-examination. On the other hand, Professor Weber's negative evidence for their non-existence seems to be of a very unreliable kind. Negative evidence has been adduced, in this volume, in respect to the admission of the doctrine of the metempsychosis by Christ. It has been contended that, as He did not preach against it, He appears to have admitted it. But then there would seem to have been every motive for His alluding to it, as it was the doctrine of those whom He was rebuking for their practices; and as allusion was positively made to it in His presence, according to the text of our New Testament. Professor Weber considers, for instance, the absence of allusion to the Mahábhárata in the remarks of Megasthenes which have descended to us, evidence for its non-existence at his time. In Ferishta's "History of Hindustan," the Mahábhárata is introduced as affording authority for the early history of the Hindus, but no allusion is made to the Ramáyana. But it cannot be asserted that the latter was not in existence at the epoch of this author. It was not indeed translated into Persian like the Mahábhárata; but Dow, in his introductory dissertation to his translation of Ferishta, says nothing of it or its religion, though commenting on the Vedas, Hindu deities, etc. It seems to be forgotten that in a region of the extent of India a literary work might be known and revered for ages without universal acquaintance throughout the country being made with it. A Hindu or Chinese visiting Europe might indite exhaustive accounts of our continent without alluding to Roman Catholic legends, or to Milton's Paradise Lost, which has been almost held sacred amongst us; or without mentioning Dante, or Camoens, or Goethe. It may be urged that these are not sacred; but he even might describe the outer forms of our religion without alluding to the Bible, in Roman Catholic countries at all events. Rama and Krishna may have been adored for ages before the Ramáyana and Mahábhárata were accepted as sacred accounts of their incarnations. The New Testament was extant in at least the time of Irenæus, at about 180 A.D., but was little put forward by the Church for the many mediæval centuries; till the printing press aided Protestantism, and it became the constant authority of a great part of Christendom. In ancient as in modern days it is not unreasonable to surmise that time added sanction to an author. Shakspeare only seems to have been fully appreciated, in his entireness as a poet, in our epoch, two centuries and a half after his own age. An acquaintance with his works can hardly be said to be general throughout our continent, but time may render them as familiar upon the shores of the Mediterranean as in northern Europe. If Krishna became adored as divine only on account of the description of him in a poem, many centuries must surely have been required to invest it with this sanctity in a large portion of this region of 200,000,000 inhabitants. If this should indeed have happened since the commencement of our era, it is a curious and instructive testimony to the spread of Christ's teaching, though in a foreign form. The educated throughout our quarter of the globe would now respond to enquiries concerning Virgil, but within a few hundred years after his time there would have been a much more circumscribed European acquaintance with him. The Mahábhárata and Ramáyana, or other works or ideas concerning the incarnations, etc., may have been held in esteem, or venerated as sacred, in Indian territories as large as Italy or England, for centuries; without their being acknowledged in other equally extensive territories, and becoming current throughout the land. MSS. could not multiply of course so rapidly as modern printed editions, nor reciters learn their tasks in such numbers as to diffuse the knowledge of literary works through the country with the rapidity of modern times. Many traditions must long have continued local, but at length have spread. Then the acknowledged antiquity and authority of a book, when once it is admitted, may perhaps even occasion few observations to be made upon it, on account of allusions to so well-known a work seeming trite. A writer on grammar might consider the forms contained in it too old-fashioned for his illustrations, or they might not be sufficiently antique if he were illustrating bygone forms. In fact, negative evidence must be unreliable unless a motive should appear actually to exist for allusion to the topic in question. This must especially apply to a period 2000 years ago. Of course many allusions may have been made and lost in so considerable a lapse of time.

While asserting interpolations in these poems, Professor Weber appears to argue questions of the antiquity of their general matter upon words which may themselves be interpolations according to him; and which, therefore, cannot be decisive as to whether other portions are older or more recent—as to whether those portions are interpolations or appertaining to the first edition of the work.

As negative evidence the fact that the origin of a literary work is enveloped in mystery is as good evidence for the antiquity claimed for it, as the non-mention of it, in writers of any given period, for its not existing at their time; unless, of course, they professed to give an exhaustive list of the books of the period. Even then an Indian writer might only enumerate the books in circulation in his own country. A writer in Bahar might no more allude to a work of the ancient Oujein, than a modern Frenchman to a German publication.

The general aspect of these books, and the general evidence concerning them, seem to testify to their having been written in their general form at some such remote period as the tenth or twelfth century B.C., *i.e.* at about the Homeric age, rather than at a more recent epoch.

When, in addition to these literary productions of vast dimensions and unknown age, we find in India mysterious artistic works, such as the excavated temples and more modern temples, constructed in what seems to be autochthonous antique form—it seems reasonable to conclude that they indicate a civilised antiquity beyond our old historical dates. This is corroborated by the fact that the records of foreigners show us the people of the country under much the same aspect 2000 years ago as at present. The 120,000 verses of the Mahábhárata and the mile of excavated temples in the granite rocks of Ellora, seem to display advanced stages of culture, at epochs coeval with David and Moses rather than Constantine or the Ptolemies.

CHAPTER LX.

The Darwinian missing link to be found in the Tropics—Aryan literature continuing in India when the Roman Empire was declining—England ought to translate Indian works.

To the Vedic literature Professor Weber seems to allow autochthonity on, or extending eastwards from, the banks of the Indus; and he observes that "we are fully justified in regarding the ancient literature of India as the most ancient literature of which written records, on an extensive scale, have been handed down to us, not on account of Indian tradition or astronomical evidence, but because a series of centuries must have elapsed to effect the Brahmanising of Hindustan, which was clearly completed by the time of Megasthènes."

He states that direct evidence of ancient commercial relations between India and the West has been recently found in hieroglyphic texts of the seventeenth century B.C. What he classes as the Vedic literature seems, as has been observed, to have been compiled in his opinion, in its general bulk, at several centuries B.C. We must consider that this literature is admitted to be autochthonous in the eastern Aryan race, and that we have not allowed that direct divine revelation which is asserted by the Hindus. We ought to ascribe a period to the growth of such an elaborate and voluminous body of literary works, undoubtedly far transcending the old dates assigned to our dawn of historical knowledge. Four Vedas, each divided into Samhitás, Bráhmanas, and Sútras, *i.e.* into psalms, commentaries connecting the sacrificial songs and formulas with the sacrificial rite by pointing out their mutual relations and symbolical connections; with linguistic explanations and philosophical speculations, etc. etc. These, with much literature which appears to have been lost, seem to indicate a growth of centuries, which it can scarcely be ridiculous to reckon by thousands; considering that they had to arise out of such culture as we find amongst those whom we term savages. They had to be developed amongst themselves, or amongst prehistoric, or, more correctly speaking, pre-existing geographical times. Technical names of metres, observes Professor Weber, are found in the later songs of the Rig Veda. Investigations were made into the literal meaning of the prayers, as the sense, in course of time, became somewhat obscured. "Several hymns of a speculative purport," he remarks, "in the last book of the Rig-Samhita, testify to a great depth and concentration of reflection upon the fundamental cause of things, necessarily implying a long period of philosophical research in a preceding age. This is borne out by the old renown of Indian wisdom, by the reports of the companions of Alexander as to the Indian gymnosophists, etc."

He allows that express mention is made of "the science of astronomy," and, in particular, the knowledge of the twenty-seven (twenty-eight) lunar mansions was early diffused. They are enumerated singly in the Taittiriya-Samhita, and the order in which they there occur is one that must necessarily have been established somewhere between 1472 B.C. and 536 B.C. In a note he states, however, that these dates should rather be 2780-1820 B.C., and for a series contained in the Jyotisha, 1820-860 B.C. After this commencement in science, progress may be reasonably conceived to have been made without Greek or other influence. The Professor adjoins that they had not made much progress at this period, their observations being chiefly confined to the course of the moon, to the solstice, to a few fixed stars, and more particularly to astrology.

He allows the hymns of the Rig Veda to be older than the Zendavesta, which is rather related to the Brahmanas in respect to age and contents. Surely this existence of the oldest literature in India must indicate that the Persa-Aryans were derived from India itself. If Indians and Persians had proceeded from a common Bactrian home, each might have been expected to have been found in possession of the original compositions. Emigrants would naturally carry with them the expositions of faith belonging to their own period or sect.

Altogether it appears, even in the pages of Professor

Weber, who conceives both Greeks, and Christians perhaps, to have exercised so great an influence upon Indian thought during the few centuries preceding and following the beginning of our era, that the Indians must be credited with the commencement of educational culture at an age far more remote than our old chronological data. Even if astronomy were debited to the Chaldæans, literature, or at all events the arrangement of what now constitutes literature, for recitation, must be allowed to have originated in India. While, however, the evidence of the literary culture of the Madhyama seems reliable, the testimony which would assign the commencement of astronomical science to Chaldæa appears hypothetical—the Chaldæan civilisation, as has been observed, being likely to have come from the East, according to the evidence. In fact, the mass of testimony in the records of the past, and the living aspect of the present, seem to display in India the origin of civilisation and science. An apprehension of this fact would appear to be a key to open the way to knowledge of our primitive education. In these tropical regions surely search should be made for the missing link of the Darwinian theory also. Or if a garden of primeval bliss and ignorance, or innocence, be sought, this central region of many natural advantages, this land of the sun, midway between the great old civilisation of China and that of Europe and western Asia, seems to indicate an approximate site. On the borders of seas available for commerce, amid rivers, fertile fields, forests, and mountains, we Aryans, or Indo-Europeans, probably commenced, as we have continued, our career of constant growth in culture; notwithstanding local retrogressions. If Professor Weber be right in estimating so much of Hindu literature as appertaining to a period when the Roman Empire was declining, and the Goths with their essentially warlike institutions were becoming the ruling power in Europe, it would appear that the Aryan race was carrying on its literary links in India. The revival of science in Italy, or Europe in general, may have been largely due to the Hindus—members of our own family. The intervening Arabs have been credited with it.

It is to be hoped that translations, or the increase of education in the Sanskrit, will render us as well acquainted with the writings of the old Hindus as with those of the

Greeks and Romans. They seem more really important to us, on account of this appearance in them of leading doctrines of our faith; in closer similarity than can be recognised in the morality or mythology of the Greeks and Romans.

A Mahratta lady, Roma Bye, who recently delivered a lecture before an audience of natives and Europeans of both sexes at Calcutta, has contended that the high moral teaching of that "masterpiece," the Mahâbhârata, and the wisdom displayed in it, could only have been attained by the sage Vyasa, the author, as the result of deep learning and the experience of wide travel. She deduced from it this moral, "that a woman should seek to make herself, by culture of the mind, a more perfect wife and mother; and that that family is best regulated in which both the husband and the wife enjoy the benefits of education." "We are told," observes the "Globe," from which this has been quoted, in February 1879, that the lecture throughout was as lucid as forcible, and "bespoke a mind well cultivated and God-fearing." If the Indian incarnation theories, and the morality displayed in this poem and other literary works, when they appear to present similitudes to the life and doctrines of the Founder of Christianity, are due to the influence of His apostles in India, it is still distinctly clear, from the undoubted pre-Christian literature of India, that conceptions leading up to the Christian ideas were prevalent there. Germs of the Christian teaching existed amongst the Aryans, both in Brahminism and Buddhism; which, under the radiance of the actual Christian revelation, according to this view, expanded into buds of doctrine parallel to those of Christianity. From the appearance of our New Testament in the Greek language it is reasonable to suppose that it was the Aryan inhabitants of the shores of the Mediterranean who there embraced most numerously the religion of Christ. In fact, we see that the Jews and Semitic people reject it to this day. It has been and is essentially the religion of our race, whether revealed only in Palestine, or also apprehended, under a gradual growth and procession of ideas, in India; or adopted from the one to the other. The similarities in the stories of Christ and Krishna certainly seem too marked to be ascribed only to coincidences.

Professor Weber observes that "the literature of India

passes generally for the most ancient literature of which we possess written records, and justly so." But he appends a note in the last edition of his "History of Indian Literature," in which he adds:—"In so far as this claim may not now be disputed by the Egyptian monumental records and papyrus rolls, or even by the Assyrian literature, which has but recently been brought to light."

He thus again brings back the question to the old issue, as to whether the settlements on the Euphrates and Tigris, and the Nile, are the fountains of the world's culture; or whether the land of the Ganges, Indus, Brahmaputra, Nerbudda, Kistna, etc., is to be revered as the parent. In the two former we find comparatively restricted regions of fertile territories without forest timber, and the ruins of old civilisations, with modern states of different systems from the ancient. In the latter we find an exuberance of all Nature's gifts, a capacity of supporting a population of 200,000,000, a luxuriant ancient literature, remains of ancient works in all varieties of form, exhibiting systematic art and science, and extending throughout the country; we find conservatism which maintains the inhabitants as a body in the manner of life, and in the cultivation of the arts, architecture, and faiths which they appear to have affected 2000 years ago. And our science has pronounced those inhabitants to appertain to our own amongst the races of the world's people.

As we appear to have founded our belief in Babylon as an original, or the original, abode of scientific civilisation upon the Bible, the statement in the Bible itself that "they journeyed from the East, and found a plain in the land of Shinar, and dwelt there," would seem sufficient to indicate a legendary recollection, or revealed truth, of an Eastern origin in the case at least of that settlement. In the East they had so far advanced in science as to have been able to say, when they arrived at the site of Babel, "Go to, let us make brick and burn them thoroughly." At this place the prevalence of both Aryan and Semitic languages might have naturally occasioned, about the year 2000 B.C., much awkwardness; and suggested a legend of the confounding of speech.

India, the "epitome of the whole earth," seems to be, considering it in conjunction with the neighbouring China, and tropical islands, etc., and comparing it with western Asia, etc., not the abstract of the world's culture, but its first draft from the promptings of Nature to Humanity; when humanity was advancing beyond the comparative indolence of the tropical Eden, or the rude life of less fertile regions. It was then beginning to discern the voice of the unseen Spirit of All in the tangible material world; in the fulness of time to realise the Divine incarnate in the Human.

The Golden Key, which unlocked the entrance to the progress in civilisation of the human race, which opened the way to fields which afforded a capacity for expansion throughout all but the most sunburnt and rainless, or ice-bound and sunless regions of the earth, was the discovery and apprehension of man's capacity to produce at pleasure fire upon earth. The Golden Key which seems to open our comprehensions to the origin of our culture is the realisation of the fact that he acquired this art before he left the tropics, where the warmth and bounty of nature were sufficient for his nurture; and then that he spread forth over the world with fire in his possession. Recognising Providence in the sublimity of the life-giving sun, and grateful for this grand bounty of its flames rendered available at his will, he adored in Agni the Deity manifested to the world. From the recognition of the divine in the material fire, which imparted the requisite warmth, where the chilling air otherwise forbade existence, or only permitted it under circumstances of extreme austerity, he conceived that Deity was also to be discerned in the fire of the human intellect. In those minds which, by their powerful influence, were enabled to order their fellow-men to their advantage, and direct and sustain societies in labour-protected polities, he saw the Deity upon earth, manifested in the flesh, to guide mankind into the ways of order and righteousness. The recognition of God in man, by faith unto life eternal, had become the religion of the Aryan race. Krishna and Mithras, Apollo, Osiris, Bacchus, and Buddha, seem only various recognitions of the idea; and in Christ we adore Him, manifested in the flesh in Galilee, who may be held to have had countless prototypes in all ages and all worlds.

APPENDIX.

I.

ACCORDING to Professor Weber, the Institutes of Manu are quoted in such a manner in the Mahábhárata as to indicate that they were not settled in their present form when the poem was written.

Some passages are cited in the epic as they now appear, others are attributed to the Institutes which we do not possess, and others are differently quoted.

This may be an argument for the remote antiquity of the Mahábhárata; though its language may have subsequently become more modernised than that of the law book, the phraseology of which may have been considered more sacred.

The Code of Justinian was compiled some 200 years after the time of Constantine in the Roman Empire; but, as Gibbon observes, "the magistrates of Justinian were not subject to the authority of the Church; the emperor consulted the unbelieving civilians of antiquity, and the choice of matrimonial laws in the Code and Pandects is directed by the earthly motives of justice, policy, and the natural freedom of both sexes."

The religion of Krishna may have been spreading in India, but Brahminical sages of the law, in compiling or abbreviating or condensing their code for the region in which it was published in its present form, may have ignored the belief of Vishnu incarnate in Krishna.

The incarnation theory is clearly suggested in the Institutes.

As Professor Weber seems to hold, they must be the condensation of laws, traditions, devotional observances, and religious and secular life and education of the period succeeding that of the Vedic poems and ordinances, when Brahmanism had become established in the north-west of India.

Their language and general characteristics would certainly appear to take them back, as a code, in main resemblance to their present form, to at least the period originally assigned to them by Sir W. Jones, viz. the ninth century B.C. If the Chinese had a code at about 2000 B.C., as has been affirmed, these Institutes—taking the various evidences into consideration of the old connection between India and China—may be reasonably held to have been a still earlier promulgation.

The Vedic deities, or emanations from the Supreme Spirit, as given in Manu, are not incompatible with a further belief in that universal Supreme Spirit becoming personified in Vishnu, and incarnate in Krishna. But the laws were promulgated under the ancient authority of the Vedic religion, in which Brahmanism had become systematised.

The code of Yájnavalkya is allowed, by Professor Weber, to be posterior to Manu. He says, however, that the earliest limit which we can fix for this work is somewhere about the second century A.D., seeing that the word *nánaká* occurs in it to denote coin, and this term, according to Wilson's *conjecture*, is taken from the coins of Kanerki, who reigned until A.D. 40.

This conjecture does not appear to be evidence, according to the legal point of view.

Indeed the Professor afterwards seems to assign Yájnavalkya, according to Buddhist legend, to the same period as that attributed to Buddha, which cannot be placed later than 370 B.C. So that the Institutes of Manu may reasonably be considered earlier, at all events, than this epoch. If later, as he has suggested, than the Mahábhárata, this throws back the date of that poem, or, at all events, those didactic portions of it which deal with the topics of the Institutes.

II.

THE Institutes of Manu have been said to corroborate the notion of the foreign origin of the upper castes; but it would rather appear that they contain no suggestion of any but an autochthonous origin. Chap. ii. 17, 18 have been cited; but these verses, with their context, do not seem to bear any such inference.

Manu ii. 16. "He whose life is regulated by holy texts, from his conception even to his funeral pile, has a decided right to study this code, but no other man whatsoever."

17. "Between the two divine rivers Saraswati and Drishadwati lies the tract of land which the sages have named Brahmáverta, because it was frequented by Gods."

18. "The custom preserved by immemorial tradition in that country, among the four pure castes, and among those which are mixed, is called approved usage."

19. "Curucshétra, Matsya, Panchála or Canyacubja, and Surasena or Mathura, form the region called Brahmarshi, distinguished from Brahmáverta."

20. "From a Brahman, who was born in that country, let all men on earth learn their several usages."

21. "That country which lies between Himawat and Vindhya, to the east of Vinasana, and to the west of Prayága, is celebrated by the title of Medhyadésa or the central region."

22. "As far as the Eastern, and as far as the Western Oceans, between the two mountains just mentioned, lies the tract which the wise have named Arya varta, or inhabited by respectable men."

23. "That land on which the black antelope naturally grazes is held fit for the performance of sacrifices; but the land of Mléch'has, or those who speak barbarously, differs widely from it."

24. "Let the three first classes invariably dwell in the before-mentioned countries; but a Sudra, distressed in subsistence, may sojourn where he chooses."

25. "Thus has the origin of law been declared to you," etc.—*Sir W. Jones' translation*, collated with the Sanskrit text by G. C. Haughton, M.A., F.R.S.; re-edited by S. G. Grady, barrister-at-law.

The mention of Mathura suggests that Krishna ideas may have been gaining ground, which were innovations objectionable to the Brahmins of the Institutes.

Surely a conquering invading race would have a traditional idea of the benefits of extension rather than confinement.

The superiority of the Brahman to the Kshatrya is drawn as sharply as between the three twice-born classes and the Sudras.

135. "The student must consider a Brahman, though but ten years old, and a Kshatrya aged 100 years, as father and son, as between these two the young Brahman is to be respected as the father."

It must be remembered that the soul may change caste in its transmigrations. Neglect of the proper rites can degrade the three upper classes.

It is said that "elephants, horses, men of the servile classes, and contemptible Mléch'has or barbarians, lions, tigers, or boars," are the mean states produced by the quality of darkness. According to whether goodness, passion, or darkness preponderates, will be the ordering of the ensuing transmigration. The Sudra may become exalted by goodness to the Brahmin, and the latter debased.

The including of merchants in the three twice-born classes does not seem to indicate an aristocracy of warlike conquering immigrants from an inland region. Again, if the Arya varta had been conquered, by immigrants, from the Mléch'has, it must still have been considered the home of the latter, even if the ownership of the land was claimed by the conquerors.

We appear to draw much the same distinction between our three upper classes, viz. the warlike, and literary or professional gentry, and the merchants; and the fourth, whom we have lately termed "working men." The ordinances of Manu seem intended to keep the "working man" contented or subservient in his position; just as we expect our servants, mechanics, etc., to keep at a distance from us, and serve us respectfully and carefully.

The river Saraswati is praised as protecting from eastern enemies, but these are not necessarily of different race. Have we not lauded the Channel for separating us from the Continent?

III.

It is said in Manu, "that man only is perfect who consists of three persons united—himself, his wife, and his son."

The ancient Egyptians venerated a Trinity of this kind in Osiris, Isis, and Horus. Abraham evidently entertained strongly this Brahminical or Indian feeling.

IV.

The use of letters was apparently common at the epoch of the Institutes of Manu. Reading the Vedas in them appears not to mean reciting merely. Chap. ii. v. 76, "Brahma milked out, as it were, from the three Vedas, the letter A, the letter U, and the letter M, which form by their coalition the trilateral monosyllable, together with three mysterious words—*bhu*, *bhuvah*, *swer*, or earth, sky, and heaven." But repetition is much insisted upon. So in our own day our schools have largely retained repetition.

In chap. ii. v. 105, it is said, "In reading the Vedangas, or grammar, prosody, mathematics, and so forth, or even such parts of the Veda as ought constantly to be read, there is no prohibition on particular days, nor in pronouncing the texts appointed for oblations to fire."

A teacher of the Veda is said to be an image of God. Professor Weber seems to have found the commencement of the use of writing for the sacred works enveloped in uncertainty. He observes that the third stage in Vedic literature is represented by the Sútras; and that this word means thread or band, possibly analogous to the German *band*, volume, and that this necessarily presupposes the existence of writing, as probably the term *grantha*, first occurring in Panini. "The oldest inscriptions, according to Wilson, date no earlier than the third century B.C. Nearchus, however, as is well known, mentions writing, and his time corresponds very well, upon the whole, to the period to which we must refer the origin of the Sutras. But as these were composed chiefly with a view to their being committed to memory—a fact which follows from their form and partly accounts for it—there might be good grounds for taking exception to the etymology just proposed, and for regarding the signification 'guiding line,' 'clue,' as the original one." "Goldstücker contends that the words *sutra* and *grantha* must be absolutely connected with writing. It seems, at all events, to be a fact that the aphorisms were inscribed upon leaves and strung together. It appears reasonable to suppose that songs and poems may have been retained only in the head, to be recited, as was done by our mediæval bards. And even in our own age extra merit is attributed to Mr. Brandram's admirable Shakspearian readings because he recites his plays throughout, without the assistance of a book. But when, in the Yaju edas, sentences in prose became mingled with the verses, writing seems likely to have come into vogue. The second part of Vedic literature, as Professor Weber styles it, the Bráhmanas, signifying that which relates to prayer, *brahman* (brahman means drawing forth, creating, elevating in a spiritual sense, etc.) certainly appear to infer writing in their contents. Containing linguistic explanations, traditional narratives and philosophical explanations, analytic or dogmatic in illustrating the sacrificial rites, etc., as the Professor says, they originated from the opinions of individual sages; imparted by oral tradition, and preserved in families and by disciples. But surely they were written before they assumed these elaborations. He observes that it remains uncertain whether they were actually written down or still transmitted orally only. The common name for the Bráhmana literature is *Śruti*, hearing, *i.e.* that which is the subject of hearing. Now to argue from this word that the literature was not such in the strict sense would seem likely to be as erroneous as to hold that our "lectures" were the vehicles of reading only, and not discourses; from the signification of the word, as agreeing with the French *lire*. Certain Sutras bear the title of Smárta Sútras, *i.e.* Sutras founded on Smriti, memory. But this signifies, in the Professor's opinion, that they were the property of the whole people; supported by the consciousness of all, not needing to be specially inculcated, and, in this, different from *Śruti*, hearing only. As, even in the nineteenth century, many of the inhabitants of Europe cannot read, and yet, by memory, may be sufficiently acquainted with the doctrines and formulas of our faith to be termed Christians, and with our laws to avoid trespassing against them, so may the uneducated amongst the old Hindus have become partially learned in the knowledge requisite to their civilisation. In the Smárta Sútras, he remarks that we have to look for the beginnings of the Hindu legal literature. He says, "the statement of Megasthenes that the Indians in his time administered law only "ἀπὸ μνήμης, from memory, I hold to be perfectly correct." The Institutes of Manu were at least older than the time of Megasthenes, but it is of course probable that the Judges administered the law, especially to armies and their followers in the field, without recourse to books. In fact, our judges, sitting *in banco* at Westminster, may be said to administer the law "ἀπο μνήμης, in making their decisions according to judicial precedents; and although our lawyers are assisted by recorded decisions and text-books, they are supposed to carry the law in their heads, not merely to be able to point to the passage in which it is laid down. Indeed, as we have no authoritative code, our whole law may be said to be administered "ἀπο μνήμης."

The argument of the non-existence of writing amongst the early Vedic poets or philosophers seems to depend upon the negative evidence of allusions to it not being distinctly apparent. The negative evidence may also be adduced that, if writing had come into use as a novelty after an oral collection of the Vedas in the fourteenth century B.C., or thereabouts, some distinct account of it might have been expected. Commerce would suggest archaic writing.

The origin of this art in India altogether would appear to be lost in the mists of antiquity previous to the fifteenth century B.C. The hymns of the Vedas seem likely to have acquired their sanctity and been orally transmitted from many centuries later back, with other poems, traditions, etc. By the fifteenth century B.C., at about the time of Moses, writing would reasonably seem established, but doubtless its use was not universal, even amongst the poets.

Throughout Europe in the present day a large number of persons of both sexes fulfil useful avocations in life without knowledge of letters. They may, however, possess some literary fragments by rote. In our mediæval ages it was both honoured and despised as a clerical accomplishment.

Few of us nowadays comprehend the mysteries of the science of mechanics beyond the section of the world's workers who employ them as necessities. The Buddhists have traditions of the handing down of their sacred books by memory to an extent which appears to be remarkable from the internal evidence. Mr. Rhys Davids observes, in his work on Buddhism, that "even though they are well acquainted with writing, the monks in Ceylon do not use books in their religious services, but repeat, for instance, the whole of the Pátimokkha on Uposatha (Sabbath) days." The Mahavansa relates that "the wise monks of former days handed down by word of mouth the text of the three Pitakas, and the commentary upon them. Seeing the destruction of men, the monks of this time assembled, and, that the faith might last long, they wrote them in books." Mr. Davids observes that if all the printed copies of the Vedas were destroyed, they would still be preserved in the memory of the priests. Of course this idea would be still more cogent in the days of MSS. only; though writings were in use to aid the student, he would still have been bound to learn by heart the sacred books. The epithet "divine city" was given to Sanskrit writing.

The Pāli alphabet was brought by Asoka's son to Ceylon in the third century B.C. It has been thought doubtful whether the art of writing was known in the southern valley of the Ganges at Gautauma's epoch, about two centuries previously. Asoka's remarks, however, as to the Scriptures of the Law in the Edict of Babra suggest no novelty in writing.

V.

MRS. MANNING quotes a curious passage from Vedic literature, in which the sun is said never to set:—

"The sun never does set or rise. When people think that the sun is setting (it is not so). For after having arrived at the end of the day, it makes itself produce two opposite effects, making night to what is below and day to what is on the other side."

VI.

MRS. MANNING observes that in the Presidency of Bengal the worship of Siva appears to have been from a remote period what it is now, "the religion of the Brahmans." Sambhu is the name by which Siva is called in the dramas, and "Sambhu," says Professor Wilson, "is declared by Manu to be the presiding deity of the Brahmanical order."

In fact Siva, the auspicious one, or Sambhu, or Mahadeva, are really mere names of the supreme spirit Brahm. If the Brahmins of Bengal can be actually said to have adored God in Siva, his dome-shaped emblem may, not unreasonably, be supposed to have been in use. The system of Buddhism appears to have arisen on this side of India, and, as Mr. Rhys Davids has remarked, Buddhism was the child, the product, of Hinduism. Many of Gautauma's chief disciples were Brahmans; he always classed them with the Buddhist mendicants, as deserving of respect, and used the name Brahmans as a term of honour for the Buddhist saints. This symbol would seem likely to have been continued in the dhagob, with or without its umbrella at the top. These excavations, classed as Buddhistical, may either appertain to this order of the Brahmins or to the Buddhists. In the mingling of the two styles, generally suggestive of the Egyptian or classic and Gothic respectively, may be merely seen the same conjunction as may be observed in Christendom, where the Classic and Gothic, the ritualistic and the non-ritualistic schools are brought into apposition.

Mr. Davids observes that "there was not much in the metaphysics and psychology of Gautauma which cannot be found in one or other of the orthodox systems, and a great deal of his morality could be matched from earlier or later Hindu books. . . . Buddhism grew and flourished within the fold of the orthodox belief. So far from showing how depraved and oppressive Hinduism was, it shows preeisely the contrary; for none will deny that there is much that is beautiful and noble in Buddhism. . . . Gautauma's whole training was Brahmanism; he probably deemed himself to be the most correct exponent of the spirit as distinct from the letter of the ancient faith." His recourse to parables is curiously prototypical of Christ. We find the parable of the sower and seed, etc. etc., somewhat different, but eminently suggestive.

VII.

THE Malay archipelago, Java and Borneo, etc., are thought to have been, until geologically recent times, the southern portion of the Asiatic continent, on account of the identity of their flora, while the seas are shallow which divide them from the mainland.

Australia seems to be distinctly separate; to be regarded as a continent of the Secondary or early Tertiary period, now disappearing. There are indications of a former connection with Africa.

VIII.

IT is curious that in the code of Yájnavalkya, which seems to be later than that of Manu, but earlier than that of the Roman Justinian, the number of judges ordained to form a court corresponds to the number accustomed to sit *in banco* in our Courts at Westminster. "Four learned in the Vedas and in the Law form a Court or Traividya. Whatever is declared by this Court, or by a single person who has in an eminent degree knowledge of the soul in its relations, the same should be held as law."

Mrs. Manning observes that writing is referred to as freely as if the work had been composed at the present time.

"The representation, as made by the plaintiff, is to be put in writing in presence of the defendant; the year, month, half-month, day, names, caste, etc., being given," and a written statement must be furnished by the defendant in support of his assertions. Legal proofs are stated to be "writing, possession, and witnesses." But while in many respects the ordinances anticipate our own, in others they return to what we consider the darkness of our Middle ages. Trials by ordeal, walking through fire, carrying red-hot balls, etc., submergence in water, etc., are ordered; but women, children, aged men, the blind, the lame, Brahmans, and those afflicted with disease, are to be placed in scales, and utter an invocation:—

"O scales! made by the gods of old, the abode of truth; therefore do ye, propitious ones, declare the truth and liberate me from suspicion. If I be an evil-doer, then bear me down, O mother! If I be pure, carry me upwards."

IX.

In Professor Wilson's translation of the Rig Veda we read, "He who, accepting the rites dedicated to him, knows the twelve months and their productions, and that which is supplementarily engendered." Wilson comments on the importance of this passage, as indicating the concurrent use of the lunar and solar years at this period, and the method of adjusting the one to the other. Mrs. Manning observes that the name for the moon in Sanskrit, Greek, and German is derived from a root signifying to measure. "The close connection between the names for moon and month makes it probable that a certain knowledge of lunar chronology existed, even before the separation of the Indo-European family," or before the people emigrated from the old civilisation of the Indian continent, to become Greeks and Germans respectively.

The Hindu astronomer Aryabhata, whose birth is assigned to A.D. 476, wrote:—

"The terrestrial globe, a compound of earth, water, fire, and air, entirely round, encompassed by a girdle (the equator), stands in the air in the centre of the stellar sphere. Like as a ball formed by the blossoms of the nauclea kadamba is on every side beset with flowerets, so is the earth-globe with all creatures, terrestrial and aquatic;" and also, "The sphere of the stars is stationary, and the earth, making a revolution, produces the daily rising and setting of stars and planets."

Varáha-mihira, born A.D. 530, says:—"In an eclipse of the moon he enters into the earth's shadow; in a solar eclipse the same thing happens to the sun."

X.

The Greeks do not appear to have advanced beyond the ideas of Pythagoras in regard to the revolution of our globe, but rather to have retrograded. Pythagoras, either from the brilliance of his own genius, or from light obtained in Egypt or the East, made the sun the centre of the planetary system, and the earth revolving round it. But his views met with little or no support till the time of Copernicus, in our fifteenth century. To the Alexandrian school, owing its existence to the Ptolemies, the credit of making the first systematic observations in our western world is held to be due. The positions of the fixed stars were determined, the paths of the planets carefully traced, and the solar and lunar inequalities were ascertained; but the system was not so true as the Pythagorean. The Ptolemaic system placed the earth immovable in the centre of the heavens, making the entire heavens revolve around it in twenty-four hours.

With Hipparchus of Bithynia has been said to have commenced the real written history of scientific astronomy. He calculated 1081 stars, and determined the length of the year, the mean motion of the moon, the equation of her centre and acclimatisation of her orbit, etc., and he employed processes analogous to plane and spherical trigonometry, etc.

He appeared in an Asiatic Greek colony, and it is not impossible that he obtained Oriental knowledge. Altogether there appears little evidence of such advancement in astronomy in Greece as to have been likely to have materially affected the science of the Hindus.

In regard to the signs of the zodiac, attributed by Professor Weber to the Greeks, Professor O. M. Mitchell is quoted in Blavatsky's "Isis Unveiled," as stating that "upon the coffin of a mummy now in the British Museum was delineated the zodiac, with the exact position of the planets at the time of the autumnal equinox of 1722 B.C. Professor Mitchell had calculated, and found that on the 7th October 1722 B.C. they had occupied the precise points in the heavens indicated.

If Varáha-mihira, however, in or about the sixth century A.D., was influenced by the Greeks, as Professor Weber affirms from recognising a number of astronomical or astrological terms taken by him from the Greek, it is evidence of the intimate acquaintance existing between the East and West, although, at this period, the political power of the Greeks in India would seem to have departed.

Buddhism was prevailing, side by side with the other Hindu religions, and it is subsequently to this date that the system of the Roman Pontiffs appears, with the analogies of its ritual to that of Buddhism. Greece was, at this time, abandoning its ancient deities, just as India was abrogating the Vedic forms. Whatever may be urged in regard to the possibility of the more sacred aspect of the Incarnation doctrine in India being derived from Christianity, at all events the monasticism of the East preceded that of the West. There was reciprocity of ideas. If Varáha-mihira used some Greek words, he, at all events, accompanied them with imagery from his fatherland.

He says that the astrologer must be well born and of good figure, regular in his devotions, and well acquainted with the text and commentary of established works on scientific astronomy and natural horoscopy.

This infers a considerable astronomical literature in India, and that it was no novelty there; and he mentions several predecessors.

The following instances of his directions for the guidance of astrologers are quoted by Mrs. Manning:—

"When Mars has a large bright surface, and the colour of the flowers of the *Butea frondosa*, or red asoca . . . he brings blessing to kings and satisfaction to their people."

"When the moon appears white as hoar frost, the jessamine flower, the white lily or crystal, and looks bright as though polished, because she knows that at night she will adorn the head of her beloved Siva, she brings happiness to mankind."

"When the sun resembles a banner or a bow, is trembling and rough, battles are at hand. A black line on the luminary shows that a royal councillor will kill the king."

It appears that Varáha-mihira himself "attempted a Sanskrit derivation" for the word *hora*, which he employs for his "Astrological prediction by configuration of planets;" but modern science has concluded this not to be conformable to Sanskrit etymology.

XI.

ARTIFICIAL magnets, and the properties of the loadstone, appear to have been known to the Hindus by at least the eighth century A.D.

Mrs. Manning observes that "the indirect evidence afforded by the presence of India's products in other ancient countries, coincides with the direct testimony of Sanskrit literature to establish the fact that the ancient Hindus were a commercial people. The code of Manu requires the king to determine the price of commodities, and also the trustworthiness of the weights and measures used. And that the transactions contemplated were not restricted to local products, is evident from reference to the charges for freight for articles in river boats, and the undetermined and larger charges to which sea-borne goods were liable."

XII.

IN Wilson's translation of the Rig Veda a passage is cited (R. V. i. 84, 17), in which a man places his elephant side by side with his son, as an object to be prayed for. Mrs. Manning observes that elephants, which were scarcely known to the ancient Egyptians, were the cherished friends of the Indian household; and a variety of names are used in Sanskrit for this sagacious beast, whose head was bestowed upon the image of the Deity of Prudence. It is difficult to conceive that people, entering the country from the north, can have, within the periods which have been assigned for the immigration and for the composition of these hymns, learnt to regard the elephant with such affection.

It is to the south of the Himalayas that he has been subdued and rendered useful to man. The tropical forests are his home. A race of conquering immigrants would surely not have so soon domesticated him, or fondly adopted him from the crushed aborigines. He was styled *várana*, as bearing and protecting the king. Mrs. Manning quotes Lassen in saying that the Hindus were too much attached to their elephants to kill them for their tusks. When they required more ivory than natural deaths afforded, they imported it from Ethiopia.

XIII.

SINCE the days when Origen appears to have acquiesced in the Oriental doctrine of the metempsychosis in the first half of the third century A.D., our European civilisation has become divided into four great encampments of theology or philosophy. Two of these are held by the well-disciplined armies of the Greek and Roman Churches; the third occupies several smaller camps, the largest of which is the Church of England; while the fourth is held by the heterogeneous forces of the men of science, and of what is called religious indifference, infidelity, or scepticism. All of these have their differences and quarrels, but the several encampments possess bonds of union. The three first contend that a Divine Ordainer and Dispenser, a personal God, has created man, with the animals and vegetables, to serve him for a probationary existence in our world, for the deeds in which he will be relegated for ever to a spiritual or spiritualised material existence in a heaven of joy or hell of despair. This has been tempered by the purifying process in purgatory, to fit for heaven those not absolutely irreclaimable in, or unpardonable for, their wickedness. Faith in the actual and necessary atoning power of the blood of the sacrificed Incarnation of Deity is held to be requisite in these communions; Protestantism even maintaining that hell awaits all who have not, in what has been termed "saving faith," taken to heart in a special manner the manifestation of suffering Deity. Blood-shedding is taught to be the necessary price of Divine mercy; the costliness of the one sacrifice on the Cross being henceforth sufficient atonement for the world. The philosophers of the fourth camp, for the most part, regard transcendentalism of any kind as effete. They consider that brain, nerves, and stomach form the thinking process, that soul is a delusion, and that man is simply a creature of hereditary instincts and objective education, acting and reflecting under the impulses of the combined bodily functions. They appear to assert that he begins and ends his individuality with the birth and death of his present body. The ancient and modern inhabitants of India, virtually as large as Europe without Russia, and those of China, virtually twice as numerously populated, the ancient inhabitants of the Grecian Pythagorean settlements, and the Egyptians, Pharisees, and others have continued, since a period at least some centuries B.C., to profess the intermediate idea that the soul, the *I am*, the *I think*, prolongs its existence in a succession of bodies; wearing many of them out, just as the body uses up many garments. And they have also conceived heavens, and hells corresponding rather to purgatory than to our merciless abyss of eternal flames, moral or actual.

Christ is held to have taught, as God upon earth, escape from hell and hope of heaven through His own mediation. The heaven and hell, of reward and punishment, is not suggested in the first part of the Bible, except in the translation of Enoch to heaven, and subsequently of Elijah in a chariot of fire, and is barely set forth in the later portion of the Old Testament. It may therefore be averred that the utterances of Christ upon this point, as subsequently sustained by St. Paul and the Apostles, constitute, at all events in the Protestant Churches, our authority for maintaining it. The Roman Church may hold the Pope's authority sufficient, as that of God's vicegerent upon earth. But Christ's words by no means appear to teach the doctrine definitely.

He distinctly represents the rich man as being in "Hades" (ἐν τῷ ᾅδῃ), while the poor man is in "Abraham's bosom" (Luke xvi. 23). Upon other occasions He speaks of the wicked being cast into the unquenchable flames of Gehenna, or into æonian punishment, upon which remarks have been made upon pages 183 and 335 of this book; but neither Hades nor Gehenna correspond to our hell. As argued upon page 336 *et al.*, there is certainly nothing contrary to an obvious interpretation of His words, as recorded in the New Testament, in the assertion that, although He held forth a spiritual future, He also acquiesced in, or admitted, this doctrine of the transmigration of souls; which existed not obscurely in the place and period of His manifestation.

Gautauma Buddha, some 500 years previously, in the Indian civilisation, had taught the absolute certainty of the doctrine of the metempsychosis, and the possibility of the recollection of former existences. His followers had adhered to it as a matter of distinct faith. In obedience to His command of making His doctrine universally known, Buddhist missionaries have been found to have arrived in Asia Minor, while Pythagoras had promulgated the doctrine, in an equally matter-of-fact manner, in Southern Italy at nearly the same epoch as that assigned to Gautauma Buddha in India. It must certainly be admitted that its diffusion was likely to have been sufficient to render it not unworthy of the attention and reprobation of St. Paul if he disapproved of it. He is also not recorded to have impugned it.

In the Buddhist doctrine it does not appear to be conceived that an actual soul quits the tenement of the old body, existing, perceived or unperceived, by itself, till it re-enters the flesh, but that the deeds and thoughts of the lifetime, by a sort of reflex action, will return and centre upon the new body. The old intrinsic being will revive under the new material circumstances. All the actions and conceptions of the former life bear their fruits in the ensuing, both under the system of Buddha and of the Indian Krishna. Buddha is related to have systematically taught this doctrine in parables. For instance, "The holy sage Pandu Kabra, as a consequence of the sin of his having, when he was a carpenter, pierced a fly with a splinter of wood, had, while engaged as a holy sage in the performance of good works, to suffer the torture of being impaled."

The story of the impalement also appears in the Mahábhárata, under a different form, as related on page 197. In the Institutes of Manu, the doctrine of rising or falling in *caste* as a reward or punishment for the transactions of this life is very distinctly set forth. Goodness may elevate to the angelic, according to this pre-Christian doctrine or to the Brahminical class, badness debase to the demoniacal or the lowest forms of earthly life, even to the vegetable. The strictness of caste limitations became tolerable to the lower classes when promotion might result from fulfilment of duty in a servile, and degradation follow from unworthy conduct in a higher caste. The sensuous Brahmin and the degraded but righteous sweeper might exchange places in the next life.

Gautauma Buddha is narrated, in the Buddhist sacred scriptures, to have said to his disciples, "My dear sons, whoever takes life, when he dies out of his present existence, will appear again in hell, and afterwards in the state of an animal. After being freed from hell and the condition of an animal, even when he reaches the state of man, he will have but a short life."

Professor Max Müller has quoted Buddha as saying, after he had become "enlightened," "Without ceasing shall I run through a course of many births, looking for the maker of this tabernacle, and painful is birth again and again. But now, maker of the tabernacle, thou hast been seen, thou shalt not make up this tabernacle again. All thy rafters are broken, thy ridge-pole is sundered; the mind, being sundered, has attained to the extinction of all desires."

In the extinction of all desires *nirvāna* is reached upon earth, and the heaven of rest in the future seems left to the imagination, as in Christianity. The question of the manner of the personality in consciousness, when the nirvāna of heaven is attained, seems left in obscurity or vague shadowings forth, as in our religion. The heavens and hells of Buddhism seem not eternal, but intermediate states between transmigrations. In the religion of Krishna as propounded in the Bhagavad Gita, as in Buddhism, release from the recurring incarnations upon earth is offered by faith in divine manifestation in the flesh; which Buddha appears, *in effect*, to be. While Christ undoubtedly preached the spiritual life, He may, like Krishna, Buddha, and Pythagoras, have admitted the possibility of many terrestrial existences as a preparation for it, upon the strength of the arguments which have been adduced—viz. His apparent reference to the doctrine in the case of Elias and John the Baptist, and His uttering no word against it, notwithstanding its prevalence.

Of course millions of terrestrial existences with intervals of oblivion, as preparation for a life of never-ending consciousness of joy or misery, would be of little account when their end arrived; and the spirit, freed from the trammels of matter, became embarked upon the limitless ocean of eternity—the endless, in which, after millions of waves had been passed, the shore would be no nearer.

Christianity has taught that new beings are continually ushered into the world, endowed with souls which are to live in the body for some seventy years as a probation; and then that they are to spend a never-dying life in the spirit, according to the manner in which they have employed these seventy years, and accepted Christ as their Redeemer. But of those nominally born within its folds increasing numbers seem of late years to have rejected any idea of life beyond the present. They consider that the *ego*, the *I am*, the *I think*, is simply created out of, and that it is dependent upon, the *one* body. The mind of the promising genius may be dissolved into nothingness before its buds have opened, by some dissolution of ever-changing matter. Statesmen and poets, and reflecting and planning beings in general, may be all abruptly and prematurely terminated by the neglect of a railway pointsman. They hold that the faith of the religionists is a delusion, and that the mind which has left no children or actual works, after the destruction of the body becomes extinct; except in so far as its words and actions may have influenced its associates.—In conceiving that this immaterial thinking process, which takes place under action in the brain, nerves, blood, etc., can exist as an individuality without a body, we certainly seem to transcend all the ideas by which we have apprehended the finite. We have learnt to posit and measure by terms which are applicable to the material. We may be able to realise infinity by its contrast to that which is finite, and as we can perceive no actual limitations to our thinking process, we conceive that to partake of the infinite. We cannot point to any precise boundary to our ideas. Our thoughts appear to be formed in the material substance of the brain, but to be in themselves immaterial, partaking of that to which we can affix no limits. We recognise that our individuality is bounded by the body, but our thoughts contemplate the illimitable outside ourselves. But if we hold that the soul, released from the body, can exist as an individual without the material, we seem to limit that which appears in its contrast to matter to be spiritual and illimitable. We give to the immaterial the limits or individualising which we have only observed in the material. Christianity, however, has rather held forth the hopes of existence in a glorified body. Its substance is to be no longer gross or earthly, still it is to be substance, though ethereal. St. Paul speaks of a spiritual body, but then our modern spiritualists call that a spiritual body which is capable of doing material things, such as rapping or lifting a table, writing names, etc. The spiritual bodies are conceived to become partially materialised in the medium's atmosphere before they can be cognised by, and placed in communication with, our earthly selves. This somewhat corresponds to the theory enunciated by Socrates in Plato's "Phædo." He declares therein that the sensuous soul, when departing life impressed with that which is corporeal, wanders amongst monuments and tombs as a shadowy phantom, visible by partaking of the bodily nature, till such time as it again returns actually into the flesh ("Phædo," caps. 69, 70).

This conception may be applied to account for what we term ghosts.

Blavatsky, in "Isis Unveiled," remarks that Aristotle laughed at Strabo for believing that particles of matter *per se* could have life and intellect in themselves sufficient to fashion by degrees such a multiform world as ours.

Socrates said—"Each pleasure and pain, having a nail as it were, nails the soul to the body, and fastens it to it, and causes it to become corporeal, deeming those things to be true whatever the body asserts to be so. For, in consequence of its forming the same opinions with the body, and delighting in the same things, it is compelled, I think, to possess similar manners, and to be similarly nourished, so that it can never pass into Hades in a pure state, but must ever depart polluted by the body, and so quickly falls again into another body, and grows up as if it were sown, and consequently is deprived of all association with that which is divine and pure and uniform."

And again—"It is not lawful for any one who has not studied philosophy and departed this life perfectly pure to pass into the rank of gods, but only for the true lover of wisdom."

According to his ideas, those who had sufficiently purified themselves by knowledge would live without bodies throughout all future time. But if we admit that the spiritual or immaterial partakes of the infinite, *i.e.* of that which is not limited, as individuality seems to involve the notion of limitation, the renewed individualism of the thinking self after death would seem to require some sort of material body, although possibly glorified and ethereal.

But as this must partake of the universe of matter in general, which is constantly in a condition of change, it would appear, as the Brahmins and Buddhists have conceived, to be finite. And it would seem reasonable to hold that the *will* or *desire* may cause the return of the thinking self into a body as we know it, instead of into some hypothetical body. Seers and spiritualists have informed us of the actual existence of etherealised bodies, but the mass of humanity remains unacquainted with them. Religious hopes are, however, entertained that they may be found in heaven by those who discredit their appearance on earth; and the soul feels a natural reluctance to return to the grossness and pains of its present tenement, although a scrutiny of desires may evince that our thoughts are in general still of this world as we know it.

We see that, under mesmerism, the soul or thinking process seems to communicate with or obtain power over other souls by abnormal channels of communication, not dependent on the ordinary transfer of ideas by tongue or touch. We perceive that ideas such as panics seem to pervade multitudes with sudden and mysterious force. It cannot be *primâ facie* ridiculous to maintain that the *I am*, which by its will-power can conquer nervousness and subdue the brain's unwillingness to work, which can conceive immaterial laws and forces as governing a material world, such as attraction and repulsion, universality and individuality, can *will* itself from a worn-out or suddenly-destroyed body into a new one. Some body, adapted by its situation and parentage to the hopes, aspirations, or sympathies of the soul, may be conceived as necessarily to attract it as the magnet draws the steel. If we become diseased or intoxicated or excessively fatigued, some time will elapse before the *ego* can induce the brain and body to do its bidding, though circumstances of extreme excitement or interest may rally the system with what almost seems preternatural effect. If our brain and body decay entirely, it does not seem irrational, upon the mere exoteric aspect of the case, to argue that, by force of the same nature as the mesmeric, the soul-self may settle upon a new being, still unborn in self-realisation. It must go through the dream of childhood; and childhood sometimes seems a dream, especially the childhood of genius, when quaint fancies or earnest predilections and capacities astonish the parents or friends.

To show that the will can work upon the unconscious mind, when the body, in dreamless sleep, is dead to realisable thought, the desire that it shall awake at an unusual time will often occasion its so doing. Especially, perhaps, in childhood, but also later in life, seeming memories of events, conversations, and places mysteriously come over people. And civilised humanity has generally accepted some religion offering a future life. This may be the mere expression of desire to live; but then it is contended that it is that very desire to live which can carry the reflecting and wanting self over the bridge of death into a new material existence.

It is this constant pressing onwards, or intellectually upwards, of individual life, through all phases of material being, which has given us our system. Morally advancing or retrogressing, the thinking worlds still crave the knowledge of the Divine or Absolute soul, of which all thought is part; akin to fire or electricity. But it is fire in self-realisation, and ruling the matter by which it is trammelled; but which it still moulds eventually to its purpose.

But the European science of our age, in great part, says No—

your soul, your thinking process, your *I am*, is of the body only. It is of brain and nerves, stomach and blood. In moments of excitement the mind may seem to command the body, to urge the enfeebled limbs, or jaded brain, to renewed exertion, but the stomach, or some other material organ, will be found to be at the bottom of it. You marry, and to the descendants of your body your ideas will be transmitted, according to the hereditary or traducionary theory. You write a book or erect an edifice, or utter a discourse, and the ideas will again be transmitted. But the will, the I am, which throws off these without loss of energy, still retaining to death the fulness of original ideas in the vessel which threw them off, cannot retain any for the soul-self which cognises, feels, and uses them. The extracts survive, and may descend in germs through many bodies, but the essence dies with the one body, in the process of earth to earth, or ashes to ashes. It can impart its mental characteristics, in conjunction with other impartances of ancestry or parents, to mature in a child or descendant. It can represent them in material objects such as a painting. It can fertilise with them the world of ideas for the period of its one body's existence, which may be briefly determined by extraneous accident; though the ideas in the mind seem great in growing vigour. Till death seizes the body they may pass into life partly created from its breath. The acquired learning may revive in instincts in child or succeeding generation, but death dissolves it into space, and the *Ego* may not hope to realise it again for itself. The ideas leave extillations to flourish, but they expire in essence. The parts of the soul-self may live in work which represents more or less of its ideas, but its essential character or individuality ceases to be, according to Positivism or Materialism.

In answer to these propositions it may be inquired—What is the decay and death of the body? Is it not corporeally destroyed to rise again? From death springs life, vegetable and animal. If burnt, the body's vapours mingle with the sustaining air of the material world. The child is born, and unconsciously cleaves to its earthly nourishment; for animal is supported by animal and vegetable, and heat, wooing damp, brings into play the germs of life in all nature. Soon the new being begins to cognise itself as apart from the outer world, of which it takes notice. If the ideas of a deceased body can have passed to its descendants, why can they not also have unconsciously existed in the return to the material universe of the substance or vapours of those nerves, brain, etc. etc., in which they were formerly resident? Then as a new birth occurs, adapted for them because it is created of germs issuing from sympathetic beings, they concentrate upon it, constitute its soul-self, and gradually awake to power, enlarged or deteriorated by the circumstances under which they may be placed; or according to the tendencies of the soul itself in the previous life. The will-power may thus work the new body to its aims, for good or evil, progress or retrogression, without recognising in memory their cause. The accretion of ideas acquired in many lifetimes may form a character; but the body of the time must always limit it. The absence of proper eyes or health may hinder the accomplishments of certain desires, or render their attainment hopeless in the life of that body; but we see how genius can triumph over bodily defects. A blind man has made roads; and those deaf, dumb, and blind, in combination, from birth, have still acquired education.

But it may be simply replied that, when the brain is partially destroyed the mind partially decays, therefore that, when the brain is entirely destroyed in death, the mind, *i.e.* the thinking process, is entirely abrogated with it.

It may again be argued that the brain, nerves, blood, and stomach act upon and influence one another, and that the *Ego* is the mere creature of these material things. Genius betokens a high degree of brain-receptivity, and delicate nervous organisation. Music, by the same process, must be held to be produced from certain combination of wires, or brazen tubes, etc., not from eternal laws of the universe, which seem to regulate the motions of the spheres; which give us the modulations of harmony, in accordance with the properties of numbers, and in adaptation to which these wires are regulated. We may, of course, trace to greater or less extent the man in the parent or progenitor. The executive musician may be father of a great composer, or the latter may have a son who is an excellent mathematician. Some kindred ability or physical likeness may be observed in an ancestor. It has been said that the hereditary or traducionary theory can be remarked even in twins. Mr. Galton has informed us, as quoted in an article against the metempsychosis theory in the "University Magazine" of January 1879, that when they are contained in two sacs, and therefore the result of separate ova, they present ordinary family likeness, but when in one sac, that they are invariably of the same sex and exceedingly alike in body and mind.

Pythagoras declared that there must be a sympathy between the parents and the soul that is to come into their child. Undoubtedly the nervous system of the parents seems in great part to be inherited; but there is still the distinct individuality. Some characteristics may be inherited, or acquired by education or association; but the intrinsic soul-self will have taken them as an estate, settled on the soul in that body, but which is not the soul itself. From the citizen of Stratford-on-Avon, who may have had a superior and romantic wife, and perhaps with poetical talent in himself, repressed by the nature of his necessary avocations—emerged Shakspeare. Can it be that some germ, descending from the ever-widening platforms of the ascending, ancestral pyramid—in which we have four grandparents, eight great grandparents, sixteen, thirty-two, sixty-four progenitors within six generations, 126 in all—so fructified in this worthy and perhaps intellectual couple, who seem to have abided in the citizen life of Stratford? With the objective inspirations of strolling players, a masque at Kenilworth, the exterior aspect of Elizabeth's court in London, etc. etc. did this germ, or some combination of germs, produce the author of Hamlet, etc.?—A tune of music exists unperceived in the mind, and is recalled to material life when the chords of the instrument are awakened. Under the transmigration theory a soul may be conceived to have laboured in king, prelate, noble, or student, before, in pursuit of aspirations, consciously or unconsciously entertained, of authorship, it came into the body of the quiet citizen's son of the rural, river-adorned Stratford; with its sylvan vicinage and central English situation. The tune, or essence of life and character, the chords of the soul, which had given glorious sounds before, now reproduced them in the poet's and dramatist's art as the attributes to others; sometimes suggested by their imputed histories, or sometimes creations of the imagination. Unconsciously influenced by the old transactions in which it had been engaged, and by the old ideas which it had acquired, the soul vented them in the dramas suggested by its present situation. This really seems to be materialism, *i.e.* the spiritual connected necessarily with, and working in, the material; but, while recognising the constancy of the laws which regulate matter, it affords a continuance for the thinking self.

The truths of geometry can only be conceived by the mind as absolute and self-existent, though the matter of the universe were jumbled into chaos. We cannot but suppose that the forces which now keep the world revolving in its orbit, regularly as if trammelled by a material chain, would again reduce them into order. So out of the decay of its microcosm the force of the thinking self will reduce a new material being into subserviency with its wishes, so far as is compatible with the changefulness inherent in matter.

This certainly seems to account for the strong impulses and individuality of genius more reasonably than the notion of some ancestral germ or germs bearing magnificent fruit, after passing through other beings in which their nature would seem to be merged. To conceive that the germ of ancestral power can lie dormant in parents, whose abilities or impulses do not cause them to be marked amongst humanity, and then come out with startling vigour, seems more difficult to credit than the passage of the mind, which has lost its body while its own desires are unabated, into another body adapted to those desires. Sympathy attracts two minds in living bodies. It would seem that sympathy may attract the unconsciously existing mind, in the universe of mind working in matter, into the unconscious child; the thoughts which have centred on the old brain reviving in due time on the new brain.

If education, merely, acting on the instincts inherent in the germ, produced the activities and aspirations of life, it might be conceived that the child of a Shakspeare's parents, brought up amongst courts and camps, and possessing the poetical instinct through the parents, would develop it in the form suggested by the education, though foreign to its birth. But Shakspeare seems to have married before he left Stratford and commenced his London career. Within a few years after this event we find him, inspired not to recollections of his Warwickshire home, but to Venus and Adonis, etc. Meres, in the "Wit's Treasury," 1598, says that "as the soul of Euphorbus was thought to live in Pythagoras, so the sweet witty soul of Ovid lives in mellifluous and honey-tongued Shakspeare. Witness his Venus and Adonis; his Lucrece; his sugared sonnets amongst his private friends." He occasionally introduces a simile suggested in the Stratford-on-Avon neighbourhood, but the general spirit of the poems is classical, tinged with the knightly romance which lingered in his day. He seems in them to have emerged completely from the youth of the country town; though he shows in his plays that he can depict the country gentleman or clown when he chooses, but in himself, he is not of the place in which he was born and bred.

He appears to have had ideas of the alleged possibility of remembering former births, in his mind, when he makes Rosalind say—"I was never so berhymed since Pythagoras' time, that I was an Irish rat, which I can hardly remember."—Of course the twins born in such close connection as to have closely similar bodies, would naturally attract kindred minds. The tune must be performed on an instrument with a due compass of notes; and such twin bodies would seem especially to suit two souls desiring unison. It was said, however, that the Siamese twins had different dispositions, although positively linked in the flesh. If it can be shown that twins can exist in almost complete mental identity, a philosophical motive may appear to be present in the ancient Indian story of the Preserving Spirit of Deity becoming simultaneously incarnate in Krishna and Bala-rama (see page 31). One spirit may become divided in the flesh, and appear in two kindred beings.

A feeble frame, and the loss of limb, cannot check a Nelson's valour and enterprise. Intensity of will seems to have impelled him to his career. Surely it was not some mere ancient germ, but a deeply-feeling self, which burnt so fiercely in the heroic soul of the Norfolk clergyman's son. And his mother was daughter of a church dignitary. But then there was a valiant maternal uncle of the navy, and the same germ which produced his gallant soul may be thought to have fructified in Nelson's mother, to result in him.

The grand heroism, and ardent sense of duty in a Nelson would seem to argue an idiosyncrasy grown out of a fixed purpose, engendered in former life rather than the product of an ancestral germ mingling with other germs, and thus fructifying. But the family spirit which was evinced in the naval uncle afforded the requisite attraction to the individual spirit which became Nelson.

Although individual, we are only part of one universal spirit; in whom we live, move, and have our being. But, while under the universal rule, our *differentia* give us individuality; and it is in the desire, carrying on the individuality from life to life, that the *differentia* become more marked.

It may be urged, however, that it is a fortunate combination of the material living germs of parentage and ancestry, which creates a prominent man. Out of the body formed from these, issues a thought-being who realises that he has a brain and body, and, having done so, he must be merged in a comparatively short time. Under the religious idea, germs continually create new souls for eternity. Under the positive doctrine they occasion mental combinations which, in their turn, as has been observed, send forth extracts from their essence. Then, although this essence does not appear to have diminished thereby, they lose it entirely for themselves, in the intermingling of their bodies with the material universe. In fact self is a delusion, according to this view. The sense of eventual reward which causes men to work against present hope, to do their duty unto death, is a vain emotion. Patriotism and self-sacrifice are mere excitations of the stomach or nerves. We think that we are cognising ourselves as individuals; but it is the aggregate of notions in the organisations which have descended upon us, which causes the illusion of personality.

It may be so, but it is difficult to imagine spirits intermingling, ancestry in parents, and then that some ancestral germ can survive and emerge in strong individuality. If spirit accompanies the germ, its particularity must surely become lost in transmissions, and parents or children would seem to become the only likely donors or recipients of mental force. Certainly genius has neither seemed to require parents in whom the same was observed, nor children to succeed to it; although intelligent souls will naturally come into intelligent families, just as a clever youth of a certain position will go to a certain college. And so there will be sequences in professions and trades. Still genius and individualities will be observed to stand in distinctness.

Under the idea of transmigration from body to body, the spirit may be conceived as cleaving to matter, and awaking in life fitted for it, remaining as a unit. Individual mind, existing unperceived, for greater or less periods, in the universal mind, appertains to universal matter, till it resumes its individuality and consciousness in a new organisation. So the tune lives in the individual mind, an immaterial existence till materialised on the instrument. Our emotions are as its chords. If the mind is the parental product only, talent rather than cogent genius ought surely to be the highest mental progression in the child. And people, having it in their minds to desire male offspring, ought not to have female, as is sometimes the case; for in this case the germ appears not to have been influenced by the mental impressions, and it therefore seems dubious as to whether it can convey them, or mental attributes in a general way.

The same tune can be played on many instruments, in different keys, yet remain the same tune; so the thinking self may pass through many bodies, and perform in many varieties of circumstances, yet remain intrinsically and consciously the same. This seems easier to believe than that some mental attribute, accompanying a material germ, if the sex happens to suit its bias, produces a statesman, warrior, or financier, etc. etc. The great men who illumine the world seem thus relegated to accident. Even the religious theories also seem to admit the material formation of the body, in which is placed the soul destined to eternity, and born under the curse of original sin. It may be said that the Creator makes us; although two beings may apparently unite and under this notion produce an immortal person. Under the transmigration theory, the genius, a great soul, is the result of the systematic pushing forward of the mind through many careers, in which it unconsciously absorbs and reproduces experiences. Its hopes and ideas are scattered in death, but they survive in the eternal soul, which rules and lives in the material organisations of the universe, and, when the fitting birth takes place, they regain in it their self-consciousness by the law of attraction; which we see working in all nature. Under this the orbs of the starry systems revolve; and all living organisations appear to experience attraction and repulsion.

The sympathies and aversions of life seem distinctly facts, though they can scarcely be said to be always due to bodily impulses. They must be sometimes allowed to arise from mental conceptions only. The question seems to return to this: Can the *I am* disseminate ideas through a life of seventy years, and then die, with the mind still retaining them, in virtually undiminished fulness and strength, yet be unable to preserve them in abeyance, as in dreamless sleep, till a new body is obtained? Is it not rather the increasing strength of individuality in successive births, commencing with mere sensual aspirations, and enlarging them to philanthropical considerations as it progresses, which is the system of our life? This seems to afford a key to unlock the mystery of our existences, universal and individual. By attraction of spirit to matter we became units.

As children are born to the parents, these parents' bodies must gradually decay till death. The qualities of mind may also deteriorate as advanced age affects the brain; but in great part of a life the body may grow feebler, while the mind becomes firmer. This may be referred to the accretion of experiences, not to the concentration of will-power; but experiences are interpreted according to the individuality. Those who are strong in mind may survive in intellect the weakening of the body's health. The latter may cause depression, but it does not overcome the soul. Blood, nerves, and stomach affect the brain; but the strong will keeps it in working order till the decline of the whole system undermines it, and it dies with it. The brain appears to be the centre upon which the will concentrates its ideas. It cannot be said that they are actually written there. It cannot be the mere matter of the brain which discerns the image in the eye. It must be the soul-self, partaking of universal light and inhabiting that brain, while it is inhabitable, which perceives that image, and, in a healthy brain, reflects upon it, and deduces consequences from its appearance.

In the midst of intellectual activity the sudden destruction of the body may occur. Cannot then this *I am*, this self, which thinks and hopes, evolve itself by the unconscious *will*, which can rule it in sleep, and in mesmerism work upon other minds, out of the universality of mind and matter into which itself and its body have returned? Can it not, must it not, by the force of its own desires —which will usually be found to cleave to the world, however much it may seem at times to be scorned—awake in the new life of the yet unthinking body adapted to it? So have thought a large portion of the men who may be called civilised. And thus we can account for the innate powers more especially noticeable in what is termed genius, also for the revivalisms of the spirit of past ages.

Who could have supposed that the last generation of Englishmen could have produced our present ritualistic revival? The spirit of the sixteenth century would particularly seem to be revived in our own, combined with other past ages.

We must live in material organisations; but the *I am* survives their destruction. One contemplates the outer world. Under the religious idea one will, in future, contemplate it from heaven or hell. Under the *positive* theory it will shortly again become nothingness to oneself. The rational mean seems attained, and an explanation afforded of our aspirations and mental powers, by assigning them to the unconscious accretion of memories of past existences. The moral effect of this doctrine does not seem to be otherwise than beneficial. It teaches that every deed and thought, for good or evil, must necessarily be followed by a chain of events, not only in this life, as we of course perceive with our senses; but in successive existences to be discerned in our mental attributes. And our situations in this life, though affected by the parents' lives and positions, and by extraneous circumstances, are, in their essential properties, due to our own acts and desires in previous existences. We forget the circumstances o. our bygone lives in passing the river of oblivion in death, but they continue to affect our beings. They have been said, however, to be occasionally susceptible of recollection, as has been remarked.

The affection between parents and children does not seem to be diminished by this attributing to the child an essential being of its own. Both in India and China the parental ties are most sacred and enduring; and the laws of Manu, which teach transmigration, equally enforce the filial duty.

The erring, unreflecting soul, will naturally revive in a diseased or deformed body. The sins, which are deformities of the mind, will naturally conduce to a corresponding body. Those who in this life escape punishment for their crimes will receive it in some way in the next. Rank and station may be exchanged, and the king may become a beggar, the beggar a king.

Not, of course, that deformed or diseased bodies have necessarily sinful souls. They may be needful preparations for a higher life—trials to purify the soul. The mind, rising superior to disadvantages, will be schooled by them. Even in our present lives many circumstances are influencing us which we have forgotten. We sometimes unconsciously follow out a train of thought, conceiving it to be our own, in unconscious plagiarism, unmindful of the occasion when it was suggested to our minds from another. Our school work is supposed to form our minds, not to be entirely and actually remembered. Between the idea of the eternity of conscious individuality after this life, and that of absolute nothingness, the metempsychosis seems to account for the phenomena of genius, tastes, predilections, etc., and to be a reasonable explanation of past, present, and future life. The *I am* (the deity which speaks in us) may revive in a new body, just as a tune can be repeated on a fresh instrument of fitting compass, when the chords of the old one are broken. According to Christ, and to the words attributed to Krishna, Buddha, and Socrates, those who seek only holiness or wisdom can attain the *eternal* rest, in consciousness of knowledge and happiness.

THE END.